W. E. H. Lecky

FOR PEIG

W. E. H. Lecky

Historian and Politician
1838–1903

Donal McCartney

The Lilliput Press

First published in 1994 by
THE LILLIPUT PRESS LTD
4 Rosemount Terrace, Arbour Hill,
Dublin 7, Ireland

A CIP record for this
book is available from
The British Library

ISBN 1 874675 22 8

Jacket design by Conor Lucey
Set in 10½ on 12 Adobe Garamond by
Koinonia Ltd of Manchester
and printed in Ireland by
Betaprint of Dublin

Contents

Illustrations between pages 136 and 137

Acknowledgments

For their generous assistance in helping to transform my labours into book form, I am indebted to several people including Antony Farrell and his staff at The Lilliput Press; W.J. Mc Cormack, David Dickson, Oliver Snoddy, Tom Turley, Jonathan Williams, Brian Kennedy, Louise Richardson, Breidge Doherty, Jennifer O'Reilly, and my colleagues and friends in the History Departments of UCD and TCD.

I am grateful to the National University of Ireland and to University College Dublin for subventions in aid of publication. I wish to thank the Board of Trinity College, Dublin, for permission to quote from the Lecky correspondence and Mr William O'Sullivan for the care that he devoted to the collection. I also wish to acknowledge the help I have received from the staff of the various libraries containing Lecky material listed in my bibliography.

To do any serious historical writing Lecky had always sought freedom from noise. For much of the time that I worked on his intellectual biography his equable spirit had to share a home which often echoed with the sounds produced by several children. My wife, while encouraging me to persevere, struggled patiently and successfully to provide Lecky's spirit with at least some degree of the calm it craved. Neither could it have been easy for her to find over long periods Lecky and her husband strewn all over the breakfast-room table. It is, therefore, a great relief all round to be able to provide for Lecky a calmer and more comfortable abode on the book shelves of the study.

To Peig, for all patience and encouragement, this book is dedicated.

Donal McCartney
University College, Dublin
March 1994

Introduction

The Man and the Age

William Edward Hartpole Lecky (1838-1903) was an eminent Irish Victorian, born the year after Victoria ascended the throne and dying two years after her death. What distinguished him from other eminent Victorians in England was his Irishness; and what distinguished him most from the majority of his fellow Irishmen was his Victorianism.[1] For an insight into the Victorian mind, and especially its intellectual preoccupations, Lecky is a rewarding study, and is more representative than many of his contemporaries. His life and work give us a deeper understanding of the Irish question in the nineteenth century and after than do the careers of leading participants in the political drama.

As simple biography, however, his career might be described as ordinary and dull. Lecky was born into a not very significant or wealthy Anglo-Irish landlord family; he had an undistinguished academic career at Trinity College, Dublin, and after graduation travelled for a few years in Europe, spending much of his time alone and in libraries. He sat in parliament for a few years when he had lost much of whatever political ambition he had once had, and at a time when much of the excitement had gone out of parliamentary politics following the Parnellite split. He had never been an O'Connell, formulating Irish public opinion and leading a nationwide agitation that captured the attention of contemporary Europe; he was no Parnell, acting out a tragic role at centre-stage of the imperial parliament; and he was surely no conspiring Young Irelander or Fenian, willing to sacrifice life or liberty in the interests of his country's independence.

Yet Lecky's career was spent consciously wrestling with the powerful forces of his time — democracy, nationalism, socialism and liberalism. Never remotely a leader of Irish public opinion, he devoted more objective thought to the subject than did any of its acknowledged leaders, and closely analysed its texture and content. His life was his books and the 'Irish question'. The one cannot be separated from the other: the books on history and his attitudes to politics overlapped and intertwined inextricably. The process enriched his politics while at times diluting the historiographical vocation. The reputation that he had made for himself, however, was based on his historical works, all of which have gone out of fashion. Yet Lecky's historical writings continue to demand serious attention a century after their publication. His industry is measured by the following milestones in his career: *The Religious Tendencies of the Age* (1860); *Leaders of Public Opinion in Ireland* (1861; 1871; 2 vols, 1903); *History of the Rise and Influence of the Spirit of Rationalism in Europe* (2 vols, 1865); *History of European*

Morals from Augustus to Charlemagne (2 vols, 1869); *History of England in the Eighteenth Century* (8 vols, 1878-90, cabinet edition *England,* 7 vols, 1892, *Ireland,* 5 vols, 1892); *Poems* (1891); *Democracy and Liberty* (2 vols, 1896); *Map of Life* (1899); *Historical and Political Essays* (1908).

Two of these, *Rationalism* and *Morals,* were pioneering adventures into the new sociological history of ideas. Here Lecky was straining at the very frontiers of knowledge, striving to establish the laws that governed society and struggling towards a new methodology of history. If writers in English held the lead over their continental colleagues in the history of ideas down to the 1930s it was, as Momigliano said,[2] because of a handful of historical works, including Lecky's *Rationalism* and *Morals.* For his more substantial and enduring work, *England,* he avoided the temptations of too raw a sociology, narrowed its scope to a single century and a single political entity and was widely and justly acclaimed for the manner in which the author stamped his judicial interpretations on personalities, events and movements. His Irish chapters were even more original than those dealing with England. The *History* as a whole, though important in any survey of the course of British historiography, has long been replaced as the leading textbook on England in the eighteenth century. Only at their peril, however, may historians even today ignore Lecky's *Ireland.* His contribution included his *Leaders,* biographical sketches of Swift, Flood, Grattan and O'Connell. The three editions of this important book faithfully reflected Lecky's progress both as historian and Irishman.

While his stature as historian continued to grow during his lifetime, his nationalism diminished in inverse ratio to his scholarship. Yet, ironically, Lecky was among the most authoritative and influential literary contributors to Irish nationalism. *Leaders,* even when directly advancing the unionist case, indirectly encouraged people to take pride in the political evangelists of the past, and to live in expectation of an Irish political hero who would lead the people to a promised land of national reconciliation and independence. To counter the nationalism he had helped foster in his books, he turned to unionist propaganda. But Lecky, unionist pamphleteer, was no match for Lecky, nationalist historian.

Politically the current of the times was against him. He had been both formed and inspired by Ascendancy patriotism of the age of Burke and Grattan. The gentle, literary and non-sectarian nationalism of Thomas Davis, without the treasonable republicanism of John Mitchel, appealed to him. But the combination of democracy, nationalism and socialism which produced Parnellism found in him a horrified and determined opponent. His opposition was not restricted to the manifestations of democracy, socialism or nationalism within Ireland, but tended to become universal. As a mid-nineteenth century liberal, Lecky was ideologically opposed to socialism. He distrusted state intervention, including welfare politics. He disliked intensely the levelling-down notions of egalitarianism. He saw the Land League as socialism at work in Ireland and therefore denounced it in the strongest language he could command. Nationalism and democracy, which he had once praised, had developed in Ireland into Fenianism and the home rule agitation.

In Lecky's view, socialism, nationalism and democracy had entered an unholy alliance against liberalism. The role that he cast for himself in the end was that of defender of individual liberties, and minority rights in a pluralist society. He was brushed aside by stronger forces in the Ireland of his own day. An Ireland that has now emerged from the more intense nationalism of the independence struggle may be in a mood to examine this profoundly intelligent historian more objectively.

Chapter 1

Formative Influences 1838–61

Edward Lecky was born on 26 March 1838 at Maesgwyllydd House, Newtownpark, Co. Dublin. The Leckys, of Scottish origins, had settled in the north of Ireland by the early seventeenth century and became prominent in the public life of the city of Derry. Several members of the family served as mayor, and Lecky Road still commemorates the family's connection with the city. Robert Lecky, born in the mid-seventeenth century, moved from Donegal to Carlow and established the branch from which the historian sprang.

His paternal grandfather, John, married Maria Hartpole who belonged to a family once prominent in the affairs of the neighbouring Queen's County (Laois). The Hartpoles had held office under the Crown, one of the family becoming Constable of Carlow Castle and Governor of the Queen's County in the days of the Elizabethan conquest. George, the last male representative of the Hartpole family, Lecky's great uncle, was a member of the late eighteenth-century Irish parliament.

George Hartpole was described by Jonah Barrington as the inheritor 'of a large territory, a moderate income, a tattered mansion, an embarrassed rent role and a profound ignorance … of business in all departments.' His 'tendency to rustic dissipation' led to two ill-fated marriages; provision had to be made for two wives. When Hartpole, who suffered from consumption and a nervous complaint, died young and without issue, his property was divided among his two sisters, the elder of whom was Edward Lecky's grandmother. The £6,000 left to his attorney, Jonah Barrington, was unsuccessfully contested on behalf of the two sisters by their uncle, Lord Aldborough. Aldborough maintained that the will, which also bequeathed the estate to Barrington should the Hartpole sisters die without issue, had been obtained by undue influence.[1]

At the time of his marriage to Maria Hartpole, John Lecky lived at New Garden, Carlow, close to the site of the present sugar factory. The Hartpole family resided at Shrule Castle on the west bank of the Barrow, about two miles north of Carlow town. The Castle was sold by Lecky's grandparents who then bought and went to live in Cullenswood House in Ranelagh, Dublin, later famous as the original home of Patrick Pearse's Scoil Eanna.

The Hartpole and Lecky property on both sides of the river Barrow was inherited by the historian's father, John Hartpole Lecky. Relatively modest in extent, this property was sufficient to allow Lecky's father to live as a gentleman of independent means without having to practise at the bar. The Hartpole part of the property that Edward Lecky inherited amounted in 1878 to 1236 acres in Queen's County. His property in Carlow was 721 acres, with practically the same valuation as the property in Queen's County. The total — nearly 2000 acres — had a letting value calculated at £1759. Edward Lecky was also entitled to part of the rents from at least six premises in Townsend Street, Dublin; there was a family living in County Cork;[2] and sensible marriages had added to the family's favourable social circumstances.

The historian's mother, Mary Anne Tallents, was daughter of a Newark solicitor who was the law agent of the Duke of Newcastle and who had also acted as agent for Gladstone in his first election contest. The Tallents had produced academics and divines associated in the seventeenth century with Magdalene College, Cambridge. Land and learning and the professions and politics all formed part of Edward Lecky's comfortable inheritance. Birth in Dublin to an English mother, into a family of Scottish ancestry and in a home with a Welsh name, portended a natural pride in citizenship of his country — the United Kingdom of Great Britain and Ireland.

Lecky was only a year old when his mother died. Two years later his father married Isabella Eliza Wilmot, daughter of Colonel Wilmot of Queen's County. Edward was a boy of fourteen before he was told that the person he regarded as his mother was in fact a stepmother. He attended schools in England and Ireland as the family moved from Newtownpark to Graigavoran in Queen's County, to Perthshire and Sussex and back again to Ireland to Longford Terrace in fashionable Monkstown, south of Dublin. As a boy, Lecky spent a good deal of time visiting his stepmother's relations, the Wilmot Chetwodes, at Woodbrook, Portarlington. Jonathan Swift had been a frequent visitor to Woodbrook, and had corresponded with the Knightley Chetwode of the time, just as Lecky did with a later namesake. It was at Woodbrook that Lecky first became interested in Swift as a friend of the family.

He was fourteen and a half years old, and had been at Cheltenham College only a short time, when his father died. A gentle, shy and not very robust boy, his hobbies were geology and writing poetry. He liked to spend time alone with the collection of rocks which his grandfather, John Lecky, had given him, and showed no great interest in winning school prizes. He spent three not very happy years at Cheltenham before going to a tutor near Gloucester to prepare for the Dublin University matriculation. In Gloucester he acquired a copy of Burke's *Reflections on the French Revolution* which remained a constant companion for life. That same year his stepmother married Thomas Henry Dalzell (1797-1867), the seventh Earl of Carnwath, whose first wife, Mary Anne, was the daughter of Henry Grattan. The family moved to Enniskerry, Co. Wicklow, near Grattan's home; and Edward Lecky, having acquired this tentative yet symbolic connection with Grattan, began to look upon him as the greatest of Irish statesmen. It is not surprising, therefore, to find that a year before he entered Trinity College, Dublin and still a couple of months short of his seventeenth birthday, he noted in his diary: 'Enthusiastic over an old history of Ireland.'

He matriculated in 1855, obtaining tenth place among forty candidates, and entered Trinity College in February 1856 as a fellow commoner; this meant that, by paying double fees, he could dine at the Fellows' table. He enjoyed Trinity to the full, especially friends whom he entertained in his book-lined room where they talked about politics, theology, literature and philosophy. His close circle of friends included young men who had strong family associations with Irish politics: David Plunket, Gerald Fitzgibbon, and two sons (Edward and Aubrey) of William Smith O'Brien, the 1848 leader.

It was in Trinity and among such friends, and especially in the College Historical Society — the premier college debating society — that Lecky's patriotism blossomed. He explained his moderate achievements in examinations thus: 'Circumstances and temperament made me perhaps culpably indifferent to college ambitions and competitions.' While the hardworking J.P. Mahaffy was winning a studentship, Lecky was content to take a pass degree in 1859, having attended courses in Latin, Greek, Mathematics and Philosophy. He studied Divinity during the academic year 1859-60, with the intention of taking the family living in County Cork.

Lecky has left nothing of substance on record about his teachers, nor did he name any of them as contributing to his intellectual formation.[3] He followed his own bent and read widely, experiencing at Trinity the sort of liberal university education which Newman in these very same years was expounding at the newly opened Catholic University in nearby St Stephen's Green.

On 18 November 1857 Lecky was elected to membership of the Historical Society. Among the new members was J.P. Mahaffy, who forty years later, speaking at a state banquet in Trinity to commemorate the centenary of the death of Edmund Burke and proposing a toast to the Society that Burke had founded, recalled the time when he had 'the intellectual treat' of hearing 'the most brilliant group of men' that he supposed had ever come together there — David Plunket, Edward Gibson, Edward Lecky, Gerald Fitzgibbon and Thomas Dudley.[4] During his membership (1857-60), Lecky participated actively in the Society and spoke regularly on the national and liberal side in the debates. He served on the committee, took the chair on occasions and won the Gold Medal for Oratory in 1858/59.[5] On the night of his Gold Medal presentation, Lecky heard his close friend, David Plunket, auditor of the Society, declare:

> There is indeed but one responsibility I know of that you incur on entering our guild: it is to be patriotic Irishmen ... if you are cold to patriotism, I have no wish that you should become one of us.[6]

What did Plunket and his friends in Trinity understand by these words? Clearly these young men were proud of their own Society's past. 'Manfully and proudly inscribe your names as members of the society of Burke, of Grattan, of Plunket and of Bushe', Edward Gibson asserted in his 1858 address.[7] 'Did not the eloquence of Burke preserve for England that constitutional freedom of which his speeches are at this day the text-books?' asked David Plunket in 1859.[8]

The study of the past was warmly commended to members.[9] Gibson made a special plea for the cultivation of Irish history. Forty years later, as Lord Ashbourne, he would play an enthusiastic part in the Irish language movement. Let Irishmen but open their history, he said in his student days, and they would find in its earlier pages legends as strange and mystic as any classic fable; adventures more exciting than the story of the fall of Troy. What could be more heroic than the legends of the Red Branch rallying round the sunburst banner and driving the invader from the shore? What could be more interesting than the fortunes of the Great O'Neill?[10]

These young men were the descendants of eighteenth-century patriots, and were proud of their national and liberal achievements. Referring to Grattan and the Volunteers, Gibson declared: 'This is the Golden Age of Irish history — here is the true type of an Irish patriot'.[11] In this era, he said, would be found exemplified the moral that Grattan had so often and so eloquently inculcated; namely, that Ireland is only prosperous when she is united. In the following year's address, it was David Plunket's turn: 'Is not the name of Henry Grattan, the watchword of Irish nationality?'[12] The course of Irish history had blossomed briefly during the late eighteenth-century period of independence and then had faded away into the prosaic reality of the United Kingdom.

Lecky and his friends had little to say about another famous ex-auditor of the Historical Society — Wolfe Tone, the originator of Irish republicanism and the doctrine of total separation from England. Robert Walshe regretted Tone's 'misguided patriotism', declaring that his name might have been among Ireland's greatest had his lot been cast in less troubled times.[13] The young patriots of Trinity in the 1850s and 60s stood rather for Grattan's brand of patriotism; not that they favoured a repeal of the Act of Union and a return to Grattan's ideal of two sister kingdoms. Although they sincerely admired the era of legislative independence, Lecky's associates accepted the Union as a political fact and looked for a healing of old wounds and a proper mingling of Englishmen and Irishmen. 'Let us hope that this union is accomplished', Gibson said, 'but this process of fusion must be gradual'.[14] Retrospectively they saw themselves as liberal colonial patriots, but they were striving for a future in which 'English' and 'Irish' would be terms from the political past. Many of them, in fact, were liberal unionists in the making.

They felt a political and moral duty towards the 'lower orders' in their country, expressed by Plunket:

> Gentlemen, it is into these masses of ignorance and discontent that I call upon you to go down, to stir up amongst them a spirit of self-improvement, and give it a safe direction ... and to show them that by self-improvement they may gain a nobler independence than any Young Irelander ever preached, freeing themselves not from Saxon connexion, but from Saxon superiority.[15]

Their brand of liberal patriotism found expression in the debates of the Society and the motions that won approval: public appointments should be open to public competition; a competitive system would benefit the general education of the country; the method of conducting capital punishment was objectionable; the good effects of the French Revolution outweighed the bad; Carlyle's estimate of Cromwell was incorrect; life peerages should be introduced; modern governments were justified in reappropriating ancient national endowments; Italian unification deserved support. In each of these debates, the young Lecky spoke and, with one exception, was on the winning side.[16] There were occasions when he appeared almost too liberal for the rest of the members.

Colonial patriotism also flourished in the historical motions. Absenteeism was considered such an undoubted evil that no speaker could be found to support it.[17] When the house debated the motion that, if Swift had never written, his silence ought not to be regretted, Lecky opposed, and the house rejected the motion by a strong vote.[18] The Act of Union was a popular topic for debate, and again loyalty to Grattan's parliament was always evident. On occasions, Lecky sounded rather more patriotic and nationalistic than his colleagues. He once unsuccessfully resisted a motion that the political life of Robert Peel was worthy of admiration. Another time he argued alone that the influence of *The Times* was detrimental to the interests of society.[19] His coldness towards the former British prime minister remained in his mature writings.[20] His objections to *The Times* are preserved in commonplace books and in essays; they were based in part at least on patriotic grounds.[21] His commonplace book wittily defines *The Times* as an abbreviation for the time-server.[22] In his essay on 'Clerical Influences', he objected to *The Times* and the British press generally which ceaselessly ridiculed Ireland and the Irish: the 'unwavering contempt', the 'studied depreciation of the Irish character and intellect habitual in the English newspapers'. While such a tone continued, the two nations could 'never amalgamate, or assimilate, or cordially co-operate':

> A war of recrimination is an evil, but it is a greater evil for a nation tranquilly to suffer its character to be frittered away by calumny veiled in sarcasm, and by a contemptuous suppression of all facts but those which tell against itself. As long as Englishmen adopt a tone of depreciation in speaking of the present of Ireland, Irishmen would betray their country were they to suffer the curtain to fall upon its past.[23]

In these Historical Society debates, questions of nationality and politics were never far from Lecky's mind. In June 1859 he was the first speaker to a motion which claimed that the growth of journalism was beneficial to society. This speech amounted to a survey of the relationship of political and sectarian public opinion to the struggle for nationality in Ireland:

> The dead are still our masters,
>   and a power from the tomb
> Can shape the characters of men, their
>   conduct and their doom.

This was typical of the kind of poetry Lecky was composing. However indifferent it may have been as verse, it was an accurate description of his politics. As an undergraduate, he considered himself to be in the tradition of Grattan and of

Young Ireland. He admired especially Thomas Davis and Gavan Duffy and their newspaper, *The Nation*, John Kells Ingram and William Smith O'Brien, 'the man in Ireland he most wished to know'.[24] In his day, Davis had been auditor of the Historical Society and once had claimed that Irish nationalism had been born in the Historical Society of Trinity College.[25] The nationalism propagated by Davis and his friends in Young Ireland during the 1840s was non-sectarian and liberal; it encouraged education, self-reliance, national pride and the union of hearts between Irishmen of all creeds, classes and racial origins. Ingram, the ex-Young Irelander, and author of the stirring patriotic ballad, 'Who fears to speak of '98?', was at this time a junior fellow of Trinity College and professor of Oratory and English literature.[26] He was specially favoured by the young men of the Historical Society and was a popular chairman at their meetings.[27] Lecky admired him very much.

The lack of a native parliament worried Lecky. He declaimed: 'It is a bad sign when the genius of the country ceases to interest itself in the ordering of that country's affairs',[28] and 'It is a great misfortune when the enthusiasm of a nation is naturally hostile (as in Ireland) to the existing government.'[29] 'A good government is that which is in accordance with the wishes of the people.'[30] He regarded sectarianism as Ireland's greatest evil, and saw it as the cause and the result of the absence of a parliament around which a national spirit could flourish: 'A national spirit is the great corrective for sectarian animosities'.[31] He believed that the political weakness of Ireland was perpetuated by sectarian divisions, and in an entry entitled 'Ireland's strength' he wrote: 'Next to the Omnipotence of God is the will of a united people.'[32]

Although he sometimes adopted a bantering, anti-English stand, Lecky was no rebel and decidedly no advocate of physical force. In a comment in his notebook on 'John Mitchel and Co.', he stated: 'There are some quack doctors who have but one remedy — bleeding.'[33] Each successive appeal to arms had only riveted Ireland's chains the more firmly and forced the national party to retreat. But liberty had never fled from the prayer of peaceful and united patriotism.[34]

The tinsel of Lecky's patriotism, modelled as it was on the rhetoric of independence favoured by Grattan and his contemporaries, was too easily transcribed into poor Young Ireland rhyme. Under the pseudonym 'Hibernicus', Lecky published a slender book of mainly patriotic poetry, in 1859. In a poem explicitly entitled 'Patriotism', he reiterated the theme of so many Historical Society speeches and notebook entries:

> Woe to the land where Patriotism dies —
> … Unless the soul of nationhood be there
> Its end is ruin, misery, despair.

The moral was intended for his own countrymen, as the very first poem, 'Pictures of Fancy', had made abundantly clear:

> Oh! Gone for ever are those bright days,
> When glory beamed with undiminished rays,

> When Independence flourished in our isle
> And patriotism bloomed beneath her smile ...
> Still Fancy walks creative through the tombs
> Till heroes wake and ancient glory blooms ...
> One all absorbing passion fills man's breast
> — To free his land, to give his nation rest.

Patriotism had at least the more immediate effect of interfering with his intention of becoming a clergyman. For he was none too happy with the role which the clergy — Church of Ireland as well as Roman Catholic — had played and were playing in the national life. Grattan and Young Ireland had taught him that being Irish was more important than being catholic, protestant or presbyterian. Lecky noted in his commonplace book: 'In Ireland the aversion of the protestant towards his neighbour as a Roman Catholic is greater than his attraction towards him as an Irishman.'[35] He also asserted that the Irishman who made a friend of a fellow countryman who professed a religion different from his own was a benefactor of his country.[36] He blamed the clergy for the divisions among Irishmen, and noted that it was important to remember that, while the clergy were the descendants of the apostles, the apostles had included in their number the traitor, Iscariot:[37] 'It is a great misfortune when the clergy become the leaders of public opinion in any nation.'[38] Sectarianism fanned by the clergy had become the bane of Irish society. 'The great desideratum in Ireland', he wrote in his commonplace book, 'is a lay public opinion'.[39] To his fellow students he proclaimed:

> I fear that as a general rule — subject of course to brilliant exceptions — both the Roman catholic priest and the protestant levite would permit their wounded country to bleed to death before they would disburse the twopence necessary for its relief.[40]

Lecky's patriotism was clearly already sprouting a certain anti-clericalism. Nor was this tendency solely the result of his nationalist views. The prospect of a career as a clergyman had begun to repel him in its more professional aspects too. The standard of contemporary preaching was poor. The intense dullness of the clergy was almost an inducement to enter the profession, for by that means one could escape the necessity of hearing them, and become one of the tormentors instead of the tormented.[41] And he despised the contemporary manner of theological controversy:

> I observe that the clergy conducting their controversies accuse each other of dishonesty more frequently than perhaps any other class of men. Indeed if one were to believe the clergy a more dishonest body of men do not exist — out of a jail.[42]

In the Historical Society, Lecky's line was not that expected of a divinity student. In his maiden speech, he spoke against the motion 'that the system of modern theatricals is detrimental to the morals of the age'.[43] It was a subject to which he returned in his *History of Rationalism*.[44] Twenty of his fellow members (many of whom were intended like himself for holy orders) voted for the motion. Lecky was one of just four on the side which lost.

It is possible to attach too much significance to a bright undergraduate's smart sentences and hammered-out epigrams or to what was said at a college debating society. But Lecky was a very serious young man; he prepared his speeches carefully (often during long walks on the west pier of Kingstown Harbour), he committed the epigrams to notebooks and used them later, and much of what he wrote as a student or uttered at meetings of the Historical Society formed the basis of his first published works.[45] Certainly the young man displayed a tendency towards the unpopular viewpoint, 'an inveterate habit, which exposed him to a great deal of misunderstanding, of defending in conversation, whatever position happened to be attacked'.[46] Face to face with a protestant, he would defend the catholic side; an hour later he would argue no less eloquently for the protestant position. But here was a broadness, an independence of mind which made ordination in a particular church difficult, at the least.

It was suspected that he was flirting with Rome. A contemporary agreed that Lecky was never infected with 'the narrow sectarian bigotry which prevailed at that time in Ireland': nor could he understand 'the extraordinary intolerance towards catholics and catholicism'. It was known among his friends that he read and admired John Henry Newman. And he 'excited some little scandal by occasionally attending the Catholic University chapel in Stephen's Green' to hear the chaplain, Dr Anderdon, a noted preacher. At a time when the Oxford Movement had not yet spent all its force, 'some began to fear that Lecky would also be lost to the enemy.'[47]

But his interest in Anderdon had as much to do with pulpit oratory as with doctrine for he admired equally the protestant preacher, Dr John Gregg, afterwards Bishop of Cork. The hours he had spent in church probably helped him win the Historical Society's Gold Medal for Oratory. Whether he went to the Catholic University chapel for the preacher's method or his message — and the motives no doubt are inextricably mixed — the outcome gave him abundant reason to consider his own suitability for clerical life in the Church of Ireland.

Meanwhile, some of the works he was obliged to study as a divinity student were exercising an unintended influence. He later wrote that Bishop Butler, 'who was probably studied more assiduously at Dublin than in any other university in the kingdom', was his first great intellectual influence. He found Butler's *Analogy* the most original if not the most powerful defence of Christian belief, though its impact was variable and even contradictory in that it had been the parent of much agnosticism. There is a personal ring to his statement that Butler's supremacy of conscience had supported many amid the dissolution of positive beliefs.[48]

Archbishop Whately's works were inspiring a love of truth for its own sake: 'the jealous maintenance of an independent judgment is the first element of intellectual honesty.'[49] And Whately's belief that 'most controversies might be resolved into verbal ambiguities.' was impressive.[50] Locke, Dugald Stewart,

Mackintosh and Mill were opening up 'wide and various vistas in moral philosophy,'[51] and sceptical writers of the Enlightenment like Bayle, Rousseau, Voltaire and Gibbon were likewise having an effect on him. But Lecky was also studying the work of French catholics, especially Pascal, Bossuet, Fenélon and Montalembert: 'I have been taking a good deal to French Roman catholicism' he wrote to a friend in November 1859.[52] During vacations on the Continent he became deeply interested in European catholicism. The central place of religion in the lives of the Spanish and Italian peasantry intrigued and attracted him. He was impressed by the role of the Virgin in the catholic religion; and he immersed himself in religious art.

Positivism also was exercising a profound influence on the formation of Lecky's mind. It was to leave deep traces in his written work, especially the *History of Rationalism* and the *History of Morals*. Its leading exponent in historical writing in England was Henry Thomas Buckle, the first volume of whose *History of Civilization* was published in 1857. This book was an event in Lecky's life, giving him an altogether new interest in history.[53] He was still a student when Darwin's *On the Origin of Species* (1859) and the publication of *Essays and Reviews* (1860) were causing, for different reasons, 'the great upheaval of beliefs in England'.[54] The intellectual atmosphere of the time was 'much agitated by the recent discoveries in geology' which had a manifest bearing on the Creation and the Fall, especially the discoveries of Sir Charles Lyell, with whom Lecky afterwards became friendly.[55]

The positivistic philosophy of Auguste Comte, which profoundly influenced mid-nineteenth century attitudes to history and religion, was making an impact on Trinity during Lecky's student days. For, apart from Comtist-influenced writers like J.S. Mill, whose work was being studied there, Comte had also a personal link with the College through John Kells Ingram, the favourite of the young men of the Historical Society. Ingram had become aware of Comtean positivism mainly through the references to it in Mill's *Logic* (1843). From his first contact with Comte's philosophy in 1851, Ingram was convinced that what mankind needed was the 'religion of humanity'. He visited Comte in 1855, the year that Lecky matriculated, and was in the full flush of Comtism when Lecky came under his influence. Half a century later, when Ingram retired from Trinity and no longer felt constrained by the responsibilities of his position, he dedicated *Outlines of the History of Religion* (1900) to the great French positivist. Ingram's Comtism — both positivistic and humanistic — brushed off onto Lecky, and reinforced the effects which his interest in the scientific progress of the time was also having on him.

The world in which Lecky, with all his intellectual curiosity, grew to manhood had been shaken to its foundations by the great discoveries in science and the arguments to which these gave rise. Lyell's *Principles of Geology* (1830-3) had shown that the earth was thousands of years older and far different in its evolution than the literal interpretation of the Bible asserted. Before Lecky left Trinity, Darwin's *On the Origin of Species* (1859) substituted for the Almighty's act of creation the notion of evolution from lower to higher forms. Between them, Lyell and Darwin replaced the biblical story of the fall of man with scientific evidence of the existence of pain, imperfection and death, stretching back for countless ages before the time when Adam was supposed to have lost paradise. As Lecky wrote much later, these nineteenth-century ideas were 'as far as possible removed from the conception of human history and human nature which christendom during eighteen centuries accepted as fundamental truth.' Contemporary theological discussion was influenced not only by the progress of scientific discovery but also by the great advances being made in historical methods generally, and by the spirit of rationalism and criticism then prevailing. Comparative mythology was showing how myths, legends and miracles were the natural products of certain stages of civilization. The 'higher criticism' of German biblical scholarship was depriving those writings of much of their assumed authority and infallibility, and secular scholarship was distinguishing the historical from the merely fabulous and miraculous. Among Anglicans, the highly controversial *Essays and Reviews* (1860), 'added to the great upheaval of beliefs.' If all of these exciting intellectual advances and theological controversies did not turn Lecky into an atheist or an agnostic, they carried him some distance from traditional anglican orthodoxy, or, as he put it himself: 'I had drifted far from my Cork living and very decisively into the ways of literature.'[56]

It was a familiar Victorian crisis of conscience. But unlike the cases of John Morley, Leslie Stephen, Frederick Harrison and James Anthony Froude, there was no family disruption for Lecky. His comfortable financial circumstances enabled him to devote all his time to literature. His decision to reject the clerical life had come before he took orders, and it was not so much a crisis as the result of a slow and largely unconscious development:

> Gradually, however, by a natural and insensible process I passed into the habit of examining opinions mainly from an historical point of view — investigating the circumstances under which they grow up; their relation to the general conditions of their time; the direction in which they naturally develop; the part, whether for good or ill, which during long spaces of time they have played in the world.[57]

Bossuet, but more especially Coleridge, had convinced him that the various religious systems were not comprehensible until viewed from within, that is, from the standpoint of their more intelligent adherents.

Where doctrinal systems were concerned, Lecky had reached the haven of historical relativity. To chart his way, he wrote a small book while still a divinity student, and had it published anonymously. *The Religious Tendencies of the Age* (1860) was the outcome of the need he felt to clear up his own position with regard to ordination and the family living. But it was not merely a digression into the field of theology, as a college friend who was more impressed by Lecky's political ambitions and by his performance at the Historical Society thought.[58] For Lecky would retain what he himself referred to as 'a strong leaning towards theological studies.'[59] *The Religious Tendencies of the Age* [60] was an attempt to give an outline analysis of the chief divisions of Christianity in Britain, to elucidate

the general principles which underlay them, and the modes of thought which
pervaded contemporary theological literature. He divided the work into chapters
on private judgment, the church of Rome, high churchism, latitudinarianism,
practical Christianity and the signs of the times.

The volume was clearly the work of a Christian, both reverent in the beliefs he
accepted and tolerant of the positions he rejected. But it was evident that the
author could never become an orthodox clergyman in any Christian church, nor
accept a doctrinal system absolutely. The motto that he affixed to the title-page, a
quotation from Coleridge, well illustrated his attitude of mind then and throughout his life:

> Let it be remembered by controversialists on all subjects, that every specu-
> lative error which boasts a multitude of advocates has its golden as well as
> its dark side; that there is always some truth connected with it, the exclusive
> attention to which has misled the understanding; some moral beauty
> which has given it charms for the heart. Let it be remembered that no
> assailant of an error can reasonably hope to be listened to by its advocates,
> who has not proved to them that he has seen the disputed subject in the
> same point of view and is capable of contemplating it with the same
> feelings as themselves; for why should we abandon a cause at the persuasion
> of one who is ignorant of the reasons which have attached us to it?[61]

Nothing, it seemed to Lecky, was more certain than that Christianity was true;
nothing more uncertain than what Christianity was.[62] Of all the modern
churches he had least sympathy with High Churchism: logically it must necessarily end in the Roman Catholic church.[63] At the other extreme, he was critical of
the puritan denial of the world and urged instead a practical Christianity leading
to participation in secular life and pleasures, in lawful ambition and in the full
use of talents.[64] Roman catholicism possessed great charms for the young Lecky.

What possible influence could Rome have had on the affections of an Irish
protestant divinity student of that day? After all, it was the era of Paul Cullen, the
catholic Archbishop of Dublin. Relations between Roman Catholic clergy and
the established church were severely strained. Disestablishment, denominational
control over education, proselytism and the relations between protestant landlord and catholic peasantry were live and divisive issues. Sectarian controversy
raged between the two priesthoods at all levels from the bishop's pastoral to the
parish pulpit. The 'Cullenization' of Ireland brought closer discipline with Rome
and a hierarchy notoriously ultramontane. Triumphantly emerging from the
black night of the penal era, Irish catholicism, proud to the point of arrogance,
was at its most aggressive. A Catholic Defence Association, out of which grew the
Independent Irish Party, had been organized in the 1850s; an Irish papal brigade
fought in Italy on the non-popular and non-liberal side; and the clergy had
begun to exercise an influence in Irish politics greater than had ever before been
attained.

It was not catholicism as he knew it in Ireland, but catholicism in its continental setting which attracted him. His letters as a student during holidays on the

Continent, as well as *Religious Tendencies*, displayed a sympathy with Spanish and Italian peasants worshipping within their churches and praying as they walked in processions.[65] At another level he was excited by the intellectualism of the French church and of Newman and his friends. The result was a warmly sympathetic chapter on Roman catholicism, providing able and simple answers to the more common protestant objections to catholic doctrines and practices: 'the gorgeous beauty of its ceremonies',[66] the rich symbolism, the art which integrated with the faith, the place allotted to the Virgin. The church of Rome was what it had always been — 'the leading fact of Europe'.[67]

But Rome, too, had its repulsive side, its despotism,[68] its idea of infallibility and doctrine of the real presence.[69] The developments in French catholicism were certainly hopeful and encouraging, but those of the highest intellectual calibre had failed signally to connect the Roman system with the spirit of the age — men such as O'Connell in Ireland (whom Lecky placed first in his list), Lamennais, Lacordaire, Montalembert in France, and Ventura in Italy.[70] Lecky could not embrace the catholic faith through admiration of the Roman catholic ritual: to subscribe to what was known to be false could never be other than wrong.[71]

The outcome of Lecky's examination of conscience in *Religious Tendencies* was that he would neither become a protestant clergyman nor would he follow the path to Rome. He would remain unobtrusively a protestant of latitudinarian views. There had been many men of vast intellect, profound erudition and intense piety, who had arrived at conclusions diametrically opposite to his.[72] Not for him the clerical system of the established church designed, it seemed, to paralyze genius by obliging the minister to speak continually to the same audience and do interminable parish duties with no time for the cultivation of his own peculiar talent, no time to keep pace with the progress of the age. Thus fluent platitudes became a substitute for thought.[73] Pulpit statements were taken with great latitude; the churches were being deserted by men; and congregations were being addressed as if they were composed entirely of women; the clergy were losing all hold upon the minds of the gifted men and the educated and were becoming more and more alienated from the progressive intellect of the country. Lecky regarded this diminution of clerical influence as one of the most significant signs of the times.[74] As a young man of strong ambition, he aspired to a power and influence that he felt could never be attained as a clergyman.

Although remaining a protestant, he did so on his own terms. Protestantism was 'a series of theoretical opinions, not demonstrated facts ... a measure of uncertainty and difficulty is its legitimate concomitant.'[75] 'Protestantism', he said, '... is a principle, and not a church.'[76] In Lecky's view, each Christian church was true in so far as it was Christian, but false in so far as it was too systematically and dogmatically a distinctive church. 'I believe', he wrote, 'that one of the very greatest dangers with which Christianity is menaced in the present day arises from the passion for defining.'[77] His own standpoint was that of Christian latitudinarianism — by which he meant a religious, moral and humanist attitude pervading every church, but which was not a distinct religious system.[78]

The Christian latitudinarian was of course a protestant, but Lecky implied that far from there being anything wrong about being a protestant-Roman catholic, the attainment of that stage in religious development was most desirable. The latitudinarian believed that protestantism (in Lecky's sense) and dogmatism — even the dogmatism which insisted on the infallibility of private judgment — were logically incompatible.[79] The latitudinarian 'cannot conceive that a man who had arrived at erroneous conclusions after a faithful and earnest investigation, can be esteemed in any sense guilty of a sin.'[80]

In *Religious Tendencies* Lecky was a missionary of Christian ecumenism a century before ecumenism had arrived. One of his objectives was that the book should help to promote charity and tolerance among Christians of different denominations: 'an impartial consideration of the weighty arguments to be urged in favour of different doctrines is calculated to foster that spirit so seldom found among controversialists — the spirit of charity and tolerance towards those with whom they disagree.'[81] Truth in doctrinal matters was for him a matter of relativity. It would be pleasant to believe that the doctrines of others were so absurd that there could be no question about the truth of one's own, but such pleasure could be purchased too dearly at the expense of truth.[82] Every man had to seek the truth for himself in icy solitude. In this respect, wrote Lecky, Ralph Waldo Emerson's precepts deserved attention, and he summarised them as follows:

> Let truth be the grand object of your research, and therefore begin by discarding all prejudices. Do not hesitate to abandon the creed you have been taught, if truth require you to do so. Shrink not, though your fathers may have died for it; though it be identified with all the glories of your country; though it mingle with the holiest recollections of your childhood.... Beware of being governed by the authority of great men. Those men were great because they were original. Men were given minds to discover truth for themselves, and they have no right to delegate the search to others and perform the duty by proxy.... Let the whole drift and tenor of your mind be towards the acquisition of truth. Make it the subject of your habitual meditation — seek for it in solitary thought.[83]

At the end of it all, however, Lecky believed that one could only be certain that whatever was found would not be absolute.

> Such is the weakness of our private judgement that a breath can cloud it; a thousand influences which it is impossible to avoid, conspire to distort it; like the lake it seems to take its colour from whatever sky is above it.[84]

Variation in personal religious beliefs was a common enough experience, so how could we be certain at any given time, he asked, that we had arrived at the last stage of our religious development?[85]

He had become deeply impressed by a saying of Carlyle to the effect that literature is the one modern church.[86] This, said Lecky, was scarcely an hyperbole. Lay writers were moulding the characters and forming the opinions of the age; their logical acumen, their learning, their eloquence and their candour were so superior to what was found in the church that it was no surprise that they had superseded the clergy in directing modern thought. The intellectuals were for Lecky the priesthood of the modern world, and among those to whom he made reference in *Religious Tendencies* were Coleridge, Emerson, Newman, Bishop Butler, Jeremy Taylor, Macaulay, Hallam, Scott, Paley, Carlyle, Hume, Locke, Bossuet, Fenelon, Kempis, Victor Hugo, Montalembert, Lacordaire, Lamennais, Voltaire, Rousseau, Niebuhr, Mosheim, Goethe and Ventura. The young man now aspired to enter this sacerdotal class.

Meanwhile, he was disappointed and a trifle discouraged that his first prose work had not found many readers. Two years after its publication, his publishers informed him that sixty-eight copies had been sold.[87] There was some compensation and enjoyment in the reactions of his friends. A contemporary at Trinity, R.K. Arbuthnot,[88] whom Lecky had proposed for membership of the Historical Society, was 'a good deal shocked'. Arbuthnot showed the book to friends who were likewise bewildered and astonished; one was writing a refutation of Lecky's chapter on the church of Rome, while another thought the author must be a Jesuit. The *Downshire Protestant* praised its arguments against infallibility, but condemned it for propagating 'much nonsense in favour of popery'.[89]

Apart from theology various passages in *Religious Tendencies* spoke loudly of Lecky's interest in politics, especially in the forces of public opinion acting beneath the surface of contemporary affairs. Both the theological and the political content showed an emerging man of letters looking upon the world of ideas mainly from a historical-evolutionary standpoint. The history of the race was 'marked by periods of infancy, of youth, of manhood and of dotage'.[90] The historical process was in a state of perpetual flux. This point of view enabled Lecky to write with considerable detachment.

He saw contemporary religious systems only as so many flowerings of certain stages in the course of human development, and as the products of certain transitory sets of conditions. The emphasis with Lecky was not so much, as in Newman's case, on the development of Christian doctrine by the gradual unfolding of divine revelation, but on the moulding of congruous ecclesiastical systems by the era in which they flourished.[91] *Religious Tendencies* was Lecky's first groping excursion into the field of historical writing. Although not a work of history, the author's approach was infused with a historical attitude of mind, imaginative, tolerant, many-sided. The use of imagination in history, in being able to project oneself into another's position remained for Lecky a historiographical principle of vast importance.[92]

Lecky had lost one vocation and was groping towards another. He was never to analyze very deeply his philosophy of history, but historical thinking had begun to encompass everything in his world, even those spheres which in the lives of others are reserved for religion. He was determined to be a man of the times. While the age in which he lived was 'a moral and a reforming and a philanthropic age', it was not a believing age.[93] And so the doctrinal systems he had examined were gently set aside, and in their place historicism began to mean for him what religion, deeply realized, meant for others. For Lecky, a theological problem had converted itself into a historical one.[94]

Lecky's student mind encompassed two major disciplines — theology and politics. Thirty years later, describing his formative influences, he concentrated on the theological,[95] excusing his omission on the grounds that 'to write effectively it is necessary to take a single line, and I think that of theological development is the most important, and also the one most likely to interest a far-off public, who certainly could not care about debating societies or rhetoric'.[96] But the debating society, the political influences, the rhetoric and the patriotic poetry were significant for his political development generally, and for his *Leaders of Public Opinion* in particular. His friend Arthur Booth realized this:

> His main enthusiasm was directed to the literature and politics of Ireland. He studied the speeches of the principal orators and could repeat by heart many passages from them; he was thoroughly acquainted with the history and especially the 'wrongs' of the country; he was saturated with the writings and poetry of the patriotic party. ... His library was full of the speeches of the Irish orators.

Booth shrewdly added: 'We suspect that the material for the *Leaders* ... was collected at this period, and probably the essays themselves were outlined if not actually written.'[97] Indeed, a college notebook contains Lecky's notes for *Leaders* and many of the epigrams entered in it were incorporated into the essays. A speech he delivered to the Historical Society was clearly the basis of the famous concluding chapter, 'Clerical Influences', published only in the original edition.[98]

Lecky put the finishing touches to *Leaders* while on a visit to Italy during 1860/61; both the book and his letters of the time reflect the enthusiasm and poetry animated by the *Risorgimento*. Years later he could still give expression to the feelings which the Italian wars inspired in him and many of his generation:

> The regeneration of Italy ... gave popularity to the doctrine of the rights of nationalities. It was one of the most genuine of national movements, and very few who were young men when it took place, still fewer of those, who, like the writer of these lines, then lived much in Italy, can have failed to catch the enthusiasm which it inspired. ... It was the one moment of nineteenth-century history when politics assumed something of the character of poetry.[99]

The Leaders of Public Opinion in Ireland was Lecky's first book on a historical subject. It was the product both of his schooling in patriotism in Trinity's Historical Society and of the nationalist enthusiasm stimulated by the *Risorgimento*, and as such it reflected much of the contemporary spirit of European nationalism. It comprised an introduction, followed by essays on Swift, Flood, Grattan and O'Connell, and a concluding essay, 'Clerical Influences'. In the introduction to the first edition in 1861, Lecky wrote that, in a diseased and undeveloped nation like Ireland, history was resolved into biography. The earlier history of Ireland had been 'almost exclusively concentrated upon a succession of warrior-chiefs, who represented in turn the principle of nationality, who carried on the hereditary war against England ... [until] the sword of Ireland was broken at the Boyne.'[100] After the Glorious Revolution, 'the true principles of constitutional monarchy' were grasped and appreciated by 'a few of the higher intellects in Ireland.... The possibility of reconciling nationality with loyalty was perceived. The reign of public opinion was inaugurated.'[101] What Lecky called nationality with loyalty — the essential position of the 'patriots' or protestant nation of the eighteenth century — was also Lecky's own political ideal. And public opinion meant for him the creation and expression by leaders of this 'nationality with loyalty'. Public opinion was not something spontaneous arising from the people, but rather the work of 'a few transcendent intellects'. These intellects formed it, fostered its growth and gave it direction, and in all its phases it reflected the character of its creators. Lecky made no distinction between public and popular opinion in these essays. Phrases such as 'confidence of the people', 'voice of the people', 'will of the people', 'public feeling', 'the popular mind', 'nation', 'national sentiment', 'national movement', 'national will' are interchangeable. He has as yet no cause to distinguish between them, because it was assumed that public opinion formed by the 'leaders' received 'popular' and 'national' support. He retained this view of the origin and nature of public opinion, but he later came to distinguish it from 'popular' opinion.[102] In 1861, however, the pattern traced out by Irish public opinion since the beginning of the eighteenth century seemed simple enough and without need of subtle qualification:

> Under Swift public opinion first acquired a definite form and an imposing influence. Under Flood it penetrated into the debates of parliament. Under Grattan it triumphed in 1782; it succumbed in 1800. ... Under O'Connell its dominion became still wider, but its spirit more narrow.[103]

In that pattern, the four leaders characterized the rise, progress, triumph, failure and decline of the national spirit. With the death of O'Connell, the political element was absorbed almost entirely in the religious, bequeathing since then what Lecky called 'a disorganized state of public opinion'.[104] One found extreme liberal politics combined with admiration of foreign despotism and aversion to everything English. This latter chapter in the phase of public opinion was described by Lecky as 'Clerical Influences'. The vacuum was filled by sectarianism.

Sectarianism was the point at which Lecky's politics and theology intersected. His *Religious Tendencies* had opposed intolerance in religion. His *Leaders* opposed clerical influences in politics. Sectarianism was the occupation by a quasi theological spirit of territory rightly belonging to the political. It was everywhere and always an evil. It was contemporary Ireland's greatest curse. Lecky's warm approval of Grattan's parliament was precisely because of its tolerance and developing liberality to the penalized Catholics. His condemnation of the Union of 1800 was partly because, in abolishing the Irish parliament, the organ of the national sentiment, it prepared the way for the sectarianism of the nineteenth century. And one of the worst features of O'Connell's career, Lecky felt, was the increase in sectarianism which had resulted from his bringing priests into politics.[105] Since then, both catholics and protestants shared the responsibility for fostering the circumstances in which public opinion was diseased and sectarian politics rampant. He hammered the Church of Ireland for its opposition to the national cause, for casting aside its nationality and for allowing itself to be placed in an obviously false political position. He rapped the Roman catholic bishops for obstructing harmony between catholics and others, and for handing over the country as a weapon in the service of the Vatican: 'We have an English party among us, and an Italian party; but we look in vain for an Irish party.'

What was the cure for Ireland's ills and for sectarianism in particular?

> The only two possible solutions of the present discontents of Ireland are the complete fusion of the people of Ireland with the people of England, or the creation of a healthy national feeling in Ireland, uniting the various classes, and giving a definite character to its policy.[106]

Many of Lecky's friends in Trinity's Historical Society would have favoured the former solution. But which one did Lecky himself approve of in 1861?[107]

Passage after passage in his book implies that the one cure for sectarianism is the creation of a national spirit through the restoration of an Irish parliament. Sometimes he is explicit. Sectarianism is:

> ... the master curse of Ireland, the canker that corrodes all that is noble and patriotic in the country, and, we maintain, the direct and inevitable consequence of the union. Much has been said of the terrific force with which it would rage were the Irish parliament restored. We maintain, on the other hand, that no truth is more clearly stamped upon the page of history ... than that a national feeling is the only effective check to sectarian passions.[108]

A closer analysis of *Leaders*, however, reveals tendencies towards unionism in certain political circumstances. In the first place, Lecky states that time could heal the retrospective discontent in Ireland regarding the union. Secondly, he has grave fears that catholic clerical influence was destroying what he called the reversionary loyalty of the Irish to the English connection, and the connection was the cornerstone of Lecky's politics. Thirdly, there are some clear indications of the budding imperialist in the work. One may usefully elaborate on these.

In one passage, Lecky characteristically quotes Grattan: 'When you banish the parliament do you banish the people? ... Do you extinguish the soul?'[109] There follows a comment which is unexpected in view of his general identification with Grattan, his own condemnation of the Union and his nationalist bias in the rest of the book. His point is that if the curse of sectarianism did not exist, the people would come in time to accept the Union: 'Discontent which was purely retrospective would hardly prove permanent.' Each year ill-feeling over the Union would grow fainter and the public mind would gradually identify with that of

England. The 'coalescing of the sentiments of the two nations': here is the language of the emerging unionist as yet scarcely discernible beneath a profusion of nationalist sentiment.

Lecky was worried by the political power assumed by the catholic clergy. They supported a papacy whose temporal power was maintained by foreign armies and against Italian public opinion. They gave the lie to O'Connell's principle that the public opinion of a nation should determine its form of government. They rejected the O'Connellite motto, 'as much theology as you please from Rome but no politics'. In O'Connell's time, there had been what Lecky called 'reversionary loyalty' among the people; 'they looked forward to the restoration of the Irish parliament as the termination of all agitation'.[110] But now, with loyalty to the Vatican in the forefront of the catholic mind, Lecky had doubts. An Irish parliament subject to this kind of clerical influence would not be desirable.

Broader concerns are also evident. Here and there in *Leaders* one stumbles upon phrases of imperialism. Lecky expressly repudiates the evangelical notion that an empire would be dearly bought by the death of a single unrepentant soldier.[111] This of course hardly classes him with Dilke, Seeley, Froude and company as a harbinger of the English imperial idea. His use of the word 'empire' in 1861 does not convey the meaning it was to have from the 1870s onwards: Lecky was thinking primarily of what later would be regarded merely as the core of the empire — the British Isles. Loyalty for Lecky included loyalty to the empire in this restricted sense of the United Kingdom. He condemned sectarianism because it prevented Ireland from acting 'in harmony with the rest of the empire'. And the continuance of sectarianism in an expanding democracy threatened the united parliament with a more numerous Irish party whose primary wishes were not attached to the interests of the empire.[112]

Although Lecky's essays had roundly condemned the union policy and the methods of 1799-1800, he was no repealer or doctrinaire anti-unionist:

> If a legislative union could have been effected between England and Ireland with the full consent of the Irish people ... there can be no doubt that such a union would have consolidated the empire and strengthened the connection.[113]

But neither was Lecky the loyal unionist under a nationalist skin. He strongly resented the remedy of Union in the circumstances of 1800 and regretted the ill effects that he claimed had flown from it. Patriotism in the future would look back in admiration to Grattan's parliament:

> ... the enthusiasm and the national feeling of Ireland will long revert to the period of its independence as forming one bright parenthesis in a history which is covered like the prophet's roll with lamentation and weeping and mourning.[114]

Whatever unionist tendencies appear in *Leaders,* and one must note them, they are effectively obliterated by other passages and by the general thesis. Thus, given that retrospective discontent over the Union would fade if sectarianism were eliminated, the cure for sectarianism was a national spirit cultivated by a restored parliament. And though clerical influence might destroy the reversionary loyalty to the crown, it was a fear, not a fact. Again, the improvement of Ireland's condition, meaning recognition of the national spirit, was in the best interests of the empire. Paradoxically, Lecky was an imperialist who believed in the rights of nationalists — Italian, Polish and Irish.

Not only did he answer his own unionist tendencies, but in other and more numerous passages he was manifestly nationalist. In the essay 'Clerical Influences', he held that the goal towards which Europe was moving was the universal recognition of the rights of nationalities;[115] that the public opinion of a nation should determine its form of government;[116] and that 'the present form of government in Ireland is retained in distinct defiance of the principle ... that every nation had a right to a form of government in accordance with its will'.[117] Irishmen would betray their country if they were to allow the curtain to fall upon its past,[118] 'a tissue of brutality and hypocrisy scarcely surpassed in history'.[119]

> Ever since the dawn of public opinion there has been a party which has maintained that the goal to which Irish patriots should tend is the recognition of their country as a distinct nationality, connected with England by the crown ... to this party all the genius of Ireland has ever belonged. ... The enthusiasm which springs from the memory of the past will ever sustain it ... the enthusiasts of the land will ever struggle against a form of government which was tyrannically imposed.[120]

Lecky's position in 1861 clearly was not that of a nationalist in any republican or separatist sense. He fully accepted Grattan's ideal of a sisterhood relationship between Ireland and England — a connection based on independence and mutual respect. He wrote that each country without the other was imperfect, and that 'the old dream of a republic has long since passed away'.[121] Equally emphatically, Lecky was not unionist, certainly not in the sense in which he became one during the home rule struggle. He was more nationalist than unionist; the nationalism is patent, the unionism has to be elicited. But there is just enough hint of a mind not yet resolved.

Lord Acton, in a letter to Mary Gladstone, described Lecky as one who composed while another tune was running through his head.[122] It might be argued that *Leaders* was written in such circumstances: obviously nationalist, but the first faint notes of the unionist were forming. In the last pages of his book, Lecky looked forward 'with unshaken confidence' to the advent of a leader who would follow in the footsteps of the leaders of the past: 'The mantle of Grattan is not destined to be forever unclaimed.'[123] His bird's-eye view of Irish history was in a recognizable tradition: the past was full of wrongs perpetrated by England, the present was unsatisfactory because Ireland had no parliament of its own, and the future — and this was his distinctive contribution — was pregnant with confidence about the birth of another Grattan. More than any other writer of his time in Ireland, Lecky consciously cultivated the hero and hero-worship.

The new leader was to be in the tradition of the four men whose contribution to Irish nationality Lecky had outlined. He must be neither a lawyer nor a lay-preacher, like the contemporary clerically influenced politicians.[124] He should be broad-minded enough to unite the whole country, catholic and protestant, in a non-sectarian national movement. But who was he to be? And where was he to come from? Lecky had noted in a poem he wrote at this time:

> Alas! how few still guard the patriot flame.
> How few are worthy of the dead and fame![125]

Lecky himself seemed to possess the very qualifications he demanded in the new leader. Was he grooming himself early for a political career? He had collected the works of the Irish orators,[126] had spoken often on political subjects at the Historical Society. His notebooks and poems are replete with references to glory and fame, liberty and patriotism. Lecky was openly ambitious. Who knew better the traditions of the national leadership or was better qualified on the grounds of non-sectarianism?

In a letter on 31 January 1862 he wrote: 'The only two things I should the least care for are a seat in parliament or a position as an author'.[127] By then it was clear that *Leaders* was not going to be a success in the marketplace and he felt he had failed as an author. Similarly, the opportunity of a parliamentary career was unlikely to present itself. But the longing for such a career remained with him for some time yet. During the debate on the 1867 reform bill, Lecky wrote that he found it 'very tantalising to look at the house from a gallery but unfortunately I know no Irish liberals, have not the gift of pushing and fear that there is therefore no chance. If I went in, it should be as a liberal'.[128] His wife noted this intense ambition at the time[129] and he himself returns to the subject again and again and rather dejectedly. In June 1868 he wrote: 'There is not the smallest chance of my ever getting into parliament. I have no influence, no pushing faculty, no popular opinions and very little money.'[130] In March 1870: 'I wish I was in parliament to vote for it' [the Land Bill].[131] As late as May 1871 he was writing: 'I fear I have not quite sufficiently schooled myself to help looking with a rather envious feeling on the actors on that great stage which, I fear, it will never be my lot to mount.'[132] Arthur Booth, with whom he corresponded at this period, noted: 'Probably no other career could have so thoroughly realized Lecky's own ambition as to have become himself, the great political leader of his youthful dreams'.[133] But the seat in parliament was not available. He could not yet don Grattan's mantle. For the moment it must be the pen of Swift. As he wrote in *Leaders*: 'In the meantime, the task of Irish writers is to defend the character of the nation.'[134]

The old repealer, William J. O'Neill Daunt — the most widely respected survivor of O'Connell's movement — was charmed with *Leaders* and wrote a lengthy review for the *Cork Examiner*. He noted the hopeful expectation of a new leader.[135] He suspected that the anonymous author was connected with Trinity College, a 'most cheering symptom of healthy political life in quarters where we scarcely were prepared to suspect its existence.'[136] In his *Journal*, O'Neill Daunt confided that he had reviewed the book 'as a labour of love ... being anxious that

the brilliant abilities of a young protestant nationalist should receive appreciation'. Lecky wrote to him from Naples, making himself known. He assured
O'Neill Daunt that his national principles 'are neither so unknown nor unpopular in Trinity College as the reviewer appears to suppose'.[137] O'Neill Daunt
replied that no earthly cause was so dear to him as the legislative independence of
Ireland and that he was anxious that the political principles Lecky upheld should
be brought before the Irish public. He hoped it would not be the last work that
Lecky would write about Ireland in the eighteenth century.[138]

Apart from this review, the book was hardly noticed. In *Leaders* Lecky warned
that the prophet of the future might lead a big Irish party in parliament, pursue
obstruction, upset the balance of power, and be aided by the Irish in America.[139]
He argued that the situation was so grave in Ireland that the possibility of future
rebellion should not be discounted. His prognosis turned out to be remarkably
accurate in a man of twenty-three. The Fenian rising, strongly aided from
America, took place within a few years of his writing. The further extension of
democracy did result in an Irish party under the leadership of Parnell deciding
the balance of power in parliament and making use of obstruction tactics.
Parnell, in many respects, was the fulfilment of Lecky's dream.

For the moment, however, there seemed little prospect for Lecky in either
politics or literature. John Murray, the publisher, had rejected *Leaders*. He did
not feel sanguine about the success of such a work and advised Lecky to consult
other publishers.[140] Macmillan and Co. regretted that the work would not suit
them and mentioned considerable difficulty in reading the manuscript — anyone who has tried to read Lecky's hand will appreciate their point.[141] So, Lecky
returned to Saunders Otley and Co., a company that had published his earlier
work at his own expense.[142] They expressed gratification at Lecky's continued
confidence and said that his work would cost £100, for which amount Lecky had
a receipt back within a week.[143] It is ironic that *Leaders* — which became one of
the great controversial works in Irish history and was used in the home rule
debate as an arsenal for the arguments of both English and Irish politicians —
had been rejected by two leading publishers and eventually was issued at the
author's own expense. Only 34 copies were sold.[144]

The essays on the four leaders were hardly biographical at all: at least they
contained very little about the private lives of the subjects. This is especially true
of Grattan — the one whom Lecky admired most and the essay he considered the
best.[145] Grattan disappeared for pages while Lecky condemned the penal laws and
sang the praises of nationality. On these discursive subjects, however, his views
coincided with those of Grattan. This method allowed him great scope in later
editions to expand his personal views.

Lecky himself was the first to admit that 'biography is not in my line'.[146] His
forte was historical analysis and imagination (already in evidence in *Religious
Tendencies*). This is especially the case in the essay on O'Connell.[147] A historian in
the Young Ireland tradition would probably have denounced O'Connell in the
strong language of Mitchel or by the more subtle methods of Gavan Duffy. A
unionist would have employed the language of *The Times*, or, of those Irish

protestants who regarded O'Connell 'with feelings of mingled hatred and terror that almost amounted to a superstition'.[148] But, while sharing some of the protestant revulsion to O'Connell, and accepting some of the Young Ireland criticism, Lecky was genuinely impressed by O'Connell's place in history and by a greatness in personality which bore more similarities with Martin Luther than with anyone else.[149] As a breakthrough in historical understanding, 'O'Connell' was Lecky's best essay. This was so despite obvious weaknesses and Lecky's inability to determine whether a preponderance of praise or blame should be attached to O'Connell's name.

As on other issues, in the end the two tunes had intermingled in Lecky's mind. Yet he had succeeded in carrying into historical writing what Lord Acton was to preach: that one should put the other's case even better than he could put it himself. The result was a case for O'Connell stronger than anything that had yet appeared.[150]

Chapter 2

In Search of a Philosophy

For the sons of Anglo-Irish gentlemen the choice of career was restricted by tradition. The eldest son succeeded to the family estate which he might administer as resident or absentee landlord. Younger sons had the army, the law, the church or, occasionally, some other respectable profession. Business was for enterprising foreigners and improving catholics. Politics and literature were merely suitable for the dabbler although offering to the ambitious and intellectual more satisfying distractions than hunting or the endless pursuit of leisure in the health resorts of continental Europe.

By the time he had left Trinity in the summer of 1860 Lecky had decided definitely against the church. 'Feeble and picturesque minds united with a certain emotional excitability are evidently destined for the Church',[1] was his comment to a younger cousin in 1869. His friends from the Historical Society had been attracted to the bar where already Gibson, Plunket and Fitzgibbon were giving indication of the success they were to achieve in the legal profession. 'Pushing, eloquent and logical people should become lawyers,'[2] Lecky said. He was convinced that he himself lacked the first of these characteristics. Besides he hated the idea of getting himself mixed up in other people's quarrels. The army was for non-intellectuals who had energy and fire. As far as he himself was concerned, he said, he would just as soon shoot himself at once. And the prospect of a career as a resident landlord held no attractions whatever for him, for he had no intention of being transformed into another Nebuchadnezzar who became a beast and ate grass.

Residency had not been part of his upbringing. As a child and young adult he had known several homes in Ireland and England, none of them for any considerable stretch of time. As a university student he had kept up his travels, often spending his holidays on the Continent where his step-parents now lived. He left Dublin in the summer of 1860 and spent the greater part of the decade wandering about Europe from one hotel to the next, and from one library to another. The letters which he wrote during this time, especially to his college friend, Arthur Booth, and to his cousin, Knightley Wilmot Chetwode, chart his geographical and intellectual progress. They offer tantalising glimpses of a wandering Irish scholar retracing the steps of his fellow countrymen, those medieval monks who had travelled all over Europe as *peregrini Christi*. These letters reveal a kindly man, with a gentle sense of humour and simple needs, who was thrilled with his experiences and eager to share them with his friends. The correspondence with his cousin, six years his senior, often takes on the form of an exchange of sermonettes: the cousin, in the first couple of years of the correspondence, evidently a bit anxious that Lecky had not yet decided on a stabilizing career for himself, and Lecky for his part, trying to persuade his rusticated correspondent in Portarlington to do some serious reading.

For the first year and a half or so Lecky's wanderings had no other purpose beyond that of self-directed liberal education. Beginning with London in July 1860, he travelled to Paris, Switzerland, Bavaria, the Tyrol and Italy. The greater part of this first year abroad was spent in Milan, Florence, Perugia, Rome and Naples. He spent his time visiting churches, picture galleries, theatres, beauty spots, historic sites, or listening to famous preachers like Dupanloup in Rome or Père Félix in Paris. The different schools of painting of the cities he visited was the only thing he studied any way systematically. After a few months' interval in Monkstown during the summer of 1861 for the proof-reading and publication of his *Leaders*, he returned to the Continent, first to the French Pyrenees, then to Spain — Madrid, Burgos, Toledo, Valencia — and once again to Italy for the first half of 1862. Next to reading, he said, he considered travelling one of the pleasantest occupations. The brigand-infested streets of Bologna which frightened off the more sober minded did not intimidate him unduly. He suffered greater loss in Rome where, walking in a trance, thinking of all things in heaven and earth except those immediately around him, he had his smart umbrella twisted out of his hand by a man who ran off down a lane. And although he acquired a pair of pistols in Spain to protect his person and property, he never bought the gunpowder for fear of accidentally shooting himself.

In Bavaria he found the Oberammergau passion play, performed by the local peasants and lasting seven and a quarter hours, 'extremely beautiful',[3] and interesting to a degree he had hardly imagined possible. Florence enchanted him as 'the most classic place in the whole world'.[4] Although Naples was delightful, he thought the Neapolitans the least civilized people he had ever seen. Every second man wore a red shirt in honour of their hero, Garibaldi. He visited Gaeta shortly after its capture and came to the assistance of a gang of small boys whose hammering on a shell had caused an explosion only a few yards from Lecky and severe burns and cuts to themselves. At Milan he went to see the great actress, Ristori, who haunted him so much that he went to see her again at Genoa. In later years he described her as an old flame of his, and after he had come to know her personally he entertained her in St Moritz and in Dublin. Rome was like a great museum which took him more than one visit to explore. He liked to attend the Easter ceremonies there, presided over by the pope, Pio Nono, and enjoyed also the music in the churches, especially the singing of the eunuchs.

In Spain the attractions were the schools of painting, the sculpture, the gothic architecture, the good theatre and the comic opera. The number of miraculous images bewildered him. He was amazed at the uncommonly good theological digestions of the Spanish people on the one hand, and, on the other, the ridicule which their plays poured on the clergy. Apart from the bull-fights, cafes and theatres, the Spanish seemed to have very little else to do but stare at foreigners.

But then, Lecky did his own share of staring at the Spanish ladies dressed in their graceful mantillas, endlessly waving their fans and walking in 'the most killing manner'.[5] In the Introduction to his *History of Morals*, and elsewhere, he was later to apologize in a rather priggish fashion for introducing the delicate subject of women. It is not without its own small charm, therefore, that privately he was human enough to admire Spanish beauties and Italian prima donnas, and to discover that women were 'a permanent perturbing element'.[6]

At a hotel in Florence he was entertained by 'a very immoral gentleman', who gave him 'interesting information on very improper subjects.'[7] At the same hotel he was both impressed and amused by the stories told by Gavazzi, the Italian priest, orator, actor, '48 rebel, ally of Garibaldi and convert to evangelicalism, who, at the invitation of the Irish evangelicals, had preached in Dublin's Rotunda in the 1850s where Lecky had first heard him. With the exception of Dean Kirwan, Lecky said, Gavazzi was the only man of talent, not notoriously of bad character, in the last one hundred and fifty years who had become a protestant. He also became friends with the Irish novelist, Charles Lever, a British Vice-Consul in Italy, a household word in Victorian fiction and an impressive swimmer. On one occasion, during the summer of 1866, when he found himself staying in the same hotel on Lake Geneva as John Henry Newman, one of the people he most wished to meet, he was not bold enough to introduce himself. Newman in any case did not look engaging. He was very melancholy, gazing into the bottom of his teacup, and he was in the charge of a keeper, a 'stupid-looking person named St John.' Newman, he wrote, 'has a very large nose bending about … in different directions to economise space … and there is something very wrong indeed in the junction of his trousers and boots'.[8] For the two or three days while they shared the same hotel Lecky found it tantalizing not to be able to speak to Newman, so he '… thought of an Irish saint … who whenever … she was in love used to put her feet in the fire in order that one fire might drive out another; and I got Buckle from the … library and always brought him down to tea.' Eventually, the presence of a band drove Lecky from this hotel. Since he enjoyed doses of perfect solitude there were always those others whom he wished to avoid. On one occasion he went to Pau to get away from his relatives for a while and be near a library. At meal-time in his hotel, however, he was placed beside an evangelical lady, 'a veritable pythoness', who 'poured forth loud threnodies on the abominations of popery and the demerits of bishops.'[9]

After a year and a half of these wanderings, and the tremendous impact which several readings of Buckle's book had on him, his travels assumed more purpose. He grew weary of reading about art, reverted to history with all of the enthusiasm of someone who had just seen the light, and began the researches into what became his first full-length book, the *History of the Rise and Influence of the Spirit of Rationalism in Europe*. His step-parents had settled in Bagnères de Bigorre in the autumn of 1862. This resort in the French Pyrenees had not only the advantages of an agreeable climate but it also had a very good and little-used library. He spent part of every year over the next few years reading and writing at Bagnères. From here he launched out into the libraries of France, Spain and Italy 'indulging', as he said, 'in an immense amount of literary vagabondage.'[10] Pau was close by, and in the library there he read a volume a day over a few weeks. Then he went to Paris to read in the library of the Rue Richelieu and the Bibliotheque Imperiale. He also used libraries at Montpelier, Avignon and Toulon. In Spain and Italy libraries had been formed from the books of the recently suppressed monasteries and these were particularly useful for Lecky. So, in Granada, Malaga, Cadiz, Seville, Toledo, Madrid, Barcelona, Florence, Rome and Naples, librarians stared at the young Irish scholar who requested the curious old Latin books of the early monks. As his excitement grew he quickly buried himself in the next library and, as he said, 'a night in a locomotive chair takes one very far'.[11] It was what he called 'half vagabond, half bookworm existence, diving into half the libraries of Europe and breaking unhappy porters' backs with boxes of books'. And yet he had been at the same time so much alone, sometimes not conversing with anyone for days, that writing became for him 'almost a necessary vent'.[12]

In October 1866 Lecky took a bachelor apartment in London to be near the British Museum reading room. While his many books were thus conveniently housed he continued to travel a great deal abroad doing the research for his next book on European morals. During all of his travels he was also feeling his way towards that philosophy of history which inspired his work.

For the two months of 1861 while he wandered through the Pyrenees, 'admiring the scenery and reading Spinoza',[13] he was getting 'exceedingly enthusiastic about the scenery and exceedingly perplexed about the difference between Hegel and Schelling.'[14] His intention was to learn Spanish before going south, but 'having discovered the first volume of Buckle in the circulating library I am immersed (for I don't know how many'th time) in it.'[15]

The trip to Spain was Lecky's road to Damascus. Buckle had burst upon him like the sudden revelation of a great truth:

> I have no hesitation in saying that I believe him to be the very greatest thinker and scholar now living. There is to my mind something almost miraculous in the combination in one man of such extraordinary subtlety of thought and reasoning, such boundless learning, such a keen appreciation of every side of every subject, and such clear and transparent eloquence. ... It is perhaps the most suggestive book I have ever read.[16]

This was superlative praise indeed, especially when it is remembered that Lecky already had given indications of that coldly analytical and impartial caste of mind for which he was soon to be noted. The infatuation with Buckle was not simply a lightning flash. Six months later, from Sorrento near Naples, he wrote to the same friend:

> I have a greater faith in his [Buckle's] intellect than in that of any living man, a very profound belief in many of his principles, and an admiration for his book which was almost stronger after the fifth reading than after the first.[17]

Lecky was back in Dublin in the summer of 1862 when he read about Buckle's sudden death at the age of forty-one:

> I confess I can hardly think of anything else, and except a few very near friends have never been so sorry before. To people who have my way of life a very great writer becomes an object of affection which it is difficult for the mere 'reading world' to conceive, and there is no one who has been for so many years before the public whom I admire so deeply, whom I should have so wished to know, and from whose book I have gained so much of thought and knowledge. I have long been convinced that he was one of the very greatest men that England has produced and one who was destined to throw light on some of those questions which are still in the most chaotic condition ... .[18]

An immediate consequence of Lecky's discovery of Buckle was the renewal of his faith in a literary career. The dark doubts that had beset him after the indifferent public reception of his first two prose works were soon dissipated under the influence of Buckle's strong light. At the time of Buckle's death, Lecky was already engaged in a major study of rationalism in Europe, and his letter to Chetwode concluded with a personal act of faith:

> ... to my mind nothing can be more noble or more sublime than the student life directed solely to the attainment and the diffusion of truth, bursting through the bonds of every ancient prejudice, expatiating over every department of the vast field of knowledge, and carried on without pause or without deviation till the curtain of death has fallen.[19]

Lecky was so impressed by Buckle that he was eager to share the discovery with others. In several letters to his cousin, Knightley Wilmot Chetwode of Portarlington, he pleaded with him to read Buckle which he said was possibly the best book (except perhaps Macaulay's *Essays*) to introduce people who read little or no literature to general knowledge.[20] Lecky's promotion of Buckle, backed up by suitably chosen scolding fits, eventually proved effective. Yet his praise of Buckle was not intended merely for a rural cousin's benefit, as letters to more intellectual friends show.

Lecky had already been exposed to similar intellectual experiences as Buckle, although in varying degrees: Darwin and Lyell's scientific discoveries and their effect on the biblical cosmogony; the positivism of Comte; the enlightenment of the French historical writers, especially Bayle, Montesquieu and Voltaire; the famous third chapter of Macaulay's *History of England;* and the excitement of Gibbon's discussion of the relationship between Christianity and European political and social developments. But there is no reason to believe that Lecky would have written his books on rationalism and morals without being fired by the example of Buckle's *History of Civilization.* Buckle had given concrete expression to intellectual trends, and the achievement made Lecky's next attempt that much easier to accomplish.

The first volume of the *History of Civilization* had appeared in 1857 and the second in 1861. Lecky considered the second even better than the first.[21] Buckle, who, as Acton noted, was very much under the influence of Comte,[22] complained that while in other fields of inquiry the need for generalization had been universally admitted, this was not the case with the study of history, and he proposed to remedy that situation in his own historical work. The mere compilation of fact by historians was not enough. He proposed instead a 'science of history', or the discovery of the general laws of human development:

> ... I hope to accomplish for the history of man something equivalent, or at all events analogous, to what has been affected by other inquirers for the different branches of natural science.[23]

An isolated and neglected figure in Victorian literature, Buckle had no British antecedents, was almost without disciples, and has attracted few sympathetic commentaries. Yet he had made a meteor-like appearance in the world of English historiography. The effect of the *History of Civilization* on Lecky was to communicate to the young man still in search of a career some of Buckle's own high sense of purpose, of novelty and originality of approach. The first chapter of Buckle was an eloquent plea for the necessity of wide preliminary study which would enable historians 'to grasp their subject in the whole of its natural relations'.[24] Here was the conviction that 'as yet scarcely anything had been done towards discovering the principles which govern the character and destiny of nations'.[25] History was still 'miserably deficient'[26] and awaiting generous intellectual enthusiasms. Buckle's ambitious phrase about 'solving the problem of the universe' was something Lecky still remembered a couple of years after the publication of the two books he wrote under Buckle's spell.[27]

Even today, and despite the fact that many critics have commented adversely on Buckle's ambitious scheme, it is possible to sense the intellectual excitement of his writings. Lecky was attracted by the 'scope and unity of his system'; by his erudition; by 'the wonderful discrimination and depth of his literary criticisms'; by 'the extraordinary beauty of his style'.[28]

What most attracted, perhaps, was the feeling of intellectual kinship. Lecky had been trying to say things in his writing which he found better expressed in Buckle:

> I naturally admire him [Buckle] rather more than you would for I had worked out many of his views for myself ... and I have read, very extensively many of the subjects he treats of.[29]

Lecky was very pleased to find that Buckle and he held the same views about the 'secularization of politics'. He said that he had tried to embody in *Leaders* certain theories of his own about the relationship of patriotism to sectarianism, but had found it much better expressed in Buckle.[30] On another occasion he wrote:

> His central principle — that the secularization of politics is the chief measure and condition of political progress — is also that of my *L[eaders of] P[ublic] O[pinion]*.[31]

Buckle's inspiration, together with Lecky's own theological and historical interests and his purposeful travels — both intellectual and geographical — through modern and medieval Europe, eventually resulted in the *History of the Rise and Influence of the Spirit of Rationalism in Europe.* It appeared in January 1865, the first of Lecky's books to be published under his own name. The object, explained in the preface, was to trace the transition in the European mind from the age of superstition to the age of reason. Lecky noted how dogmatic theology, religious persecution and acceptance of the miraculous and superstitious gradually had succumbed to the dictates of reason, conscience and the laws of science. This change in the intellectual climate, he argued, owed less to logical argument than to the congruence of favourable circumstances. The Enlightenment had discovered that 'every great change of belief had been proceeded by a great change in the intellectual condition of Europe'. The success of any opinion therefore depended much less on the force of its arguments, or upon the ability of its advocates, than upon the 'pre-disposition of society' to receive it, or upon the intellectual type of the age. This type was the product of the intellectual and social tendencies of a period.

Religion and the religious belief of any given period, therefore, could not be left entirely to the theologian, nor even to the ecclesiastical historian, who might see himself performing much the same function as the theologian. Changes in the habit of thought and in the 'climate of opinion', and not theological truth or falsehood, were the province of the new history that Lecky eagerly embraced. Despite his strong theological interests, he saw himself as a historian of opinions, concerned with the rise and fall of those doctrines that were to be found in the general intellectual condition of an age. His book aimed to be what he called the 'psychological history of Europe', seen, however, in the whole sociological environment. Separate chapters dealt with the declining sense of the miraculous; with magic, witchcraft and idolatry and their gradual dispersal by the advent of the rationalist spirit; the relations over the centuries between religion and art, religion and science, religion and industry; the moral development that accompanied intellectual progress; the causes, course and decline of religious persecution; and the secularization of politics. As the book makes clear, the spirit of rationalism had contributed to some of the greatest triumphs of civilization: the destruction of witchcraft and religious persecution; the decay of those 'ghastly notions about hell which had diseased the imagination and embittered the characters of men'; the abolition of the guilt of error and of asceticism, which between them had paralyzed mankind's intellectual and material progress.

The buoyancy of the mid-Victorian era, the idea of infinite progress and the inevitability of limitless improvement flowed freely through Lecky's book. It was in essence an act of faith in the achievements and promise of the nineteenth century. Liberty was its great enthusiasm — liberty of the spirit and the mind from theological obscurantism, liberty of the individual from the political, economic and intellectual tyrannies of the Dark Ages. Democracy, especially the 'democratic union of nations', was 'the last and highest expression of the Christian ideal of the brotherhood of mankind'.[32] The principle of the rights of nationalities was championed as the basis of political morality.[33] Lecky's enthusiasm for nationalism was go great that he overlooked the fact that it was among the most powerful threats to peace. Political economy, he confidently predicted, would in time eliminate war, and the industrial element was 'destined one day to become the dominant influence in politics'.[34] The secularization of society was upheld as the great virtue and guarantee of the future. 'Liberty, industry and peace', Lecky wrote, 'are in modern societies indissolubly connected and their ultimate ascendancy depends upon a movement which may be retarded but cannot possibly be arrested.'[35]

Rationalism was an ambitious book, and Lecky was aware of the enormity of the task he had set himself. He realized, he said, that what he had to deal with were forms of belief which had no living representatives; he had to reconstruct modes of thought of long vanished superstitions; he had to uncover in the obscurity of a distant past 'the hidden bias of the imagination' which determined remote beliefs and dogmas; he had to bring together the different departments of classical, medieval and modern intellectual life. The project could have been undertaken only by a man of immense self-confidence, infused with the idea of progress and convinced that the all-embracing laws of history, like those of the physical sciences, were there to be discovered.

The book was acclaimed. Longman, the publisher, told Lecky that the editors of two of the leading literary magazines, Reeve of the *Edinburgh Review* and Froude of *Fraser's Magazine*, had been 'particularly emphatic in their eulogies.'[36] A short time later Longman forwarded a letter he had received from H.H. Milman, the Dean of St Paul's and a noted ecclesiastical historian, explaining the pleasure he had derived from the book, and his admiration for its literary merits: 'It is the book which if I had been younger I might have attempted to write, but which I rejoice to find has fallen into such hands.'[37]

Froude had once quoted Goethe to the effect that, as soon as a man had done anything remarkable, there seemed to be a general conspiracy to prevent him from doing it again: 'He is feasted, feted, caressed: his time is stolen from him by breakfasts, dinners, societies, idle businesses of a thousand kinds.'[38] It was Lecky's turn to discover that London society was anxious to fete a new literary star. 'Longman', he wrote to a friend, 'threatens me with dinners.'[39]

The chorus of praise which greeted the *Rationalism* was started by Reeve, whose review began:

> We opened these volumes never having heard the name of the author, and entirely ignorant of his pretensions to a place in English literature. We closed them with the conviction that Mr Lecky is one of the most accomplished writers and one of the most ingenious thinkers of the time, and that the book deserves the highest commendation we can bestow upon it.

One note of commendation which would have particularly pleased Lecky read: 'No other Irishman since Burke has devoted his talents with equal success to political philosophy.'[40] Several pages in many other journals were devoted to reviews of *Rationalism*.[41] The *Edinburgh*, the *Westminster*[42] and the *Athenaeum*

were the most praiseworthy. Lecky's strengths and weaknesses were nicely balanced in John Tulloch's review article in the *Contemporary*.[43] The *Spectator*,
Dublin Review, *British Quarterly*,[44] and James Fitzjames Stephen in *Fraser's
Magazine*, while acknowledging the book's great merits, concentrated more on
its defects. The most hostile review was George Eliot's in the *Fortnightly Review*.
It was both waspish and patronizing: Lecky was not so much an original mind as
a popularizer of the findings of recent scholarship and science. She described the
'general reader' as one who possessed a 'spongy texture of mind', who was
opposed to nothing in particular, whose only bigotry was against any clearly
defined opinion, whose only stand was for the 'utmost liberty of private hazi-
ness', and who in matters of religion felt attracted only to an undefined Christianity. Clever and fair-minded authors, who were very much above the 'general
reader' in knowledge and ability but not too remote from him in their habits of
thinking, would provide for him acceptable infusions of history and science.
Among such writers, said Eliot, *Rationalism* entitled Lecky to a very high place.[45]

Lord Acton thought that Eliot had been 'barely just' to Lecky,[46] but she had
pointed to a very important element in his success. His book had widespread
appeal and had struck a chord in the Victorian mind. This was partially at least
what Acton himself was thinking of when he described Lecky's *Rationalism* and
its successor, *Morals*, as not rising much above the 'vulgar level'.[47] Milman
pinpointed the same phenomenon of its appeal, although more generously, when
he described it as the book 'which was wanted — especially wanted at the present
time'.[48] Many years after its publication, Lady Stanhope asserted that the young
people of her generation owed Lecky a special debt of gratitude for the book: 'I
can well remember how it focused and clarified the feelings which were everywhere in the air and which in this work found their reason and their record.'[49]
That neither Lecky nor his wife made any reference to the Eliot review may
indicate that her hostile remarks had cut deeply. On the other hand, he could
well afford to take a balanced philosophical attitude towards the reviews. He
preferred the intelligent if critical notices to those by which he had been 'stupidly
puffed'.[50] The first edition was soon sold out. Seventeen subsequent editions were
to be published mostly in Lecky's own lifetime. Two separate German translations appeared. The book was translated into Russian, but was put under clerical
supervision there because it was seen as an attack on Christianity. Lecky at
twenty-seven had become a Victorian man of letters.

Lecky's next book was a logical projection of *Rationalism*. In the latter, he had
outlined the history of the decline of certain theological beliefs. His new book
examined the imposition of those beliefs and the circumstances which had
favoured their general acceptance. *History of European Morals from Augustus to
Charlemagne* was published in the spring of 1869. It dealt with the changes that
had taken place in the moral standard and in the moral type in that timespan. By
the moral standard Lecky meant the degree to which in different ages virtues had
been enjoined by moralists and practised among the people. By the moral type he
meant the relative importance that had been attached to different virtues in
different ages. Thus the changing moral standard was reflected in the successive

moral types, such as the classical hero, the medieval ascetic, the chivalrous knight and the gentleman scholar. The historian of morals had to discover in each period the rudimentary virtue — patriotism, chastity, charity, humility — for it regulated in a great degree the position assigned to all the others.

Rationalism had ended with a reference to the one dark shadow on an otherwise brilliant horizon: the reaction to the spiritualism of a more theological age had led to an increase in materialism expressing itself philosophically in utilitarianism. *Morals* opened with a chapter on the nature and obligations of morals, in which Lecky examined the rival theories of the utilitarians and the intuitionists. He came down decisively in favour of the latter. Chapters dealt with morals in the pagan empire and their influence on legislation and literature; the conversion of Rome to Christianity; the church as a moral agent in society; and morals in the medieval empire. A final chapter treated the changes that had taken place with regard to women. He apologized for having to dwell at such length on a subject so sensitive to Victorian ears.

The book ranged over ground that was familiar to his educated readers. Its originality lay not so much in the facts that Lecky had gathered, sometimes from obscure sources, as in the manner in which these facts were grouped and in the significance he ascribed to them. The search for the laws of history and the influence of Henry Buckle were as much in evidence as in *Rationalism*, and once again the book created a great stir in the literary world — fifteen editions were issued. *Morals* remained his own favourite of his books. It is also the one that is now perhaps most dated.

Sections on art and the theatre in *Rationalism* were intended to illustrate how the particular intellectual climate under discussion was reflected in the contemporary world of the artist and dramatist. Lecky's interest in these subjects, and his feeling that it would be a pity not to make use of notes made during his wanderings through Europe, led him to incorporate into his argument essays which, however pleasant, were not strictly necessary. Similarly, in *Morals* the drift of the argument sometimes disappeared for pages while Lecky meandered along, mixing significant and insignificant detail indiscriminately. In his anxiety to show that the biographical counted for less in history than had been supposed, he sometimes underrated the effects of rational argument, free will and human passion. Theological systems, not individuals, were blamed for the sins of persecutors. He assumed too stark a contradiction between reason and religion. Because he believed it to be the business of history to generalize, he sometimes was too quick to do so, occasionally on very slender evidence indeed. He was easily seduced by the spirit of his own age, so that what he wrote had too contemporary a ring to last, but by the same token it was bound to achieve popularity in its own time. His faith in the idea of progress did not always allow him to see the complexities of a historical situation.

It was impossible for Lecky to write about rationalism and morals without the question of his own religious beliefs becoming an issue with his readers. Organized religion had no great appeal for him, and there is little evidence that it played a significant part in his life. Few references to church-going occur in his correspondence, and where they do, they relate as much to aesthetic or scholarly motivations as to religious ones. Much later in his career, at a time when political opponents tried to describe him as an atheist, a supporter vouchsafed that she had seen him at church. He regarded himself as a Christian, but Auchmuty goes too far in asserting that Lecky did not deny any article of Christianity.[51] While this may be true, the point is that he did not consider any dogma as essential or unchanging.[52] It is evident from what he wrote about transubstantiation, the damnation of unbaptized infants, the Calvinistic doctrine of reprobation and the doctrine of infallibility, that Lecky not only did not hold with these dogmas, he abhorred them. *Morals* was more directly anti-catholic than any of his other works, and because it also appeared to several reviewers to be anti-Christian in its tendency, he was taken to task by catholics, protestant fundamentalists and orthodox anglicans, as well as by the utilitarians, 'The chief meaning of fame,' Carlyle wrote to him, was to have 'all the owls of the community beating at your windows.'[53] Many regarded Lecky as a Victorian heresiarch, a nineteenth-century counterpart of his favourite Pelagius. Others saw a protestant divine gone astray in him, one who might have graced the great tradition of Berkeley, Butler and Whately, if only he had taken orders.

A mind that was secularist, rationalist, relativist, and yet in its own committed way also moralist, was revealed in these two books. Lecky's personal moral base, however, lay not in any dogmatic scheme emanating from religious principle, but rather in the standard of society. The real virtues were those of Victorian England: work, economy, temperance, moderation, philanthropy, truth, reason, tolerance, education, cleanliness, patriotism, liberalism, progress. Just as he distrusted dogmatic theology, he also distrusted unassisted individual reason, and regarded the collective wisdom of mankind — displayed in history — as the surer guide. When he described his ideal type of the mid-nineteenth century as someone with the accomplishments of the scholar and the refinement of a gentleman blending with the noble qualities of a moral teacher unsullied by fanaticism,[54] he was merely looking in his mirror. It has been well said that it was Lecky, not Marx, who was the representative of the general beliefs of his time.[55]

The mid-Victorian mind, leavened as it was with evangelicalism, was in no mood to accept the agnosticism or atheism or the pernicious implications for religion that seemed to be associated with the recent discoveries in the natural sciences. Many were suspicious of the application of the methods of the natural sciences to the study of man, society and religion. They rejected the rationalism of the age which sought the dethronement of God (and of God's age-old establishment). The scepticism of Bayle, Descartes, Montaigne and Voltaire belonged to an earlier age and to another climate. The longing for God and religion ran deep. Any reconciliation with science and reason which did not represent a total capitulation was welcome.

Against this background, Lecky's contribution to the intellectual life of the mid-Victorian era was significant indeed. His *Rationalism* and *Morals* were read voraciously. Sugar-coated with a veneer of Christian belief, the scepticism, rejected when it appeared in more bitter treatises, was successfully dispensed by

Lecky to an expanding and eager middle class. Montaigne's statement that it was setting a very high value on our own opinions to roast men alive on account of them, was made more palatable when quoted in the context of Lecky's historical treatment of theological systems. Readers were relieved to discover that the rationalism of Lecky's title had nothing to do with the cynicism of those German professors who, in their scholarly footnotes, had divested Christ of his divinity. Reason had nowhere been proclaimed god in Lecky's gospel, certainly not in so many words. The absence of any such proclamation reassured the more religious and orthodox among his readers. Providence was described as manifesting itself in history through the development of the spirit of rationalism, and it was this affirmation that helped the propagation of reason as religion. Those who could no longer accept God, the miracle-worker, manifesting himself at every turn of the season and in every incident of life, but who, at the same time, craved for a god in their world, welcomed Lecky's providence of history as a new messiah. Banished by science and rational explanation from everyday life, the finger of God was now seen, instead, tracing a way for the progress of man's reason and man's morals over the long course of history. God, reason, morals and history all gained from this juxtaposition. The idea of history as the true revelation of God was enormously enhanced by Lecky's *Rationalism* and *Morals*.

The traces of the influence of Buckle's *History of Civilization* on Lecky's own work were many and deep. There are numerous instances in *Rationalism* and *Morals* where Lecky expressed views already advanced in Buckle's book. It would be too hasty to conclude that in any of these cases Lecky first found the idea in Buckle and merely made his own of it. Buckle had gathered into his work much that was already in the air around him, and if Lecky had never read Buckle, he would have found it comparatively easy to express ideas that both men imbibed from the prevailing intellectual atmosphere.[56] Lecky himself was conscious of this when he referred to the difficulty

> ... that all who have been much occupied with a single department of history must sometimes have, in distinguishing the ideas which have sprung from their own reflections, from those which have been derived from books.[57]

Often, then, where we find Lecky expressing the same view as Buckle, the most likely explanation is that both writers used the same source. Some leading ideas of both men were derived from Burke, Adam Smith, Mill, Whately,[58] Mosheim, Hallam,[59] and Carlyle.[60] Lecky was well acquainted with the work of these writers long before he became enthusiastic over Buckle. There were occasions when such a discovery led to a toning down of Lecky's high opinion of Buckle's originality, as when he realized the extent of Buckle's borrowing from Montesquieu on the influence of climate in history.[61]

Some thirty years after his first acquaintance with Buckle's work, he drew A.S.G. Canning's attention to it. Canning was then writing *Literary Influence in British History*, and Lecky said that he would find in *History of Civilization* much of value.[62] Lecky recommended one chapter in Buckle as 'admirable', 'painted with great power', and illustrated 'with ample learning',[63] and another chapter as 'most eloquent'.[64]

But it was not so much the eloquence of the style, nor any specific historical facts or interpretations that most influenced Lecky. Rather, it was Buckle's general approach, his philosophy of history. One thing both men were convinced of was that history was not what both Seeley at Cambridge and Freeman at Oxford as late as the 1890s believed it to be — merely 'past politics'. Buckle and Lecky consciously strove to break away from all such narrow conceptions of history's sphere.

Buckle claimed that it was the French historical writers — Voltaire, Montesquieu and Turgot — who had taught historians to concentrate on matters of real importance and to neglect the idle details of monarchs and battles.[65] This idea, however, had become widespread during the eighteenth century and was to be found in the works of Vico, Hume, Herder and carried very effectively into practice in the nineteenth century by Michelet. There is no doubt that, before he had ever read Buckle, Lecky had been exposed to the idea of a history that was wider than the merely political. He would have experienced it in Macaulay — whom he had read as a youth — in Hume and in Hallam. In his longest and best-remembered work, his history of the eighteenth century, Lecky explained that he had found it 'necessary to suppress much that has a purely biographical, party or military interest': 'It has been my object to disengage from the great mass of facts those which relate to the permanent forces of the nation, or which indicate some of the more enduring features of national life.'[66]

Of his contribution to European intellectual history, he wrote:

> Both books belong to a very small school of historical writings which began in the seventeenth century with Vico, was continued by Condorcet, Herder, Hegel and Comte, and which found its last great representative in Mr Buckle (from many of whose opinions I widely differ, but from whom I have learnt very much).[67]

Chapter 3

The Laws of History

The examination of large spans of both time and space has always fostered belief in the notion of laws of history, and has encouraged historians to generalize. And Lecky had chosen a big canvas. *Rationalism* and *Morals* ranged over European history from the classical period of Greece and Rome, through the Christian Middle Ages and down to the current industrialization and secularization of society.

Besides, the age in which he wrote was extremely law-conscious. Boyle's law, Newton's laws, Galileo's laws, which had already described the phenomena of the physical universe, created an intellectual fashion and encouraged the search for economic laws such as those propounded by Adam Smith and Gresham, the population laws of Malthus and the laws that governed society. Buckle had written about the need to discover the general laws operating in history in the same way as they had already been discovered for physics, and made some show of formulating these laws himself by the empirical methods of science. Lecky, on the other hand, simply assumed that the case for the need to discover these laws had been made, and so proceeded to incorporate general laws into his narrative.

His theory of history commenced with a bowing of the head to Providence. Buckle, at least by implication, had excluded Providence from his scheme: it was enough for him to feel that, as the laws of physics explained the physical world, so too the science of history would unfold all there was to be known about the world of man, without any reference to the guiding hand of God. Buckle maintained that theologians had obstructed the study of history, and was pleased that the supernatural interference in which Bossuet delighted was absent from Voltaire's historical work. Bossuet's method, he said, however suitable for theologians, was fatal to all independent inquiries.[1] Lecky, too, distinguished between the sphere of the historian and the sphere of the theologian;[2] but he, more than Buckle, was influenced by the fathers of the church, as well as by the writings of the great modern divines, including Bossuet.

Lecky did not exclude the possibility of divine interference with the order of physical nature. A world governed by special acts of perpetual intervention, such as that which medieval theologians imagined, was perfectly conceivable, but he believed that this was not the system of the planet inhabited by man.[3] By analogy, therefore, miracles were not impossible in the relationship between God and man. Lecky, however, created the strong impression that this argument for the feasibility of miracles was merely similar to that for the existence of ghosts or fairies, namely, that no one could prove that there were no such things.[4]

There was some truth in the *British Quarterly*'s comment that in *Rationalism* Lecky had not taken up the supreme anti-supernatural position in so far as he allowed that an omnipotent God could reverse his own laws.[5] But Lecky's general tendency was to exclude Providence from the whole of nature. He thought it primitive of people to imagine that rain, for example, was the result of arbitrary interposition in answer to prayer.[6] Physical science, he said, had disproved the theological theories which attributed all natural phenomena to isolated acts of divine intervention.[7]

More positively, Lecky's position was that Providence guided evolution and therefore progress. There was a law, watched over by Providence, which regulated the orderly and progressive transformation of the general intellectual condition of society. Great laws of eternal development presided over and directed the progress of belief, infused order into seeming chaos and revealed in every apparent aberration a purpose and a meaning. As in the laws of matter, Providence, tending ever to perfection, destroys every obstacle and confounds those who seek the arrest of progress.[8] The intellect of man, therefore, moved ever onwards in a given direction, under the influence of general laws. While this order and sequence in the progressive history of opinion could not be destroyed by man or by man's institutions, nevertheless he did retard, accelerate or modify its course. Man might be carried along by the force of a general current, but he was no helpless leaf upon the stream of history.[9] Lecky was even prepared, occasionally, to spell out his conception of a Providence guiding progress with specific illustrations. In his vision, it was providential that the downfall of Spain came about in the sixteenth century, thereby removing a grave barrier to the general advancement of Europe.[10]

Thus far, then, Lecky had a lawgiver in history guiding a slow, evolutionary process. It was a lawgiver not altogether dissimilar to Herbert Butterfield's concept of a Providence which guided human history like a parent with a hand on the saddle of the child's bicycle and 'allowing a considerable elasticity in regard to the general drift and direction of the whole expedition.'[11] But where Lecky's notion differed from Butterfield's was in assuming (like Acton and other Victorians) that what he regarded as progress was also the manifestation of Providence, and that divine ways, at least after they had happened, were scrutable to mankind.

In Lecky's view, law in history was also to be found on another level. Here the influence of Buckle and of his mentors, especially Comte and Montesquieu, was quite pronounced in Lecky's work. With these earlier writers, Lecky held that race, climate and geographical features were among the great external influences which determined the characteristics of different civilizations and societies.[12] Differences in climate and temperature, he said, affected the incidence of vice and virtue, or 'moral statistics'[13] — a phrase he probably owed to Buckle,[14] who in turn had been greatly impressed by a work bearing that title and written by A. Quetelet.[15]

So convinced was Lecky of the influence of climate upon morals that he wrote:

The rivers that rise and fall with the winter torrents, or the summer drought; the insect life that is called into being by the genial spring and destroyed by the returning frost; the aspect of vegetation, which pursues its appointed changes through the recurring seasons: these do not reflect more faithfully or obey more implicitly external influences, than do some great departments of the acts of man.[16]

He accepted that the evidence produced by the 'moral statisticians' was 'so ample that it enables us, within certain limits, even to predict the future'.[17] Enthusiastically he wrote:

the time may come when the man who lays the foundation-stone of a manufacture will be able to predict with assurance in what proportion the drunkenness and unchastity of his city will be increased by his enterprise.[18]

The claim that the occurrences of history could be tabled in statistics and formulated into a law, thereby raising history to a science like physics — which would enable historians to predict the future — was precisely the point that roused many critics against Buckle. Indeed, Buckle made no bones about the point and attacked the idea of free will as a force in history much more vehemently than Lecky ever dared.[19] On the contrary, Lecky declared his belief in free will; the proof he offered was that of Locke, namely, that its existence was demonstrated by the fact that we are conscious that we are capable of pursuing a course of action which is extremely distasteful rather than another course which would be extremely agreeable.[20] That there were influences independent of human control which contributed largely to the regularity of the course of vice, said Lecky, in no way destroyed the freedom of will.[21]

Once again, then, as in the case of Providence in history, Lecky had stopped short of advancing all the way with Buckle's philosophy. Beyond recording his general agreement with the idea of the significance of the influence of climate on human history, Lecky did not elaborate.[22] By implication, however, general principles derived from the observation of relatively large expanses of history. Thus, he believed that an examination of the history of morals over one thousand years of European history could furnish the historian with the general principles about the processes involved.[23]

Within this framework provided by Providence and climate, the gradualness of the slow, evolutionary processes of history was a basic tenet of Lecky's philosophy. Gibbon and Voltaire, two of the great eighteenth-century influences on Lecky, accepted the notion that history changes by revolution.[24] Exposed as he was to the advances of nineteenth-century science, Lecky held that evolution, not revolution, was the engine of history and the manner in which it progressed.[25] Thus, in the speculation of the schoolmen of the Middle Ages was to be found 'the first link of a chain of principles that terminated in the French revolution.'[26] He also wrote about 'a long train of circumstances culminating in the Reformation',[27] and claimed that we could dimly descry in the period before Charlemagne the first stages of what was to emerge as the divine right of kings and reverence for aristocracies.[28] When he came (in *Rationalism*) to account for the rise of the spirit of rationalism in Europe and the overthrow of superstition, or to unfold (in *Morals*) the progression of moral types, each an advance on the preceding one, or to trace (as in *Leaders*) the emergence of a more advanced, secular, and liberal public opinion, evolution from lower to higher types was the method he followed.

The general tendencies of the age,[29] therefore, not particular events, however momentous, nor individuals however great,[30] nor arguments however powerful and convincing in themselves, were the chief concern of the historian.[31] Laws and statesmen for the most part, Lecky said, indicate and ratify but do not create. They are like the hands of the watch which move obediently to the hidden machinery within.[32] The significance of the general tendencies in history, and of the successive moral types, 'climate of opinion'[33] and characteristics of each era, was that they created a qualitative difference between one age and the next. Hence Lecky advised 'every sincere student' 'to endeavour to understand what is the dominant idea or characteristic of the period with which he is occupied....'[34]; and the historian of morals had 'no more important task' than to discover in each period the 'rudimentary virtue', 'for it regulates in a great degree the position assigned to all others'.[35]

Lecky regarded it as the historian's task not merely to narrate the fluctuations of intellectual progress, but to seek 'to throw some light upon the laws that govern them'.[36] In accounting for these transitions that had taken place in opinion between one stage of development and the next, he lay down the principle that 'the study of predispositions is much more important than the study of arguments.'[37] It was a principle he never wearied of repeating.[38] In societies and eras, as well as with individuals, there operated a 'hidden bias of the imagination'[39] which ran deeper than any strife of argument, and had a much greater influence upon the sequence of opinions than any display of logic. This 'bias of the imagination' was dependent on what Lecky called 'the law of congruity'.

Thus it was, Lecky said, that idolatry fitted in so naturally with the prevailing conceptions of the Middle Ages that no process of direct reasoning could overthrow it. Only by a fundamental change in the intellectual condition of society was idolatry finally subverted.[40] Similarly, it was intellectually and morally impossible that any religion which was not superstitious and material (in the sense of encouraging material images, pictures and ceremonies) could have triumphed as catholicism did in the Middle Ages.[41] By the operation of the same law, 'Protestantism could not possibly have existed without a general diffusion of the Bible, and that diffusion was impossible until after the two inventions of paper and of printing.'[42] In the same way bull-baiting, bear-baiting, cock-fighting and similar amusements were once the pastimes even of the most refined and humane. The change in society's attitude to these sports came not by an increase of knowledge, or a process of reasoning, but simply by the gradual elevation of the moral standard.[43] The decline of witchcraft under the influence of the great rationalist movement which, since the seventeenth century, had on all sides encroached on theology was, according to Lecky, a fine illustration of 'the laws of intellectual development'.[44] So, too, was the decline of religious persecution — the result of the slow secularization of society.[45]

Therefore, profound changes passed over public opinion, not as a consequence of immediate conviction by the force of argument, but gradually and by 'the silent pressure of civilization'.[46] An opinion, a creed, or an attitude of mind that was opposed to the spirit of the age and out of harmony with it, incapable of modification and an obstacle to progress, perished more often by indifference than by controversy. Advancing civilization simply made it obsolete.[47] Even when, as sometimes happened, the old words were retained, they no longer presented the old image to the mind, or exercised the old influence upon life.[48]

That an idea, or an attitude, or a creed must be in harmony with the prevailing intellectual spirit, and in keeping with the moral type of that age to survive, was for Lecky 'one of the general laws of historical development.'[49] Closely allied with this law was another which loomed very large in Lecky's thought. This postulated the interdependence of each department of knowledge and each sphere of thought and action in any given age.[50] He noted as 'a general law of the human mind' that the soldier, lawyer, scholar, mathematician or fiddler acquired a peculiar cast of thought which he would display on all subjects. So, too, an age immersed in theology will judge by a miraculous standard, while an age that is secular will judge by a secular and rationalistic one.[51]

The different elements of our knowledge were so closely united that it became impossible to compartmentalize them and make a spirit of credulity preside over one, while a spirit of enquiry was animating the others.[52] The study of physical science, inventive skill and industrial enterprise were, for example, connected by this law of congruity, for the same cast or habit of thought developed itself in these three forms.[53] Virtues also were grouped according to 'principles of affinity or congruity'.[54] All minds', wrote Lecky, 'are more or less governed by what chemists term the laws of elective affinity'. 'Like naturally tends to like.'[55] It followed, therefore, that every profound intellectual change produced some modification of all facets of speculative belief.[56] Enterprise called into existence in one sphere was soon communicated to all[57]; 'it is impossible to lay down a railway without creating an intellectual influence'.[58] The formation of new habits of thought in one discipline ends by affecting all our judgments.[59] What takes place in history, then, in the initial stages of all the great transitions of opinion, is a transfer of skill from one sphere to all the rest, until finally a different cast of mind is formed and civilization progresses to the next stage.[60] As John Bowle has pointed out, Lecky was fascinated by the effect of environment on ideas, and he constantly related the change in the climate of opinion to the total environment.[61]

Lecky believed that those who contributed most to the formation of the progressive stages of civilization were the philosophers whose ideas were seized upon and popularized until they eventually permeated and influenced the thought of a whole society.[62]

Men like Bacon, Descartes and Locke have probably done more than any others to set the current of their age. They have formed a certain cast and tone of mind. They have introduced peculiar habits of thought, new modes of reasoning, new tendencies of enquiry. The impulse they have given to the higher literature has been by that literature communicated to the most popular writers; and the impress of these master minds is clearly visible in the writings of multitudes who are totally unacquainted with their works.[63]

The latter part of this statement was a fairly apt description of Lecky's own role. He had become with his books on rationalism and morals an eminently popular author and one of the most successful propagators of mid-nineteenth century ideas about history, political economy, the secularization and industrialization of society, rationalism, Victorian morality, religious tolerance, political liberalism and progress. He was not so much the philosopher as the *philosophe*, the exponent and popularizer of the opinions of more original minds.[64]

Apart from 'laws' governing the movement of history, there were a number of general observations, the strength of which had impressed themselves on Lecky. These, too, took on something like the force of separate and individual laws in his mind. He held that terror was everywhere the beginning of religion, and that when religion rested on terror, it always engendered belief in witchcraft and magic.[65] Another of these general principles was that sectarianism could not survive contact between members of different creeds.[66] A law he saw constantly manifested in history was that good men in an evil age often attained a degree of moral excellence greater than that achieved in a comparatively better age.[67] Outbursts of luxury, he believed, were usually the precursors of intellectual or political change.[68] Madness was always frequent during great religious or political revolutions.[69] And in a phrase reminiscent of Acton's famous aphorism, he wrote: 'Power, when once enjoyed, is scarcely ever voluntarily relinquished.'[70] Lecky was still sufficiently under the influence of Emerson's style that he sought to formulate his generalizations within an epigram.

Yet so well blended were these general observations on the processes of history with Lecky's narrative and analysis that the impression is created (perhaps more so in *Rationalism* than in *Morals*) of a writer who had a profound feeling for and an awareness of the forces of history. It is in this blend of narrative and generalization, rather than in any bald enunciation of the 'laws of history', that Lecky was most valuable. It is here also that any case there may be for originality in Lecky's *Rationalism* and *Morals* is to be found. Because of the popular appeal of the two books in which he elaborated his 'laws of history', it is possible that Lecky 'greatly enriched current ideas on the mysterious causes of the transformation of the tone of thought'.[71] But what in fact Lecky personally got from his search for these laws was a set of hypotheses, or models, which unconsciously guided his own historical narratives. Again, as with his earlier *Religious Tendencies*, he may not have written as he originally intended, but the exercise had helped to give him a clear impression of the ways in which he felt history worked. The apprenticeship was to be useful for the author of the history of the eighteenth century.

Lecky began his literary career from an intellectual frontier. It was the moment when transition from history to sociology was occurring simultaneously to a few minds elsewhere in Europe. Comte in France, Spencer and Buckle in England, Dilthey and later Troelsch, Meinecke and Max Weber in Germany represent the transition that was taking place. Lecky's *Rationalism* and *Morals* were the product of a pioneering historico-sociology and bear witness to that distinctive stage of transformation reached in mid-nineteenth century historiography.

A writer like Lecky, who was historicist and relativist in his attitude to the old religious dogmas and also greatly impressed by the new certitudes and methods of physical science, was peculiarly exposed to the attractions of the young sociology. It was also easier for him to move from history into sociology as one who had not been exposed by academic training in history to any straitjacketted concept of what history was. The alluring prospects of the new worlds of sociological and intellectual history appealed to anyone who had the spirit to embark on a voyage of intellectual discovery. Part of its temptation was that it offered a new credo in place of the old. The traditional school of political and military history must be replaced by the history of society as a whole; battles could be replaced by the struggle of ideas; individuals could be classified in types, and particulars could be enumerated until their sum added up to the dignity of generalizations. Many whose faith had been shaken in the fixed values and in the natural law of Providence were groping their way back to a rational universe by attempting to discover the laws that governed society.

Lecky's interest in the relationship between ideas and environment, and in a proto-version of Weber's concept of the 'ideal-type', his concern with the laws of development in history, and the generalizations he made, align him with the sociological-historians. The tools he employed for the understanding of change and development in history were also being taken up by some of his contemporaries and were in time to become part of the stock-in-trade of sociology. Moreover, he seems to have felt that one of his most important and original contributions to historical writing was his analysis of the changes in the moral-type.[72]

Buckle had denied that there could be such a thing as a history of morals. Lecky's *Morals* was an act of faith in the opposite point of view, and his two volumes were the superstructure raised upon the idea that different moral types and different moral standards succeeded each other in the progress of history. This concept of successive types, upon which he elaborated in *Morals*, had already been anticipated in *Rationalism*. There he referred to 'the moral type', 'the type of virtue', 'class-type', and 'type of each succeeding civilization'.[73] Indeed, in his earliest publications he had shown himself impressed by the notion of type.[74]

In so far as the idea of typology was becoming a part of the intellectual atmosphere of the post-Hegelian period, Lecky was less original than his disagreement with Buckle on this issue may have led him to believe. He was conscious that Richard Whately had pointed out that certain virtues belonged to particular stages of civilization.[75] But it was Michelet, perhaps, who had brought the concept of successive moral-types most dramatically and impressively to Lecky's notice. At least immediately after he had stated that 'each successive stratum of civilization brings with it a distinctive variation of the moral type', he proceeded to back this assertion with a quotation by Michelet.[76]

Among Lecky's contemporaries who, like himself, were also influenced by the Positive school, Taine writing in French and Burckhardt in German were similarly addicted to the search for 'types' in history, and regarded the type they discovered as the representative of the age. By the end of the nineteenth century the 'ideal-type' of the sociologist, Max Weber, had had a considerable number of eligible parents — Lecky among them — in the sociological historians of the mid-nineteenth century.

The attempt to establish a sociological school of history in England, however, did not meet with a great deal of success. Herbert Spencer's sociology, with its emphasis on a biological approach and its greater 'emphasis on the present rather than the past', was too remote and foreign for British historians. Buckle was closer than Spencer to historiographical practice, and his 'science of history', when discussing not theory but particular historical problems, was often indistinguishable from the traditional approach. What the more traditional historians objected to was Buckle's theory of history, which claimed that there could be a 'science of history' in the sense that there was a science of physics with discoverable general laws that would enable man to predict the recurrence of events in given circumstances.

Most of the major British historians refuted Buckle's philosophy. A succession of the professors of history at Oxford severely criticized his 'science of history'; Goldwin Smith, Stubbs, Freeman and Froude all strongly contested Buckle's claims.[77] Two remarkable essays, attributed at least in part to Acton, did much to discredit Buckle with later generations of British historians.[78]

Besides, historical writing in the nineteenth century was increasingly dominated by the influence of the German academic schools. This influence, partly through Acton, became a powerful factor in England and operated to the detriment of any possible breakthrough along the sociological lines suggested by the work of Buckle and Lecky. By comparison with the great German professors of history — Ranke, Niebuhr, Mommsen, Treithschke, Dollinger — Buckle and Lecky were amateurs in Acton's eyes. Buckle, said Acton, was 'neither wise himself, nor likely to be the cause of wisdom in others'.[79] On the contrary, Acton pronounced him pretentious, and said that 'learned ignorance' was the origin of his many errors: 'He never goes to the best authorities; he scarcely ever consults the originals'.[80] The two works that Lecky produced very much under the influence of Buckle did not, according to Acton, 'really rise much above the vulgar level'.[81]

Many, as Lecky pointed out, shrank in alarm from the concept of the universe as an organism — as distinct from a mechanism — where its adaptations and complexities were rather the results of gradual development from within than of interferences from without, under the impression that it destroyed the argument from design and almost amounted to the negation of the Supreme Being.[82] The analogy of a mechanism still held considerable influence over many historians' thinking. J.F. Stephen suggested that the habit of expressing the findings of physical science in metaphysical language led to the assumption that the 'laws' of nature blindly obeyed the dictates of a First Cause, a Creator, who had wound up the clock in the beginning and who had since kept a vigilant eye on his mechanism.[83]

People had to be sceptical about a watchful, interfering Providence and also, perhaps, possess a well-informed grasp of modern science before they could regard the laws of physical science as man-made, that is, in the sense that it was man who generalized from observation. Buckle's theory of a science of history, Stephen's speculative defence of its possibility, and Lecky's attempt to follow Buckle cautiously with an illustration of the laws of history operating in practice, all grew out of the increasing scepticism with regard to Providence and a deep realization of the implications of modern scientific developments. The work of these men added their personal contributions to the swelling streams of scepticism and scientific progress.

The failure of Buckle and Lecky's history to catch on in any significant way in Britain may be partly attributable to something else. Both writers were fully conscious that they were swimming against the flow of traditional British historical writing; and they made no apologies in this regard. Lecky wrote of Buckle's *History of Civilization*: 'It is a book which cannot take its legitimate place for some time for it disregards many current opinions but I have a fine faith in its future.'[84] They felt, however, that a far greater barrier to the serious acceptance of their speculations was the fact that the force of the inductive method in the British intellectual tradition was ranged against them.

If Lecky and Buckle failed to establish a sociological school of historical writing in Britain, they likewise failed to bequeath directly to others their own interest in intellectual history. More than a century after Buckle and Lecky, Isaiah Berlin has asserted — and with justification — that intellectual history and the history of ideas have found but few practitioners in England.[85] In 1857 Buckle pointed out how the German intellectuals outstripped German society generally, causing a division between the 'speculative classes' and the 'practical classes', and how the latter remained 'uninfluenced by their knowledge and uncheered by the glow and fire of their genius'.[86] Whatever the truth of this observation, something similar to it, although on a much smaller scale and within a narrower field, took place in English historiography. Buckle and Lecky, although very much in the swim of the immediate currents — positivistic, Comtist, sociological, Darwinian (Lecky if not Buckle) and sceptical — were yet outside the mainstream of historical writing in England. Their fate was to be brushed aside as driftwood, yet Buckle had created such a stir in his own short lifetime that, as Acton noted: It must have powerfully appealed to something or other in the public mind, or tell something or other very important, which people wanted to know, in order to win so rapid a popularity.[87]

George Eliot said more or less the same thing about the immense popularity of Lecky's *Rationalism*.[88] One explanation of this is that both Lecky and Buckle expressed in intelligible popular form some of the dominant myths of the age — the beliefs in progress, prosperity, science and liberalism.

A century later, however, Buckle's works had fallen out of favour so rapidly as to merit only a brief reference in G.P. Gooch's *History and Historians in the Nineteenth Century*. And if today Lecky's contribution to history has been more often remembered than Buckle's, it is mainly because of his work on the political aspects of the eighteenth century. The two books he wrote while he was more directly the disciple of Buckle enjoyed a great popular, if not academic, success in their own time, but have exhibited none of the staying qualities of his more orthodox history of the eighteenth century.

The sociological history of Buckle and Lecky was something of a false start. Lecky had been a pioneer in this field and for a brief spell had received a great deal of encouragement. H.C. Lea, the American historian, expressed the hope that he would follow up his *Rationalism* with other books in the same genre and thereby 'aid in the development of a school in which history may be taught as it should be'.[89]

When Lecky finished his *Morals*, however, he felt that his debt had been paid not only to the Middle Ages but perhaps even to sociological history. Lea's pleading in subsequent correspondence could not move him back from his later interests in modern and more political history. When Lecky refused the offer of the chair of History at Oxford in 1892, the last hope passed that he might found a school of 'psychological history' which might have counterbalanced the influence of the diplomatic, constitutional and political history of Lord Acton at Cambridge and of German scholarship generally in Britain. But long before he declined this invitation to Oxford Lecky had already drifted a good deal from Buckle's 'science of history' and from the more extreme notions of sociological history.

As the early enthusiasm for Buckle began to wane, Lecky became more aware of the other's limitations. His letters of 1861 show how much he was under the spell of Buckle and admired his achievement, but even then he could write:

> I do not agree with all his views, for I believe in free will and in the influence of race etc., and I think he has exaggerated the effect of physical geography.[90]

From the beginning of 1862 the commentary on Buckle grew more critical. Lecky had become aware of the derivative nature of Buckle's ideas and also his tendency to concentrate on a single aspect of his subject matter.[91] By the time *Morals* was published, Lecky was repeating that, although he had learned 'very much' from Buckle, he also 'differed widely' from many of his opinions. And by contrast with *Rationalism, Morals* contained only about half the number of references to Buckle.[92] A few years later he wrote: I quite think, with Grote, that the master-error of Buckle was his absurd under-rating of the accidents of history.[93]

In an essay entitled 'The Political Value of History',[94] Lecky recalled Pascal's dictum that if Cleopatra's nose had been shorter, the history of the world might have been different. Voltaire, too, he wrote, was never tired of dwelling on the small springs on which the greatest events of history turned. And he quoted Frederick the Great approvingly: 'The older one becomes the more clearly one sees that King Hazard fashions three-fourths of the events in this miserable world.'[95]

Collingwood, Oakeshott and others have regarded such references to the 'accidents' of history as indicating the 'bankruptcy of historical method'.[96] However, when Lecky gave his approval to the notion of 'accidents', it was as an antidote to what he called Buckle's 'kind of historical fatalism'.[97] Lecky's position on this issue, as in so many other spheres, was to adopt a via media between the extremes of the 'fatalist' and accidental views of historical causation. He held that, although there are 'certain streams of tendency' and a steady and orderly evolution, which in the long run are impossible to resist, yet individual action and even mere accident had borne a very great part in modifying the direction of history. None could escape the all-pervading force of gravitation; and so it was with history. Yet man was not

> a mere passive weed drifting helplessly upon the sea of life, and human wisdom and human folly can do and have done much to modify the condition of his being.[98]

Besides, there were periods when the human mind was in such a state of pliancy that a small pressure could give it a bent for generations:

> If Mohammed had been killed in one of the first skirmishes of his career, I know no reason for believing that a great monotheistic religion would have arisen in Arabia, capable of moulding for more than twelve hundred years not only the beliefs, laws, and governments, but also the inmost moral and mental character of a vast section of the human race.[99]

Lecky thought that Gibbon was probably right in his conjecture that if Charles Martel had been defeated at the famous battle near Tours, the creed of Islam would have overspread a great part of what was now Christian Europe and might have ruled over it for centuries. Numerous instances of the same kind, said Lecky, would occur to every thoughtful reader of history.[100]

Lecky was trying to strike a balance between historical determinism and contingency. His concept of the historical process was based on two presuppositions. First, he presupposed 'streams of tendencies', where an inevitable, deterministic cause-and-effect relationship operated. Secondly, he presupposed particular moments of history at which the logical development had been or could have been modified or diverted so as to alter the course of history. At a given moment, history carried onward by its own momentum nevertheless could move forward in a number of different ways. The actual direction it took was often determined by as small a thing as an individual will. Thus, he argued, a French revolutionary movement of some kind was the 'normal result' of the 'tendencies of the age' — change must necessarily have taken place, but it was a question of great importance into whose hands its guidance was to fall'.[101] This twin principle of 'streams' and 'accidents' is a remarkably close foreshadowing of the explanation of change in history given by Lecky's younger contemporary and fellow graduate of TCD, J.B. Bury, especially in the essay on Cleopatra's nose.[102]

The insistence on the role of the accidental emphasized the extent to which Lecky had moved away from Buckle's science of history. Contingency was an important concept for him and influenced his writing of history, perhaps leading him astray in particular instances. In his anxiety to deflate the principle of determinism, he was more apt to be sidetracked when he interpreted the 'accidental' in a given situation as due to human folly or the lack of moderation. He wrote that if the spirit of moderation, statesmanship and compromise had prevailed, the benefits of the French Revolution could have been attained without bloodshed, and a gulf need not have been created between England and her American colonies.[103] This was Lecky's way of reducing the great events of the French and American revolutions to the 'accident' of the presence of human folly in critical situations.[104]

It is as if Lecky could not understand why the men of the past were not as moderate, judicious and as politically wise as himself, Edmund Burke and Thomas Jefferson.[105] It is as if Lecky's historical imagination sought to expurgate the blunders, emotions and irrationalities from what he felt should have been the real history.[106] This rejection of the emotional and blundering factor was also behind Lecky's ascribing the disturbed state of Ireland in his own time to an 'artificial agitation', the work of professional demagogues.[107] Unconsciously, he was reluctant to admit the strength of non-articulated convictions and fears; and this weakness and limitation of the imagination was carried over into his historical writing.

The notion of 'accident' in history, therefore, occasionally restricted Lecky's understanding of a historical situation, but it also served to widen the gulf between him and Buckle's science and sociology of history. What validity could there be in a science of history once one admitted 'accident' and chance, free will and Providence? These concepts played havoc with any idea of such a science. And Lecky's 'general laws of history', once the influence of Buckle began to recede, could be seen to be less analogous to the laws of physics and more in the nature of the commonsense assumptions or observations of the well-read man. When this stage had been reached, Lecky's career tapered off into the more traditional channels of political and constitutional history.

Lecky's most mature verdict on Buckle was incorporated into an essay entitled 'Formative Influences'.[108] There, in his catalogue of Buckle's defects, he listed colourblindness in matters religious; little power of projecting himself into the beliefs, ideals and modes of thought of other men and ages; unqualified and indiscriminate contempt for the 'ages of superstition'; his doctrine that there was no history of morals; his exaggerations in excluding the influence of individuals and accidents in history; his unfortunate representation of man as essentially the creature of circumstances and the exclusion of hereditary influences, the importance of which Darwin showed only a couple of years after the publication of

Buckle's first volume; the limitations of a writer who had mixed little with men and whose mind had been formed almost exclusively by solitary, unguided study; an imperfect appreciation of the extreme complexity of social phenomena; an excessive tendency to generalization; an arrogance of assertion; and at times an indiscriminate mixing of good and bad authorities.

In spite of this litany of 'extraordinary defects', Lecky remembered that they were balanced by 'extraordinary merits'. These included a brilliancy and power of expression; a wide and multifarious knowledge; a vast range of topics which he illuminated with fresh significance; and a noble enthusiasm for knowledge and for freedom. Lecky claimed that Buckle had 'opened out wider horizons than any previous writer in the field of history':

> No other English historian had sketched his plan with so bold a hand, or had shown so clearly the transcendent importance of studying not merely the actions of soldiers, politicians, and diplomatists, but also those great connected evolutions of intellectual, social, and industrial life on which the type of each succeeding age mainly depends.[109]

With the passage of years, Lecky had drifted a long way from Buckle, but he could still recall how the *History of Civilization* had been to many contemporaries an epoch in their lives, and one, moreover, that had imparted 'an altogether new interest in history'.

What had really drawn Lecky to Buckle was not so much the 'science of history' as Buckle's large canvas and scope, which caught up so much more than the merely political. Other writers had attracted Lecky because of the breadth of their interests; their influence helped to detach him from a too fatal attraction to Buckle's rigid philosophy and method. They made Lecky aware of opposite schools of history and of other ways of looking at the past. There is no doubt that the historians of the Enlightenment made Lecky independent of Buckle in the matter of the 'accidents' of history, and some of these — Voltaire, Gibbon — were to remain firm favourites of Lecky.[110]

Among the historians writing in English in the nineteenth century whom Lecky admired at least partially were Macaulay, Carlyle, Froude and Milman. Each helped to convince Lecky of the extremism of Buckle's method. Macaulay, for example, had illustrated in the famous third chapter of his *History of England* on the condition of the country in 1688 how something more than mere political history could be written without recourse to anything resembling Buckle's scientific thesis. Carlyle, discussing with Lecky the sociological-minded Comte, described him as the 'ghastliest algebraic factor that ever was taken for a man'.[111] And Milman, whom Lecky regarded as occupying 'indisputably the first place among the ecclesiastical historians of England and a high place among the historians of the nineteenth century',[112] had also shown without the aid of the positivism of Comte or Buckle the many indirect, subtle, far-reaching ways in which the world and the Church interacted upon each other.[113] An essay by Lecky on Milman,[114] and the tribute he paid him in the preface to the *Morals*, make it quite clear how highly Lecky thought of him. The traces of Milman's influence are evident in both *Rationalism* and *Morals*.

The impression made on Lecky by those whom he referred to as 'the long line of great masters of style who have related the annals of France'[115] was also important and partially counteracted the sociological tendencies inspired by Comte and Buckle. Since Lecky did not read German,[116] the influence on him of the historians writing in French was all the greater. His books on European history contain numerous references to the writings of the great names of the French Enlightenment. He paid glowing tributes to the inquiring, critical spirit of Descartes and Bayle; he had delved deeply in the eighteenth-century classics — Montaigne, Montesquieu, Rousseau and Voltaire — and was as widely read in the historians of the nineteenth century (his references cited the works of Thiers, Mignet, Thierry and Lamennais).

It is clear from the many references to Maury's *History of Magic* (1860) in *Rationalism* that it had given Lecky 'great assistance', and Lecky helped to popularize for English readers many of Maury's ideas. He read and admired his contemporary Renan and it was possibly Renan's remarks on the Italian painters which helped to make Lecky aware of the significance of art as a historical source.

In Lecky's opinion, first among the French historians of the nineteenth century was Michelet. His book on sorcery was a source freely used by Lecky for his own chapters on magic and witchcraft in *Rationalism*. He once confessed, 'I owe a good many of my ideas to Michelet',[117] and he was referring to Michelet when he wrote about 'the matchless vividness' of an 'illustrious writer'.[118]

Yet, while other contemporary English writers may have been coming under the spell of German historical scholarship, Lecky remained almost untouched — at least directly.[119] The German books he cited in his own works were invariably translations into either French or English. He had references to Herder's *Philosophy of History* in translation, and also to the translated work of the German protestant ecclesiastical historian, Neander.[120] For what he had to say about German biblical criticism, Lecky depended on work in French, and on a translation of Strauss's *Life of Jesus*. Where he occasionally cited major figures like Mommsen and Dollinger[121] as sources, the reference is always to translations; but the great contemporaries like Ranke and Burckhardt appear to have been little better than names to him.[122] The impact of the line of German historico-sociologists — Dilthey, Troelsch, Meinecke and Max Weber — came too late to have any effect on the ebbing of Lecky's faith in the sociological methods of Comte and Buckle.[123]

There were further indications of Lecky's drift away from sociological history. In the stand he took on morals in his book of that title, Lecky expected that he would have to contend against 'the hostility ... of all Comtists'.[124] In *Rationalism*, and while he was more strongly under the influence of the positivism of Comte and Buckle, he was prepared to concede the possibility of predicting the future.[125] In *Morals*, however, he took the opposite line. He admitted that the probable consequences of changes in contemporary society were among the most important questions that could occupy the moralist or the philanthropist, but he was positive that these predictions did not fall within the province of the historian.[126] Such a statement can be seen as Lecky's deliberate farewell to sociology. Later in his career, when he confirmed his rejection of that aspect of Buckle's 'science of history' and had completed his history of the eighteenth century, he stated categorically:

> Human affairs are so infinitely complex that it is vain to expect that they will ever exactly reproduce themselves, or that any study of the past can enable us to predict the future with the minuteness and the completeness that can be attained in the exact sciences.[127]

Apart from any natural decline of interest in the matter after the first enthusiasm had died down, there was also the very important factor that the involvement with detail which the writing of several volumes on Britain and Ireland entailed was not so conducive to a search for the 'laws of history' as were the smaller works covering centuries of European history.

Nevertheless, Lecky tried to integrate various aspects of society into his history of the eighteenth century, just as he had done in his works on European history, and in so doing, felt that he was still following in Buckle's footsteps. Buckle, as well as Macaulay, had seen that a true and comprehensive history should include the 'social, the industrial, the intellectual life of the nation as well as mere political changes'.[128] It is noteworthy that Lecky now associates Macaulay with Buckle. It indicates precisely that the 'literary' no less than 'the scientific', sociological influence played an important role in Lecky's approach to history.

The 'science of history' no longer meant preoccupation with a search for the general laws that governed society, but rather the application of the scientific spirit and approach to historical research and writing. This 'science of history' had little appeal for Lecky.[129] The proposition of J.B. Bury that 'history is simply a science no less and no more', was the kind of positivism that left Lecky cold.

Lecky's engagement with the science of history was most in evidence in the pages of *Rationalism*. The final expression of his philosophy of history is most readily available in two essays written shortly after he had completed his history of the eighteenth century.[130] In these were included comments on the theory of history which grew directly out of his own immediate experience of composing the history of eighteenth-century England and Ireland. These two essays were a statement of how he had practised his most mature historical writing, but his philosophy and his practice were intimately integrated. Here Lecky rejected the school of historical writers which deplored what it called the intrusion of literature into history. It was the conviction of the members of this school, said Lecky, that the main work of the historian was 'to collect documents with industry, to compare, classify, interpret and estimate them'. The kind of intellect which such a school valued most, he said, was that of a skilful and well-trained attorney.

After his own experience with late eighteenth-century Irish history, Lecky was prepared to admit that there were some fields of history where the primary facts were so little known, so much contested or so largely derived from recondite manuscript sources that a faithful historian might be obliged to sacrifice 'both proportion and artistic charm to the supreme importance of analysing evidence, reproducing documents and accumulating proofs'.[131] He felt that a justifiable criticism of his own account of the 1790s in Irish history — and three of his five volumes on Ireland were devoted to this period — was that he had been obliged to give much original documentation at the expense of symmetry and artistic charm. And so in the preface to *Ireland*, he apologized for finding it necessary to treat Irish affairs 'with a fulness of detail' that was not required in other parts of the book. For he found that Irish history had been 'very imperfectly written, and usually under the most furious partisanship'. He reluctantly concluded, therefore, that 'copious illustration', a 'large array of original evidence' and the collection and comparison of many letters were necessary to elucidate it.[132]

Quaint as his apology may now seem to a generation of historians reared on detail and fed upon original manuscript material, the fact remains that Lecky regarded manuscript material and documents as of far less significance than the artistic creation in historical composition. That is why he described it as a misfortune when

> some stirring and momentous period falls into the hands of the mere compiler, for he occupies the ground and a really great writer will hesitate to appropriate and plagiarise the materials which his predecessor has collected.

The compiler produced books which 'one would have wished to have been all re-written by some writer of real genius who could have given order, meaning and vividness to a mere chaos of accurate and laboriously sifted evidence.'[133]

In general, Lecky regarded the 'depreciation of the literary element in history' as 'essentially wrong'; to emphasize this point, it was necessary only to recall the names of Herodotus, Thucydides, of Livy and Tacitus, of Gibbon and Macaulay and of the long line of great masters of style who had related the annals of France. Indeed, he confidently asserted that there was no subject in which rarer literary qualities were more demanded than in the higher forms of history:

> The art of portraying characters; of describing events; of compressing, arranging, and selecting great masses of heterogeneous facts, of conducting many different chains of narrative without confusion or obscurity; of preserving in a vast and complicated subject the true proportion and relief, will tax the highest literary skill, and no one who does not possess some, at least, of these skills in an unusual measure is likely to attain a permanent place among the great masters of history.[134]

But in all this Lecky was far from saying that history should be written dramatically after the fashion of Froude. He had retained enough of what he had learned from Buckle to insist that the most dramatic incidents in history were not the most important.[135] Rather, the concept of the long chain of cause-and-effect continued to exercise a spell on him.

Moderation in all things, including history, was the ideal he set himself. At a time when documents were taking on a sacrosanct nature for the professional and academic historian, Lecky consciously reacted to what he felt might become the tyranny of the document. The extent of the critical use which Ranke had made of the diplomatic document was revolutionizing the writing of history. Ranke's achievement was loudly acclaimed by Acton, whom Lecky implied was one of those English critics who had been 'formed on German models and imbued with the German spirit'.[136] Lecky agreed that it was proper that the treasure-houses of diplomatic correspondence should be explored and sifted, but he had grave reservations about a history that was based primarily on diplomatic documents.

In the first place, he said those who were dealing with manuscript materials might be tempted to overplay the small, personal details that they might bring to light. Secondly, history written from these materials, although it had its own importance, was not likely to be distinguished by artistic form or by philosophical value.[137] Thirdly, he claimed that those who were immersed in these studies were apt to overrate their importance and the part which diplomacy and statesmanship had borne in the great movement of human affairs. Therefore, he argued, the tendency of the new school was to destroy the true perspectives of history.

Lecky was as strongly as ever impressed by Buckle's idea that political and military history, as well as the role of the individual statesman, had been given too great a significance in the story of mankind. He stressed that the part played by statesmen and legislatures was far less than usually imagined, and that the fate of nations largely depended upon forces quite different from those on which the mere political historian concentrated his attention:

> Laws and statesmen for the most part indicate and ratify, but do not create. They are like the hands of the watch which move obediently to the hidden machinery behind.[138]

As Lecky saw it, the true historian would have to strike a balance somewhere between Thomas Carlyle, who would reduce all history to the biographies of great men, and Buckle, who would essentially exclude from historical development the significance of the actions of great men.[139]

The 'document' had likewise become sacrosanct in biblical studies. Lecky acknowledged that in the nineteenth century the great German and Dutch biblical scholars had exercised a 'rare skill' in dealing critically with the early Jewish writings. Without disputing the value of their work or the importance of many of their results, he hoped that he might be pardoned for expressing his belief that that kind of investigation was 'often pursued with an exaggerated confidence'.[140]

Lecky regarded much of the German biblical criticism of the day as 'purely disintegrating and destructive'.[141] He contrasted the German school of early ecclesiastical historians unfavourably with Milman's 'strong English common-sense and grasp of facts, and his dislike of subtle far-fetched ingenuities of explanation'.[142]

Lecky's final position was that he had outgrown his early interest in Comtism and in Buckle. His engagement with historico-sociology had ended with

Rationalism and *Morals*. The great literary historians in England and France made a stronger and more durable impact on him, and asserted their sway over his later work. He rejected some aspects of the new scientific historiography that had spread outwards from Germany with Ranke's work; more especially did he fear the 'tyranny of the document'. He was a survivor from the pre-Rankean era of historical scholarship and belonged to the tradition of amateur literary historians, sharing much in common with Gibbon, Macaulay, Carlyle, Froude, J.R. Green and Milman. To a considerable extent Lecky's volumes on England in the eighteenth century were in the literary amateur tradition, and Acton's criticism of the early volumes was well merited, if somewhat exaggerated. He had, as Acton pointed out, neglected the 'inexhaustible discoveries' that awaited him in the recently opened archives; and it was somewhat 'puerile to write modern history from printed books'.[143]

Although Acton's criticism was generally well-founded, nevertheless, even in the case of the early volumes on the history of the eighteenth century, Lecky had made use of the Irish State Papers Office and the French Foreign Office. He was not, therefore, altogether as untouched by the new scientific methods as Acton's comments might lead one to believe. In any event, he was consciously and decidedly not writing merely diplomatic or political history. His later volumes, especially those chapters dealing with Ireland in the 1790s, were largely based upon original records. However, he had only reluctantly become a documents man. He had entered the field of modern methodology apologetically and then allegedly only because of the unreliability and paucity of printed material on Ireland. In his heart, he remained one of the last survivors of the great tradition of amateur historians writing in English, convinced that his work ultimately had more to do with literature than with science.

Chapter 4

Defensor Hiberniae

Lecky had spent most of the six years following the publication of *Leaders* on the Continent, but his correspondents kept him informed of Irish affairs. In 1864 he said that he and Lady Wilde were the only living specimens of that almost extinct species, the Young Irelander.[1] Fenianism had greatly shocked him. From Naples he wrote to a friend:

> Tell me something about the Fenians. They look very alarming as seen from abroad ... I was almost thinking at one time if it would not be better to transfer some money to England. What a perfectly hopeless country Ireland is! And what complete fools, how utterly impracticable, how absolutely incapable of every vestige of self-government our respectable fellow-countrymen are! ... rendering perfectly out of the question all national institutions. It is certainly rather a misfortune belonging to a country in which there is no party with which one can feel the smallest sympathy.[2]

In October 1866 Lecky settled in London. He took a keen interest in politics, and met and admired Gladstone, but still his lack of what he referred to as a 'pushing faculty' prevented him from getting into politics. Had he been possessed of political drive, he might well have reminded Gladstone that his maternal grandfather, W.E. Tallents, the Newark solicitor, had been Gladstone's first election agent in 1832. Gladstone might have been tempted to use his influence on behalf of Lecky, a Carlow landlord, to acquire the Carlow seat which until 1865 had been held by Lord Acton. This lack of push, this diffidence, was at times carried to extremes, as on the occasion, in autumn 1866, when he shared a hotel in Switzerland with Newman. There was scarcely anyone, Lecky said in a letter of 10 August 1866, whom he should have liked so much to know as Newman; he had heard that Newman had been impressed with *Rationalism*: 'Had I been more brazen I would have ventured to introduce myself.' To drive out the fire of political ambition, Lecky buried himself in the fire of literature.

There was a great deal of hero-worship in Lecky's nature which extended to the living as well as to the dead, and shortly after settling in London he struck up a close and admiring friendship with Thomas Carlyle. According to Lecky, Carlyle regretted that two of his earlier Irish friends, John Mitchel and Charles Gavan Duffy, had wasted their talents in the dead-end of Irish politics.[3] But the circumstances of Lecky's achievements in literature and his diffidence in politics made it certain that Carlyle's latest Irish recruit would not abandon literature for politics. If Mitchel and Duffy had failed Carlyle, Lecky was a safer bet.

In June 1871 Lecky married Elisabeth, Baroness van Dedem, a maid of honour to Queen Sophia of the Netherlands. They had first met at Dean Stanley's when the Queen was on a visit to the Dean of Westminster. Elisabeth was the eldest daughter of General Baron van Dedem. Besides her native Dutch, she spoke English, French and German fluently. Lecky described her as being more like his cousin, Alice Wilmot Chetwode, than anyone else he knew, though not so argumentative and, like her, a little mystical. He also said she was 'very poor'. The marriage took place at the court of Queen Sophia.

While on their honeymoon, Lecky completed the revision of *Leaders* and corrected the proofs. He thought it was an opportune moment for the issue of a second edition, and hoped that the book might prove useful for an understanding of the Irish problem. The new introduction provided an impressive diagnosis of the situation in 1871.[4] He noted that the repeal movement was manifestly reviving; that the material prosperity of Ireland was increasing; and that there were encouraging signs of a general social improvement of Ireland since the Famine. However, with great multitudes, sectarian considerations had entirely superseded national ones, and all party and political questions had been subordinated to ecclesiastical ones. The catholic leaders, while calling themselves Liberals, made it the main object of their home politics to separate the different classes during their education, and the main object of their foreign policy to support the temporal power of the pope.

Lecky believed that the ballot would give new weight and independence to the masses and that at a time when, as Fenianism showed, there existed a disloyalty more malignant than anything previously known. Further, there existed a scepticism about constitutional means, and a blind, persistent hatred of England. An alarming feature of Irish disloyalty, in Lecky's view, was its close and evident connection with the spread of education:

> Disloyalty was sustained by a cheap literature, written often with no mean literary skill, which penetrates into every village, gives the people their first political impressions, forms and directs their enthusiasm, and seems likely in the long leisure of the pastoral life to exercise an increasing power.[5]

He regarded the influence wielded by the Fenian newspaper as 'no good omen for the future loyalty of the people'.[6]

Lecky held that the circumstances he described were harmful to Ireland because they tended to debase all political life, and prevented the full flow of capital into the country. But the situation was also detrimental to England. He argued that, in time of peace, Irish discontent necessitated heavy expenditure, while emigration from Ireland multiplied England's enemies throughout the New World. In a European war, Ireland might constitute a serious threat to England, and in foreign diplomacy the country was an embarrassment. In the parliament of the United Kingdom, the Irish members introduced disharmony and forced unnatural coalitions whenever parties approached numerical equality.

England's grave mistake, he thought, was to underrate Irish disaffection and to ascribe it to transitory causes. The root of Irish discontent, Lecky maintained, was the sentiment of nationality: 'It is a question of nationality as truly as in Hungary or Poland.' Special grievances or anomalies might aggravate, but they did not cause, the discontent, and they became formidable only in so far as they were connected with it.[7] Since Lecky held that 'the present of a nation can only be explained by its past', he thought it advisable to recall in the biographical essays 'the leading facts of the great struggle of Irish nationality' and investigate the causes of the deep-seated disaffection.[8] Whether the sentiment of nationality was wise or foolish, the fact was that it existed and the great mistake of English legislation for Ireland was to disregard it.

While Lecky pleaded for some form of recognition for Irish nationality, he nevertheless deeply regretted Irish disloyalty and the fact that 'genuine national enthusiasm' did not flow in 'the channel of imperial politics'.[9] O'Connell, for all his faults, had taught loyalty to the Crown, respect for the rights of property, and a consistent liberalism, which one looked for in vain among his successors.[10] Nature and a long inextricable union of interests made it imperative for the two countries to continue under the same rule. No reasonable man could believe that England would ever voluntarily allow Ireland to separate from her, or that Ireland could ever establish her independence in opposition to England, unless through the dissolution of the empire. And even then Irish separation could be achieved only at the expense of a civil war which would drive from the country much of its intelligence and most of its capital. The arena of empire would thus be closed to Irish talent and ambitions, the energies of the people would be confined to the narrow circles of a small isolated state, and wasted in petty quarrels, inanities and anarchical passions.

Although separation was out of the question, he felt that consideration should be given to the idea of increasing home government. The three great requisites of good government for Ireland, he said, were that it should be strong, just and national. No government would ever command the real affection and loyalty of the people which was not in some degree national, 'administered in a great measure by Irishmen and through Irish institutions'. Any system which failed to recognize 'this craving of the national sentiment' would also fail to win gratitude:

> To call into active political life the upper class of Irishmen, and to enlarge the sphere of their political power — to give in a word to Ireland the greatest amount of self-government that is compatible with the unity and the security of the Empire — should be the aim of every statesman.[11]

Lecky acknowledged that this would be extremely difficult to achieve. The circumstances in the early 1870s were unfavourable because of the schism of classes which existed between landlords and tenants. Irish opinion directed by intelligence could secure the co-operation of the two countries, but this could not be achieved by unprincipled adventurers nor by unreasoning disloyalty. Besides, sectarian feeling was rising so high that the first act of an Irish parliament would be to build up a wall of separation between catholic and protestant by denominational education.

The wise thing to do, Lecky thought, would be to transfer private business gradually and cautiously from an overworked parliament to local government; decentralization by degrees might make it possible safely to enlarge Irish self-government. Meantime, his diagnosis of the situation revealed certain very hopeful signs. He welcomed the two measures passed recently in parliament — the disestablishment of the state church in Ireland, and the Land Act of 1870. And the fact that he approved of these acts means that it would be a mistake to read Lecky's introduction to *Leaders* (1871) as if it were in the same genre as the abortive effusions of patriotism published, for example, in the *Irish Times*, the *Dublin Evening Mail* and the *Daily Express*, and born 'in a fit of ill-humour'[12] directed against Gladstone's measures to pacify Ireland.

Like Acton, he was inclined to regard disestablishment as a landmark in the history of freedom.[13] He felt, also, that it removed the old lines of controversy, and noted how Irish protestants had been 'cut loose from their old moorings'. No longer having the defence of the protestant church as their main object, they were now more disposed than at any time since the Union to throw themselves into the general current of Irish sentiment. The establishment of religious equality and the settlement of the temporal power of the pope had removed grave causes of irritation, and if united education should be steadily and honestly pursued, sectarian bitterness would be assuaged, which would help to bring about the benefits of real union in Ireland.

Gladstone's Land Act, on the other hand, could not fail in time to cure the division of classes (which Lecky thought had become perhaps more serious than the division of sects). The tenant-purchase class was not yet numerous, but the Land Act had given unprecedented security and had identified the tenants' with the landlords' interests. Lecky concluded his analysis of the situation thus:

> A considerable time must elapse before the full extent of these changes is felt, but sooner or later they must exercise a profound influence on opinion; and if they do not extinguish the desire of the people for national institutions, they will greatly increase the probability of their obtaining them.[14]

The introductory essay on the state of Ireland provided an impressive display of Lecky's talent for political analysis, his commonsense and moderation; his skill in marshalling arguments; his political sensitivity; and his shrewd estimate of the probable effects of trends and of legislation. Lord John Russell described the introduction as the best short account of Ireland that he knew. Another friend wrote that it was 'like hearing you talk of Ireland'. David Plunket, a fellow liberal, also wrote to tell Lecky how much he liked the new material in *Leaders*.[15] But this introduction represented the high-water mark of Lecky's nationalism, and indicated the furthest limits to which he was prepared to go. Like Gladstone, he was anxious that justice be done to Ireland; and he argued that ultimately the cure for Irish problems might well be the establishment of Irish national government.

What did Lecky mean by national government? Not an immediate surrender to Isaac Butt's home rule demand, but rather a home rule by instalments. For he considered that Ireland was not ready for self-government. The parliament he envisaged for an Ireland of the future would be made up of the Irish gentry and more especially of those men who in the representative bodies were 'learning to assemble to deliberate upon their church affairs', and who were thus forming habits that profitably might be extended to politics.[16]

But what Lecky stood for in 1871 was federalism. And in this he was closer to the federalism of the Home Government Association than to O'Connell's earlier Repeal Movement, or, what was more or less the same as repeal, the return to the 1782 constitution. Lecky's friend, O'Neill Daunt, had joined Butt's movement on the clear understanding that he regarded the federal scheme 'as a provisional rather than a final arrangement of our relations with England, and that, if attained, it would help us to work out the rest.'[17] But Lecky chose federalism in preference to repeal and held that the 1782 constitution could not have been permanent. Instead, he maintained that if the error of the Union had been avoided, a federal arrangement would probably have been the choice of the Irish public.[18]

Acton believed in home rule because he thought that the form of government most favourable to liberty was federalism, so he used his influence with Gladstone in favour of Irish home rule.[19] But Lecky's case for federalism in 1871 rested much more definitely on the need for the recognition of the existence of Irish nationality. Naturally his position received support from other quarters. Influenced as he was by the political economists and the 'little Englanders', Lecky was opposed to the kind of imperialism they had denounced, and this strengthened his nationalist predilections for federalism. The result was that in 1871 Lecky's nationalist government idea had evolved to a more advanced state than Gladstone's. In these circumstances Lecky seemed a most likely person to be approached on behalf of Butt's Home Government Association, whose original members were more protestant than catholic, and more moderate than extreme in their nationalism.[20] No evidence has so far come to light, however, to suggest that Lecky was ever asked directly to join the home rule movement. This is strange and in need of some explanation in view of the respect in which he was held and the fact that his writings were prized as propaganda for the cause.[21]

It was typical of Lecky that the case for federalism was not stated unequivocally, and he ended what otherwise read as an argument for federalism by saying that Gladstone's remedial measures would have the effect either of creating a situation in which self-government could be conceded or else of wiping out the demand for self-government.[22] The word 'empire' was beginning to take on a meaning of considerable emotive force for Lecky. He had used it in the 1861 *Leader*, when he regretted that sectarianism prevented Ireland from acting in harmony with the rest of the empire; he meant, perhaps, no more than the United Kingdom. But in 1871 his pride in the idea of empire stood out more clearly. He wished to see genuine national enthusiasm engaged in the service of imperial politics, and it was evident that he was now thinking of frontiers wider than the United Kingdom. One of the reasons he spurned separatism was because he believed that Irish energies thereby would be confined within the limits of a small isolated state, when they could be given full play on an imperial stage.

No one was quicker than Lecky to recognize the ambiguity in his position. On 17 January 1872 he wrote to a friend about the new introduction to *Leaders*:

> You will probably think that I have a very uncertain sound, and it is quite true, for at present I feel almost hopeless about my good countrymen's powers of self-government. I don't mean (if asked) to mix myself up with Butt's movement ...[23]

Some of the differences between the 1861 and 1871 editions of *Leaders* were obvious enough. Lecky had used the platform provided by a new edition to restate his political position in the altered circumstances; he had excluded the essay 'Clerical Influences' and had made some significant additions and deletions. By excluding 'Clerical Influences' (the most unionist as well as nationalist chapter), he had removed all traces of unionism.[24] The additions, especially those in the chapter on Grattan, included a much stronger condemnation of Pitt for his role in the destruction of the Irish parliament. By putting his name to the book (it was anonymous in its first edition) Lecky merely added to the nationalist or self-government cause the weight of a reputation that had meanwhile soared with his two books on European history.

When the second edition was published, Lecky wrote:

> It has cost me a great deal of trouble, and as it embodies many sentiments I had long wished to express and a good deal of reading which is not very commonplace I have naturally a rather parental affection for it.[25]

The poor sales of the 1871 edition were therefore all the more disappointing. Longman, the publisher, informed Lecky that it had not been taken up as well as expected. Three months after publication Lecky claimed that 'rather more than five hundred copies' had been sold. Seven years later Longman had more than 40 per cent of the issue still on hand.[26] His German translator, Dr H. Jolowicz, suggested a number of shrewd criticisms. He attributed the delay in a German edition to Lecky's injunction that no alteration be made in the essays, 'although there are in them many superfluous repetitions of one and the same fact, not a few contradictions and incongruities respecting the character of the Irish people, its corrupted parliament and its catholic priests, and no regard to chronology'.[27]

Irish history had not proved to be as popular in England as Lecky had expected. He complained that, before it appeared, it had not been referred to in any of the notices about forthcoming books, and after its publication reviews were slow to appear.[28] Two months after publication, his publishers sent him eleven reviews;[29] although they were favourable, he does not appear to have been greatly impressed. Some he found short and civil, polite but insignificant.[30] A more important review by John Morley, although very sympathetic, censured Lecky's 'partisan admiration for the Irish parliament' and argued against him in favour of the Act of Union. He accurately described Lecky as the champion of the Ascendancy system.[31] In Ireland, however, as Lecky satirically noted, it did excite 'some enthusiasm among the "mendicant patriots" of my country'.[32] 'No less than three people have written to me as Irishmen and patriots asking me to give or "lend" them my book, which I think very cool and which I think is a little characteristic of my countrymen.'[33]

But, despite its relatively poor reception, its immediate political impact should not be underrated. *The Nation*, for example, then giving strong backing to home rule, devoted almost a full-page review and promised a continuation.[34] It regarded the republication of *Leaders* as 'a matter of no slight importance in connection with the political fortunes of Ireland'. The review praised Lecky's 'set of historical pictures which in vigorousness of conception, brilliancy of colouring, harmony of arrangement, and (speaking generally) accuracy of detail, are scarcely surpassed by anything in the gallery of Irish literature.' Few readers would find fault with Lecky's estimate of Swift, Flood and Grattan. The reviewer thought, however, that Lecky showed a tendency 'to contract the sympathies and narrow the judgement according as he passes from the remote to the recent, and from the recent to the present'. The result was that O'Connell, 'the Great Tribune of the people, suffers from the change'. *The Nation* stressed, however, that with that one slight qualification, Lecky's book could be accepted by the Irish reader. Nothing could be more timely, wrote the reviewer, than Lecky's vindication of the Irish parliament, his denunciation of the Union and his exposure of the methods employed to abolish that parliament.

Others, too, besides A.M. Sullivan's *Nation*, saw the propaganda value of *Leaders*. One of the earliest as well as ablest pamphlets to plead the cause of Irish federalism was J.G. MacCarthy's *A Plea for the Home Government of Ireland*.[35] In this, Lecky was referred to as 'one of the calmest and most sagacious observers of Irish life'. MacCarthy quoted with approval Lecky's statement that no government would ever command the affection and loyalty of the people which was not in some degree national, administered in a great measure by Irishmen and through Irish institutions. He also used Lecky to claim that, at the zenith of the repeal movement, O'Connell had expressed a preference for the federal plan. MacCarthy found great support in *Leaders* for his argument that federalism was the only system that enabled communities to pull together. He agreed that the dualism in the arrangement between Britain and Ireland in 1782 could not have proved permanent: it was bound to end in separation or centralization. He quoted Lecky:

> The conditions of Irish and English politics are so extremely different, and the reasons for preserving in Ireland a local centre of political life are so powerful that it is probable a federal union would have been preferred.[36]

The propagandist use that was already being made of *Leaders* was a warning of what was yet to come. For this Lecky had to thank his own indecisiveness. Politically he occupied a vague position between home rule and imperialism. Some of his statements emphasized a preference for federalism in the abstract, but he had nowhere elaborated on this; and because he was so indefinite himself, it was all the easier to make use of his work for nationalist propaganda purposes.

It should be stressed that those who employed him to this end did so sincerely, and they did not see that they might be making an unfair use of him. In the days when history was still generally held to be past politics, most of Lecky's Irish admirers were unable to appreciate how a writer who wrote so strongly in defence of the independent Irish parliament of the eighteenth century could be other than nationalist in outlook.

During 1871, while Lecky was concentrating on rewriting *Leaders* and collecting material for a projected history of England, he used to discuss Irish history with his friend, James Anthony Froude, then at work on *The English in Ireland*.[37] The friendship between them had begun as a result of *Rationalism*. They were also near neighbours when Lecky settled in Onslow Gardens, London. In July 1865 Lecky had attended a literary dinner at Longman's at which, he wrote,

> my particular magnet was Froude ... He is very agreeable, talks pictorially ... and is particularly amusing. I have seen a good deal of him, for besides Longman's, he dined this evening at the 'Literary Club' to which I was invited. ... and as Froude sat next to me and dinner lasted more than two and a half hours we talked no end.[38]

A close friendship developed since both men were also leading members of Carlyle's circle and years later were among the few invited to the great man's private funeral.

Under Carlyle's personal spell, Lecky's hero-worshipping nature flourished[39] and he found confirmation for his decision to choose literature before politics or the church. The influence of Carlyle strengthened another of Lecky's convictions: man must not lead an unproductive life.[40] Lecky was impressed with the Carlyle doctrine that the essence of sound religion is 'Know thy work and do it':

> The main and fundamental part of his teaching is the supreme sanctity of work; the duty imposed on every human being, be he rich or be he poor, to find a life purpose and to follow it out strenuously and honestly.[41]

When Carlyle held that no greater calamity could befall a nation than a weakening of the righteous hatred of evil; that the moral element is the deepest and most important, deeper and stronger than all intellectual considerations,[42] he found an echo in Lecky, who said that the strongest forces bearing nations onwards to improvement or decay were moral ones.[43] Above all, Lecky considered Carlyle 'most valuable as a moral force'.[44] This influence helps to explain Lecky's unusually strong and Carlylean denunciation of 'corruption' regarding the Act of Union,[45] and later of Gladstone's 'political morality' — soliciting votes by 'direct bribe' with the promise to abolish the income tax.[46]

Yet Lecky sharply reacted to other aspects of Carlyle's teaching. He claimed that there was in Carlyle's writing much that was exaggerated, one-sided and unwise.[47] In his view, there were grave dangers in the scale of state interference Carlyle advocated,[48] and although he thought that even the most extravagant utterances of Carlyle contained some germ of truth, he found Carlyle's 'worship of force' and his ridicule of the prison reform movement 'very repulsive'.[49] In his approach to historical writing, Lecky disagreed with Carlyle's tendency to 'reduce all history into biographies'. It seemed to Lecky that the Sage of Chelsea on occasion 'talked much eloquent and exasperating nonsense'.[50] According to William Allingham, who was also in the Carlyle circle, Lecky 'seldom if ever agrees with him', and when Carlyle spoke of Cromwell and Ireland, Lecky disagreed (in silence) with almost everything he said. Once when Carlyle made a sweeping condemnation of the Slavs as 'an ugly, ill-conditioned set of creatures with all the worst qualities attributed to the Irish and none of the good', Lecky challenged the generalization.[51] Indeed, because of Carlyle's habit of inveighing against the Irish, a temporary estrangement took place between the two friends.[52]

Gavan Duffy, who saw unmistakably Carlyle's influence on Froude's book,[53] wrote to Lecky:

> What I find hardest to endure in Mr Froude's doctrines is that instead of being convictions which he cannot repress they are mere mimickries of Mr Carlyle. One can be patient with the original sin of a man of genius, and not at all patient with the foppery which apes the offence and wears it as an ornament.[54]

Lecky, although clearly worried that there was more wrong-headed conviction than mere mimicry of Carlyle, or love of notoriety, behind Froude's ideas on Irish history, also hinted that there was something tongue in cheek about certain of Froude's attitudes. Referring to Froude's anti-catholic emancipation views, and with Carlyle also in mind, Lecky wrote:

> However much it may please literary gentlemen in search of sensational paradox to coquet with such views, any responsible statesman who acted on them would be very properly regarded as more fit for a place in Bedlam than for a place in Downing St.[55]

He realized, however, that because of the prejudices so strongly expressed and because of the claims to historical scholarship upon which his work was based, Froude's views on Irish history would have to be taken seriously and refuted rationally. Part of the significance of the Lecky-Froude controversy which ensued lies in the fact that it illustrates the schism in contemporaneous British intellectual history. Froude's work on Irish history contained matter which was a foretaste of what British imperialism in its more extreme and repulsive form was about to become. In Froude, we have the evangelical missionary who believed that the English were the chosen people with a duty to rule the Irish well, since they could not rule themselves. For him the Irish were simply the white man's burden nearer home. Lecky, still a Gladstonian liberal and not yet an imperialist, understood that *The English in Ireland* was not a mere narrative history of the dead past, but a tract advocating among other things a naked imperialism.

Besides the imperialism it inculcated, Froude's book was also a strong presentation of the case against Gladstonian liberalism, against majority rule, and religious toleration, and it included criticisms of parliamentary government and political debate while showing a clear partiality for strong government. The anti-liberal, racialist and imperial tone of the book was for Lecky its most serious aspect; he felt that, as a liberal and an Irishman, with peculiar qualifications for the task, he was called upon to defend the tenets of liberalism. In a letter to Froude, which he was careful enough to draft before finalizing, he wrote:

> Someone told me that I would never speak to you again after reading your Irish book. I am afraid that you will never speak to me again after reading my review of it in *Macmillan*. I am very sorry for this as I hate quarrels and I may say with truth there are few people with whom it would give me more pain to quarrel than with you.

He went on to tell Froude that he looked at his book as 'mischievous and misleading'.[56]

In *Rationalism* and *Morals*, Lecky had already taken his stand for reason and moderation and against dogmatism and emotionalism. Both books had been written by one who held a firm belief in the idea of progress. The general theme of the books might be said to have been the story of the gradual triumph of rationalism, liberty and tolerance in European history. There could be no going back on these advances. It had never once crossed Lecky's mind that there could be any retrogression to persecution and intolerance in Western civilization. He had written: 'Liberty, industry and peace are in modern societies indissolubly connected, and their ultimate ascendancy depends upon a movement which may be retarded, but cannot be arrested.'[57] Hence his war on what he regarded as Froude's return to a medieval attitude towards religious toleration and to a Czarist attitude towards politics. Already Lecky had lauded the Irish parliament of the eighteenth century for its freedom from religious bigotry.[58] The chapter in the *Morals* dealing with the persecution the early church had undergone, and the references in the same chapter to the Spanish Inquisition sufficiently illustrate Lecky's horror of religious intolerance. To think that a friend and man of letters could advocate similar principles of intolerance by a defence of the penal laws against the Irish catholics was very disturbing. 'His whole nature', wrote Mrs Lecky, 'revolted against the spirit of intolerance of which Mr Froude was the advocate ...'.[59] Lecky himself wrote to a friend:

> I wish I did not get into quite such a vehement state of mind about these matters but I do.[60]

In political matters Froude followed Carlyle and advertised the benefits to be derived from an enlightened despotism. The rights of man, as of nations, he had written, were not to liberty but to wise direction and control.[61] Lecky, on the other hand, who was influenced by the *laissez-faire* liberal tradition, had argued for the liberty of the individual and of nations. He had written in 1865:

> Liberty cannot be attained without a jealous restriction of the province of government, and indeed may be said in a great measure to consist of such a restriction.[62]

Froude condemned democracy, but Lecky had described it as 'an aspect of the Christian spirit' and looked forward with hope to the time when nations based upon democracies would be linked together in 'the democratic union of nations'.[63] A recurring phrase with Lecky in the first and second editions of *Leaders*, and in *Rationalism*, was 'the rights of nationalities'.[64] And Lecky had given the impression that he would be happy to see the 'rights' of Italy, Poland and Ireland respected. Imperialism meant a great deal less for Lecky at this stage than it did for Froude, and whereas Froude in his essays on the colonies had blamed the political economists for what he considered a wrong-headed attitude, which would allow the colonies to separate from England, Lecky had written that political economy had steadily subverted the idea that wealth could be gained only by conquest and displacement.[65]

The temperamental incompatibility of the two authors, and the clash of two opposing intellectual camps in Britain on such matters as democracy, imperialism, religious toleration and liberalism, were fully revealed in Lecky's review of Froude's book:

> This book belongs to that class of histories which are written, not for the purpose of giving a simple and impartial narrative of events, but clearly and almost avowedly for the purpose of enforcing certain political doctrines.[66]

What these doctrines were, Lecky outlined and condemned in his opening paragraph, and incidentally produced in the process a short charter of Victorian liberalism:

> Among the intellectual phenomena of the present day, one of the most remarkable is certainly the presence among us of a small but able body of literary men, whose repugnance to modern liberal tendencies has led them to opinions on secular policy more fitted for the latitude of Russia than of England, and on religious policy more fitted for the Middle Ages than for the nineteenth century. The two things they hate the most are civil and religious liberty. Freedom of speech, freedom of the press, representative government, the rights of nations to determine the form of government under which they will live, the rights of minorities to protection, as long as they do not injure their neighbours, the right of every man to profess the religious belief and adopt the religious worship which he considers best, are in their phraseology mere cant or shams. The two fundamental principles of all constitutional government — that the will of the majority should rule, and that the scruples of the minority should be respected — are equally antipathetic to them. The whole tendency of modern policy in their eyes is a mistake, and history has to them a certain melancholy charm as a record of religious and political despotisms which have been weakly banished from the world.[67]

According to Lecky, the underlying principle of the school of anti-liberals was that might is right, and he described Carlyle and Froude as its intellectual leaders:

No system can strike more directly at the root of all that is most noble and generous in human nature than this deification of success, this worship of force as the incarnation of right, this hatred of all that is weak and all that is unsuccessful. It makes it the function of history to stand by the scaffold and curse the victims as they pass.[68]

With such an anti-liberal and partisan frame of mind, the author of *The English in Ireland*, in Lecky's opinion, was 'not dealing righteously with history'.[69] Lecky was perturbed, however, much more by the political philosophy Froude preached than by any historical inaccuracies his book might contain.[70] Froude had falsified Irish history by his dramatic one-sidedness; Lecky dismissed *The English in Ireland* with the sentence that the book had 'no more claim to impartiality than an election squib'.[71]

The strongest support for Froude came, as might have been expected, from Carlyle:

> I have read all your book carefully over again, and continue to think of it not less but rather more favourably than ever: a few little phrases and touches you might perhaps alter with advantage; and the want of a copious carefully weighed concluding chapter is more sensible to me than ever; but the substance of the book is genuine truth, and the utterance of it is clear, sharp, smiting and decisive like a shining Damascus sabre; I never doubted or doubt but its effect will be great and lasting. No criticism have I seen since you went away that was worth notice. Poor Lecky is weak as water— bilge water with a drop of formic acid in it: unfortunate Lecky, he is wedded to his Irish idols; let him alone.[72]

Of all Froude's ideas, it is significant that his assumptions of race superiority got a large degree of general support from the English reviewers, although not from the *Athenaeum*, the *Spectator* or the *British Quarterly*. These assumptions were generally rejected by his Irish critics of all shades of political and religious opinion.[73]

Apart, however, from questions of race and empire, the reviews of *The English in Ireland* illustrated that democratic and liberal principles found many defenders against Froude's onslaughts. Most of his reviewers thought him needlessly alarmed by the spectre of democracy and they disliked his apology for the penal laws, his abuse of Roman catholicism, his partiality for strong and even one-man government, and his close linking of might and right.

His critics generally understood Froude to have said boldly and crudely that might makes right. But Froude himself drew a finer distinction: 'Among wild beasts and savages might constitutes right. Among reasonable beings right is forever tending to create might'.[74]

At the outbreak of the Franco-German war, Lecky was a near convert to this doctrine, as he revealed in a letter of the period:

> On the whole this war justifies more fully than any other I remember the doctrine of my old friend, Carlyle, that 'right is might' (which in general I don't believe).[75]

Lecky totally rejected the doctrine propounded by Froude. Both Carlyle and Froude did Lecky the honour of replying to him on this point. Carlyle, referring to the doctrine attributed to him that might is the symbol of right, wrote:

> I shall have to tell Lecky one day that quite the converse or reverse is the great and venerable author's real opinion — namely that right is the external symbol of might: as I hope he, one day descending miles and leagues beyond his present philosophy, will, with amazement and real gratification discover; and that he probably never met with a son of Adam more contemptuous of might except where it rests on the above origin.[76]

Froude, confirming what he had written in *The English in Ireland*, wrote of Lecky's objection to both Carlyle and himself:

> To me as I read him [Carlyle] he seems to say on the contrary, that, as this universe is constructed, it is 'right' only that is strong.[77]

Years later Lecky himself acknowledged Carlyle's explanation:

> He [Carlyle] was often accused of teaching that might is right. He always answered that he had not done so — that what he taught was that right is might ... truth in the long run is sure to be stronger than falsehood.[78]

But there is no indication that Lecky was ever fully satisfied with these explanations. On the contrary, he still found Carlyle's 'worship of force' repugnant, even although he believed that Carlyle's most extreme statements generally contained some element of truth. Regarding Froude's dictum that 'among reasonable beings right is forever tending to create might', Lecky would have agreed with his friend John Elliott Cairnes that the phrase was a little obscure, but that, 'whatever the precise relation between right and might, in Mr Froude's philosophy they are in effect convertible terms'.[79] Since the emphasis fell on the indispensable connection between the two words, 'right' and 'might', Lecky remained uneasy.[80]

The controversy sparked off by Froude's book pointed to the fact that most British intellectuals in the 1870s belonged, like Lecky, to the liberal tradition. The debate, however, foreshadowed the crisis of liberal conscience, provoked less than a decade later by the troubles in Ireland and by Gladstone's policies on Irish land and home rule in the 1880s. In one sense, Froude was a prophet who had forecast this crisis; in another, his book helped to contribute to the atmosphere that allowed just such a critical situation to develop. He was as much abettor as prophet.

Lecky never did descend, as Carlyle had hoped he would, the 'miles and leagues' from his political philosophy of the early 1870s. In 1878, when the first two volumes of his *England* appeared, he was still the unrepentant liberal critic of Froude; but from then on, he moved closer to Froude's position not only on imperialism, but also in his terror of Irish democracy and deepening distrust of Gladstonian liberalism. At this stage, criticism of Froude petered out of Lecky's work, and it seemed as if Carlyle's hope for Lecky was indeed about to be realized. In so far as he did move nearer to the Carlyle-Froude position, the explanation is to be found in altered circumstances in Ireland and not in any abstract conversion to Froude's line of argument. Carlyle's 'willow-pattern of a man' was always an excellent political weather-cock.

In the early 1870s, Lecky had been one of the chief representatives of tolerant Gladstonian liberalism, especially with regard to Ireland. Against Froude and Carlyle, he had defended democratic and liberal principles as well as a somewhat nationalistic interpretation of Irish history. Revolutionary developments in Ireland in the late 1870s and 1880s, however, made Lecky increasingly conservative and he was to become a leading spokesman for the landlord-unionist revolt against the new Gladstonianism. Like so many others who had once criticized Froude's ideas, Lecky now appeared as if he too was about to lie down with Froude.[81] That he did not do so was due to the fact that he was never altogether to lose the liberalism that he had once championed against the author of *The English in Ireland*.

After the publication of *The English in Ireland*, Froude continued to be the whipping-boy of Irish writers for the rest of the nineteenth century. Some of the criticisms made of him were impressive. None of his Irish critics, however, provided a full cool-headed historian's answer. Lecky wrote to a friend:

> The Irish side of things is in general so deplorably represented at present. Father Burke,[82] who is very amusing and popular, appears to have the vaguest possible notion of the difference between fact and fiction; and Mr Prendergast,[83] author of the *Cromwellian Settlement in Ireland*, and really a very competent scholar, has been writing a series of half-frantic letters in which he describes Froude as a viper, a cold-blooded hypocrite, a blood-thirsty fanatic … .

Lecky told Gavan Duffy that Burke and Prendergast had only aggravated Froude's mischief.[84] John Mitchel's sarcastic reply to Froude[85] was more of a patriotic protest than an objective historical criticism. A calmer, critical assessment of Froude was precisely what Lecky set out to do. The outcome revealed that, in their historical theories and approaches, Lecky and Froude were poles apart.

Lecky believed that there was no one best way of writing history: 'there are many different kinds of history which should be written in many different ways'. He held that there was room in historical writing for many kinds of talents; it would be idle to expect a Froude to write in the spirit of a Hallam.[86] In the preface to his *Morals*, he had paid a glowing tribute to the memory of Dean Milman. His tribute revealed the kind of virtues he admired most in fellow historians. Milman's mind, he said, was free from all disproportion, eccentricity and exaggeration; he had instead a fervent love of truth, a wide tolerance; large, generous, masculine judgments of men and things; an instinctive perception of the good that is latent in each party; and a disdain for noisy triumphs, fleeting popularity and sectarian strifes.[87] When Froude's work on Irish history appeared, Lecky found that the liberal, judicial qualities he admired in historians were altogether lacking in Froude. In this, he regarded Froude as the antithesis of Milman.

In Lecky's opinion, the most important part of a historian's business was to be 'retrospective'. By this he meant that it was the historian's chief function to explain the long course of events that produced a particular revolution, rather than concentrating on the drama of the revolution itself. For, in trying to attain a just perspective in history, 'the great dramatic incidents are not the most important'. His advice was:

> Study the slow process of growth as well as the moment of efflorescence, the long progress of decay as well as the final catastrophe.[88]

Froude, on the other hand, held that the most perfect kind of history was to be found in the plays of Shakespeare: that there were certain periods of high drama of greatest interest to mankind, the history of which might be so written that the actors would reveal their characters in their own words.[89] Froude was essentially a 'dramatic' historian. Lecky was a 'philosophic' one.

The full title of Froude's book on Ireland was *The English in Ireland in the Eighteenth Century*. What attracted the most extensive and bitter criticisms, however, were not so much his narrative of the eighteenth century as the preliminary comments on the Irish character and his chapter dealing with the 1641 Rebellion. The amount of space which Froude's Irish critics, including Lecky, devoted to his account of the 1641 uprising was not altogether misplaced. The essence of his historical methods and interpretations was highlighted in this chapter. Besides, Froude had described the Rebellion of 1641 as 'the gravest event in Irish history, the turning-point on which all later controversies between England and Ireland hinges'.

Edmund Burke had looked forward to the writing of a 'philosophic' history of Ireland which would be enlightened and impartial and which would take the 1641 affair, especially, out of the hands of the fanatics and partisans.[90] A century later, 1641 had still not found its 'philosophic' historian, for, in the early nineteenth century, protestant writers, like Musgrave and Duigenan, continued to produce melodramatic accounts of massacres perpetrated by the Irish catholics, while catholic apologists like Plowden and William Parnell asserted that rebellions had been the outcome of the misrule of Ireland.

When Froude began his study, 1641 had not yet passed out of politics into history. Froude, indeed, followed the more traditional and melodramatic protestant line laid down by Sir John Temple and Edmund Borlase in the seventeenth century, and described 1641 primarily as an unprovoked massacre of protestants by catholics, placing it in the same category as the Sicilian Vespers and St Bartholomew's Day.

Extracts from the depositions preserved in Trinity College, Dublin, concerning murders and spoliations by the 1641 rebels, given in Temple's account of the affair, formed Froude's chief source for the massacre story. Here was what Froude liked: the high dramatic content and the story told in the words of frightened participants. In Lecky's opinion, Froude's method was neither

philosophical nor judicial; his argument was that, in dealing with evidence such
as the depositions afforded, one should follow Voltaire's maxim and believe only
the evil a party writer tells of his own side, and the good that he recognizes in his
enemy. For this reason Lecky condemned Froude's reliance on one-sided evidence for the atrocities of 1641 and 1798 and his method of elaborating in ghastly
pictures the crimes committed on one side while ignoring those committed on
the other.[91] According to Lecky, Macaulay's characteristic defect had been 'the
singular absence of gradation in his mind ... the truth of an historical picture lies
mainly in its judicial and accurate shading'. A strong contrast of colour in Froude
repelled Lecky:

> An historian who gives a detailed and highly finished picture of all the
> barbarities that were committed on one side, while he dismissed in the
> briefest and most general manner those that were committed on the other,
> is in our opinion not dealing righteously with history.[92]

Lecky, in fact, had far more faith than Froude in the feasibility of establishing
scientific or objective truth in historical work. And while he held that the degree
of certainty varied in different departments, he always maintained enough of his
early enthusiasm for Buckle's science to claim that:

> The growth of institutions and laws, military events, changes in manners
> and in creeds, can be described with much confidence. ...

Biography he considered the most uncertain.[93]
    Froude, on the other hand, was far more sceptical about history as a science
and had written two articles against Buckle's theory of underlying causation and
the 'science of history':

> Thucydides wrote to expose the vices of democracy; Tacitus ... to exhibit
> the hatefulness of imperialism; ... even at the present hour, it is enough to
> know that any particular writer is a catholic or a protestant to be assured
> beforehand of the view which he will take of ... a massacre of St.
> Bartholomew.[94]

Even in matters of fact, Froude said, historical conclusions 'are at best but
probabilities differing in degree'.[95] It often seemed to him that:

> History was like a child's box of letters, with which we can spell any word
> we please. We have only to pick out such letters as we want, arrange them
> as we like, and say nothing about those which do not suit our purpose.[96]

Froude, who had what was in many ways a healthy scepticism about historical
fact, was honest to the extent of declaring his own hand to his readers on more
than one occasion in his writings. 'I do not pretend to impartiality', he said.[97]
Commenting on 'Irish Ideas', Froude confessed, 'I am in sympathy with the
protestant traditions of my country'.[98] Elsewhere he said that while Prendergast
wrote as an Irish patriot, 'I [write] as an Englishman'.[99] Lecky, on the contrary,
liked to think that he wrote primarily as a historian.

Apart from their use to him as a 'dramatic historian', another reason why Froude accepted the 1641 depositions was paradoxically because he was sceptical about historical fact; one piece of subjective evidence was no weaker than another. Froude held with subjective truth in history. Besides, he was always tempted not to spoil a good story because of awkward and dry facts which might not fit into the picture.[100]

Lecky did not accept the depositions because he was more addicted to the facts that could be established by the historical method. If it was characteristic of Froude that he should write a historical novel,[101] it was equally characteristic of Lecky that he requested Standish O'Grady *not* to send him *Ulrick the Ready*, O'Grady's historical romance.[102]

Dealing with the depositions and 1641, Lecky's method was to show that in the case of Temple, Froude's chief source, there were 'facts which throw the gravest doubt upon his veracity'; that he was a partisan and unscrupulous speculator who stood to gain materially by the acceptance of his story. A major objection Lecky raised against the acceptance of the depositions as historical evidence at all was that no cross-examination of the witnesses had taken place. As a witness on 1641, Lecky preferred to Temple either the moderate protestant clergyman, Warner — 'the best historian of the rebellion, who had himself carefully examined these documents' (i.e. the depositions) — or, the catholic, Castlehaven, who saw some good and some bad on both sides. Lecky, who provided protestant witnesses for the catholic defence, produced Clogy's *Life of Bedell* — the bishop who had been taken prisoner by the Ulster rebels — to furnish evidence of humanity on the part of the rebels and to show that the rebellion did not have the 'universally ferocious character, or the religious character' attributed to it 'pre-eminently' by Froude.[103]

Lecky also objected to Froude's references to 1641 as an unprovoked rising. He listed the 'causes' and asked:

> What can be thought of an historian who having related these very facts, proceeds to give the explanation and the moral of the rebellion: 'The catholics were indulged to the uttermost and therefore rebelled'?[104]

So strongly did Lecky resent Froude's attributing Irish rebellions solely to religious causes that he returned to this point more than once in his *History*.[105] Referring to the atrocities attributed by Froude to the Irish Catholics, Lecky wrote:

> These crimes are represented as if they were at once unquestionable, unprovoked and unparalleled. The object is to represent the Irish people and especially the Irish catholics, in the most hateful light, and accordingly everything that could mitigate or alter this impression is carefully suppressed. Such a method of manipulating the facts of history when employed by an eminently skilful writer, is no doubt very effective for the purpose for which it is intended. How far a writer who pursues it is deserving of respect or confidence as an historian is another question.[106]

There was little that was new in Lecky's own treatment of 1641 except, perhaps, a greater amount of that judicial and 'philosophic' spirit than was shown by any preceding historian. Since Froude had not personally examined the depositions in Trinity College, Lecky too considered it unnecessary to examine these manuscripts, and confined himself instead to the published works.

Temple's *History of the Irish Rebellion* (1646), and his story of a massacre of protestants, although it had been many times refuted could still be accepted in the nineteenth century — and by writers who were no mere propagandists. Hume had elaborated it with great literary skill. Voltaire had spread it on the Continent; and, more recently, said Lecky, it had received much countenance 'from such eminent writers as Hallam, Ranke and Goldwin Smith'.[107] The last-named, for example, in the 'Cromwell' essay in his book *Three English Statesmen* (1867), stated that the catholics began the war of 1641 'with a great massacre of the protestants'. Froude took Temple as a reliable source. The manner in which Lecky exposed Temple finally ensured that he could no longer be accepted as trustworthy. Even Froude seemed to realize this later.[108] Lecky, then, in so far as he discountenanced partisan accounts of 1641 and wrote it up in a less partial frame of mind, had become the 'philosophic' historian of Edmund Burke's dream.

His achievement was that he had largely succeeded in breaking out of the straitjacketed account which saw, from one camp, only a religious massacre, or, from the other, only a great lie got up by the enemies of the catholics. The breakaway was important not merely because it brought about a new interpretation (or perhaps only an old interpretation in a new spirit), but chiefly because it made possible the opening up of a whole new vista in Irish history and paved the way for responsible historical writers on the seventeenth century. Lecky, by his eminence and by his determined effort to achieve impartiality, had stamped a certain amount of his own tolerant and circumspect spirit on a subject which, until then, had merely provided the ammunition for sectarian and racial recriminations. He had released 1641 from politics into history, leaving the way open for further historical inquiries. Unlike others, he had not dismissed the depositions as a source[109] and he helped to make possible the relatively more objective and scholarly discussion of 1641 by such historians as Hickson, Gilbert, Fitzpatrick, Bagwell, Dunlop and S.R. Gardiner.

Mary Hickson's *Ireland in the Seventeenth Century, or the Irish Massacres of 1641-2* marked an advance in so far as she personally examined the TCD depositions and edited some of the more credible ones. In preparing her book, she sought and was given Lecky's advice. He tried to impress upon her that the depositions should be treated like any 'hostile witness'. She replied rhetorically: 'Is it to friends and accomplices of the murderer we are to look for evidence of his crime or to the friends of the victim?'[110] Much as it might have surprised her, Lecky's principle was that, in the case of evidence such as these depositions afforded, one could only accept with any degree of certainty the evil which his friends admitted about an accused, or, the good admitted in his favour by the friends of the victim.

The high hopes intimated by S.R. Gardiner for Miss Hickson's book were hardly fulfilled.[111] And, although Lecky described it as 'an important book', he was clearly not satisfied that it had established the case even for the more credible of the later depositions.[112]

Thomas Fitzpatrick got closer to Lecky's suggested method of handling the depositions. He critically examined some half-a-dozen dealing with one particular episode in the massacre alleged by Froude. In his book, *The Bloody Bridge*, he showed a considerable debt to Lecky and acknowledged his 'well-considered … just remarks' and his 'rare judgement and acumen',[113] just as Hickson had praised Lecky's 'candour and fairness'.[114]

The success of Lecky's contribution was generously recognized not only by Irish historical writers and by correspondents like Gavan Duffy, O'Connor Morris and J.E. Cairnes, but by some of the leading authorities on the seventeenth century. S.R. Gardiner was very impressed by Lecky's work on the 1641 Rebellion:

> I take this opportunity of expressing my extreme admiration for Mr Lecky's account of the Irish rebellion. Having examined a large mass of original material amongst the *State Papers* and the *Carte MSS*, I have been surprised to find how, even when he has not himself gone through the work of references to MS authorities, he almost always contrives to hit the truth.[115]

Gardiner, and later Dunlop, agreed with Lecky that no general massacre of protestants by catholics had taken place in 1641. Dunlop, having examined the depositions for himself, came to the same conclusion about their extreme unreliability as a source for the 'massacre' story.[116]

Quite apart from 1641, what Froude had written hung like a shadow over Lecky's pages. Froude had to be refuted by him even when not actually named. He had to be followed into the manuscript repositories and his sources checked and verified; his claim to be regarded as a historian of Ireland examined. At places in Lecky's work, the shadow cast by Froude's book became something of an obsession. But, because of Froude, Lecky's work on Irish history was all the better because more thorough and scientific.

In the process of refuting Froude, Lecky had it brought home vividly that the history of Ireland 'has been very imperfectly written and usually under the influence of the most furious partisanship'. In the circumstances, and with Froude as an example before him, Lecky found that it was no longer possible to write the Irish chapters of the *History* merely from the already published histories, correspondence, memoirs and other secondary sources. He apologized to his readers for having to rely so heavily on manuscript material and for having to quote so extensively from it at the cost of impairing the book's 'symmetry and its artistic charm'. But, he explained, in this particular case it was the one method of arriving at the truth. The use of so much manuscript material would not have been necessary 'in dealing with a history of which the outlines … were well established and generally admitted'.[117] Indeed, Lecky for the most part applied the traditional method of composing from published work to the English chapters of the *History*.

Lecky had stumbled on the 'original sources' method more by accident or necessity than by design. Clearly, Froude, through the criticism he aroused, and by his talent for sparking off retroactive power in others, had played a major role in this aspect of Lecky's development. John Mitchel had based his account of the eighteenth century on the memoirs and correspondence of participants in the political struggles.[118] Froude improved on this and gave for the first time, and from the original materials, the government side of Anglo-Irish relations. Lecky, who might otherwise have written no more than a more impartial, 'philosophic' or watered-down Mitchel, had to read Froude's sources and the result was an original history of eighteenth-century Ireland.

The very qualities that enabled Lecky to liberate 1641 into history, when employed by him on his own period of the eighteenth century turned him into an 'authority'. So, while many of the big names who came after Lecky in Irish historiography took a general look at the seventeenth century, Lecky, because of his weight and the extent of his original research, imposed his own pattern on the eighteenth. He remains the giant dominating the eighteenth century, and the special studies written since his time on this period have all tended to be supplementary to Lecky and within the framework constructed and sanctioned, first by Froude and then by Lecky. Until recently no one has surveyed Lecky's eighteenth-century framework as a whole.

For the seventeenth century especially, but also for other parts of his work, Lecky was assisted to a considerable extent by Prendergast — not only in his published work, but also by his letters replying to Lecky's queries. The relationship between the two was most significant for freeing Irish historical writing, and more especially that on 1641, from political diatribe.

While it is clear that Lecky's research on Irish history owed much to Prendergast, it would be hasty to conclude that Prendergast determined Lecky's approach to such matters as 1641, the penal laws and abductions. Prendergast indeed was the first to admit that Lecky had enhanced and added to the material which he had supplied. On the first appearance of Lecky's *England*, Prendergast wrote to its author:

> I pause half-way through your chapters on Ireland 'lost in wonder, love and praise'. In wonder at the breadth, depth and reach of your labours and your views ... . Accident, amusement, idleness have given me access to *some* of the sources you have drawn from ... . If then you have surprised me, astonished me, your book ought to astound others. ... Your book has deprived me of sleep! ... for I feel despair and remorse; despair of ever approaching you; remorse that I have not furnished a brick or two more for your building ... your noble building. ... I again and again wish I had had more opportunities of meeting you that I might have had a chance of offering you any materials I possess, or directing you to sources of information. You make such admirable use of what you read that one would be

proud of being the means of furnishing you with matter.[119]

With the Froude controversy, Lecky's place in the development of Irish historiography comes into perspective. The first Irish reactions to Froude had been the popular, screaming refutations of *The Nation*, Father Burke, Mitchel, Prendergast and others. If, as Acton counselled, we learn to look behind the great historians, then Lecky's achievement is all the more enhanced by comparison with Froude and his Irish critics. But such a comparison also serves to illustrate how much Lecky owed to the solid research work being done by a man like Prendergast, as well as to the stimulus provided by Froude.

Building upon the scholarly side of Prendergast's work, Lecky raised the tone of the controversy and produced an answer which became the most acceptable reply to Froude. His reply (in both the reviews of 1873 and 1874 and the Irish chapters of the *History of England in the Eighteenth Century*) amounted to a very important contribution to the corpus but also to the spirit of Irish historical studies. He captured the imagination of many of his fellow Irish historians and was raised to the foremost place among them. From the eulogies he received, it appears that many of Lecky's Irish fellow historical writers would have been prepared to endorse Barry O'Brien's assessment of Lecky as 'the greatest of Irish historians'.[120]

This praise trickled down to the Irish popular press. Lecky became accepted not only as the country's leading historian, but also as a defender of the Irish character and as a political philosopher offering solutions for Irish ills. The frequent references to Lecky in the nationalist press of the 1870s seemed to indicate that he was regarded as one of the intellectual leaders of Irish nationalism.

Froude's account of Anglo-Irish relations achieved precisely what had been feared by a sceptical English press on first learning of his intention to lecture on Irish history in America: in presenting a survey of Irish history before a popular tribunal, he had succeeded in raking up the past.[121] He and his critics ensured that from the start of the home rule agitation in the early 1870s the argument was going to be largely about history, or, at least, past politics. A great interest was shown in the work of those Irish historical writers who answered him, and in this aspect of the controversy Lecky had played a major role and came as near to becoming a popular hero as he ever would. During these years of debate with Froude, Lecky might still be described as an Irish liberal nationalist. Not surprisingly, therefore, he emerged from the engagement with Froude as the Defensor Hiberniae *par excellence*.

In the course of his plea for the defence, Lecky presented a summary of Irish history which impressed nationalist commentators, and which they were pleased to publicize. In this summary, circulated among a wider public by the nationalist press, Lecky looked back at ancient Ireland with affectionate admiration for the early civilization. He declared that the suppression of the native Irish in the reign of Elizabeth was 'carried on with a ferocity that surpassed that of Alva in the

Netherlands, and was hardly exceeded by any page in the blood-stained annals of the Turks'. He exposed 'the clever chicanery of Froude' on the alleged St Bartholomew's Day of Irish history in 1641 and depicted Cromwell's massacre of the catholics. He defended the Patriot Parliament of 1689 'from the aspersions of Lord Macaulay' and referred to Sarsfield as 'the Irish Bayard'. Lecky treated 'the whole penal code in the spirit of Edmund Burke and Henry Grattan' and argued that the real cause of the 1798 Rebellion was not Irish treachery, but the failure to obtain parliamentary reform and catholic emancipation, the recall of Fitzwilliam, and the desire of the government to produce an premature explosion.[122]

Irish commentators on the Lecky-Froude controversy noted that Lecky had defended the Irish from a variety of charges, stated or implied, against their national character, such as treachery, cowardice, anarchy, ungovernableness, depravity, barbarity in their uprisings, religious intolerance and massacre. More especially, Lecky, whose *Rationalism* and *Morals* had shown that he was no friend of catholic beliefs and practices, now in the course of his replies to Froude had written a historical apology for the Irish catholics. This was warmly received in Ireland. As *The Nation* (1 June 1878) put it: 'Catholics will receive with gratitude the vindication of their acts and principles.' The *Monitor* offered him 'our hearty acknowledgements for his generous and conclusive defence of the Irish Catholic Church ... .'[123] The *Dublin Review*, the organ of intellectual catholicism, was even prepared to accept Lecky's defence of the Irish catholics as part-atonement for his earlier views on catholicism. It acknowledged that Lecky on Froude

> displayed very few, if any, of those characteristics of his which every catholic regards as objectionable; while his good qualities appear in the most formidable light.[124]

Lecky's defence of Ireland and of the Irish character against Froude won the warm approval of fellow Irish writers. J.P. Prendergast, whose writings were strongly nationalistic but who personally was a unionist, was fulsome in his praise.[125] The Young Ireland nationalist and catholic, Gavan Duffy, who recently had been Premier of Victoria, wrote from Melbourne:

> I cannot refrain from thanking you ... . It is such an answer as will satisfy just and reasonable men whatever may be their national or party prepossessions ... if like Mr Froude you had 'come to the succour of the stronger party' you would have had more applause from the critics, but you would have missed the silent gratitude of men in many and far-divided countries who may never see your face.[126]

Judge O'Connor Morris, a catholic and unionist, J.E. Cairns, professor of political economy at University College, London, Sir John Pope-Hennessy from Government House, Hong Kong, and the poet, Aubrey de Vere, were among others who expressed their appreciation for what de Vere called 'the noble defence of Ireland'.[127]

One of the most respected people in the nationalist camp was W.J. O'Neill Daunt. He had been secretary to O'Connell during the Repeal agitation; in the

1860s he had been one of the founders of the short-lived National League which aimed to repeal the Union; and in the 1870s he was one of the most ardent propagandists of home rule. Lecky regarded him with a sort of filial affection ever since O'Neill Daunt had reviewed the first edition of *Leaders*. Lecky called it 'the very first really appreciative review I have ever had', adding

> though there have since been many reviews of my books which have made a good deal of noise in the world I doubt whether there have been any which gave me so much pleasure.[128]

O'Neill Daunt's appreciation of Lecky's work was expressed not only publicly, in reviews and lectures, and in correspondence with Lecky, but also privately, in the many references to Lecky which he committed to his journal. He contrasted with Lecky's *England* Justin McCarthy's *History of our Own Times*, which O'Neill Daunt considered 'not at all so valuable as Lecky's critical book'.[129]

The basis of O'Neill Daunt's enthusiastic approval of Lecky is significant. He claimed that he recognized in Lecky's work 'the combination of high literary talent with a strong spirit of Irish nationality'.[130] At a point of development in Irish history, where the relationship between literature and nationalism was very close, this combination was all the more admired. It was then, O'Neill Daunt wrote, 'a labour of love' to review Lecky's work and

> to give utterance to my appreciation of an Irish writer who was not afraid to tell English readers about the systematic brutality of English misgovernment in Ireland.[131]

Lecky's answer to Froude was quickly seized upon in Ireland as a valuable contribution to the nationalist cause. It seemed to be but a short and logical step from his literary defence of Ireland and the indictment of past English rule, to the advocacy of home government. Indeed, nationalist reviewers picked out passages from Lecky's writings which seemed to indicate that he was intellectually convinced of the case for Irish self-government.

The Nation applauded as a 'perfect truth' Lecky's statement in his first review article on Froude that the issue for centuries between Ireland and England was 'a question of nationality ... much more than of creed'.[132] Later, when Lecky reviewed the final volumes of Froude, *The Nation* again praised Lecky for his 'service to the cause of truth and justice'.[133]

In his second article Lecky strongly defended the legislative independence of Grattan's parliament and the principle of constitutional self-government. He held that the deplorable condition of Ireland at the accession of George III was to be attributed not to 'Irish ideas' and Irish anarchy, as Froude had said, but to the fact that Ireland was governed exclusively by 'English ideas' and English influence. Lecky rejected Froude's thesis, which held that in eighteenth-century Ireland no evil was so great as 'the delusion that Ireland could be honourably governed by a parliament of her own'. The fact that Grattan's parliament was a corrupt, unreformed and unrepresentative assembly was no proof of the 'incapacity of the nation for self-government'. Lecky praised the efforts of Grattan and

the 'patriots' who sought 'to make their own parliament as independent as that of England, and also a faithful reflex of the opinion of the nation'. He held that 'the existence of a strong patriotic feeling in a representative body diminishes its corruption'.[134]

The Nation freely circulated these arguments. The more extreme *Irishman* and *Flag of Ireland*, both of which were owned by Richard Pigott and sympathetic to Fenianism, also republished, and at even greater length than *The Nation*, the substance of Lecky's 'extremely able and exhaustive review'.[135] All these papers gave generous quotations from Lecky and a full endorsement of his patriotic and liberal views. In an editorial, the *Irishman* (13 June 1874) reiterated and spelled out Lecky's principles of constitutional government. Lecky had insisted on:

> The value of a representative government as *sustaining and expressing the public opinion of a country,*
> The belief that a government can only be permanently useful *which is in accordance with the wishes of the majority of the governed,*
> The conception of liberty, according to which *a people have a right to determine by their own representatives, the laws they obey, and the disposition of the taxes they pay,*
> The conviction that the best way of forming a healthy public opinion in a nation, *is to call up in turn class after class to exercise public functions,*
> That the best guarantee of the purity of an administration *is to subject it to strict popular control,*
> That the best ways of meeting dangerous political discontent is *to provide a constitutional arena in which the peccant humours of the state may find free vent, and in which every grievance may be fully discussed....*[138]

In the context in which he had written the above words, Lecky was arguing on behalf of representative government and against the Carlyle-Froude theory which, he said, held that despotism was the ideal government; that England since the time of Cromwell had been steadily declining, and that her free parliament was her greatest curse. He was not discussing the application — or, for that matter, the non-application — of these principles to contemporary Ireland. However, it was noted that he had linked Grattan's parliament with these principles, and had argued that the Dungannon resolutions of Grattan's volunteers were crude expressions of 'enthusiastic beliefs' to which liberals in England had now committed themselves. Lecky's enthusiasm for eighteenth-century Irish colonial nationalism and for contemporary liberal principles endeared him to the home rulers.

Although at this stage Lecky might be truly described as a liberal nationalist, he was no home ruler in the 'party' sense. In fact, his two review articles had ended on the same optimistic note: that the political agitation and the 'ancient animosities' were subsiding under the influence of the 'healing measures of the last few years' — Church Disestablishment (1869) and Gladstone's Land Act of 1870. It was because he held this faith in Gladstone's remedial measures that he considered Froude's statement that Ireland's grievance would be removed only

by separation from England to be much exaggerated.[137]

The indications that Lecky was not a home ruler, however, were slight in comparison with the number of statements that showed him to be a liberal nationalist. His nationalistic writing was what was noted and pressed into the service of home rule. As *The Nation* at one stage seemed to appreciate, Lecky was more of a federalist in principle than an active home ruler. But the difference, it might be argued, was merely one of degree and timing since both home rule and federalism were based upon a common measure of nationalist sentiment. Lecky had presented the most authoritative case yet on behalf of the capacity of Irishmen in the eighteenth century for self-government: there was no reason, argued the home rulers, to doubt that this capacity still existed among Irishmen in Lecky's own time.

Lecky's appeal was primarily to the moderate nationalists — men of home rule sympathies who held with constitutional means. These people welcomed Lecky, if for no other reason than the fact that Froude's point — that the Irish had always shown themselves incapable of ruling themselves — had won the full favour of such influential organs of British opinion as *The Times*,[138] the *Edinburgh Review*[139] and the *Saturday Review*.[140] There were indeed some grounds for the complaint of the *Irishman* — that Froude's pronouncement against the concession of Irish legislative independence was 'rapturously approved by the entire English press' and that his opinions

> have been most eagerly adopted ... to strengthen their argument against Home Rule and there can be no doubt that he but re-echoes the sentiments of the vast majority of Englishmen.[141]

As a result of the disagreement with Froude, Lecky had now been accepted as an intellectual leader of the moderate nationalists in Ireland, while in England he had the ear of the intelligent reading public and of the more politically liberal. Gavan Duffy bracketed Lecky with three other protestants — Parnell, Galbraith and Prendergast — for outstanding services to the national cause, and he declared them to be as Irish as O'Connell or Bishop Doyle.[142] J. Lowry Whittle[143] expressed surprise that Lecky's status among the nationalists had not won for him the offer of a home rule seat in parliament. Whittle then offered a characteristic explanation of this:

> Before Mr Parnell was ever heard of, Mr Lecky's writings on Irish nationality had excited the enthusiasm of the Irish public. A liberal in politics, a fluent speaker, enjoying literary renown, he would in any other country but Ireland have had the offer of a parliamentary seat; but Ireland has always been 'managed' ... the island has always been in the hands of one faction or another ... . At the time when Mr Lecky first became known to the public, Rome had much the same importance in Ireland as Chicago has now ... Burning as was Mr Lecky's patriotism, distinguished as were his writings, he was a protestant of independent mind and not the sort of candidate to be recommended to a 'catholic constituency'.[144]

There was some truth in Whittle's analysis. For Lecky was indeed known to be not merely 'a protestant of independent mind' but also anti-clerical. 'Clerical Influences' had denounced the political influences of the Church — both Roman and established — in Ireland, and had called for its displacement by the secularization of politics through the cultivation of a patriotic public opinion. When this early essay was not republished in the 1871 edition of *Leaders*, Gavan Duffy told Lecky that he was wise to exclude it.[145]

Lecky's exclusion of this anti-clerical chapter had nothing to do with any attempt on his part to curry favour with the clergy. *Rationalism* and *Morals* had antagonised the intellectual leaders of the catholics. His books had been condemned by the *Month* and the *Dublin Review*, the organs of intellectual catholicism, and these journals regarded him as one of the contemporary rationalist enemies of the catholic church.[146] Lecky was thought suspect by the *Irish Ecclesiastical Record* which had been founded in 1864 under Archbishop Cullen's direction and whose nephew, Dr (later Cardinal) Moran, was one of its joint editors during these years.[147]

Lecky fully realized that the leading Irish clerics feared his influence. In a letter to his friend, Booth, commenting on the slow sale of his revised *Leaders*, Lecky wrote:

> As for the Irish people, they seem to me chiefly to know me by Cardinal Cullen who is good enough to make me a standing argument in support of his denunciations of T.C.D.[148]

At the very moment of the appearance of his first article against Froude (January 1873), Lecky was known to the catholic church as an enemy of their religion. Yet at this same moment, home rulers were anxiously trying to destroy the image which Cardinal Cullen and Bishop Moriarity held of home rule: that it was simply an Orange faction supported by the Fenians and led by Trinity College intellectuals.[149] In January 1873 O'Neill Daunt, after strong representations, agreed to become secretary to the Home Government Association. He concentrated on a campaign to win over the bishops individually to the support of the home rule movement.[150] In these circumstances, it would have been far from politic to invite the author of *Rationalism* and *Morals* to become personally associated with the home rule cause. Because of his treatment of questions of religion in his books, Lecky was far more suspect than either Butt, who had taught in Trinity, or Galbraith, currently a Fellow of the college, both of whom, although regarded cautiously by influential catholic ecclesiastics, were prepared to meet the bishops halfway by supporting their demand for denominational education.

Not only did Lecky not approve of the catholic demand for denominational education, but publicly, in a strong letter to *The Times* (6 February 1873), he denounced the bishops' demand, defended TCD against their criticisms, and endorsed the plan for the abolition of religious tests in the college.

This letter, reverting as it did to Lecky's denunciation of clerical influences in Ireland, did nothing to enhance his reputation with the bishops. Nor did it, in the circumstances of the *rapprochement* between nationalists and catholic ecclesiastics, encourage home rulers to consider inviting him into their ranks, despite his public approval of aspects of the home rule movement.

Lecky's participation in the controversy over the university question was perhaps sufficient in itself to explain why, despite his intellectual standing as a nationalist historian, he was not approached with an offer of a home rule seat. Yet he would not have accepted any such offer. He could not now claim, as he did a few years earlier, that he knew no Irish liberals, and Irish politicians were certainly aware of his nationalist writings. However, as early as January 1872 he had written to an old family friend in Ireland that he had no intention of getting himself mixed up with Butt's movement.[151] From this resolve, the praise he won during the controversy with Froude did not budge him. Immersed in eighteenth-century research, he no longer desired as strongly to get into parliament. He wrote to another friend in August 1873:

> I cannot say I at all wish to go into parliament just now. My book is a task quite sufficient for what little energies I possess, and parliament is getting every session less and less interesting.[152]

His friend continued to press the consideration of a parliamentary career on Lecky during 1873/4, but Lecky replied:

> Thanks for what you say about parliament. I find now that it is a sort of conventional thing among people I know to say that they expect me to stand for somewhere, but I am not aware that anyone in Ireland ever mentioned my name; and people with my mediocrity of position and fortune can never get into parliament unless they take the line of a demagogue or have someone to help them. No one has ever really helped me, and I do not feel at all inclined to make any great sacrifices for parliament, though one might like it if it came naturally in one's way.[153]

Lecky remained sufficiently interested in parliament to attend the home rule debate of 1874, just after his second article on Froude had appeared. However, what he then experienced did not attract him to the home rule movement. He thought that Butt, Sullivan, the O'Donoghue and O'Connor Power among the Irish representatives had spoken well. Others had spoken badly and he added:

> I think the close was the most disgraceful scene I ever saw, [Major O'Brien] dead drunk making a long speech, amid shouts of laughter, about how he was a member of the great Latin race, called on by his name and lineage to defend his country; while in the midst of it, amid loud cheers—came reeling in as drunk as could be and subsided on the floor. I was told that in this latter case it was quite habitual. ... I saw Gavan Duffy, who is here, and who interests me a good deal, soon after, and found him not a little disgusted with the Irish representation.[154]

Although Lecky was, perhaps, privately more against home rule than in favour of it in the circumstances of the 1870s, this was hardly obvious to his readers, who were warmed by his display of patriotism in his argument against Froude. Lecky failed to appreciate the impact he had made on Irish nationalists. Years later Whittle wrote in correspondence with Lecky:

> As to what I have said of your popularity in Ireland, I think it is borne out by the frequent references to you to be found in nationalist papers from 1866 to 1876 ... that you were claimed as one of their intellectual leaders admits I think of demonstration.[155]

For Lecky was indeed acceptable as an *intellectual* nationalist leader, but he was not acceptable in any active political sense. His writings were politically inspiring, his arguments were borrowed, and his liberal principles were adapted in the interests of the home rule cause. All this was done freely and without any personal commitment to Lecky. It was as if the home rulers had separated part of his intellect from the rest of the man and were very happy to employ it in their cause. How deep an impact Lecky, the intellectual leader, made was to be further revealed when his usefulness as propaganda was more extensively employed after Gladstone's conversion to home rule.

Chapter 5

Intellectual Landlordism

During the hectic years of home rule and agrarian agitations, Lecky worked away at his history of England in the eighteenth century. After more than five years of concentrated research and writing, the first two volumes were published in January 1878. Volumes III and IV followed in April 1882, Volumes V and VI in April 1887 and the final volumes, VII and VIII, in October 1890. Froude had established his claim to sixteenth-century England and S.R. Gardiner was laying claim to England of the seventeenth century. Lecky, by the manner and extent of his work, became the historian of the eighteenth century and assured himself a place among the most eminent men writing in English.

The accolades that greeted the volumes as they appeared were generous. Lecky had merited comparison with Gibbon, Macaulay, Carlyle and Froude. The virtues for which he won the loudest acclaim were impartiality, judiciousness, moderation, moral tone, liberal sympathies, painstaking concern with truth, industry, sweep and fluency.

When he began his work, his intention had been to base it upon an examination of the available published material. For his Irish chapters, especially, he soon discovered that he had to investigate the primary sources upon which Froude had made his assertions, and he extended his researches to the public and diplomatic records in Dublin, London and Paris. The result was Lecky's finest and most mature historical work.

His stated aim was to illustrate the more enduring forces and features of British life in the eighteenth century. Lecky's concern, therefore, was with the monarchy, the aristocracy, the churches, parliament, the press, agriculture, industry, commerce, art, drama, manners, the history of ideas and of the colonies. His interest was in themes and much less in strict chronology; he excluded the purely military or biographical. Political, social, cultural and religious themes were interwoven, if not always successfully blended, to give a more comprehensive picture of eighteenth-century society. The twin assertion that 'No battle is described, indeed few are mentioned'[1] may not be strictly accurate, for when Lecky surveyed the 1798 Rebellion, for example, he certainly gave details of military strategy and action. Nevertheless, in the work of a writer who described the Duke of Marlborough as 'Beyond comparison the greatest of English generals',[2] it is surprising to find that the victories forever associated with the Duke's name were merely mentioned.

As early as January 1872 he had outlined his objective:

> I want greatly to write a kind of analytic history explaining as well as describing about English politics for the last century and a half, and have read a great deal for it and made quantities of notes; ... the end of life is to bring out one's capacities, and literature is the readiest, and on the whole most satisfactory way of accomplishing it, and the power of expressing in a single work a long train of connected thinking is, I think, one of the highest of all pleasures. I think I could write a tolerably good book on English politics.[3]

Lecky settled down to a routine of work, visiting libraries and manuscript repositories in the mornings and writing in the evenings. The publication date of the early volumes kept on receding and the number of projected volumes went up steadily. He wrote in September 1874:

> I find the book I have undertaken to be alps upon alps, the horizon perpetually extending and certainly shall not be able to have two volumes ready before the end of next year which seems a long time, but unlimited patience is the first condition of doing anything really worthy in history.[4]

In the spring of 1875 he worked in the British Museum on about forty volumes of manuscripts relating to Ireland. Before going on to the Record Office he commented, 'History is so long and life is so short, and some three weeks ago I passed my thirty-seventh birthday — a great age.'[5] In the early summer of 1876 he was spending three hours a day reading manuscripts in Dublin Castle. Here he found the archives much better arranged than in London and was full of appreciation for the kindly help of Sir Bernard Burke, Ulster king-of-arms and keeper of state papers in Ireland. Lecky had a comfortable room to himself and went through the correspondence between the Dublin and London government officials, and the grand jury material from various Irish counties. Froude had been over this eighteenth-century material only superficially and had not used the mass of papers on the 1798 Rebellion. Lecky also examined the 'magnificent collection' of pamphlets in the Royal Irish Academy, and the newspapers for the first half of the eighteenth century. He went to Paris to elucidate, among other details, 'the extent of Bolingbroke's relations with the Pretender'.[6] The Paris archives were closed for the vacation, so Lecky had to order copies of what he required.

Ironically, Lecky was worried that all this manuscript material would prove to be detrimental to the style and balance of his book: 'I fear it will give my Irish chapter a very disproportionate magnitude and originality of research.'[7] He was also aware that this book required a very different approach from that of *Rationalism* or *Morals*. In these earlier works, as he saw it, his concern was with general causes that determined individual events and the character of successive ages. His book on the eighteenth century started at the opposite end, dealing with an enormous amount of political and social detail or those 'accidents', which altered the whole course of history.

When he returned to Dublin Castle in September 1877 to verify some of Froude's references, he found that the manuscripts he wished to consult had been removed to the Four Courts. His visit there convinced him that Froude had suppressed material in the manuscripts that was not consistent with his own prejudices.

Volumes I and II were well received. Lecky was pleased that his friends, Reeves of the *Edinburgh Review* and Dean Stanley, liked the volumes, and surprised that Carlyle was also satisfied. He was particularly proud of the Irish chapters, which took up more than a quarter of the two volumes; he saw them as the 'first serious attempt to analyse the political and social state of Ireland somewhat philosophically.'[8] Much of the Irish part of the work was original. Lecky was conscious that he was offering interpretations of the 1641 Rebellion and of the patriot parliament of 1689 that were contrary to the received views of the biggest names in British historiography — Clarendon, Hume, Hallam, Goldwin Smith, Green, Macaulay and Froude. He had been especially anxious to refute Froude, whose single object was 'to blast the character of the people' and arouse 'sectarian passions both against and among them'.[9] The social responsibility of the historian was a matter that Lecky viewed seriously. He realized that the general public had not the time, the opportunity or the skill to investigate original historical material. Historians, therefore, were honour bound to sift the sources and interpret them with the most scrupulous honesty.

Volume II brought the narrative down to 1760, and he little thought that the remaining forty years of the century would require another six volumes. The first sixty years, therefore, were rather sketchy in comparison with the treatment he was to give to the later eighteenth century. This disproportion was in itself eloquent testimony to Lecky's character as a Whig historian. His interests were the constitutional struggle between monarchy and aristocracy, the reform of parliament, Edmund Burke, the French Revolution, American independence, Grattan's parliament, the 1798 Rebellion and the Union of Great Britain and Ireland, all of which had immediate relevance to the great questions of Lecky's own time and as such received his greatest attention.

Volume I opened with the pre-Namierite assumption of parties and their principles which distinguished between Tories and Whigs. Politics loomed larger in the narrative than one might have expected from the references in the preface to the social and economic condition of the people. Lecky dealt with the ascendancy of the Whigs, analysed their support, praised the political virtues of their aristocracy, assessed the political influence of the commercial classes, reviewed foreign policy, described Walpole's ministry and outlined the religious legislation. He attempted a social history of the period with a brief sketch of national tastes and manners in which he touched on the growth and importance of newspapers, gambling, gardening, music, theatre, spas, sea-bathing and other habits of living and uses of leisure. In Volume II he devoted a chapter to a sketch of Irish history from the Normans to the beginning of the eighteenth century, and a second chapter to Ireland from 1700 to 1760. Scotland and the colonies shared a chapter; another dealt with domestic and foreign politics in the time of Pitt the Elder. A chapter on the religious revival (largely concerned with the part played by Wesley and methodism) led to a scholarly debate with Gladstone. In an article in the *British Quarterly Review*, Gladstone disputed Lecky's account of the evangelicals: he did not believe that evangelicanism was 'dominant' in religious life before the eighteenth century as Lecky had maintained, or that it had altered the tone and tendency of preaching. Lecky's reply in the *Nineteenth Century* conceded that he had overrated the number of evangelical clergy, but otherwise insisted on his own point of view and rejected Gladstone's line of reasoning.[10]

Lecky had hoped with Volumes III and IV to cover the years 1760 to 1790. Research for these volumes brought him back to Dublin Castle, the Four Courts and the Halliday collection of pamphlets in the Royal Irish Academy — 'the best collection I have ever met with'.[11] For the period in question, this collection of pamphlets extended to about 280 volumes. Lecky worked through these at the rate of fifteen or twenty volumes a day. He also examined the private papers of Lord Charlemont, head of the Volunteers. The work was so intense during 1879 and 1880 that he was unable to stick to the routine of research in the morning and writing in the evenings. The writing fell behind as he worked himself to exhaustion reading the Irish dispatches in the London Record Office where he found the amount of material 'quite appalling, often four or five long letters a week',[12] between the Irish and English officials. There were times when he complained he got 'very weary of a book which requires for its accomplishment so long a period of most exclusive work, so rigid an abstinence from many subjects I should like to go into.'[13] The volumes, published in April 1882, brought the narrative down to 1784. Original research was much more in evidence than in the first two volumes, and his authority was all the more clearly stamped on the period.

Lecky's analysis of the Whig Party and his description of the decline of monarchical power were considered most valuable. His portrait of George III attracted attention then and since. Some reviewers considered his picture unusually severe, but it was Lecky's solemn verdict that George III, despite his private virtues, 'inflicted more profound and enduring injuries upon his country than any other modern English king.'[14] Prominent in the charges that Lecky brought against him were the misgovernment of Ireland and the mishandling of catholic emancipation, which resulted in prolonged and bitter agitation. In denying that George III had acted unconstitutionally, Lecky rose above the too simple contemporary Whig version and came close to the views of Herbert Butterfield, although the latter thought that Lecky had substituted a more subtle Whig interpretation. George III was wrong, according to Lecky, not because he violated an existing constitution, but 'because he persistently opposed all those movements which in the fullness of time were to turn the government of 1760 into the government of 1860.'[15]

Lecky was worried that his views on the revolt of the American colonies would not please his American readers. He admitted to his friend, Henry Charles Lea, the American historian, that his were the views of a somewhat conservative Irishman and were not in the patriotic spirit of Bancroft;[16] in what he wrote he was simply trying to be fair to the English and the American cause. The chapters on America were later published separately as the *American Revolution 1763-1783*

(1899, reprinted 1932) with an introduction and notes by J.A. Woodburn. The enthusiastic reception of his work in America surprised and greatly pleased Lecky. Andrew D. White, president of Cornell University, was later to inform him that Lecky's volumes were recommended to Cornell students for their judicial fairness and as the best antidote to the chauvinism of American historiography.[17] G.L. Beer, J.B. McMaster, Henry Adams, the economic historian Charles Beard and the intellectual historian Carl Becker were among the internationally known American historians who acknowledged the value of Lecky's contribution to American historiography.[18]

The inspiration of Edmund Burke's political philosophy was evident throughout these volumes. Lecky had long looked upon Burke as the greatest of political philosophers. No other politician had left behind him a 'richer treasure of political wisdom applicable to all countries and to all times.'[19] His perceptive portrait of Burke impressed some of the foremost scholars of the period, including that hard-to-please critic and high priest of historiography, Lord Acton.[20] Acton wrote to say that 'your account of Burke is masterly,'[21] and he invited Lecky to contribute chapters on the French Revolution to the *Cambridge Modern History*.

Volumes V and VI dealt with the period 1784-93, and took another five years of dedicated work before their publication in April 1887. The work in Dublin was carried out under the tense circumstances that followed the Phoenix Park murders of the newly appointed Chief Secretary, Lord Frederick Cavendish, and the Under Secretary, Thomas Burke on 6 May 1882. Lecky had come to know the latter and had a great respect for him, as indeed he had for Cavendish. Their assassinations profoundly shocked him. Once during this period, when he arrived to dine at the Viceregal Lodge, the security arrangements reminded him of a police barracks; he had to give the password for the night and pass through rows of horse soldiers. On the day Parnell unveiled the O'Connell monument (15 August 1882), Lecky was prevented from working in Dublin Castle because an attack was feared and cannon had been mounted for its protection.[22]

Lecky's major research interest in Dublin Castle was the collection relating to the last twelve years of the eighteenth century, and consisting of county magistrates' reports and letters of informers dealing with the activities of the United Irishmen. Sixty-eight boxes, sealed by Lord Castlereagh, had remained unopened until the Public Records (Ireland) Act of 1867 authorised Sir Bernard Burke to do so. Burke had arranged them chronologically, but they had remained unexamined by any historian until Lecky went through them. He made extensive use of these papers, and when he discovered in 1883 that one of his notebooks was missing and probably burned, he returned to the Castle for three weeks. When his attention focused on the non-Irish parts of the work, he admitted: 'Modern Irish politics, leaders and ideals, disgust me so thoroughly that I confess it is no small relief to me to turn away from the subject.'[23] Yet in Paris in 1885 when Tallyrand's minute handwriting did nothing for his weak eyes (he had to acquire a magnifying glass) and he was continually being struck with how badly the archives were arranged because earlier and more recent documents were indiscriminately bound together, he sighed for Sir Bernard Burke's superior archival methods and the more comfortable arrangements of Dublin Castle.

The chapters on the French Revolution (later published separately, 1904, 1908) received a great deal of notice. In a history of eighteenth-century England, the inclusion of a chapter on the causes of the French Revolution and several sections of other chapters on its progress in France and on the diplomatic and military events that were more strictly related to continental history, raised many questions of relevance. Lecky justified it by remarking on the influence that the revolution had exercised on English politics. Hedva Ben-Israel has pointed out that in the historiography of the French Revolution written in English, Lecky stands midway between those who, like Morley, philosophized about its ideals, its principles and implications, and those, like Morse Stephens and Oscar Browning, who were involved in the new scholarly research.[24] Lecky's political philosophy regarding the Revolution was inspired by Edmund Burke; and his scholarship, although heavily reliant on the best secondary sources, reflected his visits to the Paris archives.

These volumes led to yet another passage at arms with Gladstone, who had written an appreciative review but who objected to some slighting references to his own political morality. Lecky had contrasted the open and direct forms of political corruption in the eighteenth century and the more subtle methods of the nineteenth century, such as the 'class bribery' of Gladstone's election promise to abolish income tax. In *Democracy and Liberty* Lecky reviewed the debate and insisted that the course adopted by Gladstone in 1874 was a conspicuous example of the evils to be feared when ministers attempted to manipulate support by appealing to mercenary self-interest.[25]

Lecky was delighted with the favourable reviews of Volumes V and VI. (He described that in the *Freeman's Journal* as 'admirable and able',[26] and suspected that its author was Gavan Duffy.) He himself thought that they were the best volumes in the series and probably the best that he would ever do because he had no intention of undertaking again a work of such lengthy research. He dreaded the prospect of what he then thought would be a final volume on Ireland from 1793 to 1800. He felt it could not be a success because it was a tangled story of horrors and isolated insurrections, lacking any element of dignity or beauty. As the work proceeded, he was alarmed to see that it was likely to amount to two volumes. Even at the expense of being dull, he said, and of destroying the symmetry of the book, he would have to do the period thoroughly. The last disturbed years of the century had taken on 'a most alarming *actualité*'. While working on the rebellion papers during the summer of 1888 he and Mrs Lecky had to be escorted by two constables to and from a dinner party at Drogheda where the plan of campaign was in operation against a local landlord. He thought it ironic that when he began his history, his critics had complained about the length of his Irish chapters, and he suspected that most of his readers had skipped the Irish parts. Now nothing he wrote was half so much avidly read and discussed as the Irish sections.

More original work went into Volumes VII and VIII than into the earlier volumes, and for a man who had shown only scant concern with some of the greatest military events of the eighteenth century, Lecky now paid a surprising amount of attention to the military episodes of the 1798 Rebellion. He trudged over the battle sites of County Wexford. This familiarity can be easily deduced from his narrative. The result was an intimacy of dramatic incident that one does not always associate with his writing. On previous research trips to Ireland he had had the benefit of the professional assistance of, J.P. Prendergast, and of Prendergast's companionship when, for example, they visited together the historian of seventeenth-century Ireland, Richard Bagwell, at Marlfield, Co. Tipperary. That Lecky saw himself in an Irish historiographical tradition while working on his last two volumes was now symbolized in his decision to visit Donegal Abbey and pay his respects to the memory of those sixteenth-century Irish historians known as the Four Masters. 'The latest of their successors',[27] as he described himself, paid homage at the site where they had written their *Annals.*

Lecky had significantly ended the account of eighteenth-century England with the outbreak of the French war in 1793, because he felt that to deal at all properly with that war and its varied consequences would have taken him well into the nineteenth century. Symmetry was always a conscious literary objective; so, to give a completeness to the Irish sections of his book, he felt it was necessary to deal with the 1798 Rebellion and the Union.

Among the great quantity of sources which determined the content of his last two volumes were the correspondence between the English and Irish administrations in the London Record Office; the papers in the French Foreign Office which threw sidelights on problems of British administration in Ireland; the Bishop Percy and the Pelham papers in the British Museum; and a number of collections in private hands. Above all, Lecky made excellent use of the Rebellion papers in Dublin Castle. Among these were letters from magistrates and government officials in different parts of Ireland which, Lecky said, had the same kind of value as the *cahiers* describing the state of France on the eve of the Revolution, and from which the best French historians had derived some of their most valuable material.

Volumes VII and VIII at last appeared in October 1890. Lecky's public had been awaiting these volumes not only because they completed a great work of history, but because they were potentially of vast political significance. The views of this respected historian were more likely to influence public opinion on the Irish question than were all the political speeches and ephemeral partisan tracts together. The importance of the volumes for the history of Ireland was immediately recognized. Viscount Bryce, the liberal statesman, held that Lecky's Irish chapters constituted the best history of Ireland to be found in the language.[28] C. Litton Falkiner, who was to shed important new light on aspects of Irish history in the eighteenth century, wrote that the final volumes were the fullest, most accurate and most exhaustive account of any period of Irish history.[29] The reviewer in the *Irish Times,* bestowing other superlatives, said that Lecky's description of the passing of the Act of Union had an interest 'not excelled by any piece of historical writing in any language of any country.'[30]

As he concluded his account of the Union, Lecky found it impossible not to say something about its consequences. This involved some reference to the current home rule issue which, in general, he said, was not desirable. 'I cannot, however, help it,' he wrote, 'and must face the charge of writing a party pamphlet on account of two or three concluding pages.'[31] Lecky had anticipated that the volumes were certain to get him into scrapes with both unionists and nationalists. To him the Union was 'as discreditable and corrupt a transaction'[32] as could possibly have been carried. But he said this was no reason for 'expiating' the destruction of a parliament of landlords by establishing a parliament of Land Leaguers. Unionists were delighted with Lecky's political comments, yet disappointed with his history. But then it had always been Lecky's conviction that, as he put it, 'unionists defend their very excellent politics by very indifferent history'.[33] Nationalists, on the other hand, had welcomed Lecky's earliest volumes as an occasion for 'profound national thanksgiving in Ireland'.[34] The historical assessments in the last volumes were equally gratifying to them. But the home rulers found it inexplicable that, having presented Irish history so impartially, Lecky was unable to draw the obvious political conclusions. 'Was it possible,' asked a London reviewer, 'that those who wrote history so well could miss its plainest lessons?'[35] While some liberal reviewers said that Lecky had written not history but a political pamphlet,[36] this was not the verdict of Irish home rulers or indeed of historians since.

Completion of the work set the seal on Lecky's reputation as a historian. There was a certain stateliness about the structure and a statesmanlike dignity of view throughout. It was intentionally and primarily a philosophical history, and, if we exclude the Irish chapters, not one that aimed at being original by basing itself on novel primary source material. There is little point in criticizing Lecky (as Butterfield did)[37] for not treating the evidence on George III microscopically, for that was not what he had set out to do. Nor is it altogether fair to suggest that Lecky picked out evidence to fit a framework already in his mind. This is to do less than justice to a historian who was trying 'to write an analytic history explaining as well as describing English politics.'[38] His moral sympathy — 'wholesome, independent and stirring'[39] — did occasionally lead him into the ways of the Whig historians, as defined by Butterfield, who were easily tempted into pronouncing moral judgments, and who sought the ratification if not the glorification of the present.[40] Although he made an effort to accommodate social history, economic history was largely missing from his structure. Concepts such as the Industrial Revolution in England at one extreme, or the 'hidden Ireland' of Gaelic poetry and folklore at the other were foreign to Lecky's mind. His Irish chapters, based on original primary sources, had the longest life. G.P. Gooch thought that Grattan's parliament, 1798 and the Union had been done so thoroughly that they did not need to be repeated.[41] Although the modern historian might not now agree with Gooch's verdict, students of eighteenth-century Ireland cannot yet afford to ignore Lecky's contribution.

The History of England in the Eighteenth Century had devoted comparatively scant consideration to the period before 1760. Out of thirty-two chapters in the original eight volumes, thirteen were devoted to Ireland, not more than eleven to

England and another eight to Scotland, India, America, France and various continental affairs. When the cabinet edition was issued in 1892 and 'Ireland' was separated from the rest, *Ireland in the Eighteenth Century* amounted to five volumes; the rest, still called *England in the Eighteenth Century*, amounted to seven volumes. L.P. Curtis has estimated that the Irish sections constituted approximately 43 per cent of the original edition.[42] This gave some basis to the plausible suggestion that Lecky's English chapters were the offspring of the clandestine parent, Ireland.

Publication of the cabinet edition of *Ireland* occured between the defeat of the first and second home rule bills. *Ireland*, therefore, was welcomed not only for the improvement in organization (which was the result of separating the Irish from the English chapters) but because of the topicality of its political interest. But in separating Ireland from England for reasons that were purely academic, Lecky was, however unconsciously, aiding the political demand for a separate Irish parliament. Lecky's *Ireland* was the unwitting admission that in Ireland's case, unlike Scotland's, the Union with England had not been successful. Liberal leaders were more than ever convinced that English crimes of the past needed to be atoned for by the granting of historic justice to the Irish nation. In the ensuing debate between home rulers and unionists, it was Lecky's role once again to supply not only the best historical arguments for the home rulers, but also the best political arguments for the unionists. The disproportionate amount of space which Lecky had given to Ireland was a clear enough indication of where his own political as well as historical interests lay.

By Irish landlord standards, the extent of Lecky's lands was moderate. He had inherited his grandmother's half-share of the Hartpole property in Queen's County (1 236 acres), and his grandfather's lands (721 acres) in neighbouring County Carlow. The Queen's County property was mainly situated in the barony of Slewmargy. The Hartpole family residence, sold by Lecky's grandparents, was at Shrule Castle on the west bank of the Barrow, some two miles north of Carlow town. At the time of his marriage to Maria Hartpole, Lecky's grandfather, John Lecky, lived at New Garden, Carlow on the opposite bank of the Barrow. The lands in Carlow, situated at Aughanure, Bestfield, and at Killnock, Kellistown in the same county, had practically the same valuation as his lands in Queen's County — a letting value calculated at £1 759 in 1878.

Besides the landed property, however, Lecky was well-connected. The two marriages of his father, and the second marriage of his stepmother strengthened his financial resources. There is also evidence that Lecky, with others, was entitled to the rents of at least six premises in Townsend Street, Dublin.[43] Although the royalties from the sales of books were in some years substantial, it was the revenue from his Irish property which formed the basis of his social position. These rents enabled him to become an absentee landlord and to devote his time to historical studies. What evidence exists about Lecky as a landlord has to be put together from a few scattered pieces of information.

After he had finished *Rationalism*, he was ordered on medical advice not to read for some time, and took the opportunity to visit — 'I am ashamed to say for the first time' — some of his tenants. He was alarmed at the prospect, for 'when one hardly knows the difference between a potato and a turnip it is not easy to be very imposing in conversation with farmers'.[44] Four years later, after the publication of his *Morals*, Lecky was again back in Ireland performing another of the functions of the landlord, serving on the grand jury for Queen's County. What the *Leinster Express* (24 July 1869) called the 'diabolical attempt' on the life of Mr Warburton, the high sheriff, on his way to open the assizes at Maryboro, and the arrival of his carriage spattered with blood, helped to make Lecky's work on the grand jury more interesting than it might otherwise have been.[45] As a member of the grand jury, he also served on the committee on public buildings, inspected the infirmary, prison and lunatic asylum and with his cousin, Charles Hartpole Bowen, signed the committee's brief and formal report on the satisfactory management of these institutions.[46] Privately he wrote that this work as a member of the grand jury was 'a great deal out of my line';[47] and he was back on the Continent at the first opportunity.

In 1873, while on a tour of Irish beauty spots with his wife, Lecky brought her to visit his tenants. Although he lived for another thirty years, further references to him as a landlord performing his duties have not been found. This can only mean that Lecky was an absentee, content to work through an agent.[48] It does not follow that he was a bad landlord; in fact, the evidence is all to the contrary. The tenants on Lecky's property appear to have been fairly well off and respectable small farmers. In the years before the land courts reduced rents generally, Lecky had tenants of over £100 per annum, which represented good-sized farmers of a class that was well able to look after itself.

When Gladstone introduced the 1870 land bill, designed to give tenants some security against evicting landlords, and encouraging the granting of leases in place of the old system of tenants-at-will, Lecky warmly approved. He defended the government's project of helping tenants to buy out their property, for he argued that a number of peasant proprietors would be 'one of the most useful and, in the best sense of the word, conservative of elements in Irish life'.[49] Lecky also welcomed the introduction of Gladstone's 1881 land bill, hoping that it would assist tenants to purchase their holdings and further encourage the system of long leases and tenancies in fee farm.[50] Nearly all his own tenants had leases, and most held leases of 31 years.[51]

After the land courts had been set up under the 1881 Act to deal with the question of fair rents, two of Lecky's Carlow tenants, John Keppel of Killnock, Kellistown, who held almost 80 acres from Lecky for which he paid £50 per annum, and William Nolan, also of Killnock, who held 77 acres for £56, applied for a reduction of their rents. Out of a number of cases heard before a sitting of the land court in Carlow, there were twelve instances where the rent charged by Carlow landlords was higher than the valuation of the property. There were six instances where the rent and the valuation were practically equal, and six others where the rent was lower. One of Lecky's tenants paid a rent lower than the valuation, the other had a rent equal to the valuation.[52]

The facts which emerged at this hearing of the land court, although neither exhaustive nor conclusive, tend to confirm other evidence that Lecky was a good and reasonable landlord. At least he was among those who charged the lower rents. In Galway, before rents were reduced by the land court, there were extreme examples of rents exceeding the valuation by as much as 133 per cent and even 224 per cent.[53] It was also stated publicly (and not denied) during the controversy over Lecky's nomination as a candidate for a University of Dublin parliamentary seat that there were families on Lecky's lands who had been there for upwards of 150 years.[54] This too suggests good tenant-landlord relations on the Lecky estate.

Although Lecky had little practical interest in the tenants on his own estate, he was compelled by the outbreak of the land war and by the political and social implications of the land acts to become politically and intellectually involved in the Irish land question, and this gave rise to what we might call Lecky's intellectual landlordism. Lecky was always a firmly convinced upholder of the rights of private property and maintained that the educated and wealthy classes should govern the country. He upheld the sacredness of the law and the sanctity of contracts and had always believed in an Irish nationality that should be linked to the empire through loyalty to the Crown.

He had become horrified at the changes taking place in Irish politics when Fenians, Land Leaguers and home rulers were welded together under Parnell's leadership. The impact of this 'new departure' is dramatically highlighted in Lecky's correspondence during the late 1870s and early 1880s with fellow moderate nationalists like O'Neill Daunt and J.P. Prendergast. Their attitude to the 'new departure', and especially to the Land League, paralleled and even foreshadowed the split in the Liberal Party, when the Duke of Argyll resigned from Gladstone's cabinet on the issue of the Irish land question in 1881.

O'Neill Daunt, who had written a letter to *The Nation* (6 December 1879) advocating home rule and tenants' rights, forwarded a copy of the letter to Lecky. Lecky wrote a long reply which was in effect a statement of the position he had now taken up against home rule:

> I must thank you for so kindly sending me the *Nation* with your letter, but you must forgive me if I say that I entirely disagree with you. Whatever else Parnell and his satellites have done, they have, at least in my opinion killed home rule by demonstrating in the clearest manner that the classes who possess political power in Ireland are radically and profoundly unfit for self-government. That a set of political adventurers who go about the country openly advocating robbery and by implication murder ('keep a firm grip on your land' without paying rent, in Ireland, means nothing else) should enjoy an unbounded popularity and command a multitude of Irish votes; that a popular press should extol them as the true leaders and representatives of the Irish race; that great meetings should be held in which cries for murdering landlords elicit loud cheers and not a word of serious rebuke; that such a movement should have attained its present dimensions in Ireland appears to me a most conclusive proof that the very

rudiments of political morality have still to be taught. There is no civilised country in Europe where such things would be possible. Whatever else government has to do, *the protection of life and property is its first duty.* Respect for contracts, *a high sense of the value of human life,* a stern exclusion from public life of all men who in any degree coquet with or palliate crime, and a hatred of disorder and violence and lawlessness are the qualities that are found in all classes which are capable of self-government; and the freedom of a country depends mainly upon the success of its public opinion in crushing the elements of socialism and anarchy within it. Judged by such tests, the political condition of Ireland seems to me at present the most deplorable that can well be conceived, and the reputation and character of the country are rapidly sinking, not only in England, but throughout Europe. It certainly passes my intellect to conceive how men can imagine that they are improving the political condition of Ireland by instigating a fierce war of classes, or its economical condition by destroying all respect for contracts and making property utterly insecure, or its moral condition by persuading the people that dishonesty backed by intimidation is the best resource in bad times.... There is really something too ridiculous in a party preaching a furious crusade against Irish landlords and then denouncing England for 'robbing' Ireland of a parliament of landlords — creating by systematic obstruction a kind of parliamentary anarchy in England by way of showing how admirably fit they are for managing a parliament of their own! ... until this new communism is extirpated from Ireland or at least branded with the infamy it deserves, I can see no real prospect of political improvement ... .[55]

Lecky was relieved to find that O'Neill Daunt and he did not disagree as much as he had feared. But while he could admire the 'fidelity' and 'energy' with which O'Neill Daunt maintained the home rule opinions of his youth, he added:

I own I do not myself believe in democratic home rule in Ireland, and I think home rule which is not democratic would never be tolerated. At present, however, the great danger to the country seems to me this new disease of communism, which when it passes into the constitution of a nation is apt to prove one of the most inveterate and most debilitating.[56]

The big difference that emerged between O'Neill Daunt and Lecky was that O'Neill Daunt regarded home rule and the Land League as two separable facts, while Lecky saw them as inextricable. Home rule, in Lecky's view, would mean both democracy and communism at the most extreme. Lecky's rejection of home rule now became both deliberate and final. In 1871 he had advocated some measure of local autonomy for Ireland, and the earliest volumes of *England* could be taken as of great assistance to the home rule cause, but from the start of the Land League in 1879, Lecky declared unambiguously against home government for Ireland. The explanation for this stand was to be found in his intellectual landlordism. He had come to the conclusion that:

... whatever may have been the case in other days, home rule would seem to me now one of the most certain ways of driving great masses of property out of Ireland; for what sensible man would, if he could help it, leave his land or other property at the mercy of an assembly guided by 'the Leader of the Irish People' and his satellites?[57]

Yet Lecky was a moderate reformer in the Liberal tradition. He hoped that something would be done to multiply the number of peasant proprietors in Ireland without injuring the landlords' rights of property. For Lecky held that to increase the peasant proprietary would help to maintain a stable society; but, he knew, the difficulties of achieving peasant proprietary had been enormously increased by the attitude of the 'patriots' in advising the withholding of the payment of debts, and by the strong anti-Irish feeling which the proceedings of 'Parnell and Co' had produced in England. In letters on 8 and 17 February 1880, Lecky expressed the fear that one of the undesirable effects of the land agitation might well be that it would lead to a period of Tory ascendancy in government. Lecky was still a strong supporter of Gladstone and hoped that the Irish situation would improve before it damaged the cause of Liberalism.[58]

He agreed with O'Neill Daunt that it was folly for Parnell and his friends to talk about the compulsory expropriation of landlords,[59] but he took a more serious view than O'Neill Daunt did of the influence of the agitators. He regarded the immense popularity of some Land League speakers as furnishing 'a presumption against Irish capacity for self-government'. O'Neill Daunt, noting in his journal a letter he had received from Lecky to that effect, wrote:

> Lecky says that any mischief to Ireland that Froude's writings can do, is infinitesimal compared to the damage inflicted on our national character and cause by the vicious and idiotic gibberings of the extreme landleaguers — in which opinion I strongly incline to agree with him.[60]

Lecky insisted that much of the responsibility for the state of the country was due directly to the land agitators. When O'Neill Daunt was attacked in the press for expressing similar views Lecky congratulated him on being enrolled among Ireland's 'domestic enemies', adding that Grattan and O'Connell, if they were alive, would also have been placed in the same category.[61] O'Neill Daunt confessed that his life-long attachment and loyalty to the cause of a domestic parliament for Ireland was being severely tested:

> I wish I had good grounds to differ from your belief that home rule, if now obtained, would impart noxious power to the brawlers of the land agitation. It is a choice of evils. The union is a deadly blight. A domestic parliament composed of Davitts, Redpaths and similar creatures would be a very equivocal blessing.[62]

But he continued to emphasize that the root cause of the trouble was not the land agitation, but the Union and the 'heartless greed of insatiable West British landlords'.

O'Neill Daunt's attack on the 'atrocious landlords' in letter after letter ultimately elicited from Lecky what amounted to a defence of his own class:

> I do not know whether the fact that I am myself — though on a small scale
> — an Irish landlord biasses [*sic*] me, but I own I take a much more landlord
> view than you do of Irish affairs. The standard of public duty in Ireland has
> always been low, and there are great faults of negligence and extravagance
> and arrogance to be attributed to the upper classes; but I have never been
> able to discover satisfactory evidence of the atrocious rapacity, extortion
> and exterminating tyranny which it is the fashion to ascribe to them.[63]

Lecky blamed the system of subdivision and the absence of industrial habits more
than landlord misdeeds for Irish poverty. The worst class of landlords, he held,
were from among those who recently had come into possession as a result of
speculation under the Encumbered Estates Act. Lecky's proposed solution was
for the government to assist 'the better and richer class of tenants' to purchase
their holdings, to give some indirect encouragement to the system of leases and
assistance to emigration from parts of Ireland. It was essential for the prosperity
of the country that tenancies under twenty acres should disappear. But beyond
helping these developments Lecky thought the government should not interfere:

> I am old-fashioned enough to believe strongly in political economy as
> applied to land and in the extreme mischief of most legislative interference
> with private contracts.[64]

Old liberals like Lecky whose ideas about political economy had been grounded
in *laissez-faire* principles were finding it increasingly inappropriate to urge the
application of their doctrines to the existing land problem in Ireland. And as the
land war grew more violent, Lecky became increasingly pessimistic about the
state of Ireland, and more firmly entrenched in his hostility to home rule. On 11
December 1880 he wrote:

> I never expect to see Ireland really quiet again for between incapable
> governors and successful agitators the very worst spirit of communism
> seems to have past [*sic*] into the unhappy country. I wonder whether we
> shall get through this winter without a regular outbreak![65]

A few months later he was commenting that it was the persuasion of most
persons who had anything to lose that Irish politics had fallen 'to a large extent
into the hands of swindlers'

> who may be admittedly orthodox on all points relating to the Sacraments
> and the Creed but whose views about the Decalogue are peculiar and who
> certainly do not make the protection either of life or property an object of
> their policy.[66]

In these circumstances Lecky did not regard a native Irish parliament 'possibly
guided alternately by Parnell, Biggar and Dillon' as a desirable thing. Rather he
suspected that unless the Coercion Act and the 1881 Land Act restored peace and

at least partial political commonsense, the representative system would sooner or later be abolished or profoundly modified in Ireland. In his reactions to the Land League, Lecky adopted some of the views of Froude which he had attacked and condemned years earlier:

> So far from things tending towards home rule, I think you will soon find the opinion growing up on all sides that Ireland is unfit for the amount of representative government which she possesses, and that a government rather on the Indian model may become necessary.[67]

He wrote of home rule that it would be 'the most perfect of all earthly realizations of Pandemonium'.[68] Lecky could not at all agree with O'Neill Daunt 'in thinking Ireland in the present day in the least fitted for home rule'.[69] When the franchise was extended in 1884, he wrote to another friend:

> How Ireland is ever to be governed, or how parliament here is to work or party government to exist when we have eighty or ninety Parnellites (which we are very likely to have), passes my comprehension.[70]

Lecky was relieved that O'Neill Daunt had remained friendly despite their divergence on home rule. In a letter, Lecky said that he was glad that

> ... you are not very angry with the emphasis of my anti-home rule heresies. I own that the last few years have quite cured me of the notion that either property or liberty could be safely trusted to an Irish popular chamber. But however much we may differ about the present we shall I hope always find considerable sympathy in our views of the past ....[71]

Lecky's final disillusionment and abandonment of home rule resulted from the horror with which he viewed Parnellism and the Land League agitation. As this continued, one can trace in O'Neill Daunt's correspondence how he came more and more to appreciate Lecky's stand and to be influenced to some extent by his friend's arguments. O'Neill Daunt had been much more personally committed to repeal and home rule than Lecky, and Lecky had been deeply impressed by O'Neill Daunt, whom, he wrote, had 'fought the battle of repeal very long and very steadily'.[72]

The seriousness with which Lecky viewed the situation drove him to participate more actively and publicly in political and social controversy. In April 1881, when Gladstone introduced his land bill, Lecky attended the debates in the House of Commons. His letters of the time show how much he still admired Gladstone,[73] and how hopeful he was that his legislation would restore order.[74] But by November he was condemning the 1881 Land Act in strong words:

> You are fortunate in having got rid of your Irish property [he wrote to a friend in England]. It seems to me that the net result of Gladstone's legislation has been that there are now two predatory bodies instead of one in Ireland, and I do not know whether in the long run the Land Court may not prove the worst of the two.[75]

Gladstone's 1881 Land Act cost him not only the support of a powerful landowner like the Duke of Argyll, but also the backing of Old Liberals like Lecky. In letters to *The Times*, Lecky now put the case of the Irish landlords. In the first letter, he defended those landlords who within living memory under the Encumbered Estates Act, and 'by invitation of the government', had spent £52 million in purchasing estates and acquiring an undoubted legal right, the most secure known to English law. The 1881 Act, Lecky argued, destroyed the complete and exclusive ownership of land hitherto guaranteed by parliamentary title. While parliament had the right to deprive a person in part or altogether of the ownership, nevertheless, in such a case it was bound to compensate the owner for any diminution by law of the value of the private property. Otherwise the action of the government was one of simple dishonesty and confiscation, which would shake the security of every kind of property in the kingdom.[76]

Another landlord-historian, Richard Bagwell, criticized Lecky's letters on the grounds that it was wrong tactics on the part of the landlords to seek compensation only for those who had purchased under the Encumbered Estates Act, and to regard their title as more sacred than those of the older landlord families.[77] Bagwell had misunderstood Lecky. He was not, as Bagwell assumed, favouring one class of landlord against another, for he had in fact only fifteen months earlier described the worst landlords as coming from among those speculators who had bought property under the Encumbered Estates Act. In a further letter to *The Times*, Lecky explained that the only reason he had distinguished between Irish landlords was because the claim of the most recent class could be made the most universally intelligible. He added that it was not necessary that parliament should directly compensate the landlord whose property the 1881 Act had arbitrarily devalued:

> It would be quite sufficient if it gave him the means of parting with it on equitable terms and such a course might greatly facilitate the establishment of a considerable peasant proprietary, which is fast becoming the only possible solution of the Irish difficulty.[78]

It was a symbol of the stature he attained as a landlord propagandist that Lecky, a man with less than 2000 acres, should have been invited to go on Lord Castletown's landlord deputation to the government 'to represent the necessity of the government advancing more money for the purchase by tenants of Irish land'.[79] Five others accompanied Lecky on this 'central committee': Lord Castletown, the Earl of Bessborough, Sir Rowland Blennerhassett, Lord Monteagle and Mr Art MacMurrough Kavanagh. Four were titled gentlemen, while the fifth, MacMurrough Kavanagh, was very wealthy and one of the country's principal landlords.[80]

By comparison with other Irish landlords, however, Lecky was less active in the landlords' defence organizations, and more willing to achieve compromise in the land struggle. When the Irish Landowners' Convention was set up, Lecky sent his subscription to his cousin, J. Frederick Lecky of Ballykealey, Ballon, Co. Carlow, the head of the Carlow Leckys and secretary and treasurer of the Carlow

branch.[81] While Lecky could agree that 'fixity of tenure' was an interference with
the rights of property since it took from the landlord's absolute ownership, he
would concede it as a principle, providing compensation were made to the
landlord for relinquishing part of his rights.[82] Not only did Lecky outdistance
fellow unionist landlords in the policies he advocated for a settlement of the land
question, he went further than some moderate land reformers in the nationalist
camp. If Gladstone's 1881 Act and the later land purchase acts appeared much too
radical for Lecky, he nevertheless favoured an increase in the number of peasant
proprietors at a time when O'Neill Daunt, the home ruler, thought that such a
policy might be impolitic and that the recognition of tenant-right would be a
sufficient limit to measures of land reform.

It would be too simple to say that Lecky had been frightened off Irish
nationalism by the emergence of agrarianism. What was significant about his
position was not so much that he was himself a landlord, but the fact that
intellectual landlordism was the basis of his political and social thinking. The
suddenness with which socialism and democracy had displayed their force and
extremism in Ireland horrified Lecky. He had been shocked out of much of his
earlier liberalism and purged of most of his Irish nationalism. For the rest of his
life Lecky was hardly able to separate Irish nationalism from agrarianism, and his
arguments against home rule from this time forward invariably referred to the
land question, linking it with an attack on democratic and socialistic implications
in the demands of the agitators. From this period Lecky in his political writings
openly became a propagandist in the unionist and landlord interests. The experience, which so deeply coloured his political and social opinions, was also to leave
its imprint on his historical writings.

The contemplation of the trend of affairs in Ireland between 1878 and 1882
was a horrifying experience for Lecky. He was convinced that many of his
dearest-held values were being consumed in the political and social furnace of the
period. His world was beginning to crumble about him. But these were the years
when he was hard at work on the third and fourth volumes of *England*. His
hostility to developments in Ireland — to the emergence of socialist doctrines
relating to the land, and the first signs of social revolution; to democratic
tendencies and nationalist pressures — affected his historical ideas. His reaction
to the situation is traceable in his volumes and his comments on Irish landlordism, on the legislative independence of 1782, on the French and American
Revolutions, and on Edmund Burke are particularly revealing.

In these years, when the land war was raging, Lecky re-examined the question
of Irish landlordism, going deeper into its history than he had ever done before.
He discussed the landlord system, its benefits and deficiencies; he devoted a fair
amount of space to absenteeism, middlemen, rents and the conditions of the
tenantry. The emergence of certain changes of emphasis and the employment of
particular arguments illustrate the profound effect that contemporary affairs were
having on Lecky's written work.

His first picture of the Irish landlords in *Leaders* (1861) had exhibited them as
lovable rascals:

> They were men of the most reckless improvidence, of the wildest dissipation, but of almost invariable amiability and kindness. Their life passed in cockfights and hunts, in duels and in drunken revels — but also in the exercise of the most boundless hospitality and the most lavish generosity. … Their irregularities were pardoned on the score of their generosity. Their vices were of the kind that did little harm to their neighbours. Their virtues were of the most fascinating and attractive order. Their tenants regarded them with feelings of feudal affection.[83]

Despite Whiteboy activities, there was not, in the eighteenth century, the general antagonism of the classes which Lecky found around him in 1861. The class war was, according to the young Lecky, the result of the sectarianism that O'Connell had evoked. The relief bill of 1829, ending the struggle for catholic emancipation, marked a great social revolution in Ireland. O'Connell, whose 'first object was to increase the influence of his Church', replaced the landlords' authority with that of the priest, and in the process evoked that spirit of sectarian zeal which broke the bond between landlord and people. Lecky added that he was far from thinking that this severance was for the advantage of Ireland. He regretted that the landlords, whom he often referred to as 'the natural leaders of the people' and who had fulfilled their role of national leadership honourably during the period of legislative independence, should have been alienated politically from the people by the re-emergence of sectarianism.[84]

When Lecky revised his picture of the landlords for his 1871 edition of *Leaders*, he still described them as rascals, but they were not so lovable now. The deepening of the shades was produced by a more detailed elaboration of landlord vices, and by the fact that, whereas the 1861 edition had taken the virtues and the vices together, in the 1871 edition he outlined the vices first before treating of the virtues in a separate and shorter passage. To the part played by sectarianism he added other causes, emphasizing the repeal movement as a significant factor in the estrangement of the landlords:

> The attitude which the landlord class afterwards assumed during the agitation for repeal completed the change and they have never regained their old position.[85]

This language led O'Neill Daunt to believe that Lecky was reprimanding the landlords for not being nationalist enough.[86] Besides the immediate causes of sectarianism and the landlords' rejection of repeal, Lecky saw more remote influences at work. The author, who meantime had traced causes and effects through centuries in his *Rationalism* and *Morals*, now attempted something similar for the history of landlordism in Ireland. He explained that a 'train of causes' had been forging a schism between the landlords and the people. Among these he listed the diseased economic conditions to which trade restrictions and penal laws against the catholics had contributed; the absence of manufacturing industry, which had thrown an impoverished population for subsistence upon the soil; the fact that the farming classes were divided into protestant landlords

and catholic tenantry; the memory of ancient confiscations embittering differences of religion; the levying of tithes on poor catholics to support the landlords'
church; secret agrarian societies; the custom of subletting, which divided the land
into infinitesimal farms, enabling the peasantry to marry early (encouraged by
their priests) and multiply recklessly; the system of the middleman; the distress
and feeling of oppression which predisposed the people to follow leaders other
than the landlords. 'All the materials of the most dangerous social war thus
existed … .'[87] Pitt, by his Union policy and methods, 'the Utramontane policy
dictated by the priesthood', and 'the socialistic follies of Fenianism' also contributed to the division of the classes in Ireland.[88] As long as this gulf between
landlord and people continued, there could never be a successful national policy,
and the materials for self-government therefore would be wanting.[89]

Greater experience in studying the impact of historical causes, and more
extensive acquaintance with literature on the Irish land system had deepened
Lecky's knowledge of Irish landlordism. But besides this objective study, Lecky
had also become much more practically interested in the land question. Developments that had taken place in political and social life in the decade since he wrote
the first edition of *Leaders* affected his judgments in 1871. Now, for example, he
could postulate in defence of O'Connell the argument that he 'never encouraged
those socialistic notions about land which since his death have been so prevalent'.[90]

In 1871 Lecky acknowledged that the shades of his picture of the landlords
were 'sufficiently dark'.[91] Yet he also maintained that there was a brighter side to
their character:

> The noble efflorescence of political and oratorical genius among Irishmen
> in the last quarter of the century, the perfect calm with which great
> measures for the relief of the catholics which would have been impossible
> in England were received in Ireland; above all, the manner in which the
> Volunteer movement was organised, directed, and controlled, are decisive
> proofs that the upper classes possessed many high and commanding quali-
> ties, and enjoyed in a very large measure the confidence of their inferiors.[92]

By and large, however, the shades were more prominent than the lights in
Lecky's portrait of the landlords in 1871. The following year Froude approved of
the policies of confiscation and plantation in Irish history, and of the uprooting
of the catholics. Lecky answered that the same policies had resulted in the present
agrarian troubles. Despite their estrangement from the people and their many
vices, he argued, the landlords were not nearly as despicable as Froude had
painted them. The bitterness of Froude's picture, he claimed, could be accounted
for by the fact that he had relied on Jonah Barrington's sketches of their
character. Barrington, said Lecky, was not reliable; he overcoloured his subjects.

Barrington's *Personal Sketches* recounted many anecdotes of the eighteenth-
century ascendancy. Among these was one of Lecky's grand-uncle, George Hartpole,
the inheritor 'of a large territory, a moderate income, a tattered mansion, an embarrassed rent-roll and a profound ignorance … of business in all departments.'[93]

It was a sketch typical of the eighteenth-century buck and corresponded with Froude's lowest estimate of Irish landlords. Indeed, some of Froude's remarks might well have been based on Barrington's picture of Lecky's relative.

Beyond this Lecky's immediate ancestors and cousins had been the butt of Barrington's witty pen. However, there was another side to the story: a side preserved among the Hartpole papers in Lecky's own possession.[94] Among these papers is a memorandum by Lord Aldborough which denies Barrington's claim to be related to the Hartpoles, and which alleges that Barrington was paid £300 a year by Hartpole to act as his attorney.[95]

In addition Lecky had read the *Personal Sketches* and also probably the memoir of Barrington by Townsend Young which was appended to the third edition (1869).[96] This memoir had made public some of Barrington's questionable financial dealings and his appropriation of public funds while holding office in the court of admiralty. It is greatly to the credit of Lecky's moral restraint that he contented himself with saying merely that Barrington was an unreliable writer. Because of the family feud, one might have expected some animus on his part. Lecky's logic, however, was faulty because in his later work he often referred to Barrington as an authoritative source. There was no indication that in rejecting Barrington's picture of the landlords he had done so out of any anxiety to keep the family ghost, George Hartpole, safely locked away in the cupboard.

Although Lecky, in his history of the Irish landlords, had concentrated more on darkening his 1871 version, in his 1873/74 review of Froude he carefully retouched the bright spots. The outline he had given in 1871 and defended in 1873/4 continued to be the basis of his portrait of the ascendancy when he wrote his history of the eighteenth century. With Froude undoubtedly in his mind he wrote:

> A dishonest historian, who selected or conceals his facts according to the impression he wishes to convey, may, no doubt discover without difficulty authentic materials for an unqualified diatribe against the Irish protestants and their parliament; but a true picture will contain many lights as well as shades ... .[97]

But when Lecky in *England* got down to the business of depicting the 'lights' and 'shades', it was not accident, nor was it entirely for historical reasons that the volumes written before 1878 should stress the shades, while those appearing after that date and during the Irish Land War emphasized the virtues of Irish landlordism. In the volume of *England* which appeared in 1878, Lecky showed that he was not prepared to defend the Irish landlords indiscriminately. He admitted that there had been much oppression of the tenantry, but the culprits were not so much the head landlords, whose faults were rather those of neglect than of oppression, but the middlemen. The landlord vices were more or less diffused through the whole class, but they attained their extreme development in the middleman.[98] These were the small gentry, 'a harsh, rapacious, and dissipated class living with an extravagance that could only be met by the most grinding exactions ... .'[99] The negligence of the landlords themselves, on the other hand, often took the form of absenteeism, one of Ireland's greatest evils in the eighteenth century. It drained out of the country large sums of money in the form of rent. It opened the way for the disastrous agrarian system of subletting and of middlemen, who were without the 'culture and position' and the interest of the landowner in the soil and his tenants, and who were usually 'the most grasping of tyrants'.[100] With something, perhaps, of Victorian snobbery, he described them as men who 'combined the education and manners of farmers with the pretensions of gentlemen, and they endeavoured to support these pretensions by idleness, extravagance, and ostentatious arrogance.'[101] Their vices included:

> ... gambling, fighting, drinking, swearing, ravishing and sporting, parading everywhere their contempt for honest labour, giving a tone of recklessness to every society in which they moved.[102]

The faults of landlords and middlemen feature largely in the volumes that appeared before 1879. Writing before he was shocked by the violence of the land agitation, Lecky held that no one should be surprised by the existence of agrarianism in Ireland:

> No reasonable person will wonder that a country with an agrarian history like that of Ireland should have proved abundantly prolific in agrarian crime.[103]

In the volumes appearing during or after the agitation, defence of the landlords, the recounting of their virtues, and the shifting of responsibility for the diseased state of society on to the system and away from individuals, becomes more noticeable.

In the later volumes Lecky defended the landlords against the generalization that they were 'a class of rapacious and extortionate tyrants'.[104] Evicting landlords were a minority, and evictions were not a permanent feature of Irish society, for the records of most Irish estates show that a long continuance of the same families on the same estates had been at least as characteristic of Ireland as of England.[105] This was indeed the position on Lecky's own estate. Looking broadly over Irish history, he asserted that the real owners of the land rarely asked the full market or competitive rent from their tenants.[106] He tended to accept the views of Arthur Young, who had examined rents in Ireland in the eighteenth century and had concluded that they were abnormally low.[107] Fierce competition for the smallest subdivision forced up rents.[108] This was not the fault of the landowners but of the agrarian system. Despite the differences of race, creed and traditions, a strong feudal attachment and reverence had grown up in the eighteenth century between protestant landlord and catholic tenantry. The Volunteer movement had shown their qualities of leadership. 'A class who were capable of these things may have had many faults, but they can have been neither impotent nor unpopular.'[109]

Even the lower gentry, or the middlemen, who had been severely castigated in 1878, got off lighter as Lecky's history of the eighteenth century proceeded. In his discussion of Irish social conditions, he gave at some length the arguments of

Whitley Stokes in 1822, who for philanthropic reasons had defended the system of middlemen and subdivision.[110] Clearly Lecky himself preferred the case put by Young, whom he regarded 'as the first living authority on agriculture'.[111] Nevertheless, he saw that Stokes had a point; and the elaboration of the various causes favouring the subdivision of land also helped to soften his earlier criticism of the middlemen.[112] If one could blame the system, as Lecky now did, one could find extenuating circumstances, not only for the landowners but even for the faults of the middlemen. In his final picture of the gentry (in the later volumes of *England* and in *Democracy and Liberty*) they were to a great extent the victims of the diseased society that bred them, and much could be argued against any indiscriminate condemnation of the Irish landlord class.

In accounting for the change of emphasis in Lecky's references to landlordism in the volumes written during or after the Land War of the 1880s, one has to guard against attributing too much to the influence of the contemporary situation. It should be pointed out that when Lecky's history of the eighteenth century was reissued as separate volumes on Ireland and England in the 1890s, he did not make any noteworthy changes in his account of landlordism. Volume I of *Ireland* remained (like Volume II of the first edition of *England*) severe on the middlemen, while the later volumes continued to give the extenuating circumstances. It also has to be borne in mind that, in relating the misdeeds of the gentry, Lecky was describing mainly the political and social effects of the earlier confiscations from 1700 to 1760. He argued that the gentry improved in the eighteenth century, particularly during the period of legislative independence. The faults that existed among the gentry then Lecky attributed largely to the agrarian system. Further, one has to allow for the fact that the different evidence that Lecky used for the two halves of the eighteenth century tended to determine a change of emphasis. To judge from his footnote references and from his notebooks, it is clear that wider research certainly did have an influence on Lecky's changing picture of Irish landlordism.

When due allowance has been made for all these factors, however, the fact still remains that his reaction to contemporary events did have a strong influence on Lecky's historical writing. In his private correspondence he acknowledged that recent political and social developments had left their mark on his work. O'Neill Daunt pointed out to Lecky that, in *Leaders*, he had observed that the contemporary generation of protestant gentry had not inherited Grattan's national spirit.[113] In 1861 and in 1871, Lecky and O'Neill Daunt were in agreement in regretting that the protestant gentry should have found themselves in a state of political alienation. Later, however, Lecky responded that the events of the last few years had cured him of his earlier nationalism.[114] The outcome was that, while O'Neill Daunt continued to castigate the landlords and to blame them for the situation that had emerged in the late 1870s and the 1880s, Lecky defended them.[115]

The letters he contributed to *The Times* (25 January, 3 February 1882) putting the case of the Irish landlords, and likewise his private letters, were re-echoed in *England*.[116] To O'Neill Daunt, Lecky outlined those very arguments in defence of the landlords which he later developed and incorporated into *England*.[117] He admitted great faults of negligence, extravagance and arrogance, but saw no satisfactory evidence of extortion and exterminating tyranny, and blamed the system of subdivision more than landlord misdeeds.

On the question of absenteeism, Lecky does not appear to have been unduly worried that he himself was in the category of absentee landlord. In a volume of his history which appeared in 1878, Lecky gave some explanations for absenteeism, but he elaborated on its extent in eighteenth-century Ireland as well as on its evil consequences, which, he said, could hardly be exaggerated.[118] During the heat of the land agitation, when Lecky realized almost reluctantly that he belonged to the landlord class,[119] he wrote in defence of the absentees:

> When you say that Irish landlords are in the main absentees I think you over-state greatly. If you will look at Thom's *Almanack* you will see that the proportion of Irish rental which belongs to persons who live at least for a great part of the year in some parts of Ireland is very considerable. In several Irish counties — Dublin, Wicklow, Queen's County, Carlow[120] and I believe even Galway — landlords residing on the spot appear to me nearly if not quite as numerous as in most English and Scotch counties and a great part of the alleged absenteeism arises from the fact that persons who are engaged in different professions have inherited small properties often without any house in which they could live.[121] Of course I do not deny that there is a large amount of absenteeism and it will no doubt greatly increase for no sensible man would as a matter of preference live in a country where he was the object of ceaseless invectives or a member of a particular class and when neither his property nor his life were secure. Of this at least I am certain that without the concurrence of the class of county gentry no good is ever likely to be done for Ireland, for an intelligent middle-class like that of England is almost wholly wanting. ... Irish 'patriots' are at present doing everything in their power to drive capital in all its forms out of the country, to lower the value of property, to make Irish life intolerable for men of intelligence and moderation, to teach the Irish peasantry to look to systematic dishonesty and political agitation as the natural path to wealth, and in fine to destroy any vestige of sympathy and respect for Ireland both in England and on the continent ... .[122]

These arguments represented the spirit in which Lecky wrote about landlordism from 1878. The defence of the landlords in the later volumes of the history of the eighteenth century was incorporated into his *Democracy and Liberty*, as when he rejected the allegation of the American socialist, Henry George, who had referred to the Irish landlords as 'useless, ravenous, destructive beasts'.[123] In *Democracy and Liberty* Lecky showed the extent to which he was influenced by or agreed with the propagandist publications of the landlord associations of which he was a member.[124] By the time Lecky had come to write *Democracy and Liberty*, he had been long convinced that Irish sedition had taken on a new and terrible character. The evils of the old land system had been many and they had produced oppression and agrarian crime. But all this was in the past. In the

1880s and 1890s, however, theories of land socialism and political agitation, which in Ireland had become 'a large and highly lucrative trade',[125] were linked, and constituted the great dangers to life, property and political stability. In the last chapter of the final volume of the eighteenth century, Lecky described the new character of contemporary Irish sedition which had followed the linking of the agrarian and political movements. Recent work on Fintan Lalor and John Mitchel[126] had convinced him that in the writings of these two Young Irelanders was to be found the keynote of the politico-agrarian alliance which had produced the Land League. Lecky opposed this politico-agrarian sedition with his own intellectual landlordism, and the evidence of the battle lies scattered across the pages of his historical work.

He had always held that the possession of land 'never fails to diffuse through a disaffected class conservative and orderly habits'; that the possession of a moderate amount of property is the chief steadying and restraining influence in politics.[127] This principle alone, apart altogether from his liberalism and tolerance in religious matters, would account for his eloquent condemnation of those penal laws which deprived the catholics of the land.[128] He had always regretted that in the past the law had divided Irish society into protestant landowners and catholic peasants, thereby sowing the seeds of 'the most permanent and menacing divisions'.[129] The division of classes, he wrote, 'which was begun by confiscation, has been perpetuated by religion, and was for many generations studiously aggravated by law'.[130] A catholic landowning class would have been 'the natural political leaders of their co-religionists'. It was to the absence of such a class that both the revolutionary and sacerdotal extravagances of Irish politics were to be mainly attributed. Landlords were 'the natural leaders' of the people, but the tendons of society had been cut, and no fact had contributed more to debilitate the national character.[131] The result was that every national movement in Ireland had been handicapped by the division of society into protestant landlords and catholic peasants. The dread of the change of property 'paralysed every political movement by making it almost impossible for it to assume national dimensions'.[132] This 'dread of the change of property' was indeed one of the major reasons why Lecky himself could not approve of home rule, especially as linked with the Land League.

Lecky's intellectual landlordism also helps to account for changes in his interpretation of the period of legislative independence, 1782-1800. While engaged upon the research and rewriting of this period, Lecky wrote to O'Neill Daunt that he hoped that his account of 1782 — the brightest moment in Irish history for both of them — was not too tinged with his increasing conservatism.[133] The retouching of Grattan's parliament with a conservative brush, however, becomes fairly obvious when comparisons are made with the picture in the two earlier editions of *Leaders*. In his treatment of 1782-1800 in *England*, he preached political lessons that were opposed to the lessons he had earlier drawn from an examination of the same period. A younger Lecky had been something more than nostalgic about Irish legislative independence; he had looked forward to its restoration. From the period of the Land War and *England*, however, it was his conviction that Grattan's parliament was entirely different from any legislature that could now be established in Ireland.[134]

As he grew older, Lecky's picture of the patriotic achievements of the late eighteenth-century ascendancy brightened if anything, perhaps by way of compensation for his own loss of faith in Irish nationality, and his words carried more weight than ever because the picture was based upon deeper research and richer experience. On the other hand, the pessimism induced by the violence of the social revolution undermining the gentry accounted for Lecky's more numerous references to the contemporary situation, and the many passages in which he contrasted the brightness of ascendancy patriotism with the dark separatism and anarchical tendencies of his own time. In Grattan's age:

> The intellect, the property, the respectability of the country still led the popular movement, and as long as this continued no serious disloyalty was to be apprehended.[135]

Lecky never wearied of reminding his readers that Grattan had no sympathy with disorder, anarchy and democracy;[136] and when he stated the tasks facing the ascendancy parliament in the late eighteenth century, he was clearly conscious of the conditions in Ireland one hundred years later.[137] The older Lecky also often stressed the point that it was a serious delusion to suppose that Ireland was fitted for the same degree of popular government that had been accorded to England. For, he wrote:

> An amount of democracy which in one country leaves the main direction of affairs in the hands of property and intelligence, in another country virtually disfranchises both, and establishes a system of legalised plunder by transferring all controlling authority to an ignorant and excited peasantry, guided and duped by demagogues, place-hunters and knaves.[138]

Clear traces of the interaction of contemporary politics on historical writing were also apparent in his treatment of Burke's place in history. Lecky had long believed that his fellow Irishman was 'the greatest of all modern political philosophers' and the writer of English to whom he was perhaps most indebted.[139] A 'very humble little copy' of Burke's *Reflections on the French Revolution* which Lecky acquired in 1855, was for many years Lecky's favourite pocket companion in long, solitary, mountain walks.[140]

The portrait of Burke was one of the more brilliant features of Volume III of Lecky's *England*, written when the author was most deeply concerned with the Irish Land War. In the image that Lecky created, Burke was more a man for the 1880s than of the eighteenth century, and he spoke through the Burke he had thus created, sometimes indeed with Burke's own words, solemn warnings about the evil tendencies of the time. All other statesmen belonged wholly to the past. Burke alone retained an enduring interest. No other politician had left behind him such a treasure of political wisdom applicable to all times and to all countries.[141] Burke's conservatism and caution, his utilitarianism and distrust of political ideologies and popular politics had great appeal. Not that Lecky was blind to Burke's faults. Even at his most enthusiastic, Lecky could be critical, and he considered that the reverence with which Burke looked upon the British constitution, and the extreme dread he had of any change in that constitution, were exaggerated even to extravagance.[142] But Lecky agreed so far with Burke to say that:

> ... it is a dangerous thing to arrest the growth of a living organism: it is a fatal thing to disturb the foundations of an ancient building.[143]

For this reason, Lecky, like Burke, was very impressed with the significance of the role that the aristocracy, and particularly the great historical families, had to play in government.[144] Their function was to supply men who from an early age would devote their whole careers to political leadership. The policies in Lecky's own time which were undermining the aristocracy by Irish land acts and extensions of the franchise had ignored Burke's lessons and were anathema to Lecky.

Burke, wrote Lecky, had always opposed doctrinairism in political and social theory. He had refuted those whose arguments were based upon natural right and the doctrine of equality. Logic was rightly applied to reasoning, but it had no place in political institutions. Government was a matter of experience and not a question of morals. It was Burke's first principle, wrote Lecky,

> ... that government rests wholly on expediency, that its end is the good of the community, and that it must be judged exclusively by the degree in which it fulfils this end.[145]

In the early 1880s when, according to Lecky, wild communistic ideas about landownership, and extreme democratic theories about parliamentary representation were being advocated in Ireland, Burke's wisdom should be heeded and cherished. Expedience and not theory, agreed Lecky, was the basis of political and social stability, and that government is best 'which produces fewest evils and discharges the greatest variety of useful functions'.[146]

To make Burke's views clearer, Lecky thought it best to consider what were the objectives of the representative system in the England of Lecky's own time. His answer was that it must in the first place bring together in parliament men of ability, knowledge and integrity to look after the welfare of an empire which included one-fifth of the human race. He argued, however, that a high average of intelligence among the electors was required if one were to obtain a similar average among the parliamentary representatives. It was vital, therefore, that the predominating power of election should not be placed in the hands of the poorest and most ignorant classes of the community.[147] The frequency with which Lecky employed phrases like 'the ignorant masses of the population'[148] betrayed a Victorian class-consciousness in his outlook.

The chief function of parliament thus basically constituted was to see to the maintenance of personal security and to guarantee respect for private property. To begin with, parliament must be representative of the country's property. However, it should also represent other classes and interests and especially the middle-class, with its shrewd political sense.[149] Current opinions should also receive due representation, for in this way parliament could act as the safety-valve of the nation. It was a matter of no small delicacy to maintain a proper balance of class representation, but as 'the most ignorant and most incompetent portion of the community is necessarily the most numerous',[150] it was evident to Lecky, as it was to Burke, that an elective system that was at once perfectly simple and democratic would establish an overwhelming preponderance in favour of the classes least fitted to exercise political power. Political power should be mainly in the hands of those classes whose material interests were most immediately affected by anarchy and war.[151]

Lecky, who in his earlier works on European rationalism and morals had traced the effects of remote causes through centuries, always held that a piece of legislation could have remote and indirect consequences more important than its immediate effects.[152] Contemporary governments living from day to day, looking only for immediate popularity, and depending on the capricious vote of great masses, were easily tempted to sacrifice distant objectives for present party advantages.[153] As Lecky saw it, contemporary English governments, for the sake of votes and immediate advantage, tended to make concessions to Irish agitators on questions relating to the land and the franchise, and ignored all examination of the dangerous effects these concessions must eventually have on the whole empire. Apart from forecasting evil effects on the empire as a consequence of the Irish policy, Lecky also feared that parliament would decline in ability and efficiency; that it would cease to attract the country's highest intellect and the highest social eminence; that it would cease to include any considerable number of young men capable of devoting their careers to politics; that a variety of opinions would no longer be represented within its walls; that the increasing democratic spirit of the Commons would make it impossible to cooperate with the Lords; and that its character as a legislative body would be profoundly altered.[154]

Acton had been sharp in his criticism of the first two volumes of Lecky's *England*.[155] Yet he was greatly impressed by Lecky's third and fourth volumes published in 1882, and more especially by Volume III in which the portrait of Burke appeared, and in which Lecky was so apprehensive about the current Irish situation. Acton wrote to Lecky to say that he found the volumes of 1882 'fuller of political instruction than anything that had appeared for a long time';[156] Acton recommended Lecky's volumes to Mary Gladstone as 'nutritious', and he especially praised the pages on Burke, which he described as 'the best I have read in the language', and also the 'beginning' of Volume III.[157] This 'beginning' outlined the evils of political instability, condemned the habit of regarding revolution as in itself admirable and desirable, listed the objections to elective monarchy, and praised the great merits of constitutional monarchy of the British type — in all of which the influence of Burke on Lecky's ideas was plainly evident.[158]

A bond between Lecky and Acton was their common admiration for Burke's political philosophy.[159] In his generous praise as well as in his keen fault-finding, what seems to have escaped Acton's notice was the extent to which Lecky's historical writing had been influenced and acutely sharpened by his participation in the Irish controversies of the hour. On occasion (as Butterfield, in *Man on his Past* says) Acton seemed to believe that the nineteenth century provided a peculiarly favourable environment for the attainment of impartial historical study. This would partly explain why Acton overlooked the influence of the contemporary Irish environment on Lecky's work. In Lecky's volumes, what had made most appeal to Acton was the Burkean political wisdom; and he saw this wisdom as something that was permanently true and for all countries. Burke, when true to himself, was a man for all seasons.[160] Irish admirers of Lecky on the other hand were more keenly aware that Lecky intended that the political lessons he offered should be regarded as urgent, and that they were pointed directly at the contemporary Irish situation. J.P. Prendergast was more sensitive than Acton to the controversial and propagandist nature of Lecky's pages on Burke, as his letter of congratulations indicates:

> Your study of Edmund Burke shows how you are overflowing with his wisdom — never more wanted than at the present. So that your estimate of him and citations are most beneficial. We are on the road to a more Jacobinical revolution than the Jacobins![161]

It was precisely because he agreed that contemporary affairs in Ireland showed much of the worst and most dangerous features of the French Revolution that Lecky regarded himself as playing the role of a latter-day Burke called upon to interlace his volumes on England in the eighteenth century with reflections upon the Irish Revolution taking place at the time of his writing. He saw an organized and excited mob of peasants responding to the every whim of Land League demagogues. Here was agrarian outrage, murder and conspiracy; class warfare fanned by agitators; a well-drilled party machine of the home rulers throwing venerable British representative institutions into chaos by obstructive tactics; a government surrendering on questions relating to the franchise to the most extreme demands of the democrats among the home rulers, and surrendering on matters relating to the sacred rights of property to the socialistic and levelling doctrines of the Land Leaguers. The dreadful nightmare of eighteenth-century revolutionary France seemed to Lecky to be in danger of repeating itself in Ireland. The rights of property and the political liberties guaranteed under the British constitution were once again being called into question with all the attendant evils of a fierce ideological and class warfare. What was happening in Ireland, Lecky felt, was a violent revolt against a political and social order sanctioned by God, history and Edmund Burke; and, as in the case of Burke in the 1790s, Lecky's world was threatening to topple about his ears.

When he came to deal with the French Revolution,[162] Lecky was impressed by the analogy between its violence, its democratic and socialistic principles, its political upheavals and the situation in the Ireland of his own day. The result was a stronger antagonism to the French Revolution than he might otherwise have shown. Indeed, as a younger man he had supported the view that 'the good effects of the French Revolution have more than counter-balanced its evils and excesses'.[163] But in *England* he stressed the 'long train of calamities' in France, which had been 'the fruits of that diseased appetite for organic change' implanted by the revolution. Lecky wrote that blind must be the politician who had not learned from these calamities 'the danger of tampering with the central pillars of the state and letting loose those revolutionary torrents which spread ruin and desolation in their path.'[164]

Lecky felt that to appear to condone the activities of the Land Leaguers and home rulers, or to express sympathy with their aims, would be to place himself in the position of the Girondins who had fostered the French Revolution, but who had not been able to control it and who ultimately were swallowed up by its progress. This realization was the basis of his warning to his friend, O'Neill Daunt — a more persistent nationalist than Lecky, and more severe and more unrelenting in his condemnation of the Irish landlords:

> ... do not forget what was the fate of the Girondins. I hope we may both keep our heads and something at least of our Irish properties.[165]

Thus the shifting of the emphasis in his accounts of Irish landlordism; the interpolation of contemporary unionist propaganda into his later versions of the legislative independence of 1782; the portrait of Burke and the sketch of the French Revolution were those aspects of the history of the eighteenth century which exhibited the clearest evidence of the effect of Lecky's intellectual land-lordism on his historical writing. But it permeated the book. A final illustration of its effect was unconsciously provided by Lecky in his last paragraph. At the end of eight volumes, and searching about for the most important lessons which some twenty years of research and reflection had suggested to him, he wrote:

> The lessons which may be drawn from the Irish failure are many and valuable. Perhaps the most conspicuous is the folly of conferring power where it is certain to be misused, and of weakening, in the interests of any political theory or speculation, those great pillars of social order on which all true liberty and all real progress ultimately depend.[166]

It must not be assumed, however, that Lecky's increased sensitivity towards the events of his own time which influenced his writing necessarily detracted from his history. On the contrary, those episodes which in his history showed the most obvious traces of Lecky's preoccupation with the present were the very parts of his study most loudly acclaimed then and since. The fact that Lecky was keenly alive to the revolutionary tendencies of the time in Ireland only sharpened his appreciation of similar problems and episodes in the past. One of the greatest creative works ever written on Irish history, Lecky's chapters on the eighteenth century included in *England*, was the product of the time of crisis for the author's own landlord class. But while his awareness of this crisis made Lecky a better historian, it also, paradoxically, turned him into more of the politician in his historical writing. It was, perhaps, not surprising therefore, but rather the neces-sary step in a logical development that Lecky's next book after the completion of the history of the eighteenth century, his *Democracy and Liberty*, should belong more specifically to the realm of politics than of history.

Chapter 6

Defending the Union

Nothing that had taken place during Gladstone's second ministry, 1880-85, had endeared Lecky to the Liberal Party which he had earlier supported. Viewed retrospectively, it appeared to him that the land war, the Land Act of 1881, Parnellism, the Phoenix Park murders, the Reform Bill of 1884 extending the 'mud-cabin vote' to the Irish electorate, highlighted a disastrous Liberal administration. During the latter half of 1885, when a Conservative minority government was back in office, Lecky was approached to contribute to a new Liberal manifesto volume explaining why he was a Liberal. Not surprisingly, and in his own words, he 'pithily declined on the ground that I am going to vote Conservative'.[1]

Lecky could not have found it reassuring, however, when Parnell, too, only a couple of days before polling took place in the general election of November 1885, issued a manifesto ordering the Irish in Britain to vote Conservative.[2] If mystery and apprehension surrounded the political bargainings that had gone on in private between the Home Rule and Conservative leaders, the election results did not solve any of the pressing problems. True, the Conservatives had bettered their position. And the rejection of 'no less than 9 members' of the last Liberal administration, 'their own hopeless divisions', and the increased movement against them in the great towns, made a change of government 'scarcely possible at present'.[3]

From all this Lecky derived some little satisfaction and he was, indeed, even looking forward to happier times.

> Two or three years more and Gladstone must be played out, and everyone agrees that this election has profoundly discredited Chamberlain, and that the triumphant return of the three liberals he most hated — Goschen and Cowan and Forster — is a more severe blow to his party even than a Conservative victory.[4]

It was evident that there would have to be another dissolution, after which he expected — and here he showed some foresight — that a coalition would be formed of moderate Liberals and Conservatives to produce a very powerful government.

With regard to the results coming in from Ireland, Lecky considered it a strange nemesis in the light of recent politics that no Liberal had been returned. He expressed his deep regret, however, that a man of the calibre of his friend, Sir

Rowland Blennerhasset, standing as a Conservative, had been defeated in Dublin.[5] Writing to Lady Blennerhassett, Lecky said:

> You probably, however, already knew that it was a forlorn hope, and it must be some satisfaction to think that except in a few Northern constituencies the position of an Irish M.P. is fast ceasing to be tenable by a gentleman.[6]

When the final results were known, the Liberal majority had been reduced to 86, and that was precisely the number of home rulers returned. They had achieved the power to make and unmake British governments. But, as far as Lecky was concerned, worse was to follow. For shortly after the election, Gladstone's conversion to home rule was announced to the world. However much it had been privately suspected that Gladstone for some time past had leanings towards home rule, even his own colleagues were astonished by the circumstances of the public disclosure. Immediately it became the chief topic of political discussion.

Lecky wrote to a friend that he had been assured by one of Gladstone's colleagues that only Gladstone himself was in favour of the idea. Nevertheless, Lecky also reported 'alarming rumours' that Lord Spencer (who had been viceroy) had been shaken and that Lord Carnarvon had been seeing much of Archbishop Walsh and of Gavan Duffy (who had written a pamphlet 'to prove that the Tories could particularly well grant home rule').[7] A government-sponsored home rule bill in the not too distant future had become a distinct threat. Lecky was not optimistic about the situation that had arisen. In an atmosphere of increasing tension and expectancy, the new parliament met formally on 12 January 1886. And the very next day Lecky went publicly into the attack against home rule with a long, well-timed letter to *The Times*.[8] It was his first shot in a sustained and private campaign in defence of the union of Britain and Ireland.

The letter well illustrated the intensity of Lecky's reactions to the recent political and land agitations. He claimed that the home rule party was animated by two ideas: a desire to plunder the whole landed property of the country, and an inveterate hatred of the English connection. No one who had read the leaders' speeches could doubt it; the paymasters in America openly avowed it. If any English politician had doubts, Lecky asserted, let him read *United Ireland*, the organ of the party, which had preached the new nationalist doctrines with conspicuous ability. The English statesman who would read that and still hand over the government of Ireland to its writers must be either a traitor or a fool.

Repeating what he had learned from Burke,[9] Lecky argued that it was the duty of all governments to protect property and that the Irish landlords' unpopularity had stemmed from the fact of their attachment to the English connection. Fenians or separatists, he argued, had started the land agitation chiefly because they had no other hope of enlisting the farming classes without the enticement of the plunder of the landlords.[10] At the invitation of the government (under the Encumbered Estates Act), £52 millions had been invested in Irish land. Besides, the recently established Land Courts had exacted large sacrifices from the landlords. If obligations of honour were now to be neglected, no property could be held under an English government.

On the question of home rule, Lecky held that it was idle to argue that because an Irish parliament had once existed therefore one must be re-established in what were very different circumstances. He expected that people who had read his historical work knew that he was far from taking an unfavourable view of the eighteenth-century Irish parliament. But it was 'absolutely certain that a protestant parliament ... was utterly unlike anything that could now be set up.' The synod of the disestablished church bore a considerable resemblance to it.[11] That Irish parliament had many faults, but it had no elements of disloyalty and it was always ready to make sacrifices for the empire. Whether it had been wise to abolish it might be a matter of controversy, but it was certain that it could never be restored; and a democratic legislature would be under the guidance of the bitterest enemies of the empire.

A third of the population, Lecky claimed, was thoroughly loyal to the union, and it constituted what, until a few years before, would have been generally considered the natural governing body of the country. It comprised almost all the protestants, the catholic gentry, the great majority of the catholics in the professions, an important section of the catholic middle class, as well as those numerous catholics in the army and the constabulary who had shown themselves on so many trying occasions to be the most devoted servants of the crown.[12] Two-thirds of the population, on the other hand, supported the disloyal side; but among them were the poorest, most ignorant, and most dependent in a country where extreme ignorance and poverty were much more common than in England. This party had been mainly supported by foreign subsidies, and while much of the disloyalty was due to political and religious animosity, much was also due to intimidation, to hopes of plunder, or to the belief that the disloyal side was winning.

Lecky's break with Gladstone, following the Land Act of 1881, became more embittered as a result of Gladstone's home rule policy. In this letter to *The Times*, he now stated that since Gladstone had come to office the policy was to take power out of the hands of those very classes in Ireland who were attached to the connection.[13] Liberals were astonished that Gladstone's policies had still failed to conciliate Ireland. But as long as English statesmen assumed that a country with two-thirds of its population disloyal could be governed by the same institutions and the same plan of democracy as a country which was loyal, so long would Irish anarchy continue. It was rumoured that Ireland was to have the same amount of representative local government as England. What could be expected? Merely an increase in the power of the disloyal. What was wanting in Ireland was not the extension of local government, but the restoration of the liberty of the people and a state of society in which men might pursue their business and fulfil their lawful contracts without danger or molestation. Representative institutions, public meetings and juries were all excellent things, but the liberty of the individual was more precious than any of them, and there was far more of it at the present time in Russia and in Turkey than in Ireland.[14] Unless English political parties combined to restore the empire of law in Ireland, then industrial ruin must follow, and anarchy that could only be quelled by the sword.

One other essential task faced the statesman. That was to create a new social type[15] in place of that which had been destroyed, by buying out the landlords at a reasonable rate.[16] A Celtic proprietary would not bring the millennium, but if it were established on reasonable terms, it might at least give security to property, create a class with conservative instincts, and put an end to a struggle which was threatening the country with absolute ruin.

Overnight Lecky had become one of the most eminent and articulate champions of the unionist cause. In an editorial in the very next issue of *The Times* (14 January 1886) it was stated that Lecky's 'remarkable letter' had produced 'a profound impression on public opinion'. *The Times* quoted some of Lecky's sentences and added that his testimony was the more valuable because, as a historian, he had defended

> 'Grattan's parliament' and has measured swords as a champion of the Irish character and Irish nationality with Mr Froude. But Mr Lecky acknowledges that the restoration of Grattan's Parliament is impossible, and that an Irish Parliament such as Mr Parnell demands would be only an instrument ... for accomplishing separation ... .

Letters of congratulations poured in from New York, Toronto, the Hague, London and from all over Ireland — from Coleraine, Monsterevan, from his cousin in Carlow, from the protestant bishop of Limerick and from his old friend and fellow historian J.P. Prendergast.

Irish unionists were extremely pleased that a man of Lecky's eminence should have come forward publicly in defence of the Union. 'I had been wishing ... that you and one or two others who knew the natural state of Ireland ... would educate English opinion a little before parliament met' wrote one.[17] That was precisely what Lecky was now doing. To English unionists it seemed that Lecky had declared stoutly for the defence of the empire. Lord Tennyson's wife assured Lecky that her husband was most grateful for the letter to *The Times* and added; 'so are we all and so ought every man, woman, and child in the empire to be'.[18] Goldwin Smith,[19] the former professor of history at Oxford and then at Toronto, wrote to tell Lecky that he regarded his argument against home rule as 'excellent'. It appeared to Smith that the House of Commons was mad and that the nation was in a stupor. He supposed that Gladstone would have his way, but the result would be about the most stupendous lesson the world had ever received on the danger of allowing itself to be governed by rhetoric. He added an ominous note of advice:

> Save Ulster, and you may yet save all. Gladstone hates her as a rationalist and Morley as an agnostic; and both of them would like to coerce; but in the attempt they would rouse the spirit of the nation if the nation has any spirit to be roused ...[20]

A summary of Lecky's celebrated letter was published in the *New York Tribune*, not only because the author was a dignified figure in literature, 'but because he seemed to speak for the great body of the best English people'.[21] His letter, together with those of Sir James Stephen, were reprinted in pamphlet form for the Loyal and Patriotic Union, to play a more permanent role in the mounting unionist propaganda.[22] His contributions to the home rule debate were not such 'amateur excursions' into politics as he pretended.[23] In February 1886 Gladstone was returned to office. Lecky's first letter against home rule had been timed to coincide with the opening of parliament, and his second letter was timed for the eve of the first meeting of parliament under the new Liberal administration.

The second letter to *The Times*[24] was aimed chiefly at discrediting Gladstone, whose Irish policy he said, was 'the most stupendous, the most disastrous of failures'. Can it be possible, Lecky asked of the Liberal leaders, that:

> on the morrow of a general election, during which the home rule question was carefully kept out of the sight of the electors, and availing themselves of a majority which was obtained in consequence of this reticence they are about to surrender the virtual government of Ireland to men whom they have described themselves as 'the rebel party', 'steeped to the hips in treason' and engaged in a policy of plunder ...? That Mr Gladstone should be engaged in such a design is perhaps not absolutely incredible. He is the same statesman who in 1874 went to the constituencies with the promise that if he were returned to office he would abolish the income tax — that is to say with the offer of a direct and literal money bribe to every member of the class ... then dominant in the constituencies ....[25] But if Lord Spencer, if Mr Trevelyan, if Sir William Harcourt make themselves accomplices of such a design as I have described what faith can any longer be placed in English statesmen? It is surely time for these eminent men by a few plain words to clear the situation, to tell their fellow countrymen whether or not they have abandoned the opinions they have so often and so emphatically expressed — whether they are about to surrender to the National League, and by acquiescing in the dissolution of the union, to prepare the way for the dismemberment of the empire ... the next few days are likely, more than any period within the recollection of our generation, to determine irrevocably the character of the reputation of English public men.

It was a clever piece of political debating, perhaps even of special pleading. The tactics were skilful and calculated to separate Gladstone and his home rule policy from at least some of his Liberal lieutenants. And since Lecky was already aware that the prime minister was far from having the unanimous support of his cabinet colleagues, the second letter was Lecky's personal contribution of hammer blows on the home rule wedge that was splitting the Liberals apart.

So sincere was Lecky in his conviction that home rule would prove disastrous that he even overcame his nervousness about public speaking and entered the political arena in defence of the union. Some months before Gladstone's conversion to home rule had been made public, certain supporters of both the Liberals and Conservatives in Ireland had formed the Irish Loyal and Patriotic Union.

This group had one simple plank: the maintenance of the Union.[26] Its secretary was Edward O'Brien, son of the Young Irelander William Smith O'Brien, and a friend of Lecky at Trinity College. O'Brien asked Lecky to join the ILPU, the subscription to which, he said, varied from £1 to £2000. The letter to Lecky illustrated how pessimistic the secretary was with regard to the outcome before the 1885 general election: 'We shall of course be beaten hollow, and the union will come to an end after the elections.'[27]

First the election results, and then the split in the Liberal Party gave the faint-hearted ILPU a sense of respite if not encouragement. Two days after Lecky's first letter to *The Times*, he was requested to go on a delegation from the ILPU to Lord Salisbury, who was still prime minister.[28] In March he was 'inveigled' by O'Brien into speaking against home rule at a public meeting organized by the ILPU at Kensington Town Hall on St Patrick's Day.[29] Despite the rumour than 200 Parnellites were to be sent to break up the meeting, Lecky went through with the ordeal, but, he wrote to a friend: 'I don't mean to do such a thing again for a long time.'[30]

Writing was more congenial than public speaking. So, amplifying his Kensington speech into an article for the *Nineteenth Century*,[31] Lecky continued his unionist campaign in print. The article was a more detailed elaboration of the arguments he had already urged against home rule in *The Times*. In it he contrasted the protestant loyal and propertied nationalists of Grattan's time with the catholic, disaffected and democratic agitators of the National League. He conceded that a large measure of self-government would be profitable if Irish public opinion respected the law, individual liberty and loyalty to the connection, and if it were directed by men of property.

O'Connell's repeal movement, Lecky argued, had none of the more evil features of home rule. In Ireland there was now an instinctive hatred of England: if Ireland were surrendered, home rule would end in separation, and the days of the empire would be numbered. Disestablishment of the protestant church had not made the catholic priests loyal; the granting of home rule would not convert the separatists. Anarchy would reign in Ireland and economic ruin would follow. While statesmen in Germany, Italy and the USA aimed at consolidation and unity, Gladstone alone desired the disintegration of an empire; but, as Burke had taught, any organic change in a nation's constitution should always be a slow and deliberate process and not the whim of a political party.

Once again the letters of congratulation flowed in.[32] Chief Justice Morris wrote: 'I have just read your powerful article — it to my mind contains in the best form all that can be said on the principles of or rather the want of principle of the contemplated measure. ... this most profligate attempt.'[33] Lady Blennerhassett, writing from Munich, subscribed to every word of his 'simply admirable' article and added: 'Dr Dollinger, notwithstanding his old friendship for Mr Gladstone, agrees entirely with you.'[34] Sir C. Trevelyan wrote:

> It is the best statement of this portentous question I have seen and might with great public advantage be printed in a separate form and sent to all

newspapers and Liberal clubs etc. Its especial merit is that it lifts the subject out of the common muck of person and party and treats it as a vital issue affecting the whole future of our body politic.[35]

Lecky contacted Knowles, editor of the *Nineteenth Century*, concerning the separate republication of the article for distribution, but Knowles, a friend of Gladstone, declined. In a postscript he wrote: 'Mr Gladstone dined here last night and spoke to me about this article which he had read — and does not like.'[36]

The propaganda value of Lecky's manifestoes was promptly appreciated in the unionist camp. His friend, Albert Grey (later the 4th Earl Grey),[37] was one of the dissentient Liberal MPs who had voted against Gladstone's first home rule bill. Grey's plan to defeat home rule, he informed Lecky, was to get behind Parnell's supplies and cut them off. These supplies came chiefly from America, where the Parnellites had got a grip upon the press and were moulding public opinion. To stop Parnell's supplies, that impression must be removed, and this could be done to some extent at least by the publication in the American press of vigorous statements against home rule by representative Englishmen.

Grey had already made arrangements through a Mr Hurlbert[38] to have cabled to a syndicate of American journals a signed *pronunciamento* of 1200 to 2000 words against home rule twice a week. For this purpose he requested statements from notable unionists like the Duke of Argyll, Professor Huxley, and Lecky. At the end of five or six weeks he hoped to have 'a very pretty volume for home consumption'.[39]

A month after his Kensington speech, Lecky was asked to take part in another meeting planned for 4 May. He regretted that a previous engagement would prevent his taking part, but in his reply he outlined his views on Gladstone's home rule bill. The bill, he said, consisted of two parts. One reduced Ireland to the position of a vassal and tributary nation, deprived of all voice in the management of that great empire which Irishmen had done so much to create, and to the expenses of which they were still obliged to contribute. The position was one of intolerable humiliation; but it was accepted by Irish members only because they regarded the whole arrangement as a sure step to separation. The second part of the scheme seemed intended to compensate for national degradation by the increased opportunities of class plunder which would be provided by the placing of the whole internal administration in the hands of the present unpropertied agitators. The home rule bill portended ruin to Ireland and speedy dismemberment of the empire; it would leave an indelible stigma on those who proposed it.[40]

By now Lecky had become a knight-errant of unionism and was considered a worthy match for any of the opposition champions. Lord John Morley, Sir William Harcourt and Gladstone himself were taken on in turn. Morley, speaking in Glasgow in favour of home rule, reminded his audience that Lecky had called them — 'not very considerately' — 'either fools or traitors'. He pointed out the discrepancy between Lecky the paladin of unionism and Lecky the nationalist historian, and to prove his point he quoted from Lecky's *Leaders* the passages about the evil consequences that ensue from disregarding the sentiment of nationality.[41] It stung Lecky to a response. In a cogent letter to *The Times* (5 May 1886) he proceeded to elaborate on his objections to the character of men who would operate the self-government machinery in Ireland:

> I do not believe — and I do not think the people of Great Britain will believe — that the government of Ireland can be safely intrusted to the National League — to priests and Fenians and professional agitators supported by the votes of an ignorant peasantry, whose passions it has been for many years their main object to inflame.

Shortly after his exchange with Morley, Lecky was engaged in a more prolonged bout by Harcourt. During the second reading of the home rule bill, in a speech which *The Times* characterized in an editorial as 'a mass of stale historical scraps and witticisms',[42] the Chancellor of the Exchequer cited Lecky's historical work on the corruption that had been employed to achieve the abolition of the eighteenth-century Irish parliament. Lecky replied that it was difficult to exaggerate the absurdity of people like Sir William Harcourt who argued that because a parliament of landlords was corruptly abolished in 1800, a parliament of Land Leaguers should be established in 1886.[43] Harcourt's reply gave further and more copious quotations from Lecky's work in order to show that he was once a much better nationalist and Liberal than he now supposed.[44] In answer, Lecky insisted that the issue between Sir William and himself was whether there were any real differences between Grattan's parliament and that which it was now proposed to establish, and he outlined those differences of loyalty, religion, property, character and constitution which led him to admire the one and oppose the other.[45] A second letter from Harcourt and a third from Lecky brought to an end a controversy in which Harcourt had cleverly illustrated the use that could be made of Lecky's historical writings for the home rule cause and Lecky had skilfully drawn attention to the sophistry of Harcourt's tactics and had restated his own unionist stand.[46]

Six years later when Gladstone was fighting his way back into office for the fourth and last time, he, too, in a speech on home rule to non-conformists at Clapham Common, employed a passage from Lecky's early work to support his case. Lecky displayed his annoyance in a letter to *The Times*. Gladstone, he wrote, 'evidently intended to infer' that the passage quoted 'was written with some application to the present condition of Ireland'.[47] The leader-writer of *The Times* rejoiced that: 'Mr Lecky, to whose testimony Mr Gladstone appealed, rather rashly and not very fairly, has set the matter in the proper light', especially with his references to the current situation in Ulster.[48]

Lecky was often sought for unionist meetings and as a contributor to unionist literature. Lord Hartington, another of the Liberals who had broken with Gladstone, organized such a meeting at Nottingham on 24 October 1887, at which Lecky spoke. His speech, published in the *Liberal Unionist*,[49] stressed what to him was the main issue of the home rule controversy, namely, the question of what confidence there could be in the men who would form the home rule government and sit in the Irish parliament. He reminded his audience that anarchy was one of the most infectious political diseases, and that, if allowed to spring up in Mayo, might soon be found in Piccadilly. At a public meeting in Birmingham on 25 April 1889, Lecky's speech, which provided yet another pamphlet for the Liberal Unionist Association,[50] again played on the theme that it was neither wise nor honourable to turn lawbreakers into lawmakers.

Lecky always realized that Gladstone's policy would have to be countered in America, from where the home rule funds came; in Scotland, which gave Gladstone his majorities; and in Ireland which voted overwhelmingly for home rule. Early in 1891 he contributed two articles on the Irish question to the *North American Review* (edited by Lloyd Bryce).[51] In these he reviewed the history of home rule since 1886; reiterated the arguments for the maintenance of the Union; and made use of testimony that had come to light during the Parnell Commission, the O'Shea divorce case and the Parnellite split to support his oft-repeated assertion that the home rulers were disloyal and dishonest. The argument regarding the undesirability of home rule which he propounded for the Americans took on much of the unashamed aspect of party political propaganda directed against the Gladstonian Liberals. Lecky aimed his appeal specifically at those Americans whom he believed had, for sincere but mistaken reasons, supported home rule.

With a Liberal victory anticipated in the July 1892 general election, a great unionist demonstration took place in Belfast on 17 June 1892. *The Times* devoted two full pages to reporting it.[52] Unionists in the three southern provinces organized a convention for Dublin. Among Lecky's eminent friends who were members of the executive committee were Lord Castletown, Lord Monteagle, J.P. Mahaffy, the Hon. Horace Plunkett, Edward Dowden and the historians Richard Bagwell and C.L. Falkiner. Lecky's cousins were among the Carlow delegates and another friend, David Plunkett, MP for Trinty College, was one of the chief speakers.[53] Dowden, Professor of English at Trinity College and a well-known Shakespearean scholar, enlisted Lecky's support for the Dublin convention.[54] Lecky sent a letter very much in the style of 'Why I am going to vote for the unionist government', and it was read to the convention.[55] Dowden informed him that it had produced a great effect.[56] It was no doubt partly in recognition of this kind of service that a few months earlier Salisbury, with the Queen's authorisation, was pleased to offer Lecky the regius professorship of history at Oxford.[57] His unionism, however, was utterly sincere and not adopted in the hope of any rewards, and, besides, it was by no means his greatest qualification for the Oxford chair.

No apparent personal provocation or hope of reward accounts for Lecky's attack on Gladstone during the July 1892 election. The long and able letter to the *Scotsman*[58] was in fact an election squib which Lecky let go where he felt it might be most effective. Gladstone was dependent on Scottish support for a majority; he was, therefore, according to Lecky, appealing to every class of voter in Scotland with different promises and skilfully drawing a veil over other issues. To Lecky, this was political trickery and highly immoral electoral tactics. So Lecky presented the case against home rule to the Scottish public and appealed to their presbyterian sentiment and their kinship with the Ulster Irish. It is impossible to say what effect Lecky's letter to the *Scotsman* had. In the election, while the Liberals were returned with an increased majority in Scotland if not with the number of seats which they expected,[59] Gladstone's own personal vote in Midlothian was reduced. At least one of the candidates assured Lecky that the Scottish Liberal Unionist and Conservative candidates owed him their best thanks for his 'excellent letter'.[60]

With Gladstone back in office, and the second home rule bill before parliament in 1893, Lecky maintained a steady attack on its provisions as well as on the whole idea of self-government for Ireland. In a letter (4 April 1893) addressed to the Belfast Chamber of Commerce and printed in the Chamber's *Reply* to Gladstone's speech, Lecky refuted the argument which held that the prosperity of Ireland under Grattan's parliament was a guarantee of its prosperity under home rule. 'Everyone should read Mr Lecky's letter …', declared A.V. Dicey,

> and I venture to say that every page of Mr Lecky's *History of England in the Eighteenth Century* which refers to Grattan's parliament bears out the contention, that no inference can be drawn from it as to the successful working … of the legislature to be constituted under the home rule bill.'[61]

Some were encouraging Lecky to even greater efforts. A plan which Judge O'Connor Morris[62] proposed does not appear to have got off the ground. The idea was that Lecky should edit a series of anti home-rule pamphlets, as well as appeal to public opinion in newspapers and light literature.[63] At the same time Aubrey de Vere[64] was urging Lecky to write a pamphlet on the home rule issue.[65] But the encouragement was hardly necessary. He contributed a short article to the special supplement of the *National Observer*.[66] This supplement consisted of comments by well-known unionists on the home rule bill. Lecky's piece concentrated on the ruinous consequences which he alleged would accrue to Britain, especially regarding constitutional arrangements, national defence, and the welfare of the empire and of Ulster. He followed this up with an article for the *Contemporary Review* [67] which summarized all the arguments he had ever urged against home rule. It stressed, as indeed did much of the unionist propaganda of 1892/3, 'the unblushing clerical intimidation', which he said prevailed in Ireland and which had emerged blatantly in the Parnellite split.[68]

During the summer of 1893, the *Pall Mall Gazette* printed a series of articles by prominent unionists which were immediately republished in pamphlet form.[69] Lecky's contribution to this series was entitled 'The Case against Home Rule from an Historical Point of View'.[70] He argued that the parliament projected by Gladstone's scheme bore no resemblance whatever to Grattan's parliament, and could not be regarded as its lawful successor. Gladstone's scheme would be only a transition to the total separation of the two islands.

In the home rule debate there were many references to the last independent Irish parliament, for the history of which Lecky was acknowledged by controversialists on both sides as the greatest living authority. His historical work was regarded as having contributed to the momentum of the Irish self-government ideal, and his books were ransacked for home rule amunition. However, between the conversion of Gladstone to home rule in 1885, and the defeat of Gladstone's second home rule bill in 1893, Lecky participated actively in the unionist campaign with speeches, articles and letters to the press in which he offered strenuous and influential opposition to Gladstonian policy. As far as Lecky was privately concerned, therefore, the debate had gone full circle while his historical work was being cited in support of home rule, the historian had come out personally in favour of unionism and had proceeded eloquently to urge against home rule the argument from history.

Throughout his unionist campaign, Lecky urged certain important considerations against home rule. One point he never wearied of stressing was that his objections to home government for Ireland were based not on any theoretical case, but primarily on the character of the men to whom power would be given in an Irish parliament. His articles between 1886 and 1893 emphasized that the character of the home rule agitators provided the major obstacle to the concession of home rule. It was not a question of machinery, but an objection to the men who would work that machinery.[71]

Irish home rulers, said Lecky, were in the first instance Land Leaguers, and the mainspring of the home rule movement was the attack on private property, which had led to violence, robbery, intimidation, a land war and a war of classes. Coercion reigned in Ireland, but it was coercion by the land agitators and not of the legal variety instituted by the government and loudly complained of by nationalist spokesmen. The leaders of the land agitation were communists, their doctrines were 'as communistic as those of Jack Cade',[72] and Michael Davitt was the disciple of the American socialist, Henry George.[73] Lecky's published articles and letters, and his private correspondence, illustrate how his reactions to the Land League formed the basis of his attitude to home rule.[74] Scarcely an article failed to mention the agrarian issue.

The home rulers were in Lecky's eyes Fenians and separatists, financed by the American 'paymasters of murderers'[75] and inspired by an inveterate hatred of the English name and connexion. Lecky usually summed up his objections to the leaders of the national movement by describing them as 'dishonest and disloyal'[76]; they had been convicted by the 'Parnell commission' of

> treasonable conspiracy; of aggravated duplicity; of a course of conduct directly productive of perhaps as large an amount of fraud, tyranny and outrage as any movement of the nineteenth century.[77]

Lecky saw home rulers, Land Leaguers and Fenians as generally indistinguishable. This view was largely true. Indeed, the Young Irelander, Fintan Lalor, whom Lecky spotted as a philosopher of the land agitation, had foreseen how the land question would be the engine that would draw the national question in its train.[78] In the 'new departure', Parnell's political genius had successfully (albeit temporarily) linked the land and constitutional and Fenian strands of Irish nationalism. Lecky's view was not altogether wrong, only frightened and exaggerated. The prospect was an extremely gloomy one, for there could be no faith in contracts, and no order or liberty if the maintenance of the law was entrusted to men who had supported the tyranny of the Land League. Events following the Parnellite split and the struggle for power between the Fenians and the priests had demonstrated what was likely to be the anarchical state of Ireland under home rule.[79]

With some truth, Lecky argued that the home rule leaders were supported by the votes of 'the most ignorant, the most priest-ridden, the most disloyal portion of the community'.[80] They were backed by illiterates who, in some remote western county or small decaying county town were driven like sheep to the polling booth by agitators or priests.[81] On the other hand, Trinity College and the educated, the professions and the propertied classes, wealth and industry were opposed to home rule. In such circumstances, Ireland was not fit for the same degree of democratic government as England had, or as had been achieved by Grattan's parliament.

A man of Gladstone's experience in political debate was not without a retort. In one of his most eloquent speeches of the 1892 campaign — at Edinburgh on 30 June — he said:

> You are told that education, that enlightenment, that leisure, that high station, that political experience are arrayed in the opposing camp.... I cannot deny it. But ... in almost every one, if not in every one of the great political controversies of the last fifty years ... these leisured classes, these educated classes, these titled classes have been in the wrong.[82]

Gladstone's Midlothian speech, reported in the *Scotsman* on 1 July, was also a riposte:

> Let us go forward in the good work we have in hand and let us put our trust not in squires and peers — and not in titles nor in acres. I will go further and say not in man as such, but in the Almighty God, who is the God of justice, and who has ordained the principle of right, of equity, and of freedom to be the guides and the masters of our life.

To this Lecky's reply was that religion would lose nothing if sacred names and holy words were kept out of the political arena.[83] Because he genuinely wished to exclude religion from the question, he was always careful to avoid using the extreme unionist argument that home rule would be Rome rule. Leading catholic gentry, he maintained, including O'Connell's son and Grattan's grandson, were opposed to home rule;[84] multitudes of catholics in Ireland who accepted *bona fide* the pope's condemnation of boycotting and the 'Plan of Campaign', were as sensible as himself of the unspeakable infamy of placing Ireland in the hands of home rulers.[85] Even the most fervent protestant must agree with the pope's condemnation of these actions.[86] Nevertheless, there was no escaping the fact that a great portion of the priests had been allies of these disloyal men.[87] As early as 1861, in *Leaders*, Lecky had condemned 'clerical influences' in Irish politics, but, he insisted, the priests then possessed nothing like their present enormous power.

In his view, their power constituted another major objection to home rule, for Lecky always firmly held that the secularization of politics was a *sine qua non* of all political liberty and progress.

If Lecky avoided the more intolerant interpretation of the phrase 'Rome rule', he nevertheless boasted, like every other unionist, of Ulster's stand against home rule. And he had nothing to say to any charges of bigotry and discrimination made against Ulster unionists. He declared that the unionist convention held in Belfast in June 1892 seemed likely to become one of the great landmarks in Irish history.[88] So perhaps it did, but not quite in the way Lecky had hoped. Quoting Grattan, he said that the north of Ireland contained 'the active citizens of Ireland, its principal wealth, industry and spirit'.[89] He believed that the north had never rendered a better service to Ireland or the empire than by the 'firm, moderate and unsectarian attitude' it had assumed. Any Englishman going through Ulster 'which concentrated in the highest perfection all the elements and energies of the most prosperous industrial civilization', and then passing into 'the thriftless, ignorant, poverty-stricken, priest-ridden districts of the south and west' could scarcely fail to perceive the madness of coercing the former in order to place it under the latter.[90] Gladstone and his friends were committing a grave error in professing to believe that the strong, puritan element underlying the resolution of Ulster was destined to evaporate in words. Gladstone's policy had brought the country within 'measurable distance' of civil war.[91]

Lecky had parted company with Gladstone over the 1881 Land Act and became increasingly critical of the man to whom he had formerly devoted a certain amount of hero-worship. He had made up his mind to vote Conservative in the 1885 general election.[92] When Gladstone committed the Liberal Party to home rule early in 1886, Lecky became a Liberal Unionist. He was proud of the unionist alliance, an alliance that, he alleged, proved to be one of the most successful and the most disinterested in English history.[93]

He considered his new position to be analogous to that of Edmund Burke and the Old Whigs in 1791-93 when Burke's pamphlet, *An Appeal from the New to the Old Whigs* (1791), resisted the current radicalism. Indeed, Lecky's anonymous letter to *The Times* was entitled '1793-1886'.[94] In this he asked the Liberal leaders whether they had forgotten the painful but instructive episode in the history of their party in 1793 when they had committed the unpatriotic error of placing themselves on the side of the enemies of England, and which had resulted in their exclusion from office for nearly forty years. Significantly this letter was signed 'An Old Whig'. Again, when describing the events of 1791-93 in *England*, Lecky pointed out that Burke's tone was very alien from that prevailing in England in 1887, especially among the leaders of the Liberal Party. Their sentiment, he wrote, probably had been expressed with much greater fidelity by Tom Paine.[95] The Irish home rule allies of Gladstone were the heirs not of Henry Grattan and the 'liberal party' of the late eighteenth-century Irish parliament, but of the republican Wolfe Tone and his United Irishmen.[96]

A correspondent objecting to the closing passages of chapter 23 of *England* (in which Lecky referred to Gladstone's income tax promise in the 1874 election campaign) wrote with some degree of truth about these passages that they 'appear to me to disfigure the effect of the whole work and which I am sure in many minds, compromise the author's reputation for insight and liberality'. The references to Gladstone constituted 'a grave misuse of the high position of an historian', and were 'as reprehensible as a harangue on party politics from the pulpit of a church':

> I am quite sure that fifty years hence such paragraphs will be taken as symptoms of the gigantic prejudices Mr Gladstone had to overcome to persuade the English people to enter upon the true lines of their advancement.[97]

Lecky was convinced that if it had not been for Gladstone, home rule would not have had as many as fifty supporters among British MPs, and added that he had too much respect for Harcourt to believe that he would have been among the fifty.[98] Large allowance would have to be made for the effect of old age on Gladstone's judgment and character, but the fact was that he was devoting the last years of his life to sowing jealousies between the different classes, between rich and poor, between the educated and uneducated, and between different parts of the British Isles.[99] According to Lecky, the policy of home rule rested largely on a single life; and it should be remembered that home rule was the policy of an old man who could scarcely in the course of nature be called upon to grapple with the dangers he was bringing into existence. Lecky believed that Gladstone's was a nature 'by no means lacking in vindictiveness', and there were signs that his feelings towards England, because of the continued opposition of the English constituencies to his policy, had 'developed into something not far removed from positive hatred.'[100]

The profile of Gladstone in the 'Introduction' to the cabinet edition of *Democracy and Liberty* was one of the most brilliant short pieces of writing Lecky ever penned. But the brilliance was to some extent the result of scratching with a pen dipped in vitriol. Compared with the numerous eulogies on Gladstone's death, Lecky's profile had some of the luminous quality of poisonous matter, and it seems all the more bitter in that it was written the very year of Gladstone's death. The trouble between Lecky and Gladstone was that both were political moralists and each had a deep sense of righteousness. In another age they might have found themselves leading opposing religious sects and anathematizing each other from their pillars in the desert.

As Gladstone in seeking support for home rule appealed to Victorian morality, so Lecky in opposing Gladstone's policy appealed to the same authority. The problem of how both could be morally right and yet come to opposite conclusions was resolved by Lecky at least to his own satisfaction. He explained that Gladstone was essentially an honest man with a dishonest mind; a man wholly incapable of deliberate untruthfulness but one who had the habit of quibbling with his own convictions until, by skilful casuistry, he persuaded himself that what he wished was right. Yet, whatever may have been the case in the first moment of inception, Lecky had no doubt that in the subsequent stages of his

policies Gladstone was not only sincere but also in a high state of moral incandes-
cence.

Lecky would not go so far as to describe Gladstone as a hypocrite, but he
believed that, to win a majority, he was prepared to place Ireland in the hands of
the dishonest and disloyal whom he had himself condemned.[101] A parliamentary
majority was Gladstone's first aim, and for this he had to secure Irish support. He
then persuaded himself that justice to Ireland was to be among his chief contributions to political morality. Once he adopted a cause, his moral nature speedily
took fire and he was soon persuaded that he was acting under a divine impulse.[102]

Lecky's profile also hinted broadly at Gladstone's possible insanity.[103] He
added that no man was more dangerous, for Gladstone possessed the power of
moving and dazzling his contemporaries, while in soundness of judgment he
ranked considerably below the average of educated men. 'If the world could be
wisely governed by skilful rhetoric, he would have been one of the greatest of
statesmen.'[104]

Particularly annoying to Lecky was the facility with which Gladstone supported his Irish policies with references to God and religion.[105] Morality, Lecky
agreed, certainly entered into the home rule question: it was, for example, the
moral duty of the government to ensure freedom, protect property, guarantee
contracts, prevent anarchy and insist firmly on the law. A public man could
commit no greater crime than to place the government of a nation in the hands
of dishonest and disloyal men;[106] and if indeed home rule succeeded in coming
into effect, the solvency of the Irish parliament would mainly depend on the
continuance of an enormous consumption of whisky, and in such circumstances
the moral prospects under home rule could not be encouraging.[107]

Lecky waxed Actonian in defence of political morality, especially when it
came to attacking Acton's hero, Gladstone. He condemned what he regarded as
Gladstone's 'discreditable' electoral tactics — mischievously fanning the smoul-
dering jealousies between England and Wales, and England and Scotland, in
order to capture votes; bribing one class with promises regarding income tax,[108]
and seducing the uneducated with other forms of trickery by his great rhetorical
gifts. He accused Gladstone, while out of office, of trying to make the task of
governing Ireland as difficult as possible. He charged him with the responsibility
of so lowering the level of political morality in England that politicians in both
camps had gone gambling for the disloyal Irish vote. Lecky claimed that it was
difficult to overestimate the blow given to public confidence and character and
morals. 'England must indeed be much changed if such transparent trickery can
ultimately succeed.'[109] MPs might be excellent judges of their own immediate
interests, but they were apt to underrate the importance that character still
possessed in public life. It was possible for politicians to sacrifice their honour
without serving their interests.[110] Lecky firmly believed that England would not
soon forget the men who had been accomplices in the 'Great Betrayal'.[111]

Lecky's unionist pamphleteering raises the question of the extent, if any, to
which he retained his early nationalist sentiment. There is no question here about
the sincerity of his desire to see the material improvement of Ireland. In his

unionist publications, he continued to advocate that the landlords should be bought out and a new social type of strong farmer thereby created,[112] but he rejected the idea that home rule would provide the remedy for Ireland's material ills. He was convinced that the only radical cure for the impoverished social conditions in the West of Ireland was emigration. Short of this, Balfour's policy of providing light railways and his encouragement of agriculture and fisheries was a palliative if not a cure.[113]

He was not doctrinaire in his opposition to Irish self-government. He confessed that in the very different pre-Land League conditions he was 'more sanguine' than now about the success of local institutions, and he believed that national sentiment had greater prominence in earlier than in the contemporary Irish movements:

> I still, however, fully acknowledge the national sentiment and would gladly see any extension of local government, which did not weaken the unity of the empire, endanger property or threaten Ireland with anarchy and civil war.[114]

His objections as always were to the individuals and not to the principle of home rule:

> For my own part I would as willingly entrust the government of Ireland to its catholic as to its protestant gentry and I know that the law has never been more ably and more uprightly administered than by catholic judges. But I do not believe … that the government of Ireland can be safely entrusted to the National League — to priests and Fenians and professional agitators, supported by the votes of an ignorant peasantry … .[115]

Privately Lecky admitted that if Irish opinion was moulded by persons of property and responsibility, and if the government were worked by men like Gavan Duffy, he would not object to home rule in moderation.[116]

In 1887 when it was proposed to abolish the Irish viceroyalty on the grounds that it had kept alive the idea of a separate nationality, Lecky was strongly opposed to the idea. He wrote a *Memorandum* on the subject which was privately printed. One of the arguments he advanced for the retention of the office was that he believed that 'national feeling, instead of being repressed, should in every safe way be encouraged in Ireland'; the political decadence of the Irish gentry was very largely due to their neglect of that truth.[117] It seemed to him that the Irish question as it had developed in the 1880s was not so much national as agrarian, and that the effect of the Ashbourne and similar land purchase measures would be to deflate the home rule question into one of manageable dimensions. But, he added:

> If any form of home rule could be devised for Ireland which would rob no one and oppress no one, which could be guaranteed to maintain the law and act loyally in the interests of the empire I dare say a large number of us Liberal Unionists would be inclined to look upon it with favour.[118]

These were cautious words, but they showed that Lecky was not prepared to deny the usefulness of the 'national sentiment'. It was essentially this way of looking at the Irish question which led later to the abortive devolution schemes of 1904 and 1906/07 by which an Irish Council should exercise a measure of local authority and which had the support of men like under-secretary Sir Anthony MacDonnell and Lord Dunraven.

The argument against home rule based on 'the interests of the empire' was no doubt largely due to the rising tide of British imperialism. 'Nationality with loyalty' had always been Lecky's recipe for Ireland's relationship with the empire, but if in his early years the stress was on 'nationality', during the home rule controversy he emphasized 'loyalty'. Accordingly, a great point in favour of Grattan's parliament was that it was always ready to make sacrifices for the empire.[119] But if Ireland were to be surrendered to a home rule agitation, spear-headed by Fenians and separatists and financed by England's enemies in America, then the days of the empire were numbered.[120] Home rule was 'a mere step to separation and the breaking up of the empire.'[121] If the ties between England and the colonies were broken, it would be a misfortune but not a fatal wound. Ireland, however, lay at the very heart of the empire, and an Irish parliament guided by disloyal men might easily in the agonies of a great war be absolutely fatal to its existence. Wherever on the Continent men desired the downfall of the empire, they also desired the success of Gladstone's home rule policy.[122]

Lecky's status as an imperialist resulted in an invitation from the Prince of Wales (later King Edward VII) to deliver an inaugural lecture at the Imperial Institute introducing a course of lectures and conferences on the empire.[123] This lecture, in which Lecky spoke on the value and growth of the empire, reflected much of the imperialist thinking of the time. It seemed to indicate that Carlyle's hopes for Lecky of some twenty years earlier had been fulfilled to some extent; during the Lecky-Froude controversy, Carlyle had expressed the hope that Lecky would one day descend 'leagues and miles' from his current philosophy of liberalism.[124] In those days Lecky had denounced the defence of naked imperialism, strong government and theories of racial superiority in Froude's pioneering work on British imperialism, *The English in Ireland*. He had rejected Froude's condemnation of the free-traders of the Manchester school, the first Gladstonian ministry, the literary liberals like Mill, Bright and Goldwin Smith and the 'little Englanders' generally, for thinking in terms of the separation of England from her colonies.[125] Indeed, Lecky had then believed that the political economists and the extension of free trade had encouraged the tendency towards the disintegration of great, heterogeneous empires and had destroyed the argument that colonies were an advantage.

In this lecture, however, Lecky appeared more a colleague than an opponent of Froude. A strong, if recent, conviction of the significance of 'the part of England in promoting the happiness of mankind' inspired his words. He spoke warmly in support of the 'great revolution of opinion' that had taken place in favour of the retention of the colonies and against the non-imperial ideas of the free-traders. He was now as proud of England's Indian empire as ever Froude had been. To have conferred upon more than 250 million of the human race 'perfect peace', 'perfect religious freedom, perfect security of life, liberty and property; to have planted in the midst of these teeming multitudes a strong central government enlightened by the best knowledge of Western Europe', in place of the endless famines, 'savage oppressions', 'fierce anarchies' and 'barbarous customs' was one of the great glories of history.[126] In striking contrast with those politicians at home who estimated measures only according to party advantage, the Indian service had produced a long line of able administrators. India had proved to be 'a school of inestimable value for maintaining some of the best and most masculine qualities of the race'.[127]

Without any apparent realization of the fact, Lecky now followed many of the other doctrines he had once condemned in Froude. He who had once proclaimed the first principle of constitutional government to be majority rule[128] now insisted, like Froude, that all countries were not fit for the same representative institutions, or the same amount of democratic freedom.[129] He now asserted that one of the first conditions of success in India was the fact that the government had been conducted on principles essentially different from government at home.[130] Whether consciously or not, he was echoing Froude when he said that it seemed one of the greatest errors of modern English statesmanship that, during the great exodus from Ireland after the famine, the government had taken no step to aid it, or to direct it to quarters where it would have been of benefit to the empire.[131]

He did not say as baldly as Froude had that some peoples were born to rule and others to be ruled, and that success was the acid test of the ability to rule. Nevertheless, Lecky accepted that the English had a 'peculiar power both of conquering and holding distant dependencies;' that they had created 'the greatest and most beneficent despotism' the world had ever seen; and that their public servants had displayed a standard of patriotism and honour 'at least to a greater degree than most other nations'.[132] Yet, even at his most enthusiastic, Lecky was no believer in gunboat imperialism. It pleased him greatly to think that the British empire had escaped the curse of 'exaggerated militarism' — eating like a canker into the great nations of Europe. He cautioned against meddling more than was reasonable with the affairs of other nations. 'I distrust greatly', he said, 'these explosions of military benevolence. They always begin by killing a great many men. They usually end in ways that were not those of a disinterested philanthropy.'[133] Nor did Lecky accept the more racialist opinions of Froude, and especially the view that held that there was something inherently wrong with the Irish 'Celts'.[134]

Throughout his lecture Lecky had used the terms 'English race', 'British race' and 'Imperial race' interchangeably.[135] He thought of the empire as predominantly 'English', rather than 'British', and included himself in the category when he wrote about 'we Englishmen'.[136] That he was an Englishman would indeed have been the verdict if the rest of Lecky's work had been lost and one had to determine his nationality from this one lecture.

His assumption that 'English' and 'British' were synonymous was bound to lead him into trouble. Certain Scots took exception to his phraseology, and private correspondents criticizing him asked whether his language was a mere slip or employed with malice aforethought for the Scots.[137] Charles Waddie the secretary of the Scottish Home Rule Association wrote to the Prince of Wales complaining that Lecky's lecture had bristled with insults to Scotland; that it had ignored Scotland and spoken of the British empire as if it had been built up by English hands alone. Lecky's language, he said, had given the greatest offence in Scotland. The Prince of Wales replied in a conciliatory manner that he was persuaded that Lecky had no intention of casting any reflections on Scotland, or purposely of ignoring the great services the Scots had undeniably rendered towards the creation of the empire.[138]

In a letter to *The Times*, Lecky and added that if he had occasionally used the term 'England' instead of 'Great Britain' he had much too high an opinion of the good sense of his Scottish hearers and readers to believe that they were in the least likely to misunderstand him. He ended irritably that the Scots had much reason to complain of people who, professing to speak in their name, were doing all in their power to make them ridiculous in the eyes of the world.[139]

The Scottish nationalists were not appeased, and Charles Waddie pointed out that in his lecture Lecky had used the word 'Britain' or 'British' eleven times, 'England' or 'English' thirty-five times and seemed to be under the impression that they were of the same meaning. He took Lecky's last sentence, altered it in one word using 'Ireland' instead of 'England' and claimed that 'the dullest Englishman' would see the impropriety of such language. The altered sentence read: 'Again, whatever might be the humiliation of the future, *Ireland* could not be deprived of the glory of having created this mighty Empire.[140]

The phraseology may very well have been no more than a slip. But then, as Waddie pointed out, Lecky was too well read not to know the value of language. Besides, although he later revised and extended this lecture[141] for his volume of essays, he did not alter the offending phrases. One is left with the impression of a man who, having become disgusted with Irish politics, wanted with one half of his nature to regard himself as an Englishman and with the other half found some compensation for the diminution of feeling of Irish nationality in what he called 'a larger and imperial patriotism'.[142]

If Lecky did not mention the Scots, he was proud of the contribution the Irish had made to the empire, and spoke of the colonies as noble flowers which had sprung from 'British and Irish seeds'.[143] He included Ireland in a number of references to 'these two islands'[144] which were the heart of the empire. One of his objections to home rule was that it would reduce Ireland to the role of a vassal and tributary nation and deprive Irishmen of a voice in the management of a great empire which Irishmen had done so much to create.[145] That would be, he claimed, a position of intolerable humiliation. Even at his most imperialistic, Lecky had not quite banished the 'sentiment of nationality' from his political thought.

Gladstone, employing the analogy of Grattan's parliament to strengthen his home rule argument, spoke as if the age of Grattan was merely the era of home rule only a little further back in the same roll of film. Lecky, on the other hand, stressed the difference between the two periods, arguing that, in contrast with any home rule parliament that could be established, Grattan's parliament was protestant, propertied and loyal. Lecky could not be faulted in claiming protestant and propertied characteristics for the eighteenth-century Irish parliament. The question of loyalty was more arguable. In his first public attack on home rule,[146] in his replies to Harcourt,[147] and in his article in the *Nineteenth Century*[148] Lecky stated that Grattan's parliament was a body 'emphatically and exclusively loyal'.[149] Some home rule publicists — notably R. Barry O'Brien — questioned the assertion of loyalty,[150] and when Lecky returned to the subject he made some concession to his critics, saying that Grattan's parliament at the time of its extinction probably did not contain a single member who was disloyal to the empire.[151] Later still he added further qualifications and admitted by implication some disloyalty, but claimed that 'not more than two, or at the most three disloyal men appear to have sat within it'.[152]

Lecky had in mind Lord Edward Fitzgerald and Arthur O'Connor, leaders of the United Irish movement. When it was argued that the government of Ireland should be made over to men who were thus disloyally inspired as a kind of expiation for historical grievances, Lecky replied that to do so and for such a reason was to treat history in an irrational manner. Such arguments should be left to schoolboys: they were not worthy of serious and practical men.[153]

History, certainly, had its lessons for all concerned in this question of home rule. Few lessons of history, said Lecky, were more clearly taught than that whenever a restricted, mutilated and tributary nationality was set up, its first objective was to make itself whole and independent. Three times, therefore, in Irish history — in 1641, 1689 and 1782 — an Irish parliament that was severely restricted by constitutional laws had annulled its restrictions by a declaration of right. Could it be doubted that the same would happen again?[154] That separation was the only logical alternative to Union was a view that had long and strong support. It was propounded in the late eighteenth century by Lord Clare, one of the architects of the Union. Froude fully supported Clare's opinion long before Lecky subscribed to it, and it became a not uncommon viewpoint among unionists in the late nineteenth and early twentieth centuries. Arthur Balfour, for example, argued that total separation was the only logical alternative to the Union.[155]

What merits did Lecky display as a political pamphleteer? In his scholarly work he was above all else a 'historian of opinions'.[156] He disagreed with Voltaire, for instance, who dismissed the history of opinions as 'no more than a collection of human errors'.[157] But Lecky in his historical work was concerned with public, political, religious and moral opinion. His *Rationalism* and *Morals* had traced the course of 'climates of opinion'[158] over the centuries. His *Leaders* had described the formation and leadership of a national sentiment or public opinion in Ireland; and much of his *England in the Eighteenth Century* had been concerned with the influence of the political press, the orator and pamphlet. So that long before he ever began his own campaign as an anti-home rule propagandist, Lecky had been alive to the influence and to the organs of public opinion. Some of his best historical work had discussed the political pamphleteering of the eighteenth century, the age of the political pamphlet. He had examined the merits and demerits of such masters of political controversy as Addison, Steele, Swift, Molyneux, Lucas, Flood, Grattan, Wilkes, 'Junius', Burke, Chatham, Voltaire and Rousseau. His comments on the political writers of the past help us realize what it was that Lecky aimed at in his own pamphleteering.

In the first place, therefore, what Lecky brought to the unionist side was a mind that was richly versed in the masters of political controversy, and an awareness of what constituted effective political writing. It was an age when it was widely believed that the greatest value of history lay in the political lessons it taught. In these circumstances, Lecky carried great weight. Wherever the home rule debate touched on questions of history, friend and foe acknowledged Lecky as the highest authority.

Virtues that graced Lecky's historical work were also apparent in much of his political writing; a deep knowledge, an air of solemn dignity, a transparent sincerity, a rectitude of purpose, a masterly marshalling of fact and argument, a comparatively moderate tone and air of impartial judgment. If there were more sarcasm in the anti-home rule writing than in his historical books, there was also a lighter touch, more wit and even a little humour. And although his political articles were less impartial than the *History*, they never sounded so screechy and panic-stricken as his private correspondence. Because he was a partisan in the home rule controversy, the hesitation and suspended judgment which George Eliot considered a fault in his scholarly work was missing from his political writing. Instead, he came down decisively on the unionist side and urged his case all the more forcibly.

Lecky avoided what he regarded as an Irish tendency to exaggeration and bombast, and cultivated instead what he admired in Swift — the terse, homely, practical logic of arguments so plain that the weakest mind could grasp them, yet so logical that it would be impossible to evade their force. He admired Burke and Grattan for their ability to sow their speeches with 'profound aphorisms' and epigrams, and to associate 'transient questions with eternal truths' until their arguments assumed the appearance of axioms.[159] Lecky believed that the first-rate political pamphlet should aim at original views, large generalizations, political prescience, and deep and powerful thought. He felt also that it should show a wisdom ahead of its own time and that it should be argued upon the highest grounds. Hence in his own anti-home rule pronouncements, there was the striving after the political epigram; the stress upon political morality; constant concern with grand imperial designs, as distinct from local issues; an anxiety to teach contemporaries the habit of learning from the best tradition while engaged upon examining each measure on its own merits so that the future benefits of political wisdom could be distinguished from immediate party gains.

It could be argued that Lecky introduced little or nothing that was original to the home rule debate. But he possessed a virtue he ascribed to 'Junius', namely 'the art of giving the arguments on his side their simplest, clearest and strongest expression'.[160] What was more, Lecky, who in his historical work was in the habit of arranging the major causes of a particular event and of listing all the arguments on each side of a question, presented a strong and comprehensive case against home rule. His political letters and articles were representative and a summary of the best case that could be made out for the continuance of the Union. His brief against home rule included apt quotation from fellow unionists such as Chamberlain, Dicey, Goschen, Plunkett, Stubbs of TCD and even an anonymous Irish farmer writing to the *Irish Times*. His case was further strengthened by references to the findings of the Parnell Commission and the Belfast Chamber of Commerce.

Although Lecky had once described his efforts against home rule as 'amateur excursions' into politics, they were nothing of the sort. A blast from him was often calculated for delivery at a time or a place where it would be most effective. One letter was timed to coincide with the opening of parliament.[161] Another was published in the *Scotsman* on the eve of an election in which the Scottish vote counted for so much.[162] Lecky also employed the tactical device of quoting Gladstone, Harcourt, Bryce, Trevelyan and Spencer at themselves, using arguments from their pre-home rule speeches against the Parnellites and Land Leaguers. It was a game that two could play. If nothing else, the appeals made by the home rulers to Lecky's youthful work, *Leaders*, were neutralized when it was possible for the unionists to claim that the mature Lecky was on their side.

Lecky questioned the morality of Gladstone's appeals to different sections of the electorate with different promises. But his own methods bore some resemblance to the practice he condemned. He certainly trimmed his argument to suit particular occasions and, like Swift, put his case alternately to every influential section of the community, pointing out how their special interests would be adversely affected. He appealed to English good sense and practicality, or alternatively, played upon English fears. To the Imperial Institute he spoke as a British imperialist; to the Irish he appealed as one with Irish interests at heart. He praised, while at the same time appealing to the catholic gentry, moderate nationalists and comfortable farmers; and he wooed all those who were predisposed to take seriously the pope's condemnation of the Plan of Campaign organized by the land agitators.

In Birmingham he tactfully reminded his audience that the most prosperous province in Ireland, which included the one city, Belfast, which might reasonably be compared with Birmingham, was opposed to home rule. In a letter aimed at Scottish readers, he stressed the religious, spiritual and racial bonds between Scotland and Ulster. His articles for an American review were designed to appeal to American readers. Always his propaganda was intended to show that the test of a man of education, wealth, property, statesmanship, good sense, loyalty, social conscience and political morality was whether he was a unionist. The fool, the traitor, the agitator and the easily-led lower orders were on the side of home rule.

Although he was paid in the normal way for many of the anti-home rule articles he contributed to magazines and reviews, and even though his literary

income was greatest in the years of his unionist pamphleteering,[163] it would be too
cyncial, and moreover unfair, even to hint that purely selfish motives explain his
unionist stand. He possessed what he had praised in 'Junius' — enough public
spirit to want to pull down those whom he considered bad.

Alongside the merits were weaknesses which detracted from Lecky's effective-
ness as a political pamphleteer. However much he may have strengthened people
in their unionism or provided them with arguments, there is no evidence that he
ever won a convert to the cause.[164] There is evidence to suggest that his historical
work, on the other hand, had produced converts to home rule.[165] Among Lecky's
chief limitations was the fact that, while he appreciated the logical and well-
organized, he underrated the more emotional and irrational forces. He was guilty
of what Vico called the conceit of the learned: he supposed that the people about
whom he was writing or to whom he was appealing were, like himself, scholars
and people of a reflective and academic cast of mind.[166]

The solutions Lecky proposed were practical, moderate and sensible, but he
proposed them to an age that was idealistic and greatly excited. A younger Lecky
had realized that:

> ... the success of any opinion depended much less upon the force of its
> arguments, or upon the ability of its advocates, than upon the predisposi-
> tion of society to receive it.[167]

During winter 1877-8 Lecky sat for his portrait by George Frederick Watts. Mrs Lecky wrote: 'Lecky was difficult to do, and in spite of the pains Mr Watts took, the likeness is not as characteristic as that of most of the great painter's portraits.' (National Portrait Gallery, London)

No date is given for this photograph by Elliot and Fry, but it would appear to be from the early 1880s, possibly 1884.

From a photograph by Bassano, 1897.

The name here is 'Walter L Colls, Ph So'; Mrs Lecky in her *Memoir of W.E.H. Lecky* attributes it to Chancellor & Son, 1888.

'The Eighteenth Century': a cartoon by Sir Leslie Ward ('Spy'), *Vanity Fair*, 27 May 1882.

This bronze statue of Lecky by Goscombe John RA was erected by his friends and unveiled in the Front Square of Trinity College, Dublin, on 10 May 1906. At the unveiling Lecky's old college friend Lord Rathmore (David Plunket) said:

Yonder stand the statues of Oliver Goldsmith and Edmund Burke, the warders of our gate, and close at hand, in the thronging thoroughfare, the effigy of Henry Grattan, illumined through the genius of Foley with all the fire of patriotism. It is well that here within these academic courts should rest the monument of another, not less illustrious in his time than they were in theirs, the patient, the indefatigable student, the philosopher, the orator, the historian who rewrote the annals and vindicated the character of his countrymen.

'The Great Parliament of Ireland' (1790): John Philpot Curran, MP for Rathcormack, Co. Cork, addressing the Irish House of Commons. The two figures in the right foreground are Henry Grattan and Henry Flood; John Fitzgibbon, the Earl of Bristol and Lord Charlemont (seated) are in the left foreground. The painting by Henry Barraud and John Hayter was executed *c.* 1870 and hangs in Campbell College, Belfast. (Courtesy Campbell College)

Above Cullenswood House, Ranelagh, Dublin, was bought from Charles Joly by John Lecky, the historian's grandfather, in 1833. Lecky's father, John Hartpole, sold the house in 1848. As a child, the historian would have known Cullenswood well. In 1908 P.H. Pearse purchased it as a home for his school, St Enda's, and was conscious of its association: 'So our school-house has already a very worthy tradition of scholarship and devotion to Ireland; scholarship which even the most brilliant of our pupils will hardly emulate, devotion to Ireland, not indeed founded on so secure and right a basis as ours, but sincere, unwavering, lifelong' (*Collected Works of Pádraic H. Pearse: The Story of a Success*, ed. Desmond Ryan [Phoenix Publishing, n.d.], p. 5). In 1910, when St Enda's was moved out to the Hermitage, Rathfarnham, Pearse founded a sister-school for girls at Cullenswood, St Ita's, run by Louise Gavan Duffy.

Left No. 38 Onslow Gardens, South Kensington, London, where Lecky moved to in early spring 1873 and which became his permanent home, ending 'a vagabond existence'. He died in the library of this house on 22 October 1903. A commemorative blue plaque records: 'W.E.H. Lecky 1838-1903. Historian and Essayist lived and died here.' (Courtesy the author)

A portrait of Lecky by John Lavery, painted four months prior to his subject's death.
(National Gallery of Ireland, Dublin)

Chapter 7

Devils Citing Scripture

'The pleasure of quoting a unionist against himself seems to have been an insuperable temptation', wrote the Duke of Argyll.[1] Lecky's powerful unionist letters to *The Times* in January and February 1886, and his article in the April number of the *Nineteenth Century*, elicited no immediate response from the home rulers. But this turned out to be no more than a lull while his opponents closed ranks on him. J.P. Prendergast, congratulating Lecky on one of his letters to *The Times*, wrote: 'Everyone considers your letter crushing. But the Grand Old Man will blow up the bladder again.[2] Gladstone, as usual, was being underestimated, for already the previous autumn he had planned his own historiographical offensive, which was to prepare the way for his public an-nouncement in favour of home rule. Both Barry O'Brien and Gavan Duffy had been approached on the question of writing for *Nineteenth Century* a dispassion-ate historical article that asked whether the Union had been a successful experi-ment or not. This was the origin of Barry O'Brien's article 'Irish Wrongs and English remedies'.[3] In the same number of the *Nineteenth Century*, in which Lecky argued against home rule, O'Brien, in a separate article quoted from *Leaders* to substantiate his point that, under the Union, Ireland was normally governed badly and on anti-catholic principles.[4] In the *Freeman's Journal*, O'Brien undertook to answer Lecky's article against home rule mainly by quot-ing him against himself. This he did in a friendly spirit, for as he said:

> ... no difference of opinion, even on the question now at issue shall tempt us to forget how much the students of Irish history owe to the author of the *Leaders* ... and the *History of England* ... Mr Lecky the historian must never be forgotten in Mr Lecky the politician, and his severance from the national cause must be regarded without irritation if with regret and pain.[5]

After O'Brien came a flood. Lecky found that the home rulers had all hurried away to read or reread *Leaders* to gather ammunition to throw at him. Had he been a mercenary man, he would have had the consolation that the controversy helped sell his book. Longman raised the question of bringing out a cheap edition,[6] but although Lecky replied that he was prepared to defend it, he did not wish to reissue the book, since it was not altogether applicable to the existing conditions, and he was too busy to revise it. In July 1886, Longman told him that he had no copies left.[7]

Although the book was now hard to come by, political leaders quoted generously from it. John Morley read out passages for a Glasgow audience.[8] Harcourt, the chancellor of the exchequer, quoted pages from the essay on Grattan.[9] Gladstone quoted it in articles for the *Contemporary Review* and the *Nineteenth Century* and referred to it in the *Handbook of Home Rule*.[10]

The propaganda value of Lecky's historical work was especially appreciated by the home rulers among his fellow Irishmen. One of the earliest of the home rule tracts, J.G. MacCarthy's *A Plea for the Home Government of Ireland* (3rd edition 1872) had strengthened its case by quoting from *Leaders*. A.M. Sullivan's the *Nation* had done likewise.[11] After Lecky had publicly opposed home rule in 1886, he was recognized by Irish nationalists like John Redmond and Alfred Webb as one of the most distinguished of the 'paper-unionists'.[12] This fact by no means prevented their use of his historical work for their own purposes. As Webb, vice-president of the Protestant Home Rule Association, put it in 1887: '... all his historical writings so far as they relate to Ireland are perhaps unconsciously one long and most powerful argument for home rule'.[13] Redmond referred to *Leaders* in at least two of his political pamphlets and was also able to use *England*.[14] In *The Truth about '98* he quoted Lecky's *Leaders* among his authorities for alleging that Pitt had deliberately planned and brought about the 1798 Rebellion in order to advance the cause of the Union.

Justin H. McCarthy, in *The Case for Home Rule* (1887) based some of his arguments upon *Leaders*. The *Freeman's Journal* said:

> The best things that have been written about Ireland have been written by Mr Lecky; and some of the best things that have been written by Mr Lecky on the subject of English rule in this country will be found in the last chapter of the first edition of *The Leaders of Public Opinion in Ireland*.

The *Freeman's Journal* proceeded to fill two and a half columns of small type with extracts from the chapter entitled 'Clerical Influences', 'for the benefit of Mr Balfour and our Liberal Unionist friends', and commended the extracts to 'the perusal of Englishmen and Irishmen of all classes and shades of political thought'.[15] Sending a copy of the relevant issue to Lecky, and complaining of the misuse that was being made of his early historical work for home rule propaganda, J.P. Prendergast lamented:

> They know these cod mouthed priests and farmers will never enquire when your work was first published ... .[16]

Other private correspondents, however, surprised at Lecky's unionism, now reminded him of what he had once written.

As long as home rule continued to be a live issue, Lecky's work remained an arsenal of nationalist propaganda. The Irish Press Agency in London issued a series of pamphlets as part of the home rule propaganda campaign, and made considerable use of Lecky's historical writing.[17] One of the leaflets, devoted entirely to extracts from *Leaders* (1871), was entitled *A 'Liberal Unionist' Historian Answering the 'Unionists'*. The extracts were intended to show that Lecky had 'answered long ago, by anticipation, almost every part of the "unionist" case'.

Another leaflet attempted to assuage the fears of religious discrimination being fanned by the Orangemen, with a passage from *England* in which Lecky proclaimed that 'among Irish catholics at least religious intolerance had never been a prevailing vice'. Extracts from Lecky's review of Froude's *The English in Ireland* were given in another leaflet. These extracts described the atrocities of government forces in Ireland, land confiscations, massacre, destruction of Irish commerce and penal laws against the catholics. The purpose of quoting rather selectively from Lecky's word-pictures was to explain to the British public the reason why Ireland hated English rule.

Lecky once wrote that we can confidently believe the good which a party writer recognizes in his opponents.[18] As a historian, he always appreciated the value of the testimony of the hostile witness, and did so explicitly in his comments on the alleged massacre of 1641. He discovered, however, that his own earlier writings were now providing the home rulers with hostile evidence in just such an exercise. One of the leaflets of the Irish Press Agency, which reproduced a favourite excerpt from *Leaders* in favour of self-government for Ireland and the recognition of the principle of nationality, was entitled *Hostile Witnesses in the Box.*

The nationalist MP for South Tyrone, T.W. Russell, quoting Lecky's remark in *Leaders* that the Union was a crime of the 'deepest turpitude', asserted that Lecky's position 'alike as historian and politician entitles his words to the greatest weight'.[19] The fact was, however, that it was the views of Lecky the historian, and not the politician, that Russell and his home rule friends considered valuable for their cause and worthy of constant public reiteration.

J.A. Fox, another active home rule propagandist,[20] stated that Lecky, 'in his right mind', had summed up the Irish case against England. Supporting this claim with generous quotations from Lecky's *England* and *Leaders,* Fox concluded:

> No man living has done more to foster public opinion in that country than the great protestant historian.[21]

Long after his death, Lecky's historical work was still being adduced for the home rule cause. In 1911 W.E.G. Lloyd and Frank Cruise O'Brien edited the chapter, 'Clerical Influences', from *Leaders* for the Irish Self-Government Alliance, because, they wrote:

> We feel that the argument of the book, and the spacious principles, so characteristic of the author, which underlie it, possess in the political considerations of our time a value, scarcely, if at all, affected by the fact that the book was written nearly half a century ago.[22]

When the third home rule bill was being discussed in 1912, the Ulster Liberal Association published extracts from Lecky's *England* in support of the claim that the Union had been extorted by 'the most enormous corruption in the history of representative government', and that it had been preceded by what was probably the most prosperous period in Irish history and followed by one of the most miserable.[23] Similar use was made of Lecky's *England* in a history of Grattan's parliament published in 1912. Its author, M. McDonnell Bodkin, admitting that he was 'at no pains to conceal' his own strong opinions in favour of home rule, described Lecky as 'an ardent champion of the union' and 'the calmest and most impartial of historians'.[24]

The books and articles of Professor J.G. Swift MacNeill MP provide one of the most typical cases of nationalist reliance on Lecky's work. MacNeill was also, perhaps, the home rule publicist who borrowed most extensively from Lecky. In a series of publications between 1885 and 1917, the extent of his dependence on Lecky becomes progressively more obvious.[25] MacNeill used Lecky not only as his chief reference work on the eighteenth century, but also acknowledged that on many occasions he had presented the facts of history and Lecky's judgments upon these facts in Lecky's own words. The reason for this was that if these judgments had been pronounced by himself, they 'might be discounted as the utterances of a party man committed to certain party doctrines'. Given in Lecky's words, however, they would have to be

> ... considered from a far different point of view as the mature judicial conclusions formed, to use a favourite expression of Mr Lecky's, 'in the cool light of history', by one of the foremost protagonists of his generation in the defence and maintenance of the union.[26]

In an article for the *Fortnightly Review*[27] MacNeill selected five topics of Irish history that were often raised during the home rule controversy and showed that Lecky's views on them were 'nationalist' and opposed to the usual 'unionist' interpretations.

First, MacNeill pointed out, unionist speakers and writers were fond of charging the last Irish parliament of the eighteenth century with intolerance, selfishness, cowardice and corruption. MacNeill answered them by giving passages from Lecky's *Rationalism* which had argued the very opposite. The second point that MacNeill selected for illustration arose out of an assertion by Colonel Saunderson MP, leader of the Ulster unionists, during the debate on the first home rule bill on 12 April 1886. Saunderson had stated that Grattan's parliament had led inevitably to the 1798 Rebellion. MacNeill's article quoted *Leaders* on the Pitt conspiracy as the direct cause of that rebellion.[28] The third point was the question of Irish support or lack of support for the Union. *The Times*, in an editorial contradicting a statement made in a speech by Sir William Harcourt on 4 October 1889, asserted that the better half of Irish opinion at the time of the Union favoured the measure. Following the lead set by Harcourt's letter of reply (8 October), MacNeill refuted *The Times* with quotations from *Leaders*.[29]

Fourthly, unionists used the 'massacre' of protestants by catholics in 1641 as an example of the way that Irish catholics had behaved under home rule in the past. This argument had been used in a leaflet issued in support of a unionist candidate in Cheshire in the 1886 general election. Noting this, MacNeill supplied passages from *England* and *Rationalism* to show how much Lecky's views on this matter were at variance with the creed of the ordinary unionist politician.

Fifthly, the proceedings of the Irish catholic or 'patriotic' parliament of James II were sometimes held up by the unionists as a warning against the concession of home rule. At a unionist demonstration at Bodmin on 17 October 1889,[30] Chamberlain claimed that the only Roman Catholic parliament that Ireland ever had passed the most monstrous acts which had ever been passed by any parliament in the history of the world. Once again MacNeill refuted the argument by employing a number of paragraphs from Lecky's *England*.[31]

Lecky knew perfectly well that many of the home rulers praised and quoted him simply because of his propaganda value. But he was also aware of the fact that he had the sincere respect of those nationalists whose opinion he held in high regard. Stephen Gwynn assured him:

> ... it is the barest statement of facts to say that we never speak or think of your work without respect and gratitude.[32]

During a long correspondence over many years, O'Neill Daunt had left Lecky in no doubt about the high esteem in which he held him. And Gavan Duffy wrote to him about 'the respect and good will' which he had felt for him ever since he had first read *Leaders*.[33]

One of the nationalist men of letters who praised Lecky highest and often in public was the Parnellite, R. Barry O'Brien. In an article for the *Freeman's Journal* in 1886 on 'The Best Hundred Irish Books', he wrote:

> ... let me at once say that in any list of the best hundred Irish books ... written no matter by whom, about Ireland or the Irish — the first place must be given to Mr Lecky's *History of England in the Eighteenth Century*.

In the Irish chapters of this 'great work', wrote O'Brien, 'science and honesty have been for the first time combined in the writing of Irish history':

> Mr Lecky possesses in an eminent degree the qualities essential to make an historian of the foremost rank. He has the faculty of research, the faculty of style, and an inherent love of justice ... Transparent honesty, an earnest desire to be fair, and an anxiety to let no fact pertinent to the subject escape his attention, are combined with a brilliant style, the distinguishing characteristics of one who is not only the greatest of Irish historians but among the greatest of living writers.[34]

O'Brien's article was forwarded to numerous leading personalities with the request for their comments. Lecky replied that he was afraid he had been extravagantly overrated.[35] Nevertheless, it was clear that he appreciated tributes from people who differed from his political opinions. In the ensuing discussion in the columns of the *Freeman's Journal,* other leading home rule politicians, including William O'Brien and T.P. O'Connor, also praised Lecky. The old Fenian leader, John O'Leary, distinguishing the historian from the politician in Lecky, and 'the present partisan of English wrong' from 'the past upholder of Irish right', agreed that as an historian Lecky was everything O'Brien had said he was, 'and indeed far more'.

Curiously, the only reservations that were expressed about Lecky's work in the *Freeman's Journal* came from Roman catholic dignitaries. This was a reminder that they had not forgotten his books on morals and rationalism.

R. Barry O'Brien was more representative of Irish home rule opinion. At the conclusion of this discussion, he wrote that he still regarded Lecky as 'the greatest and the fairest of Irish historians'.[36]

Certain passages in Lecky's books were often repeated by the home rulers. The famous last chapter, 'Clerical Influences', now provided much of the argument for the need to recognize separate Irish nationality by the re-establishment of an Irish parliament. Gladstone wrote that the character and force of nationality was most admirably set forth by Lecky in that chapter.[37] The *Freeman's Journal* provided its readers with a full summary of it.[38] Although Lecky had made his strongest case for the restoration of an Irish parliament in that chapter, he had returned to the same theme (but more cautiously) in the introduction to the 1871 edition. This introduction provided home rulers with ammunition such as this:

> As in Hungary, as in Poland, as in Belgium, national institutions alone will obtain the confidence of the nation, and any system of policy which fails to recognise this craving of the national sentiment will fail also to strike a true chord of gratitude.[39]

In the second edition, Lecky condemned the Union, and more especially Pitt, in language which, as Harcourt said, made Gladstone's condemnation seem mild.[40] He portrayed the Union as a great Pitt-planned conspiracy: 'the union of 1800 was not only a great crime, but was also, like most crimes, a great blunder.'[41]

What was Lecky's answer to all this? His reply to those who had quoted him on the Pitt conspiracy and the Union was that it was absurd to argue that, because a parliament of Irish protestant landlords was corruptly abolished in 1800, a parliament of Land Leaguers should be established in 1886. Home rule, he said, did not mean the restoration of Grattan's parliament;[42] and in his stand against a democratic home rule, he wrote: 'I have little doubt that Henry Grattan himself would have been on my side'.[43]

Is it possible to assess the influence that Lecky's historical writing had in the home rule controversy? Theodore Roosevelt said that he had been a home ruler since reading Lecky's work.[44] Lecky's German translator wrote that he could not but profess sympathy for home rule after reading him.[45] This kind of goodwill abroad was no doubt useful for the home rulers. At home, O'Neill Daunt had reviewed the first edition of *Leaders* because he was anxious that such talent, employed in the cause of Irish nationality and advocating political principles with which he agreed, should be brought before the public.[46] No doubt similar reasons caused Justin McCarthy to claim that the book had played a considerable role in the development of the home rule idea.[47] But these men had been nationalists before reading Lecky. The most that can be claimed with any certainty is that *Leaders* confirmed nationalists in their political opinions.

During the controversy of 1886, John Morley was one of the first to commend Lecky's words on self-government. But Morley, who had reviewed *Leaders* in the

Fortnightly Review in February 1872, had then censured Lecky for his 'partisan admiration for the Irish parliament', insisting that there was a case to be made for the Union, which had placed Ireland 'in the healthier air of imperial government'.[48] There was nothing in his review to suggest that *Leaders* had made a home ruler out of Morley.

Not only do Gladstone's speeches and articles contain many references to Lecky, but, perhaps more significantly, where no references are given, Gladstone's views on Irish history are remarkably similar to the early Lecky. Gladstone's article 'The Lessons of Irish history in the Eighteenth Century' was based extensively on Lecky's *England* for the facts, but its conclusions were the same as those in 'Clerical Influences' ± namely, that bigotry could be effectively cured in Ireland only by the recognition of Irish nationality. In his first home-rule speech, Gladstone maintained with Lecky (but without any special reference to him) that laws must be not only good but native.[49] When in the same speech he commended the aphorisms of Grattan, he was only following Lecky, whose *Leaders* grew out of the original purpose of collecting these aphorisms.[50] Gladstone's views on the penal laws, Grattan's parliament, the recall of Fitzwilliam, and on the Union as a Pitt-conspiracy were similar to those expressed by the 1871 edition of *Leaders*.

When Morley denied that it was he who had converted Gladstone to the idea of historical justice for Ireland, Acton then staked his claim to the role.[51] But if any single man did so (a doubtful proposition) Lecky would have a right to be considered; and if any book more than another influenced Gladstone in this matter, a case could be made out for *Leaders*. Whatever the significance of Lecky's work for Gladstone, it is at least certain that once he had decided that the seed was ripe and had made his home rule policy public, he straightaway called Lecky to witness that what he had affirmed was true. When Gladstone's opponents sneered that Gladstone brought 'bad history to the support of bad politics',[52] he could reply that his source was the greatest living authority on eighteenth-century Ireland.

Harcourt said that *Leaders* was the best textbook of home rule that he knew.[53] And perhaps a textbook is a good way to regard it. If it is not possible to show that people read *Leaders* and, as a result, were converted to home rule, it is easy enough to show that those who were already home rulers found eloquent confirmation and eminent support for their politics in its pages. The home rulers cited Lecky's text because it admirably served their purpose.

In the final analysis Lecky had no right to complain that the propagandists had used his historical work for political reasons. After all, he believed that history held its 'lessons' for politics, that, if hearkened to, could inspire the wisest political activity. Indeed, one of his best short pieces was a lecture entitled 'The Political Value of History'.[54] It was a question of degree and not of principle which separated Lecky's philosophy of the political use of history from that of the party propagandists.

He justly complained, however, of what he regarded as the misuse of history by political propagandists quoting from his work. Politicians had every right to learn from history, but the unfortunate thing was that to many the study of history was not only useless but positively misleading: 'An unintelligent, a superficial, a pedantic or an inaccurate use of history is the source of very many errors in practical judgment.'[55] Readers without a proper appreciation of the complexities of history vainly expected it to repeat itself exactly. As an example of what he had in mind, he wrote:

> How often in discussion about the advantages and disadvantages of home rule in Ireland do we find arguments drawn from the merits or demerits of the Irish parliament of the eighteenth century with a complete forgetfulness of the fact that this parliament ... for good or for ill ... was utterly unlike any body that could now be constituted in Ireland.[56]

The best corrective to this kind of abuse was the 'really intelligent study of history'; and Lecky recommended a study of the history of institutions and of the vast revolutions for those who wished to derive political wisdom from history. He appended the advice that every sincere student should endeavour to understand the dominant idea or characteristic of the age under review. History approached in this spirit, he believed, had a great deal to teach. Besides furnishing a key to the past, it would also provide an admirable political education and a discipline for judging the present.[57]

Unlike the more obvious propagandists, therefore, Lecky did not regard history as a magical box out of which could be drawn ready-made solutions to present political problems. Its use did not lie in supplying instant answers to the questions of the hour. On the contrary, he held that it was most useful in cultivating a philosophic and reflective attitude to politics. It taught that 'the fate of nations largely depends upon forces quite different from those on which the mere political historian concentrates his attention':[58]

> History is never more valuable than when it enables us, standing as on a height, to look beyond the smoke and turmoil of our petty quarrels, and to detect in the slow developments of the past the great permanent forces that are steadily bearing nations onwards to improvement or decay.[59]

The author of *Rationalism* and *Morals* had not become submerged in the unionist pamphleteer.

Lecky never could approve of the employment of history in any partisan political manner. He especially faulted men like Swift MacNeill and Argyll who were indebted to his own work for their partisan use of history. Because he had a deeper appreciation of history than the mere political propagandist, he would have been seriously at fault to have condoned the abuse of history in his unionist allies simply because their political cause was his own. It would have been more blameworthy if he had followed their example in his own political pamphleteering. To his credit, these things he resolutely refused to do.

Nevertheless, his work was influenced by the political and social considerations of the hour. There were a few sentences in his historical writing which showed him slipping to the level of the mere propagandist. Considering the amount of his historical output, however, and the strong views he held about contemporary questions, these occasions were rare and out of character. The influence of contemporary politics on his historical writing was usually less obvious and more subtle than was the case with the ordinary propagandist. If he never treated history crudely as propaganda, nevertheless his liberal and nationalist sympathies at one time, and his landlord and unionist professions at another, coloured his historical work and inspired and restricted his interpretations of men and events in both history and contemporary politics.

Apart from his active role as propagandist, Lecky abetted, advised and tried to moderate fellow unionists in their campaign against home rule. He had always been generous when his help was sought.

One of the most cogent and moderately phrased unionist publications of the period was *England's Case against Home Rule* (1887) by A.V. Dicey, professor of English law at Oxford. While working on this book, Dicey corresponded with Lecky, requesting his advice on the constitutional position of Grattan's parliament. He referred to a speech in the House of Commons in which James Bryce, professor of civil law at Oxford and a home ruler, had talked about the existence of two crowns between 1782 and 1800. Dicey wanted Lecky's comments on Bryce's thesis. He added that, years before, Lecky's writings had convinced him that the passing of the Act of Union was an unfortunate and premature act of statesmanship. However, he wrote:

> I have never been able to see (and in this also I conceive I have the sanction of your far greater knowledge) how the fact that the abolition of Grattan's parliament was a calamity, can prove that the creation of Mr Parnell's parliament would not be an even greater calamity and this to Ireland no less than England.[60]

In his reply, Lecky mentioned the Regency crisis of 1789. Dicey agreed with Lecky's views on this, and found his letter generally 'instructive'.[61] When Dicey's book was published, he sent a copy to Lecky, assuring him that it was 'to a considerable extent, the fruit of your own writings'.[62] Later when the book received what Dicey called two interesting reviews from Ireland, probably by the same hand, he again applied to Lecky for help. The reviews claimed that Dicey had blundered in asserting that Gavan Duffy and his friends had wished for 'national independence' in 1848 in the sense of Irish separation from England. Dicey wrote to Lecky: 'Can you tell me whether I have made a blunder or not?'[63]

Dicey's scholarly temperament was closely akin to Lecky's. In his case against home rule, he continued to hold that it was not necessary to have recourse to any race theories, or to attribute more original sin to the Irish than to the rest of humanity in order to explain the failure of government in Ireland.[64] Like Lecky the unionist pamphleteer, Dicey rejected the view that the 'sentiment of nationality' lay at the bottom of Irish discontents.[65] For him, the Irish question was essentially agrarian, and the solution was not to abolish 'foreign law', but to amend the land laws.[66]

Other unionists acknowledged a similar debt to Lecky's published work and private information. Stephen de Vere[67] told him that all that was of value in the first part of his pamphlet was culled 'from your rich stores'.[68]

One of the most persistent of those seeking Lecky's help was the Duke of Argyll. Argyll entered the arena of historical argument against home rule with gusto. Although Lecky was willing to aid him with helpful replies to his questions, he was uneasy about his blatantly propagandist approach to history. He advised him on more than one occasion that the proper attitude to history required a 'judicious impartiality'. Lecky felt that his advice was especially needed on the occasion when Argyll wrote an article on Wolfe Tone. This article was an effort to redress the balance, upset, according to Argyll, by a publication of Gladstone's which implied that Tone was 'one of the noblest of Ireland's children'.[69] Argyll thought of Tone as 'an incarnate fiend', 'a villain, in short, of the deepest dye'.[70] When Lecky read the proofs of Argyll's article, he advised a more 'judicious spirit'. Undeterred, Argyll replied that the judicial spirit in history called for the black cap as well as for the ermine.[71]

When the article had appeared, Argyll again wrote emphatically to Lecky:

> From what you said to me, and from what I hear you said to others, you condemn my paper as not consonant with the spirit in which history should be written. I contest this verdict … I deny altogether that a tone of perfect indifferentism or indecision on the moral character of men's actions, is a good qualification for historical narrative.

He elaborated once more on the baseness of Tone's character. He admitted that Lecky had 'justly acquired a great reputation for impartial narrative and conscientious investigation', but, without any effort to disguise his own criticism and perhaps resentment of the way in which Lecky's historical works had played into the hands of home rulers, he issued a stern warning to him:

> I see that you are soon to be in the press [Lecky's final volumes on the rebellion of 1798 and the Union were about to go to press]. I hope you will remember that every word you say, and every defence you set up, will be the texts for — not only comments or doctrines — but for actions and for deeds.[72]

Their disagreements on the proper approach to history did not prevent Argyll from seeking further assistance from Lecky, nor Lecky from aiding him. In an article in the *North American Review*, Argyll asserted that Gladstone's oratorical version of Irish history was little better than 'inflated fiction'.[73] Challenged by Gladstone to substantiate the charge, Argyll wrote to Lecky for help after he had decided to refute Gladstone's interpretation of Irish history.

Argyll's reply to Gladstone's version of Irish history was published as *Irish Nationalism: an Appeal to History* (1893). In the earlier chapters he used Stokes, Richey and Prendergast as his authorities, while for guidance on the period since the seventeenth century he relied on Lecky's historical work. In his book Argyll said many kind things about Lecky: he described him as an 'Irish historian of the highest rank in English literature', said that the tone and balance of his mind was

judicial, that he possessed a 'spirit of philosophic equity' and of 'judicial calm-
ness', and compared him favourably with Macaulay and Froude:

> The calm philosophy of Mr Lecky's narrative is not only delightful in itself,
> but representing as it does, nearly in perfection, the temper and other
> highest qualities of the genuine historian, it is invaluable in the confidence
> with which it inspires us that all facts are truly stated — and no facts, in so
> far as known to the historian, are omitted, — that nothing is sacrificed to
> the temptations of epigram or antithesis, as is often done in the case of
> Macaulay, or to the one-sidedness of strong convictions as sometimes in
> the case of Mr Froude.[74]

However, Argyll was not sure that in trying to redress one side of the balance,
Lecky always recollected the other. By not doing so, Lecky had played unwittingly into the hands of unscrupulous politicians. No other writer, Argyll said,
had given so fair an enumeration of the 'depressing influences' at work on Ireland
in the eighteenth century. But he disagreed with Lecky's statement that 'the
greater part of them sprang directly from the corrupt and selfish government of
England'. On the contrary, Argyll held that the adverse influences were, during
at least six of the proverbial seven centuries of English misrule in Ireland 'almost
exclusively of native Irish origin'.[75] Gladstone's version of Irish history was an
'inflated fable' precisely because it propounded this idea of 'seven centuries' of
oppression by England:

> When we have to contradict and expose such passionate misrepresentations
> as the inflated fables of Mr Gladstone's speeches, it is absolutely necessary
> to dwell on aspects of the facts which lie in the region of suppressed or
> neglected elements.[76]

In such instances Argyll thought that Lecky's 'tone of perfect impartiality ... is
apt to fail in its practical application'.

Like the later Lord Acton, the independent-minded Argyll tended to think of
the personalities of the past being summoned to answer at the bar of history, and
then having moral judgments passed upon them. He would have approved of
Acton's advice to his students 'to suffer no man and no cause to escape the
undying penalty which history has the power to inflict on wrong'. 'Judicial' for
Lecky, however, did not conjure up any pictures of the hanging judge. Rather did
it mean the presentation of the two sides of any case in the strongest possible
arguments. He had once given the advice:

> When studying some great historical controversy, place yourselves by an
> effort of the imagination alternately on each side of the battle; try to realise
> as fully as you can the point of view of the best man on either side and then
> draw up upon paper the arguments of each in the strongest form you can
> give them. You will find that few practices do more to elucidate the past, or
> form a better mental discipline![77]

Lecky's primary concern as a historian was expounding the two sides of a question and trying to strike a balance between them. Argyll's concern was with the final sentence of the judge. He wrote of the 1798 Rebellion:

> It is all very well to say, as Mr Lecky philosophically does, that we may find some 'difficulty in striking the balance between the crimes of the rebels, and the outrages of the soldiers'. But we are bound to remember which of the two parties set the first example, as well as which of the two parties was representative of the highest interest of society.[78]

Lecky, despite the political arguments raging about him, made brave and successful efforts to understand and explain the past in its variety and contradictions. He did not imagine that his chief function was to judge and condemn. He tried to distinguish the role of historian from that of politician, and attempted to persuade fellow unionists like Argyll not to abuse history by approaching it in the spirit of political advocates.

If Lecky sometimes felt uneasy with his unionist allies for their abuse of history, unionists like Argyll were embarrassed by the contribution which Lecky's historical writings unwittingly had made to the home rule cause. The most severe of the castigations Lecky received on this score came from T. Dunbar Ingram.[79] Ingram, a lawyer, was the younger brother of J. Kells Ingram, the former Young Irelander and junior fellow of TCD.[80]

Ingram's books were intended as a counterblast to the historical views which were associated most prominently with Lecky's name. The thesis in the earliest of these was that the alleged corruption in the manner in which the Union had been carried rested merely on the declamatory statements of the opposition, or on one-sided books by the younger Grattan and Jonah Barrington.[81] Although Ingram cited Lecky a few times as the source of a fact, it was obvious that the argument of his work was an assault on Lecky's heroes, especially Grattan, and on Lecky's conclusions about the corruption involved in the passing of the Union.

Ingram's book drew a severe critique from Gladstone,[82] who said that, although it contained some useful information and was written with talent, it was not history at all but a piece of special pleading.[83] In the course of this review, he defended his own earlier statement by citing Lecky's *Leaders* for the fact that there were only 7000 petitioners in favour of the Union, a point which Ingram had denied on the first page of his preface.[84] Ingram replied that *Leaders* was not the fruit of ripe judgment, as was his history of the eighteenth century then in progress.[85]

In his *A Critical Examination of Irish History* (2 vols) which appeared ten years after the completion of Lecky's *England*, Ingram gave no quarter:

> Mr Lecky is the most respectable among the teachers of the doctrine that no good thing can come out of the British Nazareth, and conveys his opinions in a more polished style … Like them, too, he accepts every utterance, provided it comes from an anti-English source, as confirmation strong … .[86]

What Ingram proposed was to select Lecky's work as an example of the rest, and 'accompany him in his disquisitions on ancient and modern Irish history'.

Ingram's two volumes hardly amounted to more than a hostile commentary on Lecky's work. Numerous references were made to him throughout, and the final chapter on the legislative union was devoted almost entirely to a refutation of his views and an attack on his methods.

He described Lecky's *Leaders* as a 'crude and premature production', and as an 'amusing instance of the perfect confidence of ignorance', published at a time when 'his knowledge of Irish history was derived from a foolish and untruthful book written by the younger Grattan'.[87] Ingram suggested, and with a certain amount of truth, that the five-volume work on Grattan by the younger Grattan, himself a repealer, not only had inspired Lecky's first book on Irish history but also exercised a permanent influence on him. Ingram wrote of the Grattan book:

> Worthless as the work is, and useless for the purpose of history, it converted Mr Lecky, who considered it, as he tells us, 'much the amplest and best history of the closing years of the Irish parliament ... .' Influenced by Grattan Mr Lecky enlisted in the ranks of the detractors of the English and British government. He very soon proved himself an apt disciple of a crazy master, and devoted many years to demonstrate that the policy of the sister country in Ireland has been a selfish policy, which has prevented the prosperity and industrial development of the island.[88]

Ingram described as an absurdity Lecky's reference to the Union as 'a sacrifice of nationality'.[89] He referred to his 'groundless assertions', 'flimsy evidence' and 'infinite folly, prejudice and ignorance' in claiming that the whole intellect of Ireland favouring the Union was bribed. He wrote that his attempts at proof were 'as ridiculous as ineffectual'.[90] Ingram accused Lecky of factual error, misrepresentation and misquotation, of garbling by quoting out of context, of employing guesswork in place of fact and of omitting what did not suit his theory. He claimed that impartial reasoning was foreign to Lecky's mind.[91] Concluding the bitterest diatribe that Lecky had ever provoked, Ingram expressed an opinion on Grattan's parliament which was the direct opposite to Lecky's. He characterized it as 'the most worthless and incompetent assembly that ever misgoverned a country'.[92]

Lecky regarded Ingram's historical writing as belonging to the same category as Argyll's; and although he admitted that everything that could be said to enhance the importance of the addresses in favour of the Union and to diminish the importance of the petitions against it were to be found in Ingram's book, nevertheless he regarded Ingram not so much as a historian as a 'skilful advocate'.[93] Moreover, he refused to be drawn into a controversy. The *Pilot* requested an article from Lecky giving Dr Ingram a 'dressing' for his defence of the penal laws. Lecky does not appear to have availed of the offer.

Among contemporary Irish historians whose attitudes to history and politics Lecky could warmly approve of and recommend were Richard Bagwell[94] and C. Litton Falkiner.[95] Falkiner was a younger contemporary of Lecky whose published works served to underline the loss to historical scholarship when their author died young. Like Lecky, he was a staunch unionist and a historian, but he too distinguished sharply between his historical writing and his political support of the unionist cause.[96]

Lecky was unflinching in his unionism and supported its cause with his own pen and with a readiness to supply historical information to fellow unionists. Both publicly and privately, however, he strongly disapproved of the abuse of history in unionist propaganda. The views he held about the dignity of history and the 'judicial spirit' in which it should be written had made him condemn the obvious partisanship in the historical writing of fellow unionists like Argyll and Ingram, while approving of the work of Dicey and Falkiner. He failed to realize, perhaps, that propaganda of a more subtle kind informed his own historical writing. It may be, however, as the Italian historian, Gaetano Salvemini, stated, that the historian cannot be impartial, only intellectually honest: that honesty is a duty and impartiality a dream. Lecky constantly made the effort to be objective and expected other historical writers to do likewise. A leading characteristic of the man, whether as historian or as pamphleteer, was his intellectual honesty. In striving after impartiality, he was often limited by his prejudices, but never by dishonesty.

Chapter 8

Liberty or Democracy?

Always jealous of his time, Lecky generally had refused to give lectures or write occasional articles or reviews when engaged on a major work: 'It was my early aim in literature to turn away from the fragmentary and ephemeral and to the limit of my capacity to embody my best thoughts in complete, elaborate and well-digested works of enduring value.' Once, when refusing the invitation to write a university textbook, he explained that he had as much literary work on hand as he could manage, that he did not have the happy knack of being able to turn easily from subject to subject: 'I find that in order to do anything really well I must concentrate myself severely on my own lines of work and refuse many tempting but distracting offers.' It was a measure of the gravity he attached to the agrarian and home rule agitations that he involved himself to the extent he did on these issues.

However, after he had completed *England*, he did find the time to write various articles, especially between 1890 and 1893. Of the fourteen essays which were considered significant enough to be reprinted posthumously in *Historical and Political Essays* (1908), nine were written in these years. No less than three were devoted to reflections on history and the historian's craft. 'Formative Influences'[1] was the response to a request by the editor of an American journal to give an account of the intellectual influences which had formed him. This essay outlined how certain influences, together with his intellectual experiences in Trinity College, Dublin, and his researches on the Continent in the years immediately following graduation, shaped him into the historian who had written *Rationalism* and *Morals*. Lecky's major interests as a historian had diverged into two main streams. *Rationalism* and *Morals* had shown him to be a historian of intellectual and moral development. In *England*, his concern had been mainly with political institutions and political development.

The 'Political Value of History', a presidential address delivered before the Birmingham and Midland Institute in October 1892, was clearly the work of the more political historian. It was a philosophical treatment of the question of how history should be best studied if it were to be politically useful. Lecky's theoretical position on historical writing always clung closely to his own practice. It was as if when asked to discuss the true theory of historiography, he went off to his own published work to discover the answer. An essay entitled 'The Art of Writing History' for *Forum*[2] was based on a published lecture delivered a quarter of a century earlier to the Royal Institution.[3] The revised essay for *Forum* was the work of a man who had written both the intellectual history which the *Morals* represented and the more political history of *England*, and who held up his own art as a model to others. In this essay, Lecky expressed his appreciation of the science of history as well as emphasized the supreme importance of history as literature.

If these essays, which offered Lecky's reflections on history, contained echoes of his earlier sociological and even deterministic phase, they were also tempered by his later work which spoke of the role chance and accident play in the historical process. They also made explicit that what Newman with his *via media* was to theology, Lecky was to history. On the issue of the significance of individuals in history, he stood midway between two thinkers who in different ways had strongly influenced him. He now picked his own way between Carlyle, who tended to reduce all history to biography, and Buckle, who taught a kind of historical fatalism and saw history as the product of a long chain of mechanical cause and effect where the biographical was the mere plaything of greater impersonal forces. Rejecting both extremes, Lecky publicly advised the historian to avoid Macaulay's political Whiggery and powerful epithets and Froude's blatantly anti-Irish and anti-catholic Toryism. As to whether an act should be described neutrally as a transaction or in moral terms as a crime, Lecky's disposition was again to occupy the middle ground between Ranke's noncommittal narrative and Acton's moral judgments.

Apart from exploring the historical processes, these essays showed Lecky's continuing preoccupation with Ireland. Besides the political pieces with which he responded to the 1892 general election and to the second home rule bill, he contributed a more substantial essay to the *North American Review* called 'Ireland in the Light of History'. The history of Ireland, he wrote, was full of petty struggles and atrocious crimes. It had not exhibited the national unity, stability or continuous progress of the great nations of Europe. It had not turned on great issues, nor had it produced great intellects. The only periods of exception were the great missionary era of the sixth and seventh centuries (about which his knowledge was limited in any case) and the eighteenth century. Ireland before the coming of the Normans, Lecky said, was never a nation but a collection of separate tribes and kingdoms engaged in almost constant warfare. This, he admitted, was no different from the experience of many other countries, but development in Ireland's case was impeded by the disorganizing influence of Danish and Norman invasion, the latter of which, in his view, produced consequences that were almost wholly evil. In his comments on the centuries of Gaelic and Anglo-Norman struggle, Lecky revealed himself as a worshipper of success, an imperialist not much concerned about the cost, cultural or otherwise, so long as a *Pax Romana* was imposed on an anarchical situation.

This essay alleged that the history of Ireland was valuable primarily as a study in morbid anatomy. Irish history had shown how national character was formed by political and social circumstances. It underlined the calamity of missed opportunities and of fluctuating and procrastinating policies. It provided an excellent example of the folly of attempting to govern by the same methods and institutions nations that are wholly different in their character and civilization. Where now, one might well ask, was the idea of progress that had inspired Lecky's history of rationalism or his pride in the sense of political development that had inspired *Leaders of Public Opinion*? Even eighteenth-century Ireland, which his own work had always idealized, now exhibited signs of the generally diseased state of Irish history. He regretted the lost opportunity in the early eighteenth century of the union of Ireland and England when catholics would have welcomed the withdrawal of direct rule by their civil war conquerors, and protestants had not yet developed a distinctively national feeling. The union might have become popular if catholics had been admitted to parliament, priests paid and tithes commuted.

Despite his continued condemnation of the penal laws, Lecky was now prepared to see some justification for them on grounds of necessity and because they had produced some eighty years of 'the most perfect tranquillity'. He praised 'the great protestant force' of volunteers created for the defence of Ulster against the danger of invasion; these men had exercised a decisive influence over Irish politics. Volunteer conventions, Lecky now wrote, represented property and educated protestant opinion more faithfully than did the parliament. And while Grattan's parliament was now made to take second place to the volunteers, this essay also pointed out that that parliament was exclusively protestant and intensely loyal ('loyal' was an adjective that Lecky helped to promote in Irish unionist circles). It was precisely this kind of proud historical memory of loyal protestant volunteers which later encouraged Carson to defy home rule. Just as his *Leaders of Public Opinion* and *Ireland* had provided propaganda for Irish nationalists, the essay 'Ireland in the Light of History' was as unwitting in its encouragement of Ulster loyalism and armed defiance. The impact of a single essay, however, was a great deal more limited than the influence of his books.

In an essay that would be read primarily by North Americans, Lecky had attempted to undermine any possible support for home rule from across the Atlantic. With this readership in mind, he sounded more anti-nationalist than he was. When writing about the past administration of Ireland for English readers, however, he was always ready to underline the mistakes of government and therefore sounded more nationalist than he was. This latter aspect of his mind manifested itself in his long review article of C.S. Parker's *Private Correspondence of Sir Robert Peel*.[5] Unlike some historians, Lecky did not think Peel was one of the greatest of British prime ministers. As a political orator, according to Lecky, he lacked the imagination of the masters — Chatham, Burke, Canning and Beaconsfield; nor had he any great political foresight. The two great measures Peel had consistently opposed in his career had been eventually carried by him. He had left his own party shattered. Lecky was prepared to concede that Peel was a great administrator, a master of parliamentary management and parliamentary legislation, but he was not a great statesman. He had been disastrously wrong on catholic emancipation, the most important question of his time. Although O'Connell had dubbed him 'Orange Peel', Lecky believed that Peel had shown no sympathy with the ribbons, anniversaries, party tunes, insulting processions and language of the Orangemen. And if one were to judge by the epithets Lecky had used, neither had he any sympathy with this aspect of Irish unionism. But Peel's policy in protracting catholic emancipation and in neglecting to solve the tithe question had been one of the most fatal blots on his reputation. The sectarian trouble between catholic and protestant in Northern Ireland, Lecky said, was largely due to Peel's policies.

The essays on Peel and on 'Ireland in the Light of History' indicate that what Lecky desired most was a solution to Irish problems; he was much less concerned with the justification of any abstract principle, whether nationalist or unionist. The development of his views on Anglo-Irish relations was influenced considerably by the enthusiasm he had gradually acquired for the new imperialism of the last decades of the nineteenth century. 'The Empire, Its Value and Its Growth' (November 1893) was an address to inaugurate a course of lectures at the Imperial Institute.[6]

Another of the topics of the time in which he took a great interest, and which was considered worthy of inclusion in his collection of essays, was old-age pensions. This essay, 'Old-Age Pensions', which appeared in *Forum*[7] was based on the views Lecky had already expressed in parliament and in his minority report to the Chaplain committee, which had recommended an old-age pension scheme. *Forum* published it as a counterpoint to another article it carried on the same subject by Michael Davitt.[8]

Other short pieces Lecky wrote were in the nature of obituaries, providing him with the opportunity to assess the contribution made to politics and literature by his contemporaries and personal friends. 'Carlyle's Message to his Age', originally a Sunday address at Lambeth Polytechnic, was published in the *Contemporary Review*.[9] Although he disapproved of some of Carlyle's opinions, Lecky regarded him as one of the 'teachers of mankind'; he had opposed the dominant trends of his day, warning of their dangers, and his words spoke that kind of truth most needed. A sympathetic essay written for the *Pall Mall Magazine*[10] on the death of Queen Victoria described her as a great moral force. Lecky also wrote his reminiscences of another friend and admired statesman, Lord John Russell, for Stuart Reid's biography of the prime minister; and a critical assessment of the politics and historical writing of his old nationalist friend, William J. O'Neill Daunt, was prefixed to the published selection from Daunt's diary, edited by his daughter (1896).

One of Lecky's most important reviews was 'Israel Among the Nations' in *Forum*, a review article dealing with a book of that title by Leroy-Beaulieu.[11] Lecky expressed both sadness and concern at the wave of antisemitism sweeping across Europe. In Russia it had produced what he called a hideous religious persecution, by far the most serious of the century. The revival of the spirit of religious intolerance, the development of feelings of exclusive nationalism, and the spread of commercial envy and jealousy which combined to create this new persecution greatly offended Lecky's sense of liberalism. Lecky's objections to the recrudescence of a mythology, intolerance, fanaticism and religious persecution based on racial grounds were all the more strongly expressed because, when writing *Rationalism* a generation earlier, he had approached his subject with the conviction of a young man who believed that Europe had left behind these blotches on civilization. This essay also contained one of those predictions which Lecky believed could legitimately be made from a close study of the tendencies of the age. To the oriental Jews, he wrote, Palestine was still a land of promise. They still dreamt that it was destined to become once more a Jewish state. Few who considered the condition of the Middle East and the power of the Jewish race would think the realization of this dream impossible. It could be predicted safely, Lecky wrote, that if Palestine was ever again to become a Jewish land, this would be effected only through the wealth and energy of the western Jews and it was not these Jews who were likely to inhabit it.

The occasional pieces that Lecky wrote after 1890 reflect the breadth of vision that made him into a good general historian, illustrate the sweep of his interests and, in the case of those written between 1890 and 1895, anticipate the wide-ranging discussions of *Democracy and Liberty*. A.V. Dicey, distinguishing be-tween the historian and the historical essayist, went so far as to say that Lecky was not a historian but an essayist — the 'first historical essayist of the day'.[12] Lecky, said Dicey, lacked the historian's reliance on original documentation and had shown little concern with the telling of a story. Instead, his reflections on the secondary sources and his capacity for grouping together facts bearing on a given topic were essentially the virtues of the essayist. A more recent researcher agrees with Dicey's verdict.[13]

Of the fourteen pieces in his collected essays, five were originally addresses or speeches, four were quasi obituaries, three were review articles and only two, the 'Formative Influences' and 'Ireland in the Light of History' were commissioned essays. The fact that chapters and whole sections in all Lecky's books can stand on their own lends some truth to Dicey's point. Nevertheless, it remains difficult to avoid the conviction that Lecky needed the wide canvas and the free range of several volumes to exhibit his historiographical talents to the full. He was more the long distance man than the sprinter in his approach to history. The virtues he required for sifting through the enormous amounts of source material, the painstaking shading of opinion in which he delighted, the accumulation of causes and effects, the comprehensive marshalling of arguments which gave such authority to his conclusions, the patient impartiality with which he presented both sides of a case as if it were some carefully drawn up judgment before the courts of law, could not be seen to full advantage within the limits of a lecture or in a single essay in a journal.

In 1891 Lecky published a small volume of poems which included those already issued in his student days under the pseudonym 'Hibernicus'. There is nothing noteworthy about these simple pieces. At best they showed him as a competent versifier. Some of the sentiments expressed provided confirmation of his political views. Otherwise, they merely serve to establish his reputation as a non-poet.

When the 1892 general election raised the spectre of home rule for the second time in six years, Lecky threw himself once more into the fray with pieces of political literature. He gave his support to the great unionist conventions held in Belfast and Dublin. He wrote to the *Scotsman*, opposing Gladstone's campaign in Scotland. His anti-home rule campaign was continued with articles in the *National Observer*, the *Pall Mall Gazette* and the *Contemporary Review*, and the unionists reissued some of these in pamphlet form. It would be no exaggeration to claim that, outside the leading members of parliament who were professionally involved in the anti-home rule campaign, Lecky's contribution to unionism was the most influential and, apparently, the most disinterested.

When Lecky was deep in writing *England*, a friend had expressed bafflement at the state of mind of one who could devote the best years of his life to the study of a vanished past while so many questions of burning interest were rising around him. Lecky's defence was twofold. He argued that the study of the recent past helped elucidate the politics of the present. On a more theoretical level, he contended that in an age when there was an abundance of politicians, it was desirable that some citizens should remain outside the arena. It was to the advantage of all that those unconnected with political parties occasionally should consider such topics. They could bring to their subject a more independent judgment than the active politician.

Yet *England* had shown signs of an author champing at the bit to get on to current political controversies. Indeed, politics in eighteenth-century Ireland, England, America and France offered numerous temptations to an author to become engaged in the current manifestations of similar political issues. But since Lecky also strove to be the impartial historian, he had to hold back. Now, with his history of the eighteenth century behind him, he decided to give himself free rein on the political questions of the day in *Democracy and Liberty*, published in two volumes in March 1896. From one view, the book was a manual of old liberal political philosophy, re-echoing warnings against the dangers of democracy which had already been emerging in the work of Mill, Spencer and de Tocqueville. From another, the work belonged to that brand of conservatism which had already produced such diatribes against democracy as Henry Maine's *Popular Government* (1885), or J.F. Stephen's *Liberty, Equality, Fraternity* (1873). But whereas Stephen argued against advanced liberal thought, and Maine against democracy as a form of government, Lecky was content to condemn those specific practices of democracy with which he disagreed. He was not unduly concerned with philosophical analysis. His attitude and much of his material had been forged in the Irish land war, so that while the historian was at least as much in evidence as the political philosopher, it was the political pamphleteer — informed, discursive, committed — that dominated the pages of *Democracy and Liberty*.

The land war had convinced Lecky that a democratic Ireland was not fit for self-government, and the experience of democratic politics in his country confirmed his belief that democracy had grave faults and severe limitations, and was indeed a real threat to those concepts of liberty to which he had devoted his career. He saw land legislation and home rule bills as having much larger implications for liberty and democracy than their specifically Irish context, and it was to these broader questions that he now addressed himself. It should not be forgotten, though, that his comments on the bigger theoretical issues grew out of his experiences in Ireland. His book may be seen as the intellectualization of his Irish land war experiences.

In *England*, Lecky already had discussed questions of forms of government, the relationship between property and franchise, freedom of religion and other aspects of representative government, liberty and democracy. His new book was an elaboration of these topics, and the opening pages incorporated a summary of the guiding principles of eighteenth-century parliamentary government. Taking his cue from Burke, Lecky praised the organic nature of the British constitution, and the role played by the gentry, whom he looked upon as born to rule. He emphasized the rights of property and the wisdom of the restriction of the franchise, and described the period between 1832 and 1867 as 'the golden age of the British constitution'. A discussion of English representative government in the eighteenth century was followed by sections on French and American democracy, taxation, the relationship between taxation and class bribery, the Irish land question and other forms of attacks on property, including nationalization. Lecky outlined remedies for the ills of democracy, dealt with upper chambers, nationalism, religious liberty, catholicism and democracy in Ireland, continental catholicism, Sunday legislation, gambling, intoxicating drink, marriage laws, divorce, socialism and its impact on different countries, labour questions, factory laws, women in society and female suffrage.

Democracy and Liberty has been rightly described as a 'series of essays, essays within essays'.[14] The information was encyclopaedic and the range impressive. Lecky treated of marriage questions from Roman concubines down to the then current controversy on a man's marriage with a deceased wife's sister. But this discursiveness also meant a bulky book of 960 pages; chapters followed in no logical order and entire sections could have been transposed to other chapters without affecting the organization or the argument. Carlyle, said the hostile critic John Morley, had preached a sermon on Lecky's text nearly thirty years earlier in only fifty pages. The difference, Morley said, was that Carlyle was a carnivore, while Lecky had been assigned to the slow browsing tribe of the graminivorous. Mills's *Representative Government* was not even a third as long as *Democracy and Liberty*. But then, said Morley, one was a classic, while the other could never hope to get into that category.[15] Many of the topics discussed had only the most tenuous connection with democracy, but Lecky included in his survey any current political question that interested him. Although this method provided a panoramic view of contemporary politics, it also gave much of the discussion an ephemeral character. The book lacked organic unity and a clear definition of its subject. Democracy for Lecky was an imprecise, all-pervading, evil, yet inevitable force. He tended to identify it with state interference and with socialism. Its effects were to be traced in the internal changes in the religious, intellectual, social and industrial life of different countries and in the growth of the doctrine of nationalism. Lecky ascribed to democracy consequences that were merely part of the general state of society, failing to see that the faults he found in American or French democracy did not necessarily apply to the United Kingdom. He was ready to forget that patronage, corruption and tyranny were not the natural offspring of democracy, but had existed long before democracy ever reigned. Democratic government and the ills of society were not simply cause and effect.

When he was being more precise, Lecky defined the theory of democracy as stating that 'the ultimate source of power, the supreme right of appeal and of control, belongs legitimately to the majority of the nation told by the head — or, in other words, to the poorest, the most ignorant, the most incapable, who are necessarily the most numerous.'[16] Democracy so defined was only too often the opposite of liberty. The fundamental point of his argument was that democracy did not necessarily spell liberty, and was, in fact, frequently its antithesis. Lecky's concept of liberty was close enough to that of Mill's: he believed that we should have the liberty of doing what we like, so long as we did not harm others.[17] Yet he accepted the need for regulation and state control of gambling and alcohol. This was in the public interest. Nevertheless, the burden of his message was the supremacy of individual over collectivist rights.

The rights of the individual began for Lecky with the right to private property. Society was 'a compact chiefly for securing to each man a peaceful possession of his property.'[18] The security of private property was essential to liberty. Democracy, being a threat to private property, was also a threat to liberty. Understandably John Morley regarded Lecky's object as 'being really and in substance not much more than to show the effects of popular government upon the rights of property'.[19] The confiscation of Irish landlord rights was, in Lecky's view, not only dishonest but directly attributable to democracy.

Democracy and Liberty might be said to be one of the indirect results of the founding of the Land League, and no part of the book was more bitter than those sections in which Lecky pointed to the Irish example. He criticized democracy because it implied the destruction of landlordism. This meant not only the confiscation of the landlord's rights to private property, but the elimination of his political usefulness. Private property was a supreme political and social good, and the possession of land, more than any other property, was connected with the performance of political duties. The gentry had the leisure to devote to politics; the education and manner of life most suited to a political career; the experience of providing political and social leadership in their counties; and they had acquired a knowledge and a tact in the management of men and the conduct of affairs. The landed aristocracy had been born into the tradition of politics and the habit of government, and had inherited the virtues most needed for administering the affairs of state. Aristocratic government might have many faults, but it saved the nation from the greatest calamity that could befall it — government by fanatics, gamblers, or adventurers. The chief function of government should be getting business done, and not the pursuit of ideals and utopias.[20]

The vacuum created by the destruction of the landed aristocracy was filled in part by a corresponding increase in the power of the clergy. Clerical influence was facilitated by the fact that the church commanded a devotion at least as powerful as that of patriotism. In Ireland there was the added reason that, in every stage of the conspiracy against the landlords, the catholic priest had been a leading actor. Though he was never aggressively anticlerical, Lecky described priestly despotism in Ireland as scandalous and in need of legislation to restrain it. Clerical influence everywhere was the deadly enemy of liberty and of a healthy public opinion; and in Ireland where the priest was at once the intimidator and the intimidated, clerical coercion had become an elemental part of the prevalent democracy. The easy access to power and influence of an organized priesthood was a major reason for Lecky's hostility to democracy as a form of government.[21]

Democracy also conferred political power on the uneducated and the immoral. Lecky readily accepted the need for a primary system of secular education, but had no illusions about the dangers inherent in a state of semi-literacy. Illiteracy, he said, was no doubt a strong argument against entrusting a man with political power, but the mere knowledge of reading and writing was no guarantee that he would exercise it wisely. The half-educated were peculiarly prone to political fanaticism, and those who had learned to read under the system of national education never read anything but a party newspaper, the intent of which was to inflame or mislead.[22] (It was not lost on Lecky that the steep increase in the number of threatening letters received during the land war was one of the unintentional results of the spread of literacy in Ireland.)

Democracy, he argued, was responsible for the increase of immorality in public life. First, there was the organized ability of such popular associations as the Land League to incite to crime, encourage the non-payment of rent and the breach of contract and the other acts of lawlessness noted by the Parnell Commission, which had investigated the charges of criminal conspiracy against Parnell and his colleagues made in *The Times*. The Irish lesson was not lost on British trade unions. Secondly, for the sake of votes, political parties' leaders practised class bribery and played one class off against the other, succumbed to the demands of pressure groups and sacrificed long-term objectives and policies intended to benefit the country for immediate party advantage.[23]

Another aspect of democracy which Lecky thought endangered liberty was 'the tyranny of the majority'. Of all forms of idolatry, none was more irrational than the blind worship of mere numbers. The voice of the people had become for most politicians the sum of all wisdom, and was vested with something like the spiritual efficacy that theologians ascribed to baptism: it was supposed to wash away all sin.[24]

During Lecky's lifetime there had been an enormous increase in the enfranchised, and this power frightened him. A body elected by the widest possible suffrage, he said, could be largely returned by a single class, or by the ignorant duped by the artful, and it could fail to represent in true proportion and degree the opinions and interests of its constituents. Public opinion was not the same thing as popular opinion, and it was not to be confused with the number of votes that could be extracted from the sum of individuals who made up the nation. Time and again Lecky insisted that pure democracy was one of the least representative forms of government.[25]

Finally, in his list of criticisms of democracy, Lecky held that it carried within itself the germ of another evil. To place political power in the hands of the poorest, most ignorant and most numerous class was to put it in the hands of those who cared least for liberty, and who were most likely blindly to follow some strong leader.[26] This had been the case with Parnell, who had turned out to be a caricature of Lecky's ideal leader of Irish public opinion. Highly concentrated despotism was, for Lecky, the logical outcome of democracy, for it was susceptible to political emotions and mass hysteria, to enthusiasms and hero-worship. In democracies, reason was less influential than rhetoric. No man, therefore, was more dangerous than a Parnell or a Gladstone who could dazzle and fascinate the crowds. The parliamentary system of government, resting as it did on universal suffrage, was unlikely to be permanent, and the mild despotism of some strong executive, as in America or the French empire, was one likely result. However, one could not rule out the probable emergence of a more militaristic despotism. The natural companion of universal suffrage was conscription. Therefore, militarism and democracy for a while flourished side by side. But, Lecky asked, would the eagles of militarism always consent to be governed by the parrots of democracy, especially in view of the growing inefficiency and discredit of democratic governments?[27] He did not live to hear his own question answered in fascist Italy and Nazi Germany. Lecky had also forecast that one day in nationalist democracies the extirpation of alien types, like the Jews, would be savagely carried into practice.

What Lecky denounced loudest was the headlong rush towards egalitarianism — the political and social levelling that he had seen so much of in Ireland: clericalism, trade unionism and party caucuses which gave power to groups at the expense of individuals; the increasing power of the state; the flattery of the new electorate; the idolization of mere numbers; the temptations to corruption in public life; and, above all, the prospect of exchanging old tyrannies for new. Lecky was the champion of aristocratic paternalism and privilege against all forms of dissent, but he was to a much greater extent the champion of a pluralist society, and of individual and minority rights against all forms of collectivization. Furthermore, he was not simply burying his head in the sand and feeling a nostalgia for his doomed world, for he did recognize that 'Democracy has been crowned King',[28] and was an inevitable fact. But, like J.F. Stephen, Lecky could not see why, as he was carried along by the stream, he should be obliged to sing 'Hallelujah' to the river god.

He therefore tried to suggest ways by which the dangers of democracy could be mitigated. Many of his suggestions would never have won the approval of Irish nationalists. His first suggestion was that Irish representation should be curtailed, since it was the Irish vote in the House of Commons that recently had carried the most sinister measures. He also suggested a redistribution of Irish representation so that property, loyalty, intelligence and the 'progressive elements' could be given greater weight. More positively, he became an early and strong advocate of proportional representation. This would ensure that minorities, for whom Lecky felt a genuine liberal concern, would be respected. For him the essential characteristics of true liberty was that under its shelter many different types of life and belief could develop unobstructed. He also strongly favoured the referendum as tending to correct, by an eminently democratic method, some of the worst democratic evils. He thought it would bring into action the opinion of 'the great silent classes of the community', and reduce to their true proportions many movements to which party caucuses or noisy agitations had given undue prominence. Popular opinion was least dangerous, he said, when it was as far as possible uninfluenced by professional politicians.[29]

In expressing his criticisms of democracy, Lecky had spoken for many of his fellow Victorians, and more particularly for the largely inarticulate Anglo-Irish landlords. His literary work was the swansong of a class that had been overwhelmed by democracy. He had posed searching questions for his countrymen, but few seemed to be listening. Even his unionist colleagues were hearing only what they wanted to hear. This was Ireland's great loss at a time when she had need of men of Lecky's talent and concern for liberty. His subsequent impact on Irish politics was minimal. It is hardly more than a footnote to be reminded that de Valera's favourite among Lecky's publications was *Democracy and Liberty*, although the exact weight to be given to that footnote or the degree of influence it may have had on that august statesman is not certain; or that Arthur Griffith, another keen reader of Lecky's work, in order to reassure the unionist minority in the Free State, fully accepted some of those safeguards that Lecky had advocated — proportional representation, the referendum, and the second chamber or senate.

Chapter 9

Elder Statesman, or Among the Pigmies

Lecky was elected to parliament for the vacant Dublin University seat in a by-election in December 1895. When agreeing to stand, he explained to Alice Stopford Green:

> Certainly nothing except a most pressing request from a number of distinguished men who seem to think that my candidature would be a real advantage to Trinity College Dublin would have induced me to be a candidate for the House of Commons.[1]

Traditionally the Dublin University constituency had been the preserve of the legal profession. For a while it appeared as if Lecky might be returned unopposed, but the lawyers then nominated a Mr Wright, a member of the Munster circuit; 'Clonakilty *contra mundum*' was how Lecky's friend, Lord Morris, described the contest. The campaign became surprisingly bitter between the supporters of the two candidates. Lecky had the backing of a number of English papers, *The Times* especially. In Ireland he was enthusiastically supported by the liberal-unionist *Daily Express* (Dublin) and even by the nationalist *Freeman's Journal.* The conservative *Irish Times* leaned towards his opponent, and its letters columns became the chief source of public opposition to Lecky.

When first persuaded to go forward, Lecky had anticipated some opposition:

> Whether, however, the barristers and country clergy the least want me I do not know. If not I hope they will express their dissent as soon and emphatically as possible.[2]

Emphatic in their opposition to him some of them certainly were, and he had not long to wait for it to erupt. About 60 per cent of the electorate were ministers in holy orders,[3] and the opposition soon realized that Lecky's great weakness lay in the fact that he had written a number of volumes touching upon matters of faith and morals. His orthodoxy was questionable, and it became the most discussed issue of the campaign. His works were quoted against him: it was alleged that he was an agnostic. His friends counter-quoted to prove he was sound on religion; an editorial in the *Daily Express* said he was no agnostic, and others wrote to report that he had been seen at church. It helped Lecky considerably that the primate, Dr Gregg, was among his supporters, that Dr Gwynn, the regius professor of divinity, proposed him, and that his committee included six bishops and numerous others from among the higher ranks of the clergy.

Lecky's dignified answer to the attacks on his orthodoxy was to say that he was a Christian; that he had never severed his connection with the Irish protestant church; and that in a parliamentary contest, and standing for a non-denominational constituency, he refused to submit to any religious test or to make any declaration of his personal views on theology. He would prefer to lose the election than make any confession of faith.

Other objections raised against Lecky were that he had no interest in the land question; that he was not an orator; that his writings had aided the nationalists; that he was an absentee, and that he was not a conservative. The republication in the *Daily Express* of Lecky's unionist and landlord letters to *The Times* of January 1886 was in itself sufficient to counter the more serious of these charges. In the event, Lecky was returned as MP for Dublin University with a majority of 746 in an unusually large poll of 2,768. In his favour was his European reputation as a historian, his services to unionism and landlordism, and the fact that university representation was on trial.[4]

On his entry into parliament and with the silent approval of his parliamentary colleagues, Lecky assumed the role of elder statesman. It was a position he filled naturally. An ambition of his undergraduate days had at last been realized, and despite the understandable reluctance of a scholar to change his routine and way of life, privately he looked forward to the experience of observing political power at work from the centre. He had enjoyed writing history; now he had been given the opportunity to become a maker of history. Could Lecky make an impression where Acton had not?

His years as an MP (1896-1902) coincided with a period of relative calm and even dullness in political affairs. But political calm suited Lecky's philosophic disposition. Conservative governments under Lord Salisbury, supported by the Liberal Unionists, enjoyed a substantial majority. Home rule had been defeated and even the Liberals, now under Roseberry, had shelved the issue. Gladstone had gone from the scene and no one took up the question with even a hint of his missionary enthusiasm. Parnell was dead and the nationalist party, winded and divided, seemed determined to spend its energy creating the image of an Ireland wrangling over Parnell's corpse.[5] Salisbury's nephew, A.J. Balfour, as Irish chief secretary had vigorously put an end to the land war, and a policy of kindness and of welfare government replaced coercion. Three measures — the Land Act of 1896, the Local Government Act of 1898 and an act establishing the Department of Agriculture and Technical Instruction in 1899 — 'marked the period as being, from the economic and social viewpoint, one of the most fruitful for Ireland of the whole of the nineteenth century'.[6] In these and in other important questions in this period — university education for catholics, and Anglo-Irish financial relations, for example — Lecky played a prominent part.

Even before he had been approached to stand for the University of Dublin, Lecky had warmly defended the notion of university representation. The demand for the abolition of university representation was mounting. It was alleged that Trinity College did not represent the feeling of the country. In England radicals attacked university seats as contravening the principle of 'one man, one vote'. The real reason behind many of these attacks, according to Lecky, was self-interest and the pursuit of power. The abolition of university representation would expel from parliament a small class of members who were the political opponents of the abolitionists, and

> who from the manner of their election, are almost certain to be men of political purity and independent character, and who for that very reason, are especially obnoxious to the more unscrupulous type of demagogue.[7]

Lecky was convinced that no form of parliamentary representation could be 'more manifestly wise' than that of the university seat.[8] The basis of this belief, as in so much of his political philosophy, was to be found in the Irish experience. Loyal and well-educated citizens were swamped in three Irish provinces by the votes of 'an ignorant and influenced peasantry'. The University of Dublin had for many generations educated 'the flower of the intelligence of Ireland'. It had sent into the imperial parliament a greater number of representatives of conspicuous ability than any other Irish constituency. Its 4,300 electors, scattered over the country, were taking a leading part in the professions and industry and came into contact with a great variety of interests, classes and opinions.

Lecky had an exalted view of the functions of a university representative. The grave sense of his own importance was further enhanced by the congratulatory messages he received from various notabilities, both on his election and on the publication of *Democracy and Liberty*. Among these he treasured especially one from the head of an Oxford college who wrote that they looked upon him as the representative not of one university, but of the whole university system.[9]

Lecky's elevation to parliament was naturally welcomed by Irish unionists. As a Liberal Unionist, his support on most issues was warmly appreciated by Salisbury's government. But even his political opponents trusted him. It was Herbert Asquith, a future leader of the Liberal government, who after Lecky had made his maiden speech, welcomed him 'with the greatest gratification', claiming that he was expressing 'the universal opinion of the house'.[10] John Morley was one of the few members who was sometimes tempted to tease Lecky across the floor of the House, and was always ready to reply to Lecky's strictures on the policies of Gladstone and his friends. Yet even Morley contributed the odd glowing tribute to Lecky, as when he described him as:

> ... one of the most eminent members of this house — a man distinguished in more than one way and a member of this house whom we are always glad to hear whenever he cares to address it.[11]

However, it was from his more immediate political opponents, the Irish nationalists, that Lecky received the most generous compliments. In one way or another, Redmond, Dillon, Tim Healy, T.P. O'Connor and Swift MacNeill paid him tributes. They seemed to regard him as one whose circumstances had temporarily led him astray, but whose heart was in the right place. Their usual deferential attitude towards Lecky was expressed quaintly by Major Jameson, the whisky distiller and nationalist MP for West Clare, who in opposing a bill moved by Lecky for the extension of Sunday closing to the cities of Dublin, Belfast, Cork, Limerick and Waterford, said:

> that if it were not that he believed the honourable gentleman was entirely wrong in a great deal he had laid before the house, he would feel in voting against him, like a pagan about to plant an arrow in the heart of a medieval saint.[12]

The Irish members sometimes regarded him as an amusing oddity. Swift MacNeill recalled that one of the most amusing incidents he ever witnessed was an enforced *tête à tête* at dinner between Lecky and Davitt, whose views Lecky detested. Because of Lecky's short-sightedness, he had once occupied a seat at a table for two without realizing that the Land League leader was opposite him. The members at neighbouring tables enjoyed the spectacle of the two men passing salt and behaving towards each other with every possible formality.[13]

On another occasion in Westminster, Tim Healy was reading a severe indictment of English rule in Ireland from a book while Lecky sat wearily opposite. Healy stopped to inform the house that the author of the piece he was reading was one Lecky, and he added, 'I often wonder what has become of him'.[14]

It was, however, more the respect with which he was held than his actual contributions to the debates which helped Lecky to fulfil some of the expectations of those who were pleased at his election to parliament. For apart from the big Irish questions of the day, his contribution to parliamentary debates was negligible. Even in his capacity as a university member, part of whose function was to keep a close eye on things cultural and educational, he rarely intervened except in matters relating to Ireland.

His particular duties as MP for Dublin University he took seriously, firmly believing, however, that a parliamentary representative should never degenerate into becoming the mere mouthpiece of his constituency. A member should not leave his private conscience, his political judgment and his liberty of action outside the House. His political behaviour must not be that of a respectable Dr Jekyll in his private capacity and that of an unconsciensed Mr Hyde in parliament.

In *England*, Lecky had displayed a certain nostalgia for the older system of the eighteenth century whereby MPs were 'at least free to exercise their judgments'. The trouble with the nineteenth century was that:

> great bodies of uneducated constituents, newspaper writers, demagogues, local agitators, are perpetually interfering with each question as it arises, and putting pressure on the judgments of the representatives.[15]

Of course Lecky did not believe that the representative for Dublin University was subject to such pressures. On the contrary, his view was that only university representation encouraged the kind of political independence for which his hero, Burke, had stood. And in *England* he gave prominence to Burke's arguments against the doctrine that 'representatives are simply delegates, and must accept even against their own judgments, imperative instructions from their constituents'.[16]

He was sometimes charged by nationalist opponents with speaking on the side of protestant sectarianism. Because of the nature of his constituency, the charge was perhaps only to be expected, but it was difficult to refute. Lecky regretted the predicament in which he found himself due to Irish sectarian feeling, and from which he was not able to extricate himself. It is ironic that the only time in his parliamentary career that he was called to order by the speaker was when he appeared to be lending his weight to the protestant side in another sectarian battle of words between Irish nationalists and unionists. But Lecky recovered quickly and, extricating himself from any appearance of sectarianism, proceeded to castigate Dr Long, a Limerick protestant doctor, who had mixed theology and medicine by his proselytizing work; the catholic mob which had attacked the protestant doctor and his friends; the catholic clergy and nationalist MPs who inflamed the situation; and the resident magistrate who had advised the people from the bench to give no employment to the doctor.[17]

Lecky's relations with the Irish nationalist members were for the most part amicable. In the last decade of the nineteenth century and the first years of the twentieth there emerged, in Horace Plunkett's phrase, 'a wholly new spirit clearly based upon constructive thought and expressing itself in a wide range of practical activities'.[18] Not only was there a change in the attitude of England toward Ireland, but there was also a 'profound revolution in the thoughts of Ireland about itself', and these years saw the foundation of a new philosophy of Irish progress.[19]

Lecky was asked to subscribe to the Gaelic League by fellow-protestant Stephen Gwynn.[20] He became a patron of the Irish Literary Theatre and backed it financially. There was much in this new nationalist stirring that seemed to him generous. Its obvious parallels with the Young Ireland movement of his youth appealed strongly to his sense of patriotism which had lain unexercised during the political and agrarian turmoil of the 1870s and 1880s.

Lecky felt too old to play a leading part in the new stirrings. He was invited, but was too busy, to join Horace Plunkett's Recess committee, which aimed at furthering the ideals of the Co-operative Movement. In parliament, however, he backed its programme, supported its aims and praised the work of individuals like Father Finlay, the Jesuit, and Plunkett who were leaders of the co-operative idea in Ireland. Plunkett believed that Lecky had been an inspirer of the new spirit of co-operation among Irishmen. Indeed, his book, *Ireland in the New Century* was dedicated to the memory of Lecky, in gratitude for 'the friendship' and the 'counsel which he gave me for my guidance in Irish public life'.[21] Plunkett regarded himself as a disciple of Lecky and, like him, condemned sectarianism in Ireland, warned against the kind of agitation conducted by the demagogues, advocated the secularization of politics, and expressed faith in the benefits of higher and technical education for catholics. Both called on their fellow countrymen to show moral courage, independence of action, practical patriotism, self-reliance, moderation and reason in drawing attention to their grievances. It remains true, nevertheless, that the younger man's *Ireland in the New Century* was as optimistic as Lecky's *Democracy and Liberty* was pessimistic about Ireland's future.

The new spirit that had come into Ireland showed itself in parliament in an increasing amount of co-operation between unionists and nationalists. Perhaps more than any of his fellow unionists, Lecky represented this spirit, and was more acceptable to the nationalists than most of his colleagues. His maiden speech, a plea for clemency, was given on the question of the release of Irish political prisoners (among whom was Tom Clarke, the future 1916 leader).[22]

Nationalists and unionists acted together when Ireland had been excluded from the benefits of the English agricultural rating act. In his speech on this occasion Lecky said that he was reminded of a prediction made during the union debates, when it was held that the time might come when the body of Irish representatives would say that the system of taxation was unfair, and when they would be overridden and defeated by an English and Scottish majority.[23] The nationalist members cheered him throughout this speech. Again, when the government proposed to pay the Irish landlords in cash instead of in land stock, in what Lecky described as a shabby deal, a combined Irish vote was registered against the government. And on the big issue of the financial relations between Britain and Ireland, nationalists and unionists again co-operated. During this debate, Lecky was once more cheered when he said that unionists and nationalists were generally agreed that in financial matters, as in other branches of legislation, Ireland ought to be treated as Ireland and not as a mere group of 'English counties'.[24]

When a bill proposing to spend a substantial sum on public buildings in London was before the House, John Redmond successfully appealed to Lecky to say a word on behalf of Dublin. Lecky, speaking 'as an Irishman', obliged.[25] John Dillon was 'exceedingly glad that the honourable member for the University of Dublin has come to our rescue in this matter, thereby showing that on these questions at least the opinion of all sections of the Irish people are united'.[26]

There were indeed occasions when the coming partition of Ireland cast its shadow across the parliamentary proceedings, and then Lecky and Plunkett showed themselves to have more in common with the south than with the north. This was true on an issue like the proposed catholic university, supported by Lecky and the nationalists and opposed by the northern unionists. On the financial relations bill, Lecky and Plunkett found themselves in the same camp as the nationalists and separated from Carson and from their unionist colleagues who sat for the northern constituencies. During the debate on this question Lecky noted that the northern MPs, the Belfast Chamber of Commerce and the Belfast Liberal Association preferred to talk about the separate consideration of Ireland's financial position instead of using words like 'entity' and 'unity' which the southerners employed. When he added that he admired 'the metaphysical subtlety that could find any real difference between these two things',[27] he perhaps displayed the basic failure of all southern Irishmen fully to appreciate Ulster's stand.

Shortly after his election, and even before he had taken his seat, he wrote:

I do not however at all like the prospect that is before me and am not at all sanguine about doing much good. Publicity and public life are indeed things that I hate and I have no political ambitions.[28]

With three months of parliamentary experience behind him, he grumbled:

> I do not mean to spend all the rest of my life here. The work is physically very tiring and I often fell that a good deal of it might be done equally well with a little training by any fairly intelligent poodle dog.[29]

He complained of the many distractions of his new life and that it had thrown his correspondence into arrears; of the clumsiness of the parliamentary machine; of the unlimited possibilities for obstruction. He groused about its dreariness and especially of the fact that it had left him little time for research or writing. Eventually in 1902 he gave up parliament, 'finding that its late hours and constant excitement were quite beyond my strength and that I was becoming little more than a voting machine.'[30] Yet, in perspective, one can see that the role he had played in Westminster was a great deal more significant than he ever claimed or perhaps realized. In the midst of his many complaints about the parliamentary life, he admitted to Lea that 'one can do indirectly and quietly some real good in this place'.[31]

In his books, especially *Democracy and Liberty* and *The Map of Life*, Lecky was a reflective commentator on some of the big questions facing parliamentarians and the public.[32] As representative for a university seat, Lecky felt that he was carrying on the tradition of the more independent private members of the eighteenth century. This sense of independence enabled him to protest against the government's setting up of a third commission of inquiry into the question of old-age pensions because of political and trade union pressures and despite the fact that two recent commissions had found against the idea. Following his protest, Lecky was appointed to the Chaplain Committee. But Lecky showed his independence in drawing up a minority report.[33]

Moderation was another virtue Lecky brought to the parliamentary debates. Apart from the moderate tone of his language,[34] we find him reiterating that, while in principle he thought one way, because of the weight of practical considerations he was prepared to vote against his abstract principle. Thus, although he was opposed theoretically to denominational education, he urged the establishment of a university for Irish catholics as the most just and best practical solution of the problem. Likewise, the establishment of county councils under the Local Government Act was not much to his liking, given the political condition of Ireland, and on its own merits he said he would not have supported the idea. Yet, in the face of all the pledges that politicians of all parties had given, a democratic local government in Ireland with certain safeguards had 'plainly become politically necessary'.[35]

The statesman, Lecky maintained, had continually to ask himself whether it was not on the whole preferable to vote for a measure, even a bad one, when the nation manifestly desired it.[36] What the Irish people really wanted should be graciously conceded. He quoted with warm approval a French writer:

> The great art in politics consists not in hearing those who speak, but in
> hearing those who are silent.[37]

What the nation manifestly desired, however, was not necessarily the same thing
as the demagogues and agitators demanded, or as skilful and immoral politicians
claimed after they had bribed a majority of voters. Nobody condemned such
political 'immorality' as strongly as Lecky, yet he insisted that political life could
be carried on only by constant compromises.[38] In private life, he said, the
distinction between right and wrong was usually very clear, but it was not so in
public affairs. The spirit that should actuate a statesman, therefore, should be
rather that of a high-minded and honourable man of the world than that of a
theologian, a lawyer, or an abstract moralist.[39]

To the nationalists it readily appeared that Lecky often came to the same
conclusions as they did, but for the 'wrong' reasons. J.H. Clancy MP said that
whenever Lecky spoke on the question of the financial relations between England
and Ireland, he reminded him of the cow that kicked over the bucket of milk she
had just supplied: one part of Lecky's speech answered the other. Lecky's habit of
considering the two sides of an argument was only what he had preached about
the writing of history and practised in his own work.

He had had to curtail his writing on becoming an MP, but the historian was
never too far submerged in the parliamentarian. This may be just another way of
saying that, despite his contribution to parliamentary life, at least in his own eyes
Lecky was too old to make any outstanding mark. He was, perhaps, a bit like
Henry Flood, one of his 'leaders' of Irish public opinion, whose habits already
had been too strongly formed when he transferred to Westminster and who
failed to make the impression there that he had made in Ireland. And what,
according to Lecky, Grattan said of Flood was also true of Lecky himself — 'he
was an oak of the forest too great and too old' for the transplantation.[40]

Lecky was peculiarly well fitted to act as a parliamentary representative of the
Irish landlords when they were fighting for their very existence. Through his
letters to the papers and his books, he had become one of the leading apologists
of landlordism in the United Kingdom — reasonable, articulate and influential.
During his term in parliament he never forgot that he was the representative of a
corporation 'which was the largest landowner in Ireland'.[41]

So when the land measure of 1896 was introduced into parliament in April,
Lecky's stand on the Irish land question was already a matter of public knowledge. During the months when the bill was before the public, Lecky's views on
the wider aspects of the land question were being circulated, for his *Democracy
and Liberty* had devoted a considerable amount of space to a commentary on
Irish land legislation since 1870.

Here, apart from providing what is still a useful summary, he had articulated
the landlord's case. He showed far more concern with landlord rights than with
the great social evil of eviction, or with any of the arguments about the equitable
and moral justification of these land acts. Lecky believed that a subversive

principle — interference with property rights with no compensation to the owners — had been admitted and had become the logical premise of subsequent land legislation.

He went on to moralize on how a departure from sound principle was nearly always first advocated on the ground that it was exceptional, limited in application, certain to do no practical harm, and intended to secure practical benefit.[42] But once admitted, the subversive principle grew and strengthened until it acquired an irresistible power and its application was pushed into new fields. Lecky held that it would be difficult to find a better example of this process at work than in the Irish land legislation since 1870. But such a precedent could not be confined to land legislation, nor indeed to Ireland. Gladstone's act of 1870 had signalized the government's abandonment of *laissez faire* in regard to land ownership, and also the doctrine of the landlord's absolute rights of private ownership.

The 1870 act was, in Lecky's eyes, 'one of the most important measures of the present century'. Few people foresaw that the clauses which interfered with the hitherto acknowledged rights of the landlords constituted:

> the first step of a vast transfer of property and that in a few years it would become customary for the ministers of the crown to base all their legislation on the doctrine that Irish land was not an undivided ownership but a simple partnership.[43]

Like other Irish landlords, Lecky thought that his class had been betrayed not only by Gladstone's acts of 1870 and 1881 but by Conservative Unionist governments to whom the Irish landlords had given political support. Certain effects of the recent Irish land legislation, moral as well as material, were evident to him, and in his reckoning the evil results greatly outweighed the beneficial.[44] He was still enough of an old liberal to approve of 'the free bargaining of two contracting parties' and to resent state intervention, which prohibited 'grown-up men from making their own bargains'.[45]

If Lecky was right about the effects of the land acts on political and social morality, then Irish land legislation had contributed not only to end *laissez faire* in the United Kingdom and initiate the welfare state, but it had helped to undermine the Victorian virtues. The immorality of the agitation and of the resultant legislation was the charge he reiterated most constantly.

'Manipulations of taxation', especially Gladstone's in 1874, were 'dexterously adapted to catch in critical times the votes of particular sections of the electorate'. The Liberal Party, with the 'apostasy of 1886', had 'purchased the votes by adopting the policy of the National League'.[46] In 1887 a Unionist government had ignored the arguments of justice, precedents and guarantees because it, too, had chosen to regard the Irish land question primarily as a matter of political power and votes. Morley's land bill of 1894 was a particularly 'scandalous instance of political profligacy' with which the government had 'bought the Irish vote'.[47]

The publication of *Democracy and Liberty*, just at the moment when Lecky had entered parliament, cast him in the role of a nineteenth-century Savonarola, castigating British legislators for putting immediate political self-interest above moral principle. In describing the land acts, Lecky had employed phrases like 'essentially dishonest', 'the most questionable and indeed extreme violation of the rights of property', 'arbitrary and unregulated actions', 'distinctly calculated to encourage dishonesty' and 'an act of simple, gross, gigantic robbery'.[48]

He conceded that the legislators were men who in their private capacity probably would be incapable of an act of dishonesty. Publicly, however, they had shown themselves 'the accomplices of thieves'.[49] British statesmen of all parties had yielded weakly to the pressures from Ireland, a country where the repudiation of debts and the intimidation of creditors had become leading features of popular politics, and where the protection of property and the administration of justice might one day fall into the hands of the authors of the 'No rent manifesto' and the 'plan of campaign'.[50] British governments, therefore, which for political expediency had sacrificed the landlords, were no better than the 'defaulting governments of South America'.

His arguments amounted to a formidable indictment of the processes of democratic government in late nineteenth-century Britain. Yet his position was essentially that of the partisan rather than that of the philosophical observer. Lecky the historian was usually scrupulous about presenting both sides of every question. Lecky the landlord, in the thick of battle, saw one side only. He insisted that the basis of the land agitation in Ireland was 'cupidity'.

Such an assertion made no allowance for the misery of the tenantry, misery that was perhaps more the result of agricultural depression than of landlord oppression. Lecky did not take into account the tenants' legitimate sense of grievance or their hopes of remedying their condition through organization. It was illogical of him to exculpate the landlord class by blaming the system, while at the same time denouncing cupidity and not the system for the peasant agitation. He admitted only occasional and infrequent acts of oppression on the part of the landlords at a time when the eviction graph had risen dramatically, with a corresponding rise in agrarian crime.[51] In the circumstances, it was an oversimplification to claim that 'the true crime of the Irish landlords was their loyalty'. Even Lord Salisbury had lamented the absence of a clause in the 1887 act which would compel harsh, evicting landlords to sell out. And Salisbury's nephew, A.J. Balfour, who found the Irish landlords to be 'maddening clients', could cry out 'What fools the Irish landlords are.'[52]

If Lecky made little allowance for what he regarded as the duped peasantry, he made none whatever for their political leaders. To these he ascribed only the basest of motives, and had nothing to say about any sense of patriotism, social justice or legitimate political ambition that might have inspired them. In so far as he interpreted their actions as vote-catching devices, he did not allow much sincerity of purpose on the part of British politicians either, although it is an arguable case that they had tried to solve equitably the complicated Irish land problem.[53]

In view of all his previous comment, it was not surprising to find Lecky emerge as a watchdog of landlord interests. He was only two months in parliament when a new land bill was introduced by the chief secretary, Gerald Balfour. The pressing need for yet another land measure was admitted from all quarters, except by the representatives of the landlords, who had learned to expect only further curtailment of their power and infringement of their rights. Lecky faithfully reflected landlord feeling when he wrote to a friend:

> if we could only induce this house to leave us alone for a few years it would be the greatest boon parliament could bestow on us. [54]

The case for a new measure was not difficult to make. Land purchase, which all groups in parliament approved of in principle, had almost come to a halt, despite the £33 million provided for that purpose under A.J. Balfour's measure. Besides, the report of the Morley Commission in 1894 had highlighted various other shortcomings in the Irish land code and pointed the way to reform and a greater efficiency. A number of these recommendations were incorporated in the 1896 bill. It had the strong backing of the brothers Balfour and other members of the government. John Morley, leading spokesman for the Liberal opposition, welcomed the bill, claiming that no Irish member would deny that some legislation was needed. Among the Irish members, the Dillonites proved hostile, because the bill did not go far enough. The Healyites favoured, as did the Redmondites, *faute de mieux.*

Morley contended that the senior member for Dublin University, Edward Carson, would admit the need for a new Irish land bill. But, he added, in sarcastic reference to the newcomer and junior member, Lecky:

> It is possible that the more philosophic representative of Dublin University may protest, because he looks upon all of us poor pigmies in the house with displeasure and disapprobation [laughter] — he looks with suspicion upon this house as an institution, and he looks with particular indignation upon the attempts that have been made since 1881 to remedy the evils in the Irish land system. ... I am perfectly sure we shall hear him say before the debate closes that he thoroughly disapproves of all the propositions in the present bill affecting tenure and fair rents.[55]

The reason for the baiting of one historian MP by another is not difficult to guess. Lecky had denounced the policies of Gladstone and the Liberals in his recently published book. Lord Morley, Irish chief secretary in Gladstone's last ministry, had been the recipient of one of Lecky's most angry rebukes.[56] He had been given Lecky's book for review, but now he also had Lecky in the parliamentary arena where he himself was by far the more experienced gladiator. Apart, however, from interjecting the factual statement that he specifically praised land purchase and was not opposed to it as Morley implied, Lecky did not rise to the bait.

He busied himself instead with an able and behind-the-scenes opposition to certain clauses of the bill. Lecky wrote a memorandum on the bill which he circulated among members of the government, and which won the warmest approval of some. Lord Lansdowne, writing from the War Office, described it as 'excellent' and asked Lecky for a half-hour's quiet talk on the subject.[57] Ashbourne, Lord Chancellor of Ireland, praised its clarity and incisiveness and hoped that a copy had been forwarded to the prime minister.[58]

In parliament a mere handful of Irish unionists doggedly fought the battle against great numerical odds during two all-night sittings at the end of the session. Lecky was especially impressed by Edward Carson's knowledge of the legal technicalities. As the debate progressed, however, Carson saw each of his many amendments rejected by Gerald Balfour, and complained bitterly that the nationalist amendments introduced by Tim Healy had been accepted.[59]

The Irish unionist leader, Colonel Saunderson, opposed the bill in an entertaining and more genial manner than Carson, but he was no more successful; and he admitted to Carson, who had praised one of his speeches, that he had not talked about the details of the bill because he had not read it. With Saunderson ineffectual and Carson frustrated, Lecky's moderate arguments proved all the more significant. He made two speeches on the bill, in which he explained that, while he favoured the purchase clause, he was opposed to those aspects of it which interfered with the property rights of landlords and which continued the process of whittling away this property by making it over to the tenants.

The clause that attracted his particular fire was known as the turbary clause. The privilege of cutting turf on the landlord's property, he said, had hitherto been allowed only under supervision, so that the irregular and unrestricted cutting feared by Dean Swift in the eighteenth century would not prove ruinous. It was now proposed under the terms of this clause, Lecky claimed, to turn what was a customary favour conceded to the tenants by the landowners into a legal right. The turbary clause, he said, took away property rights, but they had grown used to that sort of thing in Irish agrarian legislation. Nevertheless, he thought it remarkable that this was now being proposed by a unionist government. Besides, the valuable principle of tenant-purchase was being cancelled by other aspects of Irish land legislation which transferred so many rights of property to the tenants that it made it better for them to remain tenants than become owners.

On 28 July Lecky moved the omission of the turbary clause. He claimed that the landlord was being deprived of a right not because he abused it, but because he had granted privileges to the tenants generously and of his own free will. The landlords were now to lose all power of supervision and control. 'It was difficult to conceive a more direct and absolute violation of the rights of property than this.'[60]

A couple of days later, the Duke of Argyll took up Lecky's case against the turbary clause in *The Times*.[61] The following day an editorial drew attention to a 'defect' in the bill which had no safeguard against the wasteful use of turbary rights and also drew readers' attention to a letter from Lecky which 'entirely agrees' with Argyll. *The Times* thought that the solution might be, as Lansdowne had said, an amendment in committee.[62]

Lecky had thus helped to draw public attention to certain aspects of the bill which he did not like. He decided to press the advantage and in his letter to *The*

Times warned that the effects of the bill would not be confined to turbary rights; a diminution of other natural resources of Ireland was likely to follow. When Ireland was in the hands of impoverished and powerless rent-chargers and small proprietors, what probability was there that the preservation of game and the suppression of poaching would be ensured? The Devon Commission, Lecky said, had shown how wasteful farming had preceded the Great Famine. The system of rent-revision and rent-fixing, extended further by the 1896 bill, offered a direct premium on bad cultivation since farmers tended to let their land run down in order to claim lower rents. The clauses dealing with the forced sale of bankrupt estates, and the evidence that the government was still tampering with contracts and property rights, would only impede the beneficial land-purchase principle. Not the gentry but the farmers had been the real rack-renters in the past, and the new landowners drawn from the gombeen class were not likely to be as indulgent as the former landlords. More constructively, Lecky added that £2 million a year should be provided over the next 15 or 20 years to create peasant-proprietorship. Finally, he strongly deplored the policy of pushing a complicated land bill through parliament during the last days of the session and by means of all-night sittings before a jaded House.[63]

Lecky's line of argument found more favour in the House of Lords where, the land bill was being dealt with 'in a manner which threatened to cause serious embarrassment to the government':

> It may also be true that, as Mr Lecky, recently said in our columns, Irish land legislation fatally tends to benefit and to promote the growth of a class of men who are or will become landlords of by no means the best type rather than simple tenants.[64]

However, *The Times* concluded that Irish tenants with grievances existed in sufficient numbers 'to form a serious disturbing element if their demands are not granted'. This was precisely the kind of organized pressure which Lecky feared and deplored. Ultimately, from the landlords' point of view, the House of Lords improved the bill in certain particulars and made the turbary clause harmless by an amendment.

When the bill had been finally passed (August 1896), Arthur Balfour wrote:

> The storm caused by the land bill is rapidly going down. There never was a more remarkable instance of the power which an able man has of doing infinite mischief. I really believe that if Carson had not put his finger in the pie, we should not have had the slightest difficulty with the measure either in the lords or commons![65]

This verdict was a misjudgment based on a serious oversimplification. In certain respects, of course, it only confirmed Lecky's opinion of the contribution Carson's legal and political expertise had made to the Irish landlords' cause. But in so far as Balfour attributed the government's difficulty to the influence of one man, he seriously miscalculated the situation and the extent of the opposition.

Balfour's verdict also implied a grave underestimate of the part played by the junior member for the University of Dublin, whose role had been far from negligible. *Democracy and Liberty*, with its searching criticism of the trend of Irish land legislation, reached out to public opinion much further than anything Carson said. Lecky's reputation for historical impartiality lent an authority to his pronouncements which Carson could not claim. His intellectual *rapport* with organs of public opinion like *The Times*, and his social and political sympathy with the gentry and with aristocratic institutions ensured for him a respectable influence whenever he chose to speak out. He had eloquently alerted public opinion to dangers that were inherent in the Irish land legislation, he had aroused doubts about certain clauses in the bill of 1896, and he had helped significantly to influence amendments to the legislation. Lecky's role in the land bill of 1896 emphasized that he was by no means ineffective as a parliamentarian.

On a few later occasions he got the opportunity to reiterate his own view of the land legislation, but he felt there was little that could now be done to undo the evil already perpetrated. Despite his pessimism, he continued a rearguard action, as the Irish landlord class retreated from the field of history. When, for example, a bill dealing with the tithe rent-charge proposing certain concessions to the landlords was introduced, Lecky spoke in its favour and claimed that it was only an act of justice since the landlords were 'the greatly injured class'.[66] When, on the other hand, Michael Davitt, backed by nationalist MPs, sought to give compulsory powers to the Congested Districts Board to acquire large grazing lands for the relief of distress, Lecky opposed the scheme. In answer to the bitter complaints of the nationalist members, he asserted that the true culprit was not the British government nor the Irish landlords, but the Atlantic Ocean, the poor soil, the bad farming and the subdivision of land. Although something might be done to enlarge holdings in the west, he would not consolidate the present smallholders on the soil. Similar areas in Scotland were prosperous because of the sporting and tourist traffic, and this should be encouraged in the west of Ireland too. But to attack the richer grazing lands, Lecky said, would be a serious mistake since the first and most vital Irish industry was the cattle trade and Ireland must be a pastoral country.

Lecky's contribution to the debate on the Irish land question contained a good deal of sense; but it was the kind of sense spoken by a clever man with long experience in making out a case for his clients. If pressed on the matter, he would probably have agreed that here, indeed, was an illustration of a point he had himself expressed: that 'public and private interest are, undoubtedly, often so blended in politics that it is not possible wholly to disentangle them', that the difference between 'low motives of private interest' and 'high motives of public spirit' was certainly very great, but that it was essentially a difference of proportion and degree.[67]

Lecky's position as landlord spokesman was not unlike that of Burke — giving up to party what was meant for mankind. For that matter, it was close enough to the position taken by Gladstone, whom he had castigated for having dared to employ God and morality in the service of his own party.

A second issue to which Lecky as parliamentarian devoted much attention was the Irish university question. Already in the 1860s the author of *Rationalism* and *Morals* had come to personify a standing argument against the education of catholics in Trinity. The *Irish Ecclesiastical Record* claimed that:

> ... the work of Mr Lecky cannot fail to convince catholics that it is most dangerous for them to send their children to protestant universities, in which opinions like his, destructive of all religion, are freely circulated and brought before the youthful mind.[68]

He had the further distinction of being named by Dr Cullen in a pastoral read in each church in the archdiocese. A passage in the pastoral described Lecky as a graduate whose published works were 'replete with the spirit of the worst German rationalism, and well-calculated to spread indifference to all religion, or infidelity through the land.'[69]

The catholic demand in higher education was for the establishment and endowment of a catholic university. However, a pastoral letter of the bishops in 1871, and many subsequent pronouncements, made it clear that catholic claims could be satisfied by alternative arrangements. A national university might be set up in which the catholics would have one or more colleges conducted upon purely catholic principles; or, the constitution of the University of Dublin might be modified so as to admit the establishment of a second college within it, in every respect equal to Trinity College, but conducted on catholic principles.

During the time of the Liberal alliance, a stage had been reached in the university question which Archbishop Walsh later referred to as 'the period of hopeful reform'.[70] It was known that Gladstone was prepared to go a long way to meet the claims of the Irish bishops, and the bishops were being urged by Cardinal Manning to accept what the prime minister had to offer.

A week before Gladstone's University bill of 1873 was introduced in parliament, a well-timed and strongly worded letter from Lecky appeared in the press. He denounced the bishops' demand for denominational education and defended Trinity against their criticisms. He had been much infected with the Young Ireland brand of nationalism, and claimed that religious divisions were the masterful curse of Ireland. To achieve the complete separation of catholic and protestant students was the bishops' avowed object, but their policy

> would do more than any other measure the wit of man could devise to enlarge and perpetuate the chasm between the two sections of Irish society.[71]

The bishops' policy, if successful, would destroy the prestige of Trinity and denationalize the talent of Ireland. Lecky argued that there should be no retreat from the liberal and secularist victory of 1869 which disestablished and disendowed the protestant church in Ireland. Instead of the retrograde step of endowing denominational education, Lecky suggested opening up Trinity to catholics, and making it truly national and non-sectarian. This indeed was the principle introduced in Fawcett's bill which was passed in parliament later that year after the bishops and the Irish MPs had rejected Gladstone's. But for reasons of practical compromise, Lecky went further and accepted a measure of denominationalism. He suggested that catholics be given the safeguard of a separate college and chapel within Trinity. In his view, the system he advocated was:

> ... peculiarly fitted for a country like Ireland where the first of all objects should be to assuage the bitterness of sect and to teach catholics and protestants to co-operate in secular politics.[72]

The *Freeman's Journal* summed up the attitude of the Catholic leaders to Lecky's proposals when it replied: 'The Catholic people know what they want far better than Mr Lecky.'[73]

Disraeli's University Act of 1879 establishing the Royal University — an examining board empowered to grant degrees — had one advantage over Gladstone's scheme in that it provided indirect endowment for the catholic university by its system of fellowships. Its big disadvantage in the bishops' eyes was that it still left the catholics with a feeling of inferiority towards Trinity.

Nobody, Lecky said, in 1879 before the university bill was introduced, was likely to ask or care for his opinion, but he had his own ideas on the subject.[74] He was prepared to admit that catholics had grounds for complaint against Trinity. Students who came from outside Dublin were obliged to reside with protestants or in lodgings; no provisions were made for their religious teaching or worship; and since ethics and modern history touched on questions of disputed theology, catholics might reasonably ask for some distinctly catholic approach to these subjects. However, the creation of a new university was not the answer. Lecky wished to see annexed to Trinity a catholic college where catholics might reside and have their own chapel. He would grant this college an endowment; but he would also endow distinctively catholic professorships in such subjects as ethics and modern history (later he was to add theology, ecclesiastical history and moral philosophy).[75]

Negotiations on these proposals might have resulted in a satisfactory compromise, but, however eminent Lecky was in the world of letters, the hierarchy thought him suspect. This situation changed when Lecky became MP for the University of Dublin in 1895.

In his speech accepting nomination, he said that it would be his duty as the representative of the university to guard sedulously its national and unsectarian character. His earnest desire was that it would never degenerate into the university of a sect. Whatever other institutions might be set up in Ireland, he said, let this at least be one where men of different religions may freely enter.

Bishop O'Dwyer of Limerick commented on Lecky's speech in a letter to *The Times*, and asserted that whatever its legal position, Trinity was in fact neither national nor unsectarian.[76] He restated the Catholic case for higher education. In reply, Lecky maintained that he had never said or written anything implying that no step should be taken in the direction which the Bishop of Limerick desired.[77] He was clearly holding out an olive-branch. To his credit, the bishop in his second letter responded in the same spirit. He praised Lecky as a fair disputant,

and hoped that, when the time came, he would show the way in fair and liberal
dealing with his catholic countrymen.[78] A dialogue had been tentatively opened,
and had the public correspondence ended at this point, something more might
have been achieved by informal talks leading perhaps to negotiations between
Trinity and the bishops, with Lecky as mediator. For, as Bishop O'Dwyer said, it
was a great pleasure for him to be able to agree with Lecky on a number of points,
including the importance of bringing members of the two creeds together in the
course of their secular education, and also that the University of Dublin should
be the university for Irish catholics.

But the public correspondence did not end until things had been written on
both sides which made informal discussion between the bishop and the MP most
unlikely. Lecky held that in controversial writing one should always aim at
understating one's own case. What Lecky had left unsaid, however, the bishop
said for him and a little more besides. Lecky's second letter, wrote his Lordship,
amounted to the charge that a priest-ridden people were being deprived of
university education at the behest of the bishops.[79] There was some justification
in the bishop's summary of Lecky's position, but there was also a great deal of
exaggeration which did nothing to encourage the latter to continue with the
correspondence. It had served to strengthen Lecky's conviction that no compromise solution on the question of Trinity and the catholics could be found, and
only what Bishop O'Dwyer had referred to as 'a Catholic University pure and
simple' would satisfy the hierarchy. The question was left once more with the
government.

When the problem came up in parliament in January 1897, what Lecky had to
say aroused a great deal of attention for he seemed to be more than fulfilling
Bishop O'Dwyer's hopes that he would lead the way in fair and liberal dealing
with the catholics. Lecky requested the government to gratify the catholics either
by giving them a university of their own or an endowed college connected with
the Royal University. He advised the government to make sure first that their
offer would be accepted; that they be cautious about the proportion of ecclesiastical influence that might be admitted on to the governing body; and, further, that
professors be given the security of knowing that they could not be arbitrarily
dismissed by some ecclesiastical authority.[80] Lecky's speech caused a sensation,
especially since he was followed by Arthur Balfour, First Lord of the Treasury,
who announced that he had modified his former views, and was prepared to
think of a catholic university rather than a college.

At a general meeting of the hierarchy that June, a statement was issued on the
university question, a passage of which read:

> We desire to mark in particular the fair and liberal attitude taken up by Mr
> Lecky. His own personal eminence, together with the special authority
> attaching to his statements as the representative of Dublin University lend
> importance to his speech, in which we very gladly observe a tone that does
> credit to himself and to the distinguished constituency which he represents
> ... we note with very sincere pleasure the practical conclusion at which he

arrived and the expression of his hope 'that the government would see their way to gratify the desire of the Irish catholics'.[81]

The statement gave an assurance that the bishops were prepared to discuss any plans with the government; that they were prepared to accept a majority of laymen on the governing body; and that they had no intention of arbitrarily dismissing professors.

Archbishop Walsh of Dublin, the hierarchy's leading spokesman, was very pleased to be able to regard Lecky's speech, 'so reasonable and conciliatory', followed by Balfour's, as placing the university question upon an entirely new footing. He also noted that, until Lecky's speech, no person competent to speak on behalf of Trinity had declared in favour of conceding the catholic demands. He gladly recognized in Lecky an accredited exponent of the more equitable spirit which had come to prevail in Trinity. Lecky was now the leading spokesman of liberal protestant opinion favourable to the establishment of a catholic university.

The pressure was now kept up and the following year a meeting was held in the Mansion House in favour of the demand for a catholic university at which a letter from Lecky was read and was widely quoted in support of the Catholic demand.[82] On 23 March 1900, he spoke in parliament in favour of the catholic claims to denominational university education.[83]

Lecky, however, had only changed tack, not his principles. He had come to the conclusion, 'with great reluctance', that it was the duty of the state to give further encouragement to denominational and practically exclusive catholic university education in Ireland. His reasons were practical ones, for he remained opposed in principle to denominational education. Trinity had shown every disposition to attract catholic students and to guard them against the smallest interference with their faith. With the exception of O'Connell, there was scarcely any Irish catholic of real eminence in the first half of the nineteenth century who had not been educated there. Nearly all the catholic judges, the leaders of the bar and of the medical profession of that period were graduates of Trinity; but within living memory the whole force of ecclesiastical influence had been employed to deter Irish catholics from attending Trinity. The result was that few received a university education.

Although Lecky advocated catholic university education, he was only half-hearted about it:

> ... there could be no greater misfortune for Ireland than that members of the two religions in their early days should be entirely separated; that young men at a time when their hearts were warm, when their enthusiasms were at their height; and when they were forming friendships which might mould their future lives should be kept apart and should know nothing of each other ... .[84]

He was sceptical whether sectarian education ever produced the highest intellectual standard. Where there was no religious test, as in Trinity, the teaching staff could be appointed on merit and from a wider circle. Teaching in a university, however, did not come merely from the professors. 'An immense proportion' came from the stimulus of the students, and 'the more they narrowed the area from which that competition was derived, the more feeble that stimulus would become'.[85] Lecky admitted that he had 'an incurable prejudice' against the secular education of laymen being entrusted to ecclesiastics, for he believed the result would be to turn out one class of mind — credulous, emasculated, stunted and prejudiced — and another and a stronger class of mind — acidulated, exasperated and inclined to go to all lengths in opposition to what they had been taught. Although he now advocated giving the catholics the university they asked for, Lecky was very much afraid that when such a university was set up, the bishops would make even stronger efforts to prohibit catholics going to any other university.

Why was this man who held such strong views about the evils of ecclesiastical influence, and who approved of aspects of French and German legislation against catholic education,[86] prepared to advocate a line of policy diametrically opposed to his political philosophy? We could accept his statements at face value and believe that he had concluded sincerely that, in the interests of the catholics and the state, a settlement should be made, and that after half a century of efforts to solve the problem along non-sectarian lines it was idle to think that the ecclesiastics, who meanwhile got control of primary and secondary education, would be satisfied until they had a corresponding influence in higher education.

Or can we read between the lines and say that what he was attempting to do was to cut his losses, or more accurately those of Trinity? The *Freeman's Journal* had suggested in 1873 that Lecky's aim was not to please the catholics, but simply to preserve Trinity.[87] In 1895 Bishop O'Dwyer wrote that the main purpose of Lecky's remarks was to preserve intact for Trinity its privileges and emoluments.[88]

The element of truth in these remarks is that Lecky's plans for the solution of the university question did tactfully divert attention from the suggestion made by the bishops to the effect that a remodelling of the University of Dublin so as to allow a catholic college on a footing of equality with Trinity College would satisfy their demands. Lecky realized as well as any of the more forthright and less liberal defenders of Trinity that, unless a university was established which would satisfy the catholics, Trinity might be tampered with by a government anxious to placate the majority and in a manner not likely to please Trinity men. Gladstone's attempt to turn the University of Dublin into a national university had not been forgotten, and the Conservatives had shown in their land legislation and elsewhere that they were prepared to outbid the Liberals.

It had been no part of Lecky's objective to save Dublin University for protestantism. His wish was to save it from ecclesiastical influence and for the nation; his dream was that it would be accepted as a truly national and non-sectarian institution. But he believed that Irishman and catholic had come to be interchangeable terms. Trinity was not to be allowed to become national while it remained unsectarian.

Lecky had always held that since 1873 Trinity was in fact, as in law, secular, and he was proud that it was so.[89] Words like 'secular' and 'non-sectarian', which to Lecky were epithets of the highest praise, were to the Irish bishops as offensive as the waving of a Garibaldian red-shirt in front of them. Bishop Healy wrote that the university question was essentially a religious question: 'it is above and beyond politics ... It is a matter that cannot be sold or bargained for ... a sound catholic education is a pearl beyond price.'[90]

Lecky's claim that Trinity was a national institution could be too easily laughed out of court by the fact that Dublin University was the only constituency in three provinces which always returned unionists. The claim that the University was non-sectarian was nullified by the virtual boycott practised by catholics. So, Lecky felt that for his time at least he had lost the battle, and he was anxious to rescue what he could for Trinity by sincerely offering the bishops the bigger bait of a catholic university. Privately he urged the provost of Trinity to appoint catholic professors of theology, ecclesiastical history and moral philosophy on the chance that if the bishops despaired of getting a university for themselves, the time might come when they would withdraw their ban on catholics attending Trinity.[91]

Because of broken health, Lecky resigned his seat in parliament in 1902 and occupied himself with completing a revision of his *Leaders of Public Opinion in Ireland*. All his life he had remained fascinated by Irish political leadership. He had concluded that leadership in his own lifetime no longer rested with liberal nationalists like Grattan or O'Connell. Rather was Irish public opinion inspired by a kind of clerical grey eminence in the person of Paul Cullen and his successors among the hierarchy.

The views Lecky had expressed over the years on the university question make it fairly safe to surmise what he would have thought about the settlement reached in 1908. He would have agreed with Archbishop Walsh's view, or for that matter Tim Healy's, that the bill was nobody's ideal.[92] He would not have been surprised at Cardinal Logue's reference to the new National University: 'a pagan bantling dropped in the midst of us; but, please God, if we can, we will baptize it and make it Christian.'[93] He would have been disappointed that Trinity had not proved to be good enough for Irish catholics, but would have congratulated his fellow countrymen on what they had achieved: if they had not been given a catholic university at least they had got a university for catholics. But he would have feared that a university acceptable to catholics might mean more stringent restrictions on catholics becoming students at Trinity. He would have been worried lest what was by charter non-denominational should turn out to be denominational in practice. He would have been pleased, however, that his own formula, national and secular, had been the basis of the settlement. And he would have been hopeful that the spread of higher education among his catholic countrymen would redress the balance in favour of lay public opinion, as against clerical influences in Ireland.

The best of Lecky's writing was now behind him. Apart from the occasional essays, published speeches and book reviews, he managed, during his years in parliament, to write essays on Gibbon and Carlyle and rewrite his earlier essay on Swift as a leader of Irish public opinion, for introductions to special editions of the works of these authors. He turned down Lord Acton's invitation to contribute to the *Cambridge Modern History* a chapter on eighteenth-century England, and especially a chapter on the French Revolution, which Acton said no one could do better than Lecky. He did agree, however, to do a chapter on Canning for Volume IX of the *Cambridge Modern History* since that was not wanted so urgently, but he never completed it. For the cabinet edition of *Democracy and Liberty* (1898), he wrote a new and long introduction, largely devoted to a critical and bitter appraisal of Gladstone. This was in striking contrast to the many eulogies that had appeared on Gladstone's death.

His longest work during these years was his *The Map of Life: Conduct and Character* (1899), based on thoughts and observations he had written down in his commonplace books over the years. The question of free will as opposed to determinism occupied a prominent place in the Victorian mind. Lecky's position was that, while the current of history, the natural environment and human physiology did severely restrict the domain of free will, nevertheless it did exist. The exercise of this free will shaped character and had an influence on the conduct of life. In *Rationalism* and *Morals* he had argued for the independence of both the reasoning and the moral faculties in man. In his political history, in his thinking about current politics and in his own political life he was greatly concerned about reason and morality in public affairs as against mass emotions, class cupidity, party and individual selfishness. *The Map of Life* was clearly the work of a historian active in public life, seeking to lay down rules for the guidance of others based upon his own experience, observations and high standards.

A good deal in the book had to do with questions of conscience, of right and wrong, of the relationship between public and private morality, and of the need for limits to moral compromise in legal, military and political affairs. His examples came not only from history, as one might expect, but especially from his own fresh experience of parliamentary life. Yet 'no doctor would prescribe for the slightest malady, no lawyer would advise in the easiest case, no wise man would act in the simplest transactions of private business or would give an opinion to his neighbour at a dinner party without more knowledge of the subject than that on which a member of parliament is often obliged to vote.'[94] He had found that experience initially 'very painful,' but had soon realized that 'for good or evil this system is absolutely indispensable to the working of the machine.' Whatever conclusion men may arrive at in the seclusion of their studies when they take part in active political life they will find it necessary to make large allowances.[95] The distinction between right and wrong, Lecky had discovered, was not so easy in public affairs as it was in private life. In *The Map of Life*, health, happiness, money, success, marriage, time and death were all touched upon in a manner that had something of the character of the lay sermon and of the Victorian manuals of good manners and proper behaviour. The provost of

Trinity College, George Salmon, wrote that if he had not given up preaching, he would have found in *The Map of Life* subjects for sermons for a long time to come. The comment was intended as a compliment and it was taken as such, but it accurately described the book's rather unctuous tone. Its theories were more appropriate to the pulpit than to the political platform. Salmon went on to say that in a literary age a lay preacher could command the attention of a larger audience than any clergyman. This must have given great consolation to Lecky, who had abandoned the idea of a clergyman's life in order to join Carlyle's literary priesthood. At the end of that career, the undisguised preaching of *The Map of Life* earned him the plaudits of those whose approval he esteemed highly. The 2000 copies of the first printing were sold out in a week.

The book reflected the public morality and dominant virtues of Victorian England. Lecky's doubts about the blessings attendant on the decline in infant mortality, and his attitude to the 'dangers of ill-considered charities' strike an odd note in the days of the welfare state. Because of the manner of its composition, *The Map of Life* reiterated many of the views that Lecky had already expressed in his earlier work. Although it had few very profound or original ideas, it had the air of a work of sound sense and of a mellow wisdom. Whenever he discussed issues of public morality, Ireland and Gladstone were never very far from his thoughts. Fenianism, the Land League and the catholic priesthood with 'the countless frauds, outrages and oppressions' that he associated with these aspects of contemporary Irish life 'supported and stimulated some of the worst moral perversions of modern times.'[96]

An attack of influenza in the spring of 1901 was followed by a weakening heart condition from which Lecky was never fully to recover. He was unable to enjoy his favourite pastime of walking, he had to restrict his attendance at parliament and curb his literary work. He resigned his seat in December 1902. In a postscript to his letter of resignation to the provost, he wrote: 'I wish TCD would carry out their scheme of giving degrees to women'.[97] He devoted much of the remainder of his invalid life to completing the revision of the third edition of his *Leaders of Public Opinion in Ireland*, an objective he had had in mind since Gladstone's conversion to home rule in 1886 had bestowed on it a sudden popularity and invested it with a unique authority. He now had the opportunity of revising a work that had given so much political 'scandal'. The revision amounted to his final testament on contemporary Irish politics, as well as on Irish history of the eighteenth and early nineteenth centuries. Since the second edition in 1871, Lecky's knowledge of the period had improved and his opinions had long matured. Unionism had developed into a leading article of his political credo. His nationalism and liberalism had contracted in the face of advancing democracy and socialism. All this was reflected in the two volumes which replaced the original single volume of *Leaders*.

Enlargement, revision and a great measure of rewriting went into the third edition published in the spring of 1903. The portraits of the leaders, although supplemented by much new material, remained essentially as they had been when outlined in 1861. Lecky's respect for O'Connell had increased with the years, although the two tunes, praise and denunciation of O'Connell, continued to run concurrently in his mind. The portrait of O'Connell had grown to a full volume; Grattan filled two-thirds of another volume, but Swift had disappeared.

A slight but very significant change occurred in the book's title. The two earlier editions had both been called *The Leaders of Public Opinion in Ireland.* The last edition omitted the definite article. That Lecky himself was in the true tradition marked out by the Irish constitutional leaders he never doubted. The illusion that it was the only line of importance or influence was no longer possible after Fenianism, Parnellism and agrarianism. Other lines besides that marked out by Swift, Flood, Grattan and O'Connell had emerged. This was the significance of the change in title.

Lecky insisted that the changes he made in the final edition were chiefly the result of his greater knowledge,[98] and it must be admitted that the historian was anxious to revise in the light of further research done for his study of the eighteenth century. The fruits of this research, however, may be seen to best advantage in his volumes on eighteenth-century Ireland and England, for the *Leaders*, being essays, provided more readily a rostrum for the expression of personal politics. The incorporation of this new material in the 1903 edition undoubtedly accounts for some alterations, but Lecky's protest should not blind us to the effects that controversy had on him, nor to the political motivation behind the revision. It is clear that he carefully retouched those passages that had given most scandal. He made his alterations in his own copies of the earlier editions, and pasted in additional pages of manuscript. Phrases in the 1871 edition such as 'the national sentiment',[99] 'the liberties of Ireland',[100] 'the freedom of his country',[101] 'the independence of Ireland',[102] 'the will of the people',[103] 'patriotism',[104] 'the patriotic party',[105] were deleted. Where 'the Irish people' had occurred, he crossed out the words and wrote 'Irish protestants'[106] instead. And the rhetoric of a phrase like 'maddened by centuries of oppression' was toned down to the prosaic 'exasperated by many grievances.'[107]

Indicative of this toning down process is the number of Grattan's volunteers given in the three editions. There were, according to Lecky in 1861, 80,000 volunteers. The passage was rewritten in 1871, some of the tinsel removed, and the figure reduced to 60,000. The passage was again rewritten in 1903, more of the patriotic enthusiasm was excluded, and the figure became 40,000.[108] These descending numerals represent the fall in the barometer of Lecky's nationalism.

Lecky had roundly condemned the Union in 1871, and although he still disapproved of the manner by which it had been accomplished, he was much more charitable towards the motives of Pitt and his colleagues and he now made it clear that he was for a united kingdom. Missing from the third edition was the grand ministerial design, beginning with the recall of Fitzwilliam and ending in the Union. The 1798 Rebellion, which had been part of the plot, was now written up as an uprising of the French-influenced sections of the people against a loyal Irish parliament.[109] Lecky was careful to blame Pitt less for his political morality than for his failure in the execution of the scheme to unite the two peoples. Indeed what Lecky had described as the 'bribery' of the borough owners in the second edition, he now justified as 'compensation' for the loss of property.[110] The Union, which had been labelled a 'crime', was now described with the neutral word 'transaction'[111] (as if the Acton in Lecky of 1871 had become the von Ranke of 1903). Pitt was portrayed as simply blundering, where earlier he had been made to appear malevolent.[112]

For the retelling of the Union story, Lecky had used a great deal of the same facts, the same pieces of the jigsaw; but they were now set in different combinations and produced an altogether different effect. The results were further coloured by his use of phrases associated more with Froude. He now wrote about the 'profound degradation of the Irish character'. In fairness, it should be added that he blamed the penal laws for this, but he could now toy with the idea that Ireland might have been raised in the scale of civilization if the penal laws had succeeded; and he reminded his readers of what might have happened if the catholic party had won in 1689.[113] The earlier Lecky had been careful to give the extenuating circumstances.[114] The 1903 edition of *Leaders* had accentuated his unionism without expressly recanting his earlier nationalist opinions.

The view taken by the nationalist reviewers was that what had been gained on the roundabout of Lecky's research and experience was a big price to be asked to pay for what had been lost on the swings of patriotic enthusiasm and imagination.[115] From the standpoint of scholarship, the essay on O'Connell, with its sober impartiality, was a masterpiece of historical insight.

Leaders was to be Lecky's last major work. He was engaged on a selection and revision of occasional pieces for a collection of historical and political essays, posthumously published in 1908, when he died suddenly in his library in London on 22 October 1903, aged sixty-five. Following the funeral service in St Patrick's Cathedral, he was buried in Mount Jerome Cemetry, Dublin. Lecky had died childless. In his will, apart from £500 bequeathed to his sister, he left the remainder of his property both real and personal to his wife, the sole executrix. The gross value of his estate at the time of his death amounted to £30,127, on which £1768 estate duty was paid.

When Mrs Lecky died in 1912, she left to Trinity College Lecky's library, and a substantial sum from her husband's Irish property and estate to endow a chair to be called the Lecky Chair of History. A line of distinguished historians has occupied this chair since its foundation — W. Alison Phillips, Edmund Curtis, Costantia Maxwell, J. Otway-Ruthven, James Lydon. Through this endowment, Lecky continues to make his contribution to the progress of historical studies.

Chapter 10

Conclusion

There was nothing particularly distinguished about Lecky's methods and techniques as a historian. He kept to a rigorous work routine and carefully rationed his social life. Unlimited patience, he said, was the first condition of doing anything worthwhile in history. He was a firm advocate of the practice of regular writing, even for moderate amounts of time. Lecky turned down numerous requests to do articles, occasional pieces, lectures and book reviews, for he believed in concentrating his energies on the particular volume on hand. His ambition was to turn from the fragmentary and the ephemeral, and to the limit of his capacity to embody his best thoughts in elaborate, complete and well-digested works of enduring value.

He read rapidly, and got through a volume a day while working on *Rationalism*. He made relatively brief notes, although in great quantities, and these were committed to notebooks that could fit into a coat-pocket. In the early years, he found himself so much alone reading his way through various libraries on the Continent that, he said, writing became for him a necessary vent. It was his experience that after a certain amount of reading his mind became so crowded with thoughts and arguments floating about half-formed that he found relief only in giving these shape and expression.

Rewriting for Lecky was an essential part of the historian's craft. He said once that he rarely finished a chapter without having to recast it thoroughly. He attributed most improvements in his own style either to condensation which, he said, was the secret of forceful writing, or to increased accuracy and delicacy of distinction. The minute alterations he made in each new edition of his works are adequate testimony of the meticulous care with which he revised.

His prose was fluent and lucid, but generally unexciting. Modelling himself on Emerson and Grattan, he tried to crystallize political wisdom in a single shining sentence, but, despite the continuous striving, only rarely did he come up with anything nearly as memorable as Acton's aphorisms. His writing lacked the dramatic and colourful quality of Froude's, but he was superior to Froude in the dispassionate analysis of long-term movements. It was a relief, said W.S. Lilly, to turn to the admirable Lecky after the brilliant but partisan Froude.[1]

Rationalism and *Morals*, belonging to the genre of the history of ideas and customs, were potentially the most seminal of Lecky's books. They made up, as J.M. Robertson said in 1895, 'the most considerable body of sociological history produced by any living English writer'.[2] The eulogy bestowed on them by many qualified reviewers was highly gratifying to Lecky. Percipient critics, like Acton and George Eliot, thought less of them, and it is true that these works have exhibited none of the staying power of his more solid history of eighteenth-century England and Ireland. In his works on European morals and rationalism, there was nothing very original about Lecky's matter, which he had gleaned from a great variety of secondary sources. His selection and combination of facts, however, had in their time a certain freshness.

It is important to remember that *Rationalism* and *Morals*, like all his books, were not written for professionals and academics but for the general educated public. Lecky has to be considered, therefore, not merely for his place in historiography, but also for his contributions as a sort of high-class journalist, popularizer and educator in the development of nineteenth-century civilization. Lecky helped to spread the leaven of historical thinking through the educated public, and thereby performed a function akin to that of the *philosophe* of the early eighteenth century, who had made society more scientifically conscious. He possessed a keen sense of the changes that take place in 'climates of opinion', and had argued that they were more often the result of general movement and of development and progress in all its related forms than of any logical argument. This had been indeed the recurring theme of both *Rationalism* and *Morals*. Literary popularization was not with him a term of reproach; it played, rather, a major role in the historical process, making possible the progress of civilization from one stage to the next and higher level.

It would be comparatively easy to list Lecky's weaknesses as a historian. Except for his narrative of the later decades of eighteenth-century Ireland, he had made little use of original manuscript material. This is to be regretted if we are to judge even by the limited use he made of material in the state paper offices of Dublin, Paris and London. He relied too heavily on the published memoirs, speeches and correspondence of people like Grattan, Charlemont and Burke, and tended to adopt their particular attitudes towards eighteenth-century questions. He paid scant attention to newspapers as a source of public opinion and information. Large sections of his volumes on Ireland in the eighteenth century were based upon the official correspondence between Dublin and London. *Ireland*, therefore, was largely the political, constitutional and administrative history of Anglo-Irish relations. Like other contemporary historians, Lecky underrated the social and economic aspects of history.

In theory, Lecky regarded the application of the moral standards of one age to another as dangerously misleading. In practice he judged the 'corruption' employed by eighteenth-century governments of Ireland very severely, and from a Whig and Victorian standpoint. His anti-democratic, landlord and conservative prejudices forced their way into his historical writing despite his best efforts to exclude them. Sometimes, therefore, he thought he was being wise when in fact he was only being biased. His attempts to look at all aspects of a question impartially, and his habit of taking in turn the best man on opposite sides led him occasionally into contradictions. Yet in spite of all his defects, *Ireland* remains one of the great books on Irish history.

To write at all, Lecky required freedom from street noises, trouble and care. His wife saw to it that he got a great deal of this freedom. She managed his domestic affairs for him, while an agent took care of his landed estate. This sheltered and cushioned life had its own nemesis: it left him unable to understand anything but the rational and organized. As a consequence he underestimated, misinterpreted or ignored the emotional storms and irrational forces in history and in his own society. These things were incomprehensible to his nineteenth-century philosophy of rationalism, liberalism and organized progress. He could believe that the 'national sentiment' in Ireland was less in the days of the home rule and Land League agitations than at any previous period. He too readily accepted the opinions of lesser and not so well informed minds about such possibilities as the killing of home rule with land reform. Although he acknowledged that 'the facts of history have been largely governed by its fictions',[3] in his own political career he failed to appreciate the depth and force of the historical myths which his work had helped to create and which inspired that Irish nationalism with which he strongly disagreed.

It was where he felt distaste and repulsion strongest that he often succeeded best. Although disgusted by O'Connell's 'vulgarity', Lecky's portrait of the catholic leader was sensitive. Although outraged by Gladstone's 'political immorality', his was a brilliant if distorted sketch of the GOM. He hated religious intolerance and yet wrote an excellent outline of the penal laws. The agrarian agitation of his own time terrified him, and yet he wrote a fine account of the Irish land troubles. Eighteenth-century Irish legislative independence aroused his most generous enthusiasms, yet he devoted much more space to its demise than to its birth. He once wrote that Irish history offered 'an invaluable study of morbid anatomy'.[4] He was himself attracted not only by the morbid nature of Irish history, but also by general subjects which to his Victorian mind were distasteful — miracles, magic, monasticism, medieval morality, theological controversy, obscurantism, religious persecution, sectarianism, massacre, democracy and socialism. More than most of his contemporaries, he succeeded in carrying into practice the dictum of both Coleridge and Acton about putting the point of view one disliked even better than it could be put by its best adherents.

Among the virtues Lecky possessed as a historian must also be enumerated the sweep of his learning; the determination to be fair; the balanced judgment; and the regard for truth as the supreme concern of the historian. There was also his conviction that history dealt with movement and not with still-life pictures, however colourful. In everything he studied, he attempted to withdraw to an intellectual height in order to get into proper focus the procession of events.

J.F. Rhodes and S.R. Gardiner both referred to his historical 'divination' even where he was short on original research.[5] Gladstone said that neither Macaulay nor Carlyle could come near Lecky in his 'real insight' into the motives of statesmen.[6] Acton thought that political wisdom might be gleaned from his history of England in the eighteenth century, and that his account of the French Revolution was the best to date in English. Americans like Becker, Beard, Beer and Henry Adams considered his discussion of the American Revolution ahead of anything else in its time.[7] Indeed Lecky's work was more highly regarded in the USA than in Britain. But although Lecky had many discriminating admirers of different aspects of his work, and could even be said to have belonged to a particular historico-sociological circle, he never created anything remotely like a school.

He was very much a man of his own time — a Victorian political moralist who chose history as the vehicle of his teaching. An essay on the Boer War was called 'Moral Aspects of the South African War'. His favourite among his own works was the two-volume history of European morals. The moralist in him denounced and censured cruelty, religious intolerance, persecution, tyranny, injustice, exaggeration and misrepresentation wherever he found them in history. He held that the strongest forces of history were the moral ones, and that by observing the moral current, one could best cast the horoscope of a nation.[8] Belief in progress, in mid-century liberalism, political economy and science, as well as in the benefits of education, dedication to one's duty, the virtues of self-help and all that passed generally for Victorian morality were strong with him.

As his work progressed, it became apparent that Lecky belonged more closely to the tradition of the English and French writers who regarded the historian more as a narrator than a scientist. He shared more in common with Michelet, Macaulay, Carlyle and even Froude than he did with Ranke, Acton, Stubbs or Bury. Although he held that the historian was a painter and not an advocate or a politician, he also insisted that the truth of the picture depended on judicious and accurate shading. He was more of a philosophic historian than a literary one, and he appreciated better than Acton all that the eighteenth century had accomplished for historical scholarship, especially in the work of Gibbon and Voltaire. He might, therefore, be described not only as one of the last of the great line of amateur literary historians writing in English, but also as one of the last of the historiographical school of the Enlightenment, which included Vico as well as Burke.

The fact that Lecky was well-informed and discriminating in his judgments about the past did not necessarily ensure accuracy in his assessments of the present. Much less was it any guarantee of political wisdom and vision. He held that great men were like great mountains, surrounded and obscured by the lower peaks, and that it was only from a distance that their true greatness could be appreciated. Yet he failed drastically to get the true measure of some of the personalities of his own time like Gladstone, Parnell and Davitt. Lecky's published condemnation of Gladstone was issued with almost indecent haste after the latter's death. He also realized that 'the great mass of obscure, suffering, inarticulate humanity' often escaped the historian's notice. However much he was himself aware of the sufferings and oppression of the eighteenth-century Irish catholics, the plight of the contemporary Land League peasants elicited little public sympathy from him.

For a man who had so successfully chartered the great movements of the past, he often failed to make out the direction of affairs in his own time. His prophesies were sometimes very wide of the mark. This should not have worried him unduly, for he believed that the man who happened to make the correct forecasts was too easily overrated. Occasionally he displayed an impressive ability to read the signs and map the tendencies of the times. Whenever he did see that the demand for home rule must end in a democratic Irish republic, all that the vision brought him was an unmitigated pessimism. Perhaps he should have remembered what he once had said, that 'chance' played so big a part in human affairs that the reckless obstructionist may prove more right than the cautious statesman.[9]

As a contemporary politician he was at his best when pleading for moderation, just dealing and common sense. These virtues were in evidence, for example, when he was found suggesting reasonable compromise solutions to the Irish university question, or again when advocating caution in the matter of land legislation, responsibility regarding the facile promises made to the new democratic electorate, and statesmanship, as distinct from immediate political advantage. Lecky's head was greater than his heart, and emotion played a lesser role than reason in his career.

Lecky's contribution to politics was a powerful one. In a nationalist and liberal tradition, he denounced British crime in Ireland. No other historical writer had contributed so much to the concept of the moral and constitutional invalidity of the Act of Union of 1800. He had made out a strong case for the granting of historical justice to Ireland and for the restoration of an Irish parliament. Although he had not become the political leader of his early dreams, and although Parnell (whose way he had helped to prepare) was far from being the leader he had hoped for, still it was Lecky who had done much to cultivate the leader-ideal in Ireland. He had underscored the dangerous political lesson that Britain only yielded to agitation.[10] Even the tactics he had described in 1861 as the probable lines of political action were followed out to the letter by the Parnellites.[11]

Lecky's contribution was all the more effective because of his literary fame and his reputation for impartiality. More than any Irishman of his time he had the ear of the intelligent English public. 'I am tempted to quote Mr Lecky against himself' Gladstone wrote.[12] *The Nation* said that wherever Lecky went wrong, he could be answered by Lecky.[13]

Thus Lecky had become a leader of Irish public opinion, but not on his own terms.

His dream had turned into the nightmare of Parnellism. His nationality principle had been taken over and used in a manner he deplored. From the late 1870s onwards whenever Lecky looked into the political mirror, what he saw there was a distortion of his own early patriotic dream. He saw not his own image but that of Parnell — like himself an Irish protestant landlord nationalist, hungry for political power; ruthless, however, in the methods by which he pursued it; and authoritarian in his leadership over a part-agrarian, part-Fenian, part-constitutional and largely sectarian movement. From this vision Lecky turned his head in disgust. The seat in parliament had evaded him while he most wished for it. His liberalism had had to come to terms with conservatism. His admiration for Gladstone had turned to bitterness. The pessimism induced by the home rule experience found expression in his *Democracy and Liberty*. He had become one of the late Victorian prophets of doom, but later generations were to be unfortunate enough to see some of his darkest forecasts more than fulfilled.

In his earlier years he would have liked to have worn what he called 'the mantle of Grattan'. In a certain sense he had worn it only too well, but it was a hundred years out of fashion, and he cut a quaint figure before political friends and foes alike, so that allies could never fully claim him nor political opponents ever reject him. He pointed out the absurdity of the home rulers who had argued that because of Grattan's parliament of 1782 there must follow a home rule parliament. But was he himself not guilty of the personal absurdity of trying to be a Henry Grattan in the circumstances of 1882? He once wrote: 'a public man who in framing his course followed blindly in the steps of the heroes or reformers of the past would be like a mariner who set his sails to the winds of yesterday'.[14] Yet this is a comment not altogether inapplicable to Lecky himself. For again, to quote verse which he wrote badly, but sometimes wisely:

> The dead are still our masters, and a power from the tomb
> Can shape the characters of men, their conduct and their doom.[15]

Lecky's message that Grattan's ideas were the ideal expression of what Ireland had ever wanted, or could in future ever desire, was not acceptable in the circumstances of an emerging democracy. Yet home rulers never mentioned him without the utmost respect because he had 'done more than any living man to keep alive the spirit of nationality amongst the Irish catholics'.[16] On the other hand, unionists like the Duke of Argyll found it hard to stomach his advice about being impartial in historical writings.[17] But Lecky lacked the sense of humour and detachment that would have enabled him to enjoy the situation in which he supplied both home rulers and unionists with the materials for their controversy. The historian, he once explained, must place himself in the point of view of the best man on both sides and bring out the full sense of opposing arguments.[18] It was Lecky's dilemma that, in the home rule argument, he was himself the best man on both sides.

Tom Kettle was once reported as saying of Lecky that 'he would have been an Irish patriot had we supported him by buying his books'.[19] What is important is that Lecky was an absentee man-of-letters with Britain as his chief market. But Lecky was never simply a landlord. He was above all an intellectual who had gathered into his own life and writings the complexities and contradictions of the contemporary situation. History, he once noted in a commonplace book, must never avoid contradictions in tendencies.[20] His own life and work were living witness to this truth. In the time of the 'pope's brassband', Lecky considered himself a repealer. In the time of the Fenians, he described himself as a Young Irelander. In the time of Butt, he was a long-term federalist. In the time of Parnell, he was prepared to be a moderate home ruler. When the majority of his countrymen were nationalists and employing his work in their cause, he had gone unionist.

With the emergence and spread of the Irish-Ireland ideal, Lecky's work began to occupy an even more remote shelf in Ireland's political library. The most influential of the Irish-Ireland social and cultural nationalists despised the eighteenth century and all it represented. The institutions, parliament and society which were so anglicized as to be unaware and unimpressed by the ancient civilization of Gaelic Ireland, were for that reason rejected by Douglas Hyde and Eoin MacNeill, the founders of the Gaelic League and advocates of the philosophy of de-anglicization. To them and their followers, the eighteenth century was the long dark winter of Irish history.

Lecky's golden century was described by D.P. Moran, one of the ablest propagandists of the Irish-Ireland ideal, as the period in which Ireland had lost its identity and direction and had gone politically and culturally astray. The socialist-republican martyr of 1916, James Connolly, in *Labour in Irish History*, referred to the eighteenth century as the *via dolorosa* of Ireland's past. And in striking contrast with Lecky, he regarded Grattan's parliament as the most unrepresentative, corrupt, partisan and miserable assembly in history.

The fact that the 'hidden Ireland' and poetry of the Gaelic-speaking peasantry was altogether absent from Lecky's account of the eighteenth century was brilliantly underscored in the work of Daniel Corkery. In most of the historical studies of the Irish-Irelanders — Alice Stopford Green's *The Making of Ireland and Its Undoing*, for example — the concentration was on ancient and medieval Ireland before its conquest through anglicization. The effects of the Irish-Ireland movement on the Irishman's attitude to his history were dramatic. Standish O'Grady spoke for all these cultural, social and literary renaissance nationalists when he said that the heroic age of Ireland was not a tradition but a prophesy as yet unfulfilled. Grattan was removed from his pedestal as national hero, and in his place was substituted the image of the legendary knight of Gaelic Ireland, Cuchulainn, giving his life-blood in defence of his people. A prosaic history such as that offered by Lecky had little nourishment for the poets and dreamers of Irish-Ireland.

In the few instances after the 1890s where Lecky's historical work was still felt as a strong nationalist impulse, his was by no means the only influence. It is said of Edward Martyn, the Galway landlord playwright, and art patron that in 1899 he read Lecky's *Ireland*, and for the first time a true conception of Irish history flashed upon him, and he became at once a nationalist.[21] The fact that soon afterwards Martyn refused to allow the British national anthem to be played in his home; that he protested against the visit to Ireland of King Edward VII; that subsequently he became president of Sinn Fein, a member of the executive committee of the Gaelic League and contributed by pen and purse to the Irish Literary Theatre only emphasizes the gulf between his kind of nationalism and Lecky's.

Similarly, the historical interpretations which lay at the basis of Arthur Griffith's Sinn Fein movement, and his dual monarchy principle in particular, owed much that was unacknowledged to Lecky's work. Griffith's paper, *United Irishman*, once conceded that Lecky had considerable merits as a historian, but thought that they had been occasionally exaggerated. The paper also looked forward to the emergence of a greater and more truly nationalist historian, and tried to twist at least one memorable passage of *Leaders* into reading that all the genius of Ireland belonged to the separatist tradition.[22]

Nations, Lecky had once written, were too often judged by the men they produced, and too seldom by the men they followed or the men they admired. The Irishmen whom Lecky most admired — Burke, Grattan and even O'Connell in the past, Horace Plunkett and Gavan Duffy in his own time — were most certainly not the men whom the majority of his countrymen in the early twentieth century idolized. It was Cuchulainn instead of Grattan; Tone, the father of republicanism, meant much more to them than Burke; and the bearers of the physical force and Fenian separatist tradition had triumphed over O'Connell.

The fusion, at white heat, of the Irish-Ireland and physical force separatist traditions is best represented in Padraig Pearse. His references to Lecky are clear indications of how the new Irish nationalists of the twentieth century regarded Lecky's worth. Pearse was proud of the fact that his Irish-Ireland school, Scoil Éanna, was first housed in Cullenswood House, which had once belonged to Lecky's grandfather. Commenting on this fact in his school journal in 1909, Pearse wrote:

> So our school-house has already a very worthy tradition of scholarship and devotion to Ireland, not indeed founded on so secure and right a basis as ours, but sincere, unwavering, life-long.[23]

During a meeting of the first Dail in 1919 Eamon de Valera quoted with approval a passage from Lecky's *Democracy and Liberty* which began: 'Every government of one nationality by another is of the nature of slavery, and is essentially illegitimate ...'[24] The mention of Lecky's name meant perhaps little more to the majority of the president's audience than just another of those curious, abstruse references they were learning to expect from the most recent charismatic leader of public opinion in Ireland, one who owed little to Lecky beyond the single quotation.

In a country other than Ireland, or in Ireland at some other time, Lecky might well have had a more direct and more lasting impact on political affairs. Had he been English, and not Anglo-Irish, he might well have made a mark alongside other literary politicians of the period. His tragedy, however, was to be born and to grow up neither Irish nor English at a time when his Anglo-Irish landlord class were being forced to make a conscious choice between the two. But Lecky, who had not got it in him to found a school of sociological history in England, or even to take up the leadership and direction of such a school where Buckle had left off, was no more capable of becoming the Irish political leader of his dreams. He was always the intellectual hermaphrodite, one side of whom cancelled out the other, just as his historical apology for Irish independence had balanced his political arguments in favour of the Union.

Given the actual circumstances in which his life was cast, his career made only a limited and indirect impact on the Ireland of his own time. He had little

influence in determining the final shape of Anglo-Irish relations and none at all
on the two Ireland's, north and south, which have emerged since his death. Of
course this may be all to Ireland's loss. Indeed, in view of the religious discrimination that has occasionally disfigured the scene during the twentieth century no
one can regard his comments on sectarianism as irrelevant to the current Irish
situation. In the revolutionary Ireland of his time, political giants dwarfed the
man of moderation. He had none of the glamour of Parnell; and his fellow
member for the University of Dublin, Edward Carson, overshadowed him in the
unionist camp.

Lecky was not the man for the intense political season in which he lived. In a
more moderate historical climate — after nationalism, socialism and democracy
have spent their early force — his old-fashioned concern for the liberty of the
individual and his warnings against the bureaucracy of the modern state and the
techniques of modern political bosses may merit more attention. A more understanding Ireland seeking to claim all the strands that have gone into its making
may do something to reinstate him in his patrimony. Otherwise his role in
history has been that of the great lost leader of public opinion in Ireland.

Appendix

Lecky, Mark Twain and Literary History

W.J. Mc Cormack

Perhaps the most appropriate concept under which to consider the life and achievement of William Edward Hartpole Lecky is one given its modern significance by Max Weber – the concept of *Beruf*, now generally translated as 'profession' but with a residual sense of 'calling'. Donal McCartney has admirably drawn attention to the decision Lecky made early in life to commit himself to literature rather than to holy orders. At first glance it may not seem that 'literature' is the aptest word, or that rejection of a clerical career constitutes a calling. Lecky wrote no novels or plays, and the few poems he committed to print were better committed to the waste-paper basket. As a writer he is remembered for his histories, and a few late essays on contemporary political questions. Moreover, his life was well upholstered; unlike the landed gentry who transmigrated into the Irish Literary Revival (Augusta Gregory, Edward Martyn, George Moore and – at a generation's distance – J.M. Synge), Lecky's real estate lay in the prosperous midlands. Yet the biographer's formulation is well focused: literature in Lecky's youth still admitted under its banner work written outside the privileged *genres*, and the nature of the historian's commitment to this kind of literary endeavour was (in the highest sense) vocational.

If this now sounds anachronistic or paradoxical, a further detail of the same kind should be promptly added so as to present the relationship of Lecky to literary history in something like its full complexity. For too long such relationships have been explored in terms of influence, by tracing the impact of the non-literary upon the literary. Nowadays, theories of intertextuality have added a more sophisticated glamour to the anxiety of influence-hunting. But it remains to the literary historian to reveal the dynamics of an evolving cultural pattern in which definitions of the literary are undergoing subtle change and the passive or secondary condition of the literary text is emancipated from the presumptions of causality. In terms of the present argument, we are concerned with the relationship between Lecky's historical writing and the last major work of Mark Twain, the problematic *Connecticut Yankee in King Arthur's Court*.

In his youth, Lecky was shy of such fame as the company of fellow writers might bestow. At the Tennysons' Isle of Wight retreat, he told William Allingham in May 1868 that he saw little use 'in knowing Authors personally', an observation not wholly convincing in the company he was then keeping. (Allingham concluded that personality did not interest Lecky in any case.) Of course he was only thirty at the time, a young man abroad and feeling distinctly negative about his home country. Ireland, he declared to the Ballyshannon man, was low intellectually, John Tyndall 'her best representative'.[1]

The idea that Ireland might be represented by an atheistical physicist is as unexpected as the declaration that historical writing should be treated as literature. These surprises are of course aspects of a more comprehensive difficulty, that of appreciating the particular social relations which constituted Victorian Ireland or, to be more accurate, constituted the full hegemony of the United Kingdom of Great Britain and Ireland. Doubtless, complex economic and political issues deserve consideration here, but it is possible to indicate outlines in less abstract fashion. Historians of English literature have noted that a radical break occurs between the generation which included Dickens, Thackeray and George Eliot and that which variously embraced the young Henry James, George Gissing and Thomas Hardy. Basically, the distinction is constructed on the greatly augmented sense of alienation among the later novelists, their lack of any broad social constituency, the absense of shared values uniting writer and reader. A not dissimilar break could be identified in Irish terms, with the clubbable Lovers, Levers, and Le Fanus being comprehensively transcended by the fractious coterie of social misfits known to the world as the Literary Revival.

Lecky came to maturity while the older of these two filiations, intellectually undistinguished as he plainly saw, was still in the ascendant. The younger was nonetheless imminent, even palpably so. Though he was more than twenty-five years Yeats's senior, Lecky was only in his mid-teens when Oscar Wilde was born in 1854. This transitional timetable conditions his work in a variety of ways, rendering him in one perspective a Victorian sage, in another a proto-modern. He tended the dying Carlyle and yet he also foresaw the ominous consequences for the twentieth century of accelerating military expenditure in the 1880s and '90s. One historiographer, writing on the eve of the Second World War, even assigned to Lecky a prophetic role, all the more ironic given W.B. Yeats's political leanings in the 1930s. B.E. Lippincott, presenting Lecky as a Victorian critic of democracy, noted that 'in his observation that propertied groups of the middle class may be driven to the use of force in order to defend constitutional liberty, he hinted at a fundamental element in fascism.'[2]

But in reading Lecky as 'a signpost to the twentieth century', Lippincott was too urgently affected by the times in which he was writing to assess dispassionately the times in which Lecky had written. It would be foolish, however, wholly to cut off the Victorian past from the succeeding age, for there is now a greater appreciation of the very early point at which the totalitarianism of the twentieth century began to articulate itself, in France and Germany, if not in Britain.

As a transitional figure, it is symptomatic that the young Lecky should have picked on Tyndall almost as a model. Thomas Carlyle had no time for evolution or agnosticism, yet he found ways of tolerating Tyndall as a companion – he was Irish 'but not an inaccurate Irishman'; he was 'jocular, and not without a touch of blarney'.[3] A generation later, Yeats could not so readily overcome his *ressentiment*, for he was unable to forgive Huxley and Tyndall for depriving him of 'the simple-minded religion' of his childhood. Instead, he sought

> a new religion, almost an infallible Church of poetic tradition, of a fardel of
> stories, and of personages, and of emotions, inseparable from their first
> expression, passed on from generation to generation by poets and painters
> with some help from philosohers and theologians. I wished for a world
> where I could discover this tradition perpetually, and not in pictures and in
> poems only, but in tiles round the chimney piece and in the hangings that
> kept out the draught.[4]

One should not pass lightly over the domestic details in this response to the
crisis of belief, even if its most significant manifestations had occurred long
before Yeats's day. They signify with precision a sense of lost intimacy which the
past allegedly had known. They mutely invoke the kitchen, couch and kirk of a
related authoritarian nostalgia. The desire to find a world where tradition might
be perpetual required nothing less than a religion. And such a creed would be
obliged to oppose itself totally to any historical inquiry which might jeopardise
the new totality. Just how thoroughly Yeats was prepared to re-write the history
of the Irish eighteenth century in his final defence of a totalitarian politics
remains of course a matter for investigation elsewhere.

Nothing of this kind was visible to the mid-Victorians. The idea that culture –
and especially literary culture – provided a substitute for religious orthodoxy in
the lives of Victorian men and women is generally associated with Matthew
Arnold. We may do Lecky a disservice by linking his name to Arnold's; *Friendship's Garland* is not in great demand just now. Yet Arnold and Lecky together
deserve more than a moment's thought. They both identified Edmund Burke as
a political thinker peculiarly relevant in the latter half of the nineteenth century.
If Lecky was the earlier in his enthusiasm, and generally the better informed of
the two, Arnold can take credit for republishing Burke's miscellaneous writings
on Ireland. Each should be read through the medium of the other: Arnold is
unlikely to have sponsored Burke successfully in 1881 had not the stage been
prepared by various other publications, including Lecky's *Leaders of Public
Opinion in Ireland*. The relationship is a fully complementary one, for the image
of Burke which first registers in the third volume of Lecky's *History of England*
(published in April 1882) and which increases in power thereafter, is supported by
Arnold's efforts to revive general interest in the Old Whig.

And yet there is also a sense in which the comparison of Arnold and Lecky is
valuable precisely because it brings out the degree to which they differed on the
great issue of the day – belief. Lecky began early as a cool analyst of superstition
and as a historian of rationalism's rise against and above supernaturalism. The
first chapter of *The History of Rationalism* attends to the concern of the early
Christian Roman emperors to combat magic; its title – 'On the Declining Sense
of the Miraculous' – anticipates Max Weber's notion of *Entzauberung*, and of the
two Lecky was less inclined to lament this modern process of 'de-sacralisation'.
He was not a dis-believer or agnostic, yet he never indulged belief. Douglas Bush,
for example, cites Lecky's *History of Rationalism* and Tyndall's Belfast lecture on
The Advancement of Science as stimuli, more likely provocations, to Arnold in his

search for a plausible modern perspective on belief.[5] Lecky moved away from this preoccupation with rationalism and religion to become increasingly absorbed in eighteenth-century history. Arnold, on the other hand, brought his career to a close in a series of publications – e.g. *God and the Bible* (1875) – in which he sought to recycle religion, having removed the difficult bits. If Arnold is out of fashion today – and he may be fortunate in this regard – it is largely because his high seriousness looks like hum-bug. Lecky departed from many of the enthusiasms of his youth; Professor McCartney is eloquent on the extent to which he came to substitute a British for an Irish badge of identity. But he retained that cool dispassionate attitude which is central to the historian's vocation.

Whereas Arnold's name now provokes little more than a smirk, Lecky's rarely achieves even that degree of recognition. It would be wrong simply to blame the absence of a contemporary reputation on the silly charge of plagiarism levelled against him in the pages of *Studies in Burke and His Time*.[6] But what successive replies to the allegation demonstrated was Lecky's transitional role not only in the intellectual life of Ireland but also in the evolution of professional history. If he failed to docket every source with the punctiliousness of an FBI agent or grad-school zealot, he also surpassed the partisanship of pre-Victorian historians. He had undertaken to answer J. A. Froude's *The English in Ireland*, principally because of his friend's subordinating of scholarship to *a priori* interpretations. Thus, at one level, the shift to political history was itself a rejection of credalism in favour of analysis. If, in the full course of his work on the *History of England* (which included the chapters later and better known as the *History of Ireland*), Lecky came to adopt an imperialist position in contemporary politics, he also progressively adopted a more thorough and intensive archival procedure than any previous historian. It's probably just as well that Karl Marx does not appear to have commented on Lecky's work. And yet, in an oddly literal way, Lecky exemplifies the truth of the observation that 'men make their own history, but not of their own free will; not under circumstances they themselves have chosen but under the given and inherited circumstances with which they are directly confronted.'[7] The neglect was not mutual, as the eighth chapter of *Democracy and Liberty* eloquently testifies.

Both Arnold and Froude had less well-known brothers to whom they related in terms of classic sibling antagonism. Oddly enough, both Thomas Arnold and Hurrell Froude acquired strong Roman Catholic associations, the latter as an intimate of J. H. Newman's and a powerful influence on the Tractarian movement, the former as Professor of English in the university college which Newman had done so much to establish in Dublin. The structure of nuclear families in the emergent modern world of the nineteenth century is not without its ideological significance, and a division between rediscovered Catholicism and secularised protestantism could be found in many instances beyond these. Lecky, again by contrast, was an only child; indeed, he found himself at quite a young age in the care of two step-parents, both of his natural parents having died. These circumstances were certainly not chosen, nor were they without influence. The absence of rivalry within Lecky's early domestic life might be read as conducive to that cool detachment already noted, but it also implicated a sense of comprehensive displacement from the roots of passionate interest. As an Irish Victorian who travelled abroad when he might have travailed at home, Lecky has been vulnerable to particular misunderstanding.

Long resident in London in his mature years, he inevitably clubbed, dined and socialised with his peers, many of them literary celebrities. The callow youth visiting the Isle of Wight in 1868 had been replaced by a figure no less angular in appearance but mentally attuned to contemporary metropolitan life. In addition to Tennyson and Allingham already noted, his associates included Robert Browning, the Carlyles, and Anthony Trollope. It still takes a conscious effort to recall that Trollope was attached to the Irish Post Office when he achieved fame as the author of the Barchester novels, that much of *The Warden* (1855) was written in Belfast or Coleraine, and that two of his three earlier novels were set in Ireland. The complex social interrelationships between Ireland and England in the mid-Victorian period have been overlooked in the excitement of later developments. One victim of this adjustment of focus has been the institution in which Lecky was educated but, as he quickly left Trinity College Dublin behind him, the distortion should be first traced elsewhere. Lecky's position at a London dinner-table is all too easily absorbed into an anachronistic view of him as a English rather than Irish phenomenon. If we were to take the hint provided in John Banim's unjustly neglected novel, *The Anglo-Irish of the Nineteenth Century* (1828), then Lecky exemplified a very different tradition. Like George Canning, John Wilson Croker, Robert Stewart, and Arthur Wellesley before him, he was an Irishman advancing himself in England, and not (as the latter-day interpretation of 'Anglo-Irish' usually connotes) an Englishman merely born in Ireland. Indeed, he forms a link between those earlier political migrants and the literary exiles of the 1890s.

Of course, association with Croker can hardly flatter. There is a larger intermediate element in this line of Tory activists omitted from the list of names just invoked, the element best exemplified in Isaac Butt. Lecky was born in 1838, when *The Dublin University Magazine* trumpeted young Butt's rebellious Toryism. He grew to maturity during years when such paradoxes as rebellious Toryism were sublimated into a cult of literature. Butt himself not only transferred his ideological allegiance from Orangeism to Home Rule, but first signalled such a possibility in his novel *The Gap of Barnesmore*. Samuel Ferguson, Sheridan Le Fanu and even (arguably) Thomas Davis elaborated a cultural programme in which nationalist emotion, resistance to modernising economic forces, and religious anxiety fused to such a degree that the inverted Toryism of Davis and the internalised nationalism of Le Fanu were virtually undetectable to their contemporaries.

Young Ireland affected Lecky though he was too young to feel its influence at the time. The decade of Fenianism and Disestablishment provided the occasion for the reassessment of various legacies from the 1840s. In particular, Le Fanu's novelistic concern with the eighteenth century can be read as a prelude to Lecky's historical inquiry, not because *The Cock and Anchor* deserves rating above the third division, but because the fiction generally reveals the interconnectedness of inquiry into the past and inquiry into supernaturalism. Le Fanu's *The House by the Churchyard* (1863) proposes an Augustan Age constructed round the concepts of guilt and concealment while Lecky's *Religious Tendencies of the Age* (1860) is openly generous towards contemporary Catholicism. When *The Leaders of Public Opinion in Ireland* appeared anonymously in 1861, the author's positive treatment of the eighteenth century (through essays on Swift, Flood and Grattan) was counterbalanced by the pathology of Le Fanu's novel, then commencing as a serial in *The Dublin University Magazine*.[8]

Yet, if Lecky studied the past with Whiggish optimism, his privately expressed attitudes towards Catholicism disclosed reservations hidden in his cheerful willingness to treat Catholic dogma on its own terms. 'These things are a great comfort to ignorant people,' he assured Allingham to whom he also remarked that 'practically these views are now inoperative.'[9] There is in this seeming contradiction something of Yeats's later blend of scepticism and zeal in his study of folk-beliefs, the occult, and parapsychology. On the occasion when Lecky provided his condescending defence of belief as a comfort to the ignorant, the conversation staggered insecurely from literary to philosophical topics.

Allingham attacked him sharply for his 'civility to Dogmatism', but Lecky saw 'much on both sides' of the argument while steadfastly abhorring the Utilitarians. Then, as a prelude to presenting Allingham with a copy of *The Religious Tendencies*, the historian of European Morals announced:

> I began to write in the usual way, with Poetry, and was much disappointed to find my poems unnoticed, I believed in them very strongly.[10]

Now, Allingham may not be the soundest witness ever sworn, any more than Lecky was the finest poet. But the evidence strongly suggests that it was the shattering of his belief in his poetry which redirected Lecky's energies and intelligence into other areas of literature. Belief, it seems clear, is characterised by a shared confidence; and when the poet found his work evoked no such response, he was obliged to turn elsewhere. The previous May (1868) he had given a lecture 'On the Influence of the Imagination on History' to the British Institution; history provided an area in which knowledge might be established which required no sanction from orthodox belief, in which the imaginative aspect of literature could be reconciled with truth.

These were not simply the conditions in which Lecky embarked on his career as historian. They constituted the theme, the material, and the methodology of his life's work, or at least of the first important phase of it. Though the titles of his major publications have been listed before, one further scrutiny of them (as a list) is instructive:

Friendship and Other Poems (1859)

The Religious Tendencies of the Age (1860)

Leaders of Public Opinion in Ireland (1861)

The History of the Rise and Influence of the Spirit of Rationalism in Europe (1865)

The History of European Morals from Augustus to Charlemagne (1869)
The History of England in the Eighteenth Century (1878–90)
Poems (1891)
The History of Ireland in the Eighteenth Century (1892)
Democracy and Liberty (1896)
The Map of Life; Conduct and Character (1899)
Historical and Political Essays (1908)

Three phases can be distinguished; the first (identical virtually with the 1860s) concentrates on the relationship between declining belief and moral practice; the second is given over to a minute examination of the eighteenth century; the third (a poor third), deals in shorter studies of late-Victorian concerns, with the rights of property always defended.

If this last emphasis seems all too redolent of the nervous conservatism which accompanied radical dismantling of the Irish landlord system, it might also be read as all too typical of a pusilaminity increasingly evident in the academy where Lecky had earlier trained. Trinity College Dublin boasted many notable thinkers in late Victorian times – Edward Dowden, John Kells Ingram, J.P. Mahaffy, George Salmon, and R.Y. Tyrrell being the best known. As political economist and mediator of Auguste Comte's positivism, Ingram had a reputation as solid as Lecky's. Salmon was a mathematician of European stature, and Mahaffy a pioneer in the study of ancient societies. Lecky was by no means remote from Trinity, even in his London-residing days. In the early 1880s, he addressed the College Historical Society – a student debating club and not a professional body – in his capacity as a celebrated alumnus. Douglas Hyde, then an undergraduate, was in the audience and overcame his timidity to interject a word or two in the ensuing discussion. Later, in 1896, Lecky supported Hyde's application for the chair of Irish against the negative decision of provost Salmon and Robert Atkinson, professor of languages, even though the obstacle to Hyde's appointment was his ardent nationalism. Lecky recognised ability when he saw it, and put professional considerations before political ones.[11]

Perhaps this did not endear him in Irish university circles. One cannot consider Salmon's provostship, or the published correspondence of the Shakespearean scholar, Dowden, without sensing a pathological withdrawal from the modern world, a disengagement of intellect from actual reality. This is discernible as early as 1877, when Dowden's duties as external examiner at Queen's University Belfast obliged him to brush up his general knowledge. Writing to his platonic confidante, Elizabeth West, the holder of the oldest university chair of English Literature in the world gave little evidence of having succumbed to Lecky's influence:

> It amuses me to see how I can now read history with tolerable interest. This results partly from the materializing of one's spiritual force with middle age – partly from one's discovering how much of spiritual virtue there is in *reality*. Then too I had never before read history except as children do – in bits and scraps.[12]

Dowden seems wholly unaware of Lecky's impact on his contemporaries, an impact which registered strikingly after the publication of his books on rationalism and the history of morals a few years earlier. Lecky later appears to have exhausted himself through arduous research on his eighteenth-century history. The personal condition, however, can be read as symptomatic of a cultural shift profound in its implications. In June 1900, Lady Gregory dined with the Leckys in London: he was kind but, as she noted in her journal 'does seem to be going backwards.'[13] By the time he came into contact with Literary Revival activists, he was already a grand old man, albeit one scarcely sixty years of age. New men, and even in significant numbers, new women were taking over. Yeats acknowledged Lecky's assistance in the negotiations which licensed the first performance of *The Countess Cathleen* in May 1899, though in his *Autobiographies* the playwright himself seems to get the date wrong. The following year, Lecky wrote to the London *Times* withdrawing his support from the Irish Literary Theatre because of 'the discreditable conduct of Mr W.B. Yeats, Mr George Moore and other prominent supporters of the movement.' The grounds for the severance were of course political, notably relating to the war in South Africa which Moore, in particular, found deeply offensive. It is revealing to compare Lecky's willingless to champion Hyde (a scholar, though also a nationalist) with his refusal to support anti-imperialists in their cultural endeavours. Lady Gregory interpreted her friend's withdrawl of support with dexterous felicity – it would 'do the Theatre no harm, rather good ... resting it on a literary basis not helped by outsiders.'[14] By this point, one can measure how definitions have shifted since Lecky's bold undertaking to commit himself to literature (rather than holy orders) in committing himself to history.

But the rift between him and the revivalists had already opened on other issues. As a parliamentary representative of Trinity College, Lecky had (in Gregory's view) leaped to the defence of professors Mahaffy and Atkinson who denied the cultural significance of the Gaelic language. Visiting Spiddal, County Galway, where Gaelic still survived with some vigour, Lecky had (in Gregory's term) *sneered* at her 'for calling Irish a modern language' though he was taken aback when their hostess pointed out that the people of the district still composed their songs in it.[15] As a public representative, he encountered not just the vestigial language of the west but the revivalist enthusiasm of genteel suburbs like Blackrock, County Dublin, from whence he had received resolutions in favour of Gaelic. In London, shortly after the relief of Ladysmith, the Leckys entertained a notable company to dinner, including Edward Carson, Augusta Gregory, Mark Twain and his wife. In their absence, Yeats, George Moore and the other 'Celtic people' were ticked off for their silly speeches. On this issue, Lecky's standing is well illustrated in a single sentence of Douglas Hyde's. Writing of an eigheenth-century statement to the effect that, in 1738, ninety-five per cent of the Irish population knew English, Hyde declared this calculation incredible 'and so utterly disproved by all the other evidence, that it is astonishing that so sound and careful a historian as Mr Lecky should have accepted it as substantially true.'[16] Hyde's tone conveys a fellow-professional's dismay at wrong judgment rather than an opponent's gleeful spotting of error. The topic, however, was not containable within academic boundaries.

A transitional figure in his youth, Lecky found himself out of kilter with the times of his (relatively) old age. Too young to have experienced the agony of a Tennyson or (more locally) a Le Fanu on issues of Christian belief, he lived to be bewildered by the new credo of cultural nationalism. When Gregory reported his 'going backwards' it is apt that the point at issue should have veered into the religious arena. The two had discussed a mutual friend's decision to enter a convent which Gregory (steeped of course in Irish evangelicalism) described as leading to a life of prayer. Given the tensions existing between protestants and Catholics, one might have regarded her comment as highly charitable and unexpectedly positive. Yet Lecky had responded that 'prayer is so unnecessary', prompting Gregory to accuse him of a 'want of faith'. When he declared himself a candidate for parliament, some electors pressed him (unsuccessfully) to provide a statement of his religious beliefs. Whether on the issue of women taking the veil or patronising (literary) revivalism, Lecky was a confirmed sceptic. In the early years of the twentieth century, this placed him unambiguously in opposition to all the mobilising forces in Ireland, Ulster unionism apart. And even in his Unionism, Lecky managed to play down its obligatory protestant element. The full force of his exclusion may be measured in Daniel Corkery's *Hidden Ireland* (1924). Lecky had been excommunicated from the canon of independent Ireland's literary history.

Given that George Bernard Shaw, Somerville and Ross, Oscar Wilde and a dozen other fund-raising demigods of latter-day Irish tourism were banished by the same edict, Corkery's dismissal of Lecky should not be taken too seriously. I don't mean to recommend *The History of European Morals* to the film-makers of Temple Bar, though Lecky's concern for property should certainly meet with the approval of those in charge of that once derelict area. Warehouses and works of imaginative scholarship are 'restored' by processes so different that use of the same term is questionable. The relationships which constitute Lecky's most complex placing in literary history were created far from his immediate surroundings. And Lecky's influence on his compatriots remains problematic, for too much emphasis should not be placed on accounts of Edward Martyn's conversion to cultural nationalism through a reading of Lecky's *History*. In contrast, very exact evidence survives of his indirect yet substantial contribution to the writing of *A Connecticutt Yankee in King Arthur's Court* which had appeared in 1889. The principal source in question was *The History of European Morals*, and Twain's heavily annotated copy has been analysed to show the extent of his borrowings both of detail and of general argument.[17]

Together with the remarks of Lippincott in the late 1930s, and evidence of this exploration from the 1950s onwards of Twain's debt to Lecky, Donal McCartney's biography rightly draws attention to the positive reception granted to Lecky in the United States, leading to the establishment of a reputation as a major historian which endured until the middle decades of the present century. There is of course a change of direction occurring within Lecky's American reputation, for it is more or less at the point where he ceases to be regarded as a major (or even model) historian that his *cultural* influence is discerned. Twain's reading of *The History of European Morals* back in the 1880s anticipated the irony of this. In the words of Harold Aspiz, Twain, as an astute reader

> recognized an ambivalence in Lecky's thought akin to the ambivalence readers may recognize in Mark Twain's own thought. Lecky's pioneer study provided more than a statement of the superiority of the nineteenth century over all other centuries and a qualified affirmation of inevitable progress. It also documented his misgivings about the upgrading of human nature as a concomitant of technical or social advancement.[18]

There is nothing uncertain about Twain's engagement with Lecky's work. A footnote to the twenty-second chapter of *A Connecticutt Yankee* casually reads, 'All the details concerning the hermits, in this chapter, are from Lecky – but greatly modified. This book not being a history but only a tale, the majority of the historian's frank details were too strong for reproduction in it.'[19] But it was not only *The History of European Morals* which contributed to Twain's time-travelling novel; *A History of England in the Eighteenth Century* is also cited in the novelist's notebooks and journals.[20] As the *Connecticut Yankee* also owes something to Oscar Wilde's 'The Canterville Ghost' (1887), Twain may be deemed lucky to have escaped censure at the hands of Daniel Corkery.

The anathemising school of literary criticism, exemplified by Corkery, operates on the basis of crude sociological observations. Lecky, first immersed in his state archives and then prominent in Unionist debate, was a ready victim. Ideological conditions in the 1920s provided the opportunity to read him out from the altar though, in the event, professional historiography was to encounter less hostility from church and state in independent Ireland than creative literature did. But even in the 1890s, when Oscar Wilde and C.S. Parnell had stamped their different yet complementary kinds of Irish genius on London's social occasions and reports of these could generate confusion at home. Without some willingless to consider evidence from the dining table *as evidence*, no judicious assessment of a cultural milieu is possible. And it is Lecky's misfortune that his publicly known work has been discounted almost as thoroughly as his American influence has been neglected.

Dining with the Leckys during the election campaign of 1895, Lady Gregory startled Sir Alfred Lyall by announcing that she had written an article about the Athenaeum Club; Lecky for his part expressed the half-hope that he might not be elected to parliament because it would 'interfere with his literary work' – he 'wished to write something about the beginning of this century in Ireland'.[21] In these pronouncements, divergent tendencies and potentialities can be discerned. Of the two, Gregory was the rising star, and with her name is associated a renewal, or more properly, a re-orientation of imaginative literature. She was not a Yeats or a Synge, but she provided 'cover' for these more subversive writers in their engagement with the social powers represented by Lecky. She was also a woman, and by the position she held in the movement for Irish literary revival she signalled a radical departure from Victorian conventions and proprieties.

Shortly after this conversation Gregory went to a Parnell family wedding, 'at the Plymouth Brethren Hall in Welbeck Street [London], a shabby-looking place'. The bride was Lady Sarah Cecilia Parnell (1868–1912), only daughter of the 2nd Baron Congleton; the groom one of the Mandevilles of Anner Castle, County Tipperary. Earlier the same day, the Irish parliamentary leader John Dillon had been married, without the benefit of Lady Gregory's attendance it seems. Dillon had postponed the wedding so long as tenants evicted from his wife's family estate remained homeless. Loyalty to Lady Cecily among her Brethren clearly came before the claims of so up-coming a political force as that represented by Dillon. Not that Gregory was hostile to the new politics, nor Lecky wholly blind to the historical pressures behind it. She retained her evangelical piety even as she embraced the additional revivalism of Cuchulain and Old Mahon. He was now dismissive of his Leaders of Public Opinion, keen only to preserve the essay on Daniel O'Connell, even to expand it, and to write 'on the Famine and the Tithe War, so little comparatively is known of them'.[22]

The seeming oddity of a Parnell cleaving to the Plymouth Brethren acts as a barrier to historical understanding only so long as it remains an oddity to the historian. Greater tolerance of such material makes the material a great deal less inscrutable. As with the sectarian antagonisms imaged in the divergent careers of the Arnold and Froude brothers, the flossy details of society weddings can respond to cultural analysis. What Lecky achieved in his best work was a demonstration of history's ability to provide, or at least guide, that broader analysis. And this remains true whether the context be early Christian Rome or Belfast in 1790. Pioneering new forms of intellectual history and historical sociology, his work made possible the study of *mentalités* and of micro-communities familiar to Irish readers today through the writings of Louis Cullen and others. In biographical terms, Lecky quickly abandoned his provincial origins and became a figure of European significance. Though his later defence of the Irish landed classes can hardly be brushed aside, it is ironic that he should be identified so rigidly with Anglo-Irish protestant ascendancy notions. His scepticism, his industry, his imaginative sympathy for the beliefs of others, all argue against such an identification.

Two factors relate him to a seccessionist party among the Irish gentry, the party of Yeats and Gregory. One is his concern almost exclusively with written evidence, with literature in its broadest definition. Painting and music play little or no part in his cultural histories, even though the history of morals is a field richly illustrated in – say – Dutch art in the seventeenth century, or the growth of portraiture generally. The second is that vocational motif which runs through all his work, a secularized attitude of devotion, or desacralized hermeneutic. These factors also characterise the early work of Yeats and Gregory, if not that of Wilde and Shaw for whom the non-literary arts were real and exciting.

A different logic to this relationship between Lecky and Yeats emerges in the 1930s. 'The Words Upon the Window-pane' (1934) in Yeats's *blindest* play, in the sense that dramatic power is directly proportional to the non-appearance of the central character. That character is Swift and Yeats claimed that, in suggesting fear of insanity as the motive for Swift's celibacy, he was following a lead set by Lecky in *Leaders of Public Opinion*. In fact, the play adopts to its own purposes a rather different aspect of Lecky's essay on Swift: the allegation of the Dean's scepticism. For it is a crucial and unstressed irony in the play that, amid all the nonsense about contacting dead relatives, and the results of future dog-races, the two most distressed figures are Christian clergymen – the visible figure of the Revd Abraham Johnson, who has lost his powers to persuade, and the invisible Swift who, being dead, has no comprehending audience whom he may persuade. Yeats's late debt to the historian with whom he had quarrelled refers to some of Lecky's earliest preoccupations, the decline of belief, the rise and influence of rational thought. Did Yeats secretly agree with Lecky, and recognize in Swift an anguished sceptic, a photo-modern?

Finally, one returns to Mark Twain who, in recent years, has been the victim of political correctness in relation to the politics of 'race' in the American educational system. The evidence of Lecky's influence on Twain does not so much contribute to American literary history, illuminating Twain's views on slavery by bringing out their shared opinion that pagan slavery had been a great deal less inhumane than its more debasing counterpart under Christianity; it exemplifies the need for an ever more receptive Irish literary history transcending the nationalist and petty-bourgeois presumptions of a Corkery.[23] Such presumptions do not always come dressed in the balaclavas of a tightly-knit community. The most recently published proceedings of the 'Cultures of Ireland Group' include an aside to the effect that '"liberal" or non-religious constituencies do not receive the attention their numbers warrant' amid the clamour of two nations and two traditions.[24] If Lecky were more widely read among the Unionists whose precursors he defended, the right to think that 'prayer is so unnecessary' might be conceivable.

Notes

1. *William Allingham's Diary*, ed. Geoffrey Grigson (London: Centaur Press, 1967), p. 177
2. Benjamin Evans Lippincott, *Victorian Critics of Democracy: Carlyle, Ruskin, Stephen, Maine, Lecky* (Minneapolis: University of Minnesota Press, 1938), p. 210. For the nineteenth century origins of fascism see the early chapters of Paul Mazgaj, *The Action Francaise and Revolutionary Syndicalism* (Chapel Hill: Univ. of North Carolina Press, 1979) and F. L. Carsten, *The Rise of Fascism*, 2nd edn (London: Batsford, 1980).
3. *Ibid.*, p. 224.
4. W. B. Yeats, *Autobiographies* (London: Macmillan, 1955), p. 399.
5. Douglas Bush, *Matthew Arnold; A Survey of his Poetry and Prose* (London: Macmillan, 1971), pp. 171–2.
6. See Jay Carlton Mullen, 'Lecky as Plagiarist; the Annual Register and the American Revolution', *Studies in Burke and His Time*, vol 13 no 3 (Spring 1972), pp. 2193–202; Norman Baker, 'Lecky and the Annual Register in Historical Perspective', *ibid.* vol. 14 no. 2 (Winter 1972/3), pp. 171–7; L.P. Curtis Jnr, 'Lecky Vindicated', *ibid.* vol. 14 no. 3 (Spring 1973), pp. 267–94.

7. 'The Eighteenth Brumaire of Louis Bonaparte' in Karl Marx, *Surveys from Exile; Political Writings vol 2* (Harmondsworth: Penguin Books, 1973), p. 146.

8. See also W. J. Mc Cormack, *Dissolute Characters: Irish Literary History though Balzac, Le Fanu, Yeats and Bowen* (Manchester: Manchester University Press, 1993), pp. 41–2, 184.

9. *Allingham's Diary*, p. 197.

10. *Idem.*

11. J.E. & G.W. Dunleavy, *Douglas Hyde; a Maker of Modern Ireland* (Berkeley: University of California Press, 1991), pp. 118, 200–1.

12. *Fragments from Old Letters: E.D. to E.D.W. 1869–1892*, second series (London: Dent, 1914), p. 134.

13. Augusta Gregory, *Seventy Years* (Gerrards Cross: Smythe, 1973), p. 371.

14. *Ibid.*, p. 368.

15. *Ibid.*, p. 319.

16. Douglas Hyde, *A Literary History of Ireland from Earliest Times to the Present Day* (London: Benn, 1967), p. 623. See Lecky, *A History of Ireland in the Eighteenth Century* (London: Longmans, 1896), vol. 1, p. 331.

17. See Chester L. Davis, 'Mark Twain's Religious Beliefs as Indicated by the Notations in his Books', *The Twainian* vol. 14 no. 7 (1955), *passim*.

18. Harold Aspiz, 'Lecky's Influence on Mark Twain', *Science and Society* vol. 26 no. 1 (1962), p. 15.

19. Samuel Langhorne Clemens [i.e. Mark Twain], *A Connecticut Yankee in King Arthur's Court; an Authoritative Text; Backgrounds and Sources; Composition and Publication; Criticism*, ed. Allison R. Ensor (New York: Norton, 1982), p. 121.

20. See *ibid.* pp. 264–8, where the editor transcribes three passages (two from *Morals*, one from *England*) on which Twain drew. See also R.B. Browning *et al.* (eds), *Mark Twain's Notebooks & Journals vol 3, 1883–1891* (Berkeley: University of California Press, 1979), pp. 416, 422–3, 502–4, 506.

21. Gregory, *op. cit.*, pp. 294–5.

22. *Ibid.*, p. 299.

23. Aspiz, *loc. cit.*, p. 17.

24. See Proinsias O Drisceoil (ed.), *Culture in Ireland; Regions: Identity and Power* (Belfast: Institute of Irish Studies, 1993), p. 179.

Notes and References

Introduction

1. On the notion of Victorian Ireland, see W.J. McCormack, *Sheridan Le Fanu and Victorian Ireland* (Dublin, 2nd edn, 1991).
2. A. Momigliano, *Essays in Ancient and Modern Historiography* (London, 1977), p. 1.

Chapter 1

1. Lord Aldborough's 'memorandum' of 27 January 1796 says £6000. A copy of instructions for a will, which was later altered, says £7000. Both documents are among the Hartpole papers in Trinity College, Dublin. See also Jonah Barrington, *Personal Sketches* (1869), pp. 322-3.
2. At the time of the disestablishment, Lecky expected his church property to realize £5000 or £6000 (H. Montgomery Hyde, *A Victorian Historian: Private Letters of W.E.H. Lecky*, p. 73).
3. The one possible exception was the junior fellow, John Kells Ingram. See above p. 12.
4. *Daily Express* (Dublin), 8 December 1897; *Memoir*, p. 312.
5. Minute Book of the College Historical Society, TCD, 26 May, 1, 8 December 1858, 16 November, 14, 17 December 1859, 18 January, 11 April 1860.
6. D. R. Plunket, *College Historical Society Address* (9 November 1859), pp. 31, 33.
7. E. Gibson, *College Historical Society Address* (10 November 1858), p. 33.
8. D. Plunket, *College Historical Society Address* (9 November 1859), p. 25.
9. See, especially, the addresses by William Barlow (1856) and Freeman C. Wills (1860).
10. E. Gibson, *op. cit.*, p. 26.
11. *Ibid.*, p. 28.
12. D. Plunket, *op. cit.*, p. 25.
13. R. Walshe, *College Historical Society Address* (9 November 1864), p. 19.
14. E. Gibson, *op. cit.*, p. 27.
15. D. Plunket, *op. cit.*, p. 18.
16. Lecky opposed life peerages.
17. Minute Book, College Historical Society, TCD, 7 April 1858.
18. *Ibid.*, 23 February 1859.
19. Minute Book, College Historical Society, TCD, 23 March 1859, 30 November 1859, 15 February 1860.
20. See, especially, his remarks on Peel in the essay on O'Connell in *Leaders*, and also on Peel in the *Essays*.
21. It is not so easy to determine on what grounds Lecky argued that the English government ought not to oppose the Suez Canal scheme, or that the English government ought not to

oppose the annexation of Savoy. In both cases, Lecky lost.

22. TCD, MS R.7.30, p. 42 and Marked 'H'. At the end of certain *pensees* in Lecky's commonplace books are found 'R.T.' or 'L.P.O.' or 'H. of R.' or 'H'. The significance of these letters is that the epigram thus marked was afterwards used in *Religious Tendencies*, or *Leaders of Public Opinion*, or *History of Rationalism*, or spoken at debates of the Historical Society.

23. *Clerical Influences*, pp. 30, 48-9.

24. *Memoir*, p. 17.

25. T.·W. Moody, *Thomas Davis*, 1814-45, p. 9.

26. Daniel O'Connell was referring to the author of this patriotic ballad when he jibed: 'The bird who once sang so sweetly is now caged and silent in Trinity College' (J.G. Swift MacNeill, *What I Have Seen and Heard*, p. 56).

27. The inaugural address of E. Gibson noted that Ingram was the only fellow of the college who was also a vice-president of the society, and the auditor requested that all medals and prizes of the society should be under the superintendence of the professor of Oratory.

28 TCD MS R.7.30, p. 112, and marked 'H' and 'L.P.O.'.

29. *Ibid.*, p. 44, and marked 'H'.

30. *Ibid.*, p. 111, and marked 'H' and 'L.P.O.'.

31. *Ibid.*, p. 43 and marked 'L.P.O.' and 'H of R'. An additional note explained 'found *afterwards* but not taken from Berkeley'. It was an idea of which Lecky was particularly fond, for not only did he employ it in *Leaders* and *Rationalism*, but he also used it in *Religious Tendencies* (pp. 303-4), which was written and published during his last years in Trinity. He wrote: 'In Ireland the cause of nationality seems to be hopelessly merged in the cause of sectarianism. Guided by their priests, the people have come forward as the enthusiastic sympathisers with Italian despotism. A eulogy of Austria will be received with acclamation by an audience who cheer the name of Davis or O'Connell. In a few months the priests have done more to render the Irish cause contemptible in the eyes of Europe and to cloud the memory of their departed leader than was affected by all the denunciations of Lord Stanley or all the sarcasm of *The Times*.'

32. *Ibid.*, p. 10, and marked 'H' and 'L.P.O.'.

33. TCD MS R.7.30 p. 72.

34. TCD MS R.7.30, p. 14, and marked 'H'.

35. TCD MS R.7.30, pp. 58-9 (under the year 1859 and marked 'L.P.O.'). A variant of the above sentence was used by Lecky in the essay 'Clerical Influences' in the *Leaders*; see W.E.H. Lecky, *Clerical Influences* (edited by W. E. G. Lloyd and F. Cruise O'Brien), p. 29.

36. TCD MS R.7.30, p. 26 (under the year 1859 and marked 'L.P.O.') cf. *Clerical Influences*, p. 53.

37. TCD MS R.7.30, p. 27 (under the year 1859).

38. TCD MS R.7.30, p. 43 (under the year 1860 and marked 'L.P.O.). Cf. *Clerical Influences*, p. 27.

39. TCD MS R.7.30, p. 27 (under the year 1859 and marked 'H' and 'L.P.O.'). Cf. *Clerical Influences*, p. 53.

40. TCD MS R.7.30, p. 8 (under the year 1859 and marked 'H').

41. TCD MS R.7.30, p. 31 (under the year 1859).

42. TCD MS R.7.30, pp. 40-1 (under the year 1860, and marked 'R.T.'). Cf. *Religious Tendencies of the Age*, p. 317.

43. Minute Book of the College Historical Society, TCD (24 March 1858).

44. W.E.H. Lecky, *History of Rationalism*, ii, 296-325.

45. Gibson, said of Lecky as a member of the Historical Society: 'he spoke with the strong conviction that he was saying what he believed to be right and what he held to be true' (quoted in Emily Lawless, 'W.E.H. Lecky: A Reminiscence', in *Monthly Review*, xiv, no. 41 (February 1904), p. 115.

46. A college friend (Arthur Booth), 'Early Recollections of Mr Lecky', in *National Review*, xliii (March 1904), p. 112.

47. *Ibid.*, pp. 111-12. Cf. also J.P. Mahaffy, a fellow student, who years later in evidence before the Royal Commission on university education in Ireland (Robertson Commission), second report (1902), p. 215 said: 'When we were undergraduates at Trinity College we used to escape from our own college and go and hear John Henry Newman preach in the Roman Catholic University that then was.'

48. W.E.H. Lecky, *Essays*, pp. 91-2.

49. *Ibid.*, p. 93.

50. *Ibid.*, p. 94.

51. *Ibid.*, p. 96.

52. Elisabeth Lecky, *Memoir*, p. 18.

53. *Essays*, p. 102. Buckle's influence on Lecky is discussed in greater detail, pp. 29-32, 37-8, 39-56.

54. *Ibid*, p. 90.

55. *Ibid.* As a schoolboy, Lecky had 'a great liking for geology, and his favourite pastime was seeking specimens for a collection which Mr John Lecky, his grandfather, had given him'. While at school in Cheltenham 'he geologised a great deal … He probably gave a stimulus to the study of geology in the college, for a little museum there dates from that time' (*Memoir*, pp. 7-8).

56. *Essays*, p. 103.

57. *Ibid*, p. 97.

58. Arthur Booth, *loc. cit.*, p. 114. This college friend also says that Lecky's letters testify to his weariness with theological discussion. But all controversy bored him, as Emily Lawless remarked, Lawless, *loc. cit.*, pp. 124-5. *Religious Tendencies* might be described as an eloquent plea against theological controversy.

59. *Essays*, p. 90.

60. The title may have owed something to the essay by Mark Pattison in *Essays and Reviews* (1860), 'The Tendencies of Religious Thought 1688-1750'.

61. *Religious Tendencies*, title-page; *Essays*, p. 96. Lecky could have found in Michelet, whom he came shortly afterwards to admire, similar sentiments: 'To penetrate into all doctrines, to understand all causes, to plunge with one's soul into all sentiments, these are the ineluctable demands of history' (quoted in P. Geyl, *Debates with Historians*, p. 75).

62. *Religious Tendencies*, pp. 148-9.

63. *Ibid.*, pp. 135-6.

64. *Ibid.*, pp. 227-67.

65. Cf. *Religious Tendencies*, pp. 24-5: 'Do not imagine that you can understand a religious system because you have mastered its history and can explain its doctrines. Your mind should be so imbued with its spirit that you can realise the feelings of those who believe in it; you should endeavour to throw yourself into their position, to ascertain what doctrines they chiefly dwell upon, what points fascinate the most, what present the greatest difficulty to their minds. You should try to divest yourself for a time of your previous notions and to assume the feelings of others. You should read not merely their standard theological works, but also their ordinary devotional manuals; you should haunt the village chapel and the village procession and endeavour in every way to enter into the

feelings of the worshipper.'

66. *Religious Tendencies*, p. 165.
67. *Ibid.*, p. 136.
68. *Ibid.*, p. 296.
69. *Ibid.*, pp. 153-79.
70. *Ibid.*, p. 296.
71. *Ibid.*, p. 209.
72. *Ibid.*, p. 60.
73. *Ibid.*, pp. 317-8.
74. *Ibid.*, pp. 319-20.
75. *Ibid.*, p. 80.
76. *Ibid.*, p. 277.
77. *Ibid.*, p. 214.
78. *Ibid.*, p. 138.
79. *Ibid.*, p. 192.
80. *Ibid.*, p. 209.
81. *Ibid.*, p. 27.
82. *Ibid.*, p. 26.
83. *Ibid.*, pp. 16-18.
84. *Ibid.*, p. 74.
85. *Ibid.*, p. 66.
86. *Ibid.*, p. 316. H. T. Buckle, too, had written that in contemporary Europe an inferior son 'is made either a soldier or a clergyman; he is sent into the army or hidden in the church.' And this, Buckle thought, was one of the reasons why as society advances, 'the ecclesiastical spirit and the military spirit never fail to decline' (*History of Civilization in England*, World's Classics edn, 1903, i, 154, 288). S. Laing, who had travelled widely in Europe in the 1830s and 1840s, had written a series of volumes incorporating his impressions. Both Buckle and Lecky quoted him in their work. One of Buckle's quotations from Laing reads: 'Ecclesiastical power is almost extinct as an active element in the political or social affairs of nations or of individuals ... and a new element, literary power, is taking its place in the government of the world' (*op. cit.*, i, 288).
87. No. 23, TCD. Cf. also a letter from Lecky dated 26 January 1861 referred to in *Memoir*, p. 23.
88. Afterwards rector of Stratford, Essex.
89. *Memoir*, p. 21.
90. *Religious Tendencies*, p. 70.
91. This emphasis became more apparent in his later books, especially *Rationalism* and *Morals*.
92. Lecky delivered a lecture on this very topic to the Royal Institution of Great Britain on 28 May 1868, which was published as *On the Influence of the Imagination on History*. This he later revised for an article for the American journal *Forum* (February 1893), which in turn was revised and published in the *Essays* as 'Thoughts on History'. In this he wrote that the historian should have enough of the dramatic element to enable him to throw himself into ways of reasoning or feeling very different from his own (*Essays*, pp. 4-5).
93. *Religious Tendencies*, p. 312.
94. A passage in *Rationalism* (ii, 93-7) dealing with the struggles of religious enquiry may well be autobiographical.
95. 'Formative Influences' first published in *Forum*, ix (June 1890) pp. 380-90 and reprinted in *Essays*, pp. 90-103.

96. Lecky to Booth, 4 July 1890 (*Memoir*, p. 221).
97. *Loc. cit.*
98. In a letter, 16 June 1859, Lecky wrote: 'Yesterday we had the closing night at the Historical ... not having the fear of conservatism and the clergy before my eyes, I had the audacity to review (in its relation to political and sectarian public opinion) the struggles for nationality in Ireland and to launch a diatribe at the political clergy.' (*Memoir*, pp. 15-16.)
99. *Democracy and Liberty*, i, 490-1.
100. *Leaders* (1861), pp. 1-2.
101. *Ibid.*, p. 2.
102. Towards the end of his life and after he had experienced the home rule and Land League agitations in Ireland, Lecky wrote: '... the public opinion of a nation is something quite different from the votes that can be extracted from all the individuals who compose it. There are multitudes in every nation who contribute nothing to its public opinion; who never give a serious thought to public affairs who have no spontaneous wish to take any part in them; who if they are induced to do so, will act under the complete direction of individuals or organisations of another class' (*Democracy and Liberty*, i, 21-2). 'Popular' opinion had now come to mean for Lecky something very different from 'public' opinion, and it was not without grave dangers for Europe (*ibid.*, i, 481). He insisted that: 'Violations of liberty do not lose their character because they are the acts, not of kings or aristocracies, but of majorities of electors' (*ibid.*, ii, 150).
103. *Leaders* (1861), p. 2.
104. *Ibid.*, p. 3.
105. *Ibid.*, pp. 181, 266.
106. *Ibid.*, 'Introduction'; see also p. 286.
107. J. J. Auchmuty, in his *Lecky*, pp. 70-3, claimed that Lecky supported the policy of 'complete fusion with England' as early as 1861. But there is nothing in Lecky's work of 1861 to warrant so definite and assured a statement. On the contrary, he did clearly state that the only effective check to sectarianism was a national spirit, and deliberately denied that a restored Irish parliament would foster sectarianism; rather, it would produce the opposite effect (*Leaders*, p. 276). Auchmuty gives no footnote references, but an important argument against his opinion is that there is nothing at all in Auchmuty's book to suggest that he had read either the 1861 or the 1871 editions of *Leaders*. Wherever he quoted from the biographical essays, he used the two-volume 1903 edition, and where he quoted from the essay 'Clerical Influences' he seems to have used the reprint, edited by F. Cruise O'Brien and W. E. G. Lloyd in 1911. A detail that helps to confirm one's suspicions about Auchmuty's procedure is illustrated in his remark that *Leaders* 'opened' with a chapter entitled 'Clerical Influences' (p. 70). Anyone reading the 1861 edition is unlikely to make this slip, for the point of this essay is that it is an epilogue describing the diseased state of Irish opinion in the absence of a leader like Swift, Flood, Grattan or O'Connell, and as such it *closed* not 'opened' *Leaders*. By ignoring significant passages in the 1861 and 1871 editions, Auchmuty misread Lecky's position and imposed the matured unionist of 1903 on the earlier books. The result was that he failed to see a nationalism that was obvious to contemporaries and only saw a unionism that was much less apparent. Because of this, Auchmuty's general summary of 'Clerical Influences' is also very misleading. It is true, for example, as Auchmuty says, that Lecky condemned the catholic priests for their part in fostering sectarianism, but he did not spare the protestant ministers. Auchmuty upsets the balance by ignoring

Lecky's censure of the protestant clergy, or rather he gives the wrong impression that Lecky condemned merely 'the protestants of the north' (p. 72). Lecky made no such distinction.

108.   *Leaders* (1861), p. 276.

109.   *Ibid.*, pp. 274-5.

110.   *Ibid.*, pp. 285-7.

111.   *Ibid.*, p. 277. He continued to argue against Newman on this same point in his *Morals*, i, 111-2, and also in *The Map of Life*, p. 83.

112.   *Ibid.*, pp. 307, 292-6.

113.   *Ibid.*, p. 155; see also p. 308.

114.   *Ibid.*, p. 152.

115.   *Ibid.*, p. 293.

116.   *Ibid.*, p. 285.

117.   *Ibid.*, p. 289.

118.   *Ibid.*, p. 303.

119.   *Ibid.*, p. 302.

120.   *Ibid.*, pp. 299-300.

121.   *Ibid.*, pp. 296, 148. Understandably, in view of the emergence of Fenianism, this last phrase about the republic did not recur in the later editions.

122.   Acton to Mary Gladstone, 25 March 1881 (*Letters of Lord Acton to Mary Daughter of the Right Hon. W.E. Gladstone*, 2nd edn, 1913, p. 63).

123.   *Leaders*, p. 306.

124.   *Leaders* (1861), pp. 305-6. In a notebook of 1859 Lecky wrote the following advice to electors: 'If you make it a rule never to trust a lawyer you will occasionally distrust an honest man, but you will be on your guard against a great many knaves' (TCD MS R.7.30, p. 112). He was evidently thinking of William Keogh of the 'Pope's Brass Band' who, although a leader of 'The Irish Brigade' in parliament and pledged to independent opposition, had accepted office as Solicitor General in the government of Lord Aberdeen.

125.   Hibernicus (i.e. W.E.H. Lecky), *Friendship and Other Poems*, 1859, p. 2. Lecky's manuscript of these poems is TCD MS R.7.69. His own copy of the published volume with manuscript alterations is TCD MS R.7.70.

126.   Booth, *loc. cit.*, p. 111.

127.   *Memoir*, p. 30.

128.   *Ibid.*, pp. 52-3.

129.   *Ibid.*, p. 52.

130.   Lecky to Bowen, 12 June 1868 (*Memoir*, p. 57).

131.   Lecky to Bowen, 30 March 1870 (*Memoir*, p. 69).

132.   *Memoir*, p. 100.

133.   Booth, *loc. cit.*, p. 116.

134.   *Leaders* (1861), pp. 306-7.

135.   He wrote in his journal, NLI MS 3041, on 11 December 1861: 'I pray that God in his own good time may raise up among us a patriot hero inheriting the mantle of Grattan ...'

136.   *Cork Examiner*, 7 February 1862.

137.   NLI MS 3041, 17 March 1862. See also O'Neill Daunt, *A Life Spent for Ireland*, pp. 189-90.

138.   O'Neill Daunt to Lecky, 16 March 1862 (TCD, no. 22).

139.   *Leaders* (1861), pp. 291-4.

140. Murray to Lecky, 29 April 1861 (TCD, no. 18).

141. Macmillan and Co. to Lecky, 16 May 1861 (TCD, no. 19).

142. Lecky continued to have his books published in this manner, for many years later he wrote to Henry Charles Lea: 'In England I have always published my books by commission (at my own expense) which is the way I much prefer' (Lecky to Lea, 22 March 1891, Henry Charles Lea Library, University of Pennsylvania). Like other English authors, Lecky was annoyed that the American copyright laws had left them previous to 1891 entirely at the mercy of American publishers.

143. Saunders, Otley and Co. to Lecky, 18, 24 May 1861 (TCD, nos 20-1).

144. Saunders, Otley and Co. informed Lecky on 10 July 1862 that thirty-four copies had been sold to date (TCD, no. 24). Lecky informed his friend, Booth, on 24 January 1872 that only thirty-four copies had sold (*Memoir*, p. 83). Lecky acquired a number of the unsold copies and made use of the pages, liberally writing in the margins and pasting passages into his manuscript when he was preparing the second edition ten years later. On 29 June 1865 Saunders, Otley and Co. regretted that it was not possible to furnish any more copies of the *Religious Tendencies* and *Leaders* because the remainder had been sold off (TCD, no. 33).

145. At least in the second edition. See Lecky to Booth, 24 January 1872 (*Memoir*, p. 83).

146. Lecky to Booth, 11 September 1861 (*Memoir*, p. 27).

147. Cf. G.P. Gooch, *History and Historians in the Nineteenth Century* (1913), p. 365: 'Immaturity is stamped on its pages and the epilogue breathes a fiery nationalism; but the essays are not without power.'

148. *Leaders* (1871), p. 224.

149. *Ibid.*, pp. 310-12.

150. O'Neill Daunt, who had acted as a secretary to O'Connell, noted in his *Journal*, 11 December 1861, that O'Connell 'receives much justice from this clever writer'. Among recent historians who have said more or less the same thing are A. Macintyre, *The Liberator: Daniel O'Connell and the Irish Party, 1830-47* (London, 1965), p. 39; and L. J. McCaffrey, *Daniel O'Connell and The Repeal Year* (Kentucky, 1966), p. xii.

Chapter Two

1. Lecky to Wilmot Chetwode, March 1869 (H. Montgomery Hyde [ed.], *A Victorian Historian: Private Letters of W.E.H. Lecky 1859-1878*, London, 1947, pp. 77-8).

2. *Ibid.*

3. Lecky to Wilmot Chetwode, December 1860 (*ibid.*, p. 36).

4. Lecky to Wilmot Chetwode, 11 January 1862 (*ibid.*, pp. 47-8).

5. Elisabeth Lecky, *Memoir*, p. 28.

6. Lecky to Wilmot Chetwode, 15 January 1869 (*Memoir*, p. 61).

7. Lecky to Wilmot Chetwode, 2 February 1862 (Hyde [ed.], *op. cit.*, p. 49).

8. *Memoir*, p. 47; Lecky to Wilmot Chetwode, 7 August 1866 (Hyde [ed.], *op. cit.*, pp. 68-9).

9. Lecky to Wilmot Chetwode, 12 February 1863 (Hyde [ed.], *op. cit.*, p. 60).

10. *Memoir*, p. 34.

11. *Ibid.*, p. 36.

12. Lecky to Tallents, January 1865 (*Memoir*, p. 38).

13. Lecky to Wilmot Chetwode, 12 September 1861 (Hyde [ed.], *op. cit.*, p. 40).

14. Lecky to Booth, 11 September 1861 (*Memoir*, p. 27).

15. Lecky to Wilmot Chetwode, 12 September 1861 (Hyde [ed.], *op. cit.*, p. 40).

16. *Ibid.*

17. Lecky to Wilmot Chetwode, St Patrick's Day, 1862 (Hyde [ed.], *op. cit.*, p. 53).

18. Lecky to Wilmot Chetwode, 19 June 1862 (Hyde [ed.], *op. cit.*, p. 58).

19. *Ibid.*, p. 59.

20. Lecky to Wilmot Chetwode, 12 September, 11 November 1861, 11 January 1862 (Hyde [ed.], *op. cit.*, pp. 40-1, 42, 45-6).

21. Lecky to Wilmot Chetwode, St Patrick's Day 1862 (Hyde [ed.], *op. cit.*, p. 53); Lecky to Addison (*Memoir*, p. 25).

22. Lord Acton, *Historical Essays*, p. 332.

23. H. T. Buckle, *History of Civilization in England* (Henry Froude, World's Classics), i, 6.

24. *Ibid.*, p. 4.

25. *Ibid.*, p. 5.

26   *Ibid.*

27. Lecky to Elisabeth van Dedem, 4 March 1871 (*Memoir*, p. 78).

28. Lecky to Wilmot Chetwode, St Patrick's Day 1862, 12 September 1861, 11 November 1861, 12 September 1861 (Hyde [ed.], *op. cit.*, pp. 54, 41, 42, 40).

29. Lecky to Wilmot Chetwode, 12 September 1861 (Hyde [ed.], *op. cit.*, p. 40). Cf. Lecky to Addison (*Memoir*, p. 25).

30. Lecky to Booth, 11 September 1861 (*Memoir*, p. 27).

31. Lecky to Wilmot Chetwode, 11 November 1861 (Hyde [ed.], *op. cit.*, p. 42).

32. *Rationalism*, ii, 228.

33. *Ibid.*, ii, 225, 358.

34. *Ibid.*, ii, 357.

35. *Ibid.*, ii, 358.

36. *Memoir*, p. 38.

37. *Ibid.*, p. 39.

38. J. A. Froude, *Short Studies in Great Subjects*, i, 3.

39. *Memoir*, p. 40.

40. *Edinburgh Review*, cxxi, no. 248 (April 1865), p. 455.

41. *The British Quarterly*, the *Dublin Review* and the *Edinburgh Review* devoted over thirty pages each to reviewing it. *Fraser's Magazine*, the *Westminster Review* and the *Contemporary Review* gave it between twenty and thirty pages each. The *Fortnightly Review*, *Athenaeum*, *Dublin University Magazine*, *Saturday Review*, *Spectator*, *Journal of Sacred Literature*, and numerous others gave it prominent notice. Norman Pilling, 'The Reception of the Major Works of W.E.H. Lecky' (unpublished M.Phil thesis [1975] of University College, London), lists thirty-eight separate journals which carried reviews of *Rationalism*.

42. Lecky's comment on the review in the *Westminster* was: an 'exceedingly remarkable and extremely flattering review, which is, however, calculated to deprive me of any little reputation for respectability I have had'. The review had come from the pen 'of the reverend author of the tract on eternal punishment' (Hyde, *op. cit.*, pp. 63-4).

43. Tulloch was the principal of St Andrew's when Lecky received its honorary degree of LL.D in January 1885.

44. Lecky's comment on the *British Quarterly* was: 'The *British Quarterly* has opened rather heavy artillery upon me, but has not done me much harm' (*Memoir*, p. 44).

45. George Eliot's review was in *Fortnightly Review*, i (1865), pp. 43-55, and is reprinted in her *Essays* (1884).

46. Lord Acton, *Historical Essays and Studies*, p. 288.

47. *Acton to Mary Gladstone*, 25 November 1881 (*Letters of Lord Acton to Mary Gladstone* ed.

H. Paul, p. 115).

48. *Memoir*, p. 39.

49. *Ibid.*, pp. 41-2.

50. This was his description of the review in the *Quarterly Journal of Sacred Literature* (Hyde, *op. cit.*, p. 64).

51. J. J. Auchmuty, *Lecky: A Biographical and Critical Essay*, p. 54.

52. *Rationalism*, i, 350-1.

53. *Memoir*, p. 58.

54. *Rationalism*, ii, 56-7.

55. John Bowle, *Politics and Opinion in the Nineteenth Century*, p. 245.

56. It was a situation that Buckle was aware of when he wrote: '… we shall find that a large share of what is effected, even by the most eminent men, is due to the character of the age in which they live' (*History of Civilization*, ii, 255).

57. *Morals*, i, xi-xii.

58. Archbishop Whately had already pointed out that the acceptance of the theory of eternal damnation made it easy to justify the religious persecution of heretics. Buckle accepted Whately's thesis and quoted Whately on the point (*History of Civilization*, i, 278-9). But it was not necessary for Lecky to borrow the thesis from Buckle since he had already read Whately at Trinity and regarded his writings as one of the formative influences in his life. Illustrations of the relationship between religious dogmas and religious persecution were taken by Buckle from the work of Bosheim, Neander and Milman (*History of Civilization*, i, 141-3). But Lecky was also familiar with these three ecclesiastical historians, and not necessarily because Buckle had drawn his attention to them.

59. A passage in Hallam's *Constitutional History* (ii, 50) dealt with the services rendered to English civilization by the vices of the English court in the time of Charles II. Buckle, acknowledging his debt to Hallam, expounded the same idea (*History of Civilization*, i, 313-4), while Lecky, clearly indebted to both Hallam and Buckle, attempted to generalize: 'That vice has often proved an emancipator of the mind, is one of the most humiliating, but, at the same time, one of the most unquestionable facts in history.' (*Rationalism*, ii, 65.) He reiterated the same idea in different words in the *Morals* (i, 37, 41), and gave Montesquieu as his authority for saying that the vices of the Roman politicians contributed to the greatness of their nation (*Morals*, i, 58).

60. Lecky and Buckle expressed similar views about the gradual diminution and near extinction of ecclesiastical power in Europe, and its replacement by a secular literary power. One illustration of this, they believed, was that people of first-rate intelligence were no longer entering the clerical profession. It does not follow, however, that Lecky got the idea from Buckle. He had been impressed rather by a statement of Carlyle's on this very subject (see above, p. 17). Buckle, discussing the topic, cited some observations of Laing on the same point (*History of Civilization*, i. 154, 288), and Lecky also read Laing as is indicated by his footnotes in *Rationalism* (i, 186; ii, 129).

61. *Memoir*, p. 30.

62. Lecky to Canning (*Memoir*, p. 210).

63. *Morals*, i, 314.

64. *Ibid.*, i, 103.

65. Buckle, *History of Civilization*, ii, 242.

66. *History of England in the Eighteenth Century* (1878), i, v-vi.

67. Lecky to 'a foreign friend' (Elisabeth van Dedem?), 30 July 1870 (*Memoir*, p. 59).

Chapter Three

1. Buckle, *History of Civilization*, ii, 239-40.
2. Lecky, *Rationalism*, i, xvii.
3. Lecky, *Morals*, i, 361.
4. *Ibid.*, i. 348, 352.
5. *British Quarterly Review*, XLII, no. 84, p. 406 (October 1865).
6. Lecky, *Morals*, i, 355. Quoting Bacon to the effect that 'men mark the hits but not the misses', Lecky continued: 'We are told of showers of rain that followed public prayer; but we are not told how often prayers for rain proved abortive ...' (*Morals*, i, 359).
7. *Ibid.*, ii, 231.
8. Lecky, *Rationalism*, i, 94, 288-9; ii, 336.
9. *Ibid.*, i, 350; ii, 3; *Essays*, p. 32.
10. *Ibid.*, ii, 336. 'Blind folly, ignoble selfishness, crushing tyranny and hideous cruelty mark every page of the history of the domination of Spain' (*Rationalism*, ii, 335). Buckle had a long chapter sketching the 'outline of the history of the Spanish intellect from the fifth to the middle of the nineteenth century', in which he described Spain derogatively as the sole representative still remaining of the feelings and knowledge of the Middle Ages (*History of Civilization*, ii, chapter 8, especially p. 471).
11. H. Butterfield, *Christianity and History* (first published by Bell & Sons, 1949, by Fontana, 1957, p. 126).
12. Buckle had a chapter entitled 'Influence exercised by physical laws over the organization of society, and over the character of individuals' (*History of Civilization*, i, chapter 2). The notion of the influence of geographical features and climate on civilization had become a commonplace since Montesquieu. The measure of civilization, said Buckle, is the triumph of mind over external agents' (*History of Civilization*, i, 119).
13. *Rationalism*, i, xii-xiv. Cf. also 'Conditions of race and climate have ever impelled the inhabitants of these lands [Western Europe] to active life, and have at the same time rendered them constitutionally incapable of enduring the austerities or enjoying the hallucinations of the sedentary Oriental' (*Morals*, ii, 178). Elsewhere Lecky referred to the influence which climate had, not only on the passions, but also in determining the 'position, character and tastes of women', and 'the classes among whom the gift of beauty is diffused' (*Morals*, i, 144-5).
14. Buckle, *History of Civilization*, i, 22-5.
15. Adolf Quetelet (1796-1874) born in Ghent; professor of mathematics; supervisor of statistics for the Belgium government; convened the first international congress of statisticians at Brussels 1853; author of *La Statistique Morale* (1848). He was fond of the word 'milieu', which Comte had popularised. Acton (*Historical Essays*, p. 317) held Quetelet in much lower esteem than did Buckle.
16. *Rationalism*, i, xiii.
17. *Ibid.* Cf. Buckle '... we are able to predict, within a very small limit of error, the number of voluntary deaths ...' (*History of Civilization*, i, 24).
18. *Morals*, i, 112. Later, however, Lecky was to deny that the future could be forecast with the minuteness that obtained in the physical sciences since history never exactly repeated itself (*Essays*, p. 23; see above, p. 54).
19. Buckle, who had leaned in his argument towards rejecting free will, finally said that it did not matter for his scheme whether it existed or not, and then proceeded without taking it into account (see, especially, chapter one of his *History of Civilization*, and Acton's comments in *Historical Essays*, pp. 312-3).

20. *Rationalism*, i, x. Acton (*Historical Essays*, pp. 312-3); James Fitzjames Stephen ('The Study of History', first published in *Cornhill Magazine*, iii, 666-80, June 1861, and republished in *History and Theory*, i, no. 2, 1961, pp. 186-201, especially p. 196) also defended free will with the same Lockian argument.

21. *Rationalism*, i, xiv.

22. One reason for the non-elaboration of the point is that Lecky was specifically concerned with the rise of rationalism in Europe and with the history of morals in Europe, and Buckle had said that the physical laws of climate were of less significance in an advanced civilization like that of Europe. 'Mental laws' were 'the ultimate basis of the history of Europe' (*History of Civilization*, i, 119). 'I have looked at civilization as broken into two great divisions: the European division, in which man is more powerful than nature; and the non-European division, in which nature is more powerful than man' (*Ibid.*, i, 195).

23. *Morals*, i, 130.

24. For this concept in Gibbon and Voltaire, see A.D. Momigliano, *Studies in Historiography*, p. 49.

25. However, he did not remain doctrinaire on this point, no more than on other matters, and later claimed that change sometimes came about by revolution, as when he wrote that the transformation of nations could be due either to the sudden, violent shock of revolution or to the slow process of evolution (*Essays*, p. 29). Lecky was influenced as much by the eighteenth-century historiography of Voltaire and Gibbon as by the nine-teenth-century scientific concepts of Darwin.

26. *Rationalism*, ii, 146-7. Cf. Acton's inaugural lecture on history: 'we dimly descry the Declaration of Independence in the forests of Germany'.

27. *Ibid.*, i, 59.

28. *Morals*, ii, 260.

29. 'The general tendencies of the age' was a pet phrase and 'tendency' a pet word of Lecky's. See, for example, *Rationalism*, i, vi, vii-viii, viii, xix, xx, xxiii, 277; ii, 234. *Morals*, i, 386. Cf. Buckle, *History of Civilization*, i, 291.

30. Comte and Buckle also liked to state that individuals were unable to alter substantially the direction of history.

31. *Rationalism*, i, xxi-xxii.

32. *Essays*, pp. 30-1.

33. Lecky was fond of the phrase 'climates of opinion' which he found in the seventeenth-century author Joseph Glanvill (1636-1680). It was a phrase which A. N. Whitehead in his *Science and the Modern World* helped to popularize in recent times.

34. *Essays*, p. 26.

35. *Morals*, i, 55.

36. *Rationalism*, i, xxi.

37. *Ibid.*, i, xvi. See above, p. 39. Lecky says that adherence to this principle was the special characteristic of that small but very definite school of historical writers which included Vico, Condorcet, Herder, Hegel, Comte and Buckle. See *Memoir*, pp. 55, 59 where Lecky attributes the idea more specifically to Comte.

38. We find it enunciated on at least eight separate occasions in this book, i.e. *Rationalism*, i, ix-x, xvi, xx-i, 222-3, 290, 302-3; ii, 98-9, 291-2. Cf. also 'The experience of 300 years has sufficiently demonstrated the fallacy of the old theory ... of the irresistible force of truth. Simple, unmingled reasoning never converts a people' (*Clerical Influences*, p. 30).

39. *Rationalism*, i, xx. Cf. also, 'It is much easier to govern great masses of men through their imagination than through their reason' (*Morals*, ii, 271).

40. *Rationalism*, i, 222-3.

41. *Ibid.*, ii, 209-11. Cf. Buckle, 'If either a religion or a philosophy is too much in advance of a nation it can do no present service but must bide its time until the minds of men are ripe for its reception' (*History of Civilization*, i, 208).

42. *Rationalism*, ii, 209.

43. *Ibid.*, i, 302-3.

44. *Ibid.*, i, 136-7.

45. Religious persecution, said Lecky, was only possible at all in a certain mental atmosphere. To engage in religious persecution, men had to have in the first place an 'intellectual antecedent' and believe, for example, in exclusive salvation within one church alone, and that it was their religious duty to persecute. Secondly, men needed an 'emotional antecedent' and be able to visualize, for example, the eternal and more extreme punishments of a future world (*Rationalism*, i, 328). Religious persecution was coextensive with clerical influence and a theological age (*ibid.*, ii, 39; i, 186-7). Gradually, however, everywhere throughout Europe ecclesiastical power had declined in inverse ratio to each country's intellectual progress. The resultant secularization of politics became the measure and the condition of all political prosperity (*ibid.*, ii, 131) and eliminated religious persecution, idolatry, superstition and witchcraft. The history of the emergence of modern constitutional governments was reduced by Lecky to a single all-embracing generalization – an age of sectarianism had slowly given way before an age of secularization (*ibid.*, ii, 136).

46. *Rationalism*, i, 303. Cf. also Buckle, dealing with 'a great change' which had been affected, 'not by any external event, nor by a sudden insurrection of the people, but by the unaided action of moral force – the silent, though overwhelming pressure of public opinion' (*History of Civilization*, i, 408-9).

47. *Rationalism*, i, xxi, 290. Cf. Buckle, '... every system must fall, if it opposes the march of opinions, and gives shelter to maxims and institutions repugnant to the spirit of the age' (*History of Civilization*, i, 407).

48. *Rationalism*, i, 350.

49. *Ibid.*, i, 223.

50. It was repeated in one form or another at least ten times, *Rationalism*, i, viii, ix, xxiii, 183-4, 290, 292, 407-8; ii, 85, 99, 210, 290.

51. *Ibid.*, i, 183-4. Lecky claimed that most writers who discussed miracles confined their attention to two points – the possibility of the fact, and the nature of the evidence. A third element of capital importance, however, was the predisposition of men in certain stages of civilization towards the miraculous (*Morals*, i, 361).

52. *Rationalism*, i, 407-8. Cf. Michelet, 'Woe to him who tries to isolate one department of knowledge from the rest ... All science is one ... subjects which seem the most remote from one another are in reality connected, or rather they all form a single system' (quoted in Edmund Wilson, *To the Finland Station*, first published by W.H. Allen, 1940, Fontana, 1960, p. 12). And Buckle had written '... to a philosophic mind every branch of knowledge lights up even those that seem most remote from it' (*History of Civilization*, i, 367).

53. *Morals*, i, 126-7.

54. *Ibid.*, i, 153.

55. *Rationalism*, ii, 99.

56. *Ibid.*, ii, 85.

57. *Ibid.*, ii, 290.

58. *Ibid.*, i, ix. Cf. Buckle, 'When you increase the contact, you remove the ignorance, and thus you diminish the hatred ... every new railroad which is laid down, and every fresh

steamer which crosses the Channel, are additional guarantees for the preservation of that long and unbroken peace which, during forty years, has knit together the fortunes and the interests of the two most civilized nations of the earth' (*History of Civilization*, i, 175).

59. *Rationalism*, i, xxiii,. Cf. 'No truth is more clearly established in history than that the political decline of a nation is never an isolated fact ... When public opinion grows faint, when patriotism dies ... a corresponding decadence will be exhibited in every branch' (*Clerical Influences*, p. 17).

60. In *Morals* (i, 45-9), however, Lecky claimed that it was possible for people to be perfectly indifferent to one particular section of human life, without this indifference extending to the others. He gave as an example the practice of the murder or exposition of the children of poor parents among the ancient Greeks, which at the same time did not exercise any appreciable influence upon respect for adult life. In the same way, religious unveracity or the propagation of useful superstition did not in any degree imply industrial unveracity. Extreme dishonesty in speculation often coexisted with scrupulous veracity in business. Cruelty to animals might exist without leading to cruelty to men. Yet, on the other hand, Lecky added that strong philanthropy could hardly coexist with cannibalism, and that the 'association of ideas' might explain why the habit of benevolence which was generated originally by the social contact of man with man might ultimately be extended to the animal world. The phrase 'association of ideas' was quite freely used by Lecky in *Morals* (i, 23, 28, 48, 63, 64, 66, 67, 94). He attributed its popularization to Locke, and traced the development of the concept among the utilitarian moralists in his *Morals* (i, 23ff).

61. J. Bowle, *Politics and Opinion in the Nineteenth Century*, pp. 242, 244.

62. Cf. Buckle, who claimed that the gigantic crimes of Alexander or Napoleon became after a time void of effect, but the discoveries of great men never leave us; they are immortal (quoted in J. Bowle, *Politics and Opinion in the Nineteenth Century*, p. 240).

63. *Rationalism*, i, viii.

64. For an illustration of the process of popularization here alluded to by Lecky, and carried out in his own writings, see the pages dealing with Bernard de Fontenelle (1657-1757) and the popularization of scientific ideas in H. Butterfield, *The Origins of Modern Science* (new edn, 1962), pp. 160-6.

65. *Rationalism*, i, 16, 12. It was a commonplace of the eighteenth century that fear was one of the most relevant of human emotions in the matter of religion. Vico, Bayle and Hume gave the emotion of fear considerable importance in the explanation of primitive religions. Buckle, too, employed this idea.

66. *Ibid.*, ii, 272. This idea was also the basis of 'Clerical Influences'.

67. *Ibid.*, ii, 234-5.

68. *Ibid.*, ii, 287.

69. *Ibid.*, i, 63. Cf. Buckle (*History of Civilization*, i, 378, footnote 453): 'All great Revolutions have a direct tendency to increase insanity, as long as they last, and probably for some time afterwards; but in this, as in other respects, the French Revolution stands alone in the number of its victims.'

70. *Rationalism*, ii, 139.

71. J. Bowle, *Politics and Opinion in the Nineteenth Century*, p. 243. The numerous, long, and for the most part favourable, contemporary reviews of Lecky's popular books on the history of rationalism and morals support Bowle's statement.

72. The concept of change in the moral-type and in the moral-standard was the basic idea of his favourite among his own works, *Morals*. The concept was also returned to in his essay, 'Thoughts on History', and in his book *Map of Life*, pp. 42ff.

73. *Rationalism*, i, 304, 350; ii, 57, 228.

74. In his essay, 'Clerical Influences', Lecky wrote of the French army: 'It is the visible type and representative of the people, the embodiment of their feelings, and the chief object of their affections' (p. l8). More than a quarter of a century later, in a private letter, he wrote of America and France as representing the two types of democracy towards one or other of which the world was tending (Lecky to Lea, 14 November 1888, Lecky-Lea correspondence).

75. *Rationalism*, i, 301.

76. *Ibid.*, i, 304. The quotation from Michelet reads: 'If the archaeologist can determine the date of a monument by the form of its capital, with much greater certainty can the psychological historian assign to a specific period a moral fact, a predominating passion, or a mode of thought, and can pronounce it to have been impossible in the ages that preceded or followed.'

77. For an account of this controversy, see J.M. Robertson, *Buckle and His Critics* (1895).

78. 'Mr Buckle's Thesis and Method', and 'Mr Buckle's Philosophy of History', in *Historical Essays and Studies* (1908).

79. Acton, *Historical Essays*, p. 343.

80. *Ibid.*, p. 340.

81. Acton to Mary Gladstone, 25 November 1881 (Herbert Paul [ed.], *Letters of Lord Acton to Mary Gladstone*, p. 115).

82. *Rationalism*, i, 288-9.

83. James Fitzjames Stephen, 'The Study of History', republished in *History and Theory*, i, no. 2 (1961), p. 196.

84. Lecky to Wilmot Chetwode, 12 September 1861 (Hyde [ed.], *op. cit.*, p. 41).

85. Isaiah Berlin, in Preface to H.G. Schenk, *The Mind of the European Romantics*, p. xiii.

86. H.T. Buckle, *History of Civilization*, i, 192-3.

87. Acton, *Historical Essays*, p. 305.

88. George Eliot, 'The Influence of Rationalism', in *Fortnightly Review*, i (1865), pp. 43-55, republished in G. Eliot *Essays* (1884).

89. Lea to Lecky (*Memoir*, pp. 44-5).

90. Lecky to Wilmot Chetwode, 12 September 1861 (Hyde [ed.], *op. cit.*, p. 41).

91. 'Buckle is, I think, a very wonderful man, but has taken of course, only one aspect of things, and has borrowed immensely from Montesquieu' (*Memoir*, p. 30).

92. *Morals*, i, 74, 75, 90, 103, 314; ii, 115. For the references to Buckle in *Rationalism*, see *Rationalism*, i, 5, 40, 63, 70, 121, 122, 330, 405; ii, 9, 126, 174, 215, 322, 340.

93. Lecky to Booth, 18 July 1875 (*Memoir*, p. 106). Already in *Morals* (i, 79 ff.) Lecky had held that many of the diversities about standards of beauty and morals in the different degrees of civilization could be traced to 'accidental causes'.

94. A presidential lecture delivered to the Birmingham and Midland Institute, 10 October 1892, and republished in *Essays*.

95. *Essays*, p. 31.

96. Collingwood, *The Idea of History* (first published by the Clarendon Press, 1946, Oxford Paperback, 1961), p. 80.

97. *Essays*, p. 29.

98. *Ibid.*, p. 32. Cf. 'There is indeed a certain order and sequence in the history of opinions, as in the phases of civilization it reflects, which cannot be altogether destroyed, it is not the less true that man can greatly accelerate, retard or modify its course' (*Rationalism*, ii, 3).

99. *Essays*, p. 32.

100. *Ibid.*

101. *Rationalism*, ii, 215-6.

102. See J. B. Bury, 'Cleopatra's Nose', in *Selected Essays*, (ed. H. Temperley, 1930). For a criticism of Bury's theory of two different but co-operative categories – cause and effect and contingency – see M. Oakeshott, *Experience and its Modes*, pp. 133-41.

103. Essays, pp. 36-7. See also Lecky's attack on the 'historical fatalists' and on the inevitability of the French Revolution in *England*, v, 441.

104. Cf. Acton's argument in his essay, 'The American Revolution', to the effect that the threepenny tax on tea 'broke up the British Empire', *Lectures on Modern History* (first published by Macmillan & Co. Ltd., 1906, first published by Fontana, 1960, p. 292).

105. Lecky quotes Jefferson as saying that compromise in 1789 could have avoided all the bloodshed which in the long run achieved only what reason could have arranged in 1789 (*Essays*, pp. 37-8). S.R. Gardiner noted Lecky's 'unusual stress on the importance of the personal element in the making of history as against general causes.' Gardiner commented: 'If the French Revolutionists refused to imitate Washington or Lord Somers, it was not because they were personally foolish or ill-advised, but because the current of feeling bred of the stress of circumstances was sweeping them on in quite another direction' (*English Historical Review*, viii [April 1893], pp. 394-5).

106. It is only fair to point out, however, that Lecky's practice was sometimes better than his theory. For example, when discussing whether the wise policies of Burke and Chatham could have succeeded, he added 'but pure reason plays but a small part in politics' (*England*, iii, 395).

107. See pp. 110, 113, 117, 123, 131.

108. This appeared first in the American review, *Forum*, ix (June 1890), pp. 380-90. It was later included in *Essays*, and the relevant sections on Buckle are pp. 100-2.

109. *Essays*, p. 102.

110. In the same letter in which Lecky once referred to the author of *The History of the Decline and Fall of the Roman Empire* as 'my favourite Gibbon', he went on to describe him as 'the standard authority for everything that happened in the last 1,400 years whose accuracy has never been seriously attacked on any subject but Christian theology, and who on that subject has been so triumphantly and unquestionably vindicated that Dr Newman, the greatest English catholic, declared some years ago that he was the only English writer who could be esteemed a real ecclesiastical historian, and Dr Milman, who ... has edited Gibbon, has prefaced his edition by a declaration of boundless admiration of Gibbon's accuracy, and has (with a candour that is quite amazing in a clergyman) devoted about half his notes to showing the gross failure and disingenuousness of Guizot's attempts to impugn that accuracy' (Lecky to Wilmot Chetwode, 2 February 1862, in Hyde [ed.], *op. cit.*, pp. 50-1). For further comments by Lecky, see his essay on Gibbon in *Historians and Essayists*, IV (Warner Classics), used also as an introduction to *The History of the Decline and Fall of the Roman Empire*, edited by J. B. Bury (New York, 1906-07).

111. *Memoir*, p. 54.

112. *Essays*, p. 264. See footnote 110 above for similar comments on Milman.

113. *Ibid.*, p. 265.

114. First published in *Edinburgh Review* and included in *Essays*.

115. *Essays*, p. 3.

116. Lecky to Lady Blennerhassett, 19 March 1886 (Blennerhassett papers, Cambridge University Library, add. 7486, no. 52 [1] E).

117. *Memoir*, p. 23.

118. *Rationalism*, i, 53, 304.

119. Indirectly German scholarship left some mark on Lecky. Dean Stanley described

Milman's work as 'the first decisive inroad of German theology into England; the first palpable indication that the Bible could be studied like another book; that the characters and events of sacred history could be treated at once critically and reverently' (Lecky, *Essays*, p. 260). Through Milman, it was possible for Lecky to make contact with the spirit of German ecclesiastical scholarship.

120.   *Rationalism*, i, 372, 374; ii, 302.

121.   *Morals*, i, 169, 230.

122.   He did, however, use English translations of Ranke's *History of Prussia, and History of England* as sources (see *England*, i, 272, 274, 391, 349).

123.   For an account of the German historico-sociologists, see Carlo Antoni, *From History to Sociology: The Transition in German Historical Thinking* (translation by Hayden V. White, London, 1962).

124.   Lecky to Wilmot Chetwode, March 1869 (Hyde [ed.], *op. cit.*, p. 75).

125.   See above, p. 42.

126.   *Morals*, ii, 372.

127.   *Essays*, p. 23.

128.   *Ibid.*, p. 4.

129.   *Ibid.*, pp. 2-3.

130.   'Thoughts on History' and 'The Political Value of History'. The first of these was largely based upon an earlier lecture entitled 'On the Influence of the Imagination in History', delivered on 29 May 1868 as a lecture to the Royal Institution. This was later rewritten as 'The Art of Writing History' for the American review *Forum*, XIV (February 1893), pp. 715-24. The second was his presidential address to the Birmingham and Midland Institute, delivered on 10 October 1892. Both were included in *Essays*.

131.   *Essays*, pp. 3-5.

132.   *Ireland*, i, Preface. For a fuller discussion of Lecky's employment of original documents, see pp. 76-7, 87, 89, 90-92.

133.   *Essays*, p. 3.

134.   *Ibid.*, p. 3.

135.   *Ibid.*, p. 10.

136.   Lecky to Lea, 21 October 1888 (Henry Charles Lea Library, University of Pennsylvania).

137.   Ranke, who, more than anyone else, was responsible for the insistence on the importance of the document, also recognised this limitation. However, the difference between Lecky and Ranke was that the latter welcomed the limitation. History, he said, did not aspire to such high offices as judging the past and instructing the present for the benefit of the future; the writing of history could not be expected to possess the same free development of its subject which, in theory at least, was expected in a work of literature. The strict presentation of the facts, however unconditional and unattractive they might be, was for him the supreme law (see the Preface to *Histories of the Latin and Germanic Nations 1494-1514*).

138.   *Essays*, pp. 11, 30-1.

139.   *Ibid.*, p. 29.

140.   *Ibid.*, pp. 8-9.

141.   *Rationalism*, i, 299-300.

142.   *Essays*, p. 269.

143.   Acton to Mary Gladstone, 14 December 1880, 27 April 1882 (Herbert Paul [ed.], *Letters of Lord Acton to Mary Gladstone*, pp. 51, 151).

Chapter Four

1. 'Early Recollections of Mr Lecky', in *National Review*, xliii (March 1904), p. 117.

2. Lecky to Wilmot Chetwode, 21 March 1866 (Hyde [ed.], *op. cit.*, p. 67).

3. *Leaders* (1903), ii, 279. Lecky's source was Froude, Carlyle, i, 399.

4. Lecky's diagnosis bears remarkable similarities to that given by Lord Derby in a speech in the House of Lords and reported in *The Times*, 10 March 1871. Derby was the friend of both Lecky and Froude, and Lecky later wrote a biographical essay on Derby (published in *Essays*, pp. 200-41). The three friends may well have discussed the question of Anglo-Irish relations. All three held certain general ideas in common on the subject. They were agreed about the evil political influence of the priests and the press in Ireland, and that the government of Ireland should be both strong and just, not submitting to Irish demands merely as a result of fear and agitation. They were sceptical that remedial measures like the disestablishment and land acts, or the increase in material prosperity, could ever cure Irish disloyalty, for at least Derby and Lecky believed that the spirit of nationality, which they traced back to the movement that had produced the legislative independence of 1782, lay at the basis of Irish disaffection. Where Lecky differed from his friends was in believing that some concessions should be made to nationality and that the Irish would be satisfied with a great deal less than the separation which Froude and Derby maintained was the objective.

5. *Leaders*, (1871), pp. xii-xiii.

6. *Ibid.*, p. xiii.

7. *Ibid.*, pp. xiv-xv.

8. *Ibid.*, p. vi.

9. *Ibid.*, pp. ix-x.

10. *Ibid.*, p. xiv.

11. *Ibid.*, p. xix.

12. *Nation*, 13 March 1869, quoted in D. Thornley, *Isaac Butt and Home Rule* (1964), p. 87.

13. Acton, *Correspondence*, i, xiii, 312-6.

14. *Leaders* (1871), p. xxiv.

15. Russell to Lecky, 8 January 1872 (Vienna); Margaret Elliot to Lecky, 28 December 1871; Plunket to Lecky 24 March 1872 (Lecky correspondence TCD nos 72, 78).

16. *Leaders* (1871), p. xxiii. Lecky was later to state that the real heirs of Grattan's parliament were to be found not in the home rule party but in the representative church body. See pp. 118, 239fn. 11.

17. O'Neill Daunt Journal, 4 July 1870 (NLI, MS 3041).

18. *Leaders* (1871), p. 197.

19. Acton, *Correspondence*, i, xiii; see also Acton's essay, 'Nationality', in *History of Freedom and Other Essays* (Figgis and Laurence [eds.]), pp. 270-300.

20. For a discussion of the original membership, see D. Thornley, *op. cit.*, p. 93.

21. For a discussion of a possible reason for Lecky not being invited to join the home rule movement, see above pp. 82-5.

22. *Leaders* (1871), p. xxiv.

23. Lecky to Wilmot Chetwode, 17 January 1872 (Hyde [ed.], *op. cit.*, p. 81).

24. It was also this chapter which had drawn attention to the sectarian nature of Irish politics. On this point Gavan Duffy wrote to Lecky from Melbourne on 7 September 1873: 'I am glad in this last edition that you have omitted the paper on Clerical Influence because it would stimulate a feeling already too strong in Ireland. That is not the scale in which it is necessary to put any weight; at all events addressing the cultivated classes in England'

(Lecky correspondence, TCD, no. 88).

25. Lecky to Wilmot Chetwode, 17 January 1872 (Hyde [ed.], *op. cit.*, p. 81).

26. Longman to Lecky, 4 January, 20 February 1872, 30 April 1878 (Lecky correspondence, TCD, nos 73, 74, 142); *Memoir*, p. 84.

27. H. Jolowicz to Lecky, 6 August 1872 (Lecky correspondence, TCD, no. 81).

28. Lecky to Booth, 24 January 1872 (*Memoir*, p. 83).

29. Longman to Lecky, 20 February 1872 (Lecky correspondence, TCD, no. 74).

30. Lecky to Booth, 24 January 1872 (*Memoir*, p. 83); Lecky to Wilmot Chetwode, 17 January 1872 (Hyde [ed.], *op. cit.*, p. 81).

31. John Morley, 'Irish Policy in the Eighteenth Century', in *Fortnightly Review*, new series, xi (February 1872), 196-203.

32. Lecky to Booth, 16 March 1872 (*Memoir*, p. 84).

33. Lecky to Wilmot Chetwode, 11 February 1872 (Hyde [ed.], *op. cit.*, p. 83). One of the three was M. F. Cusack, the famous Poor Clare, the 'Nun of Kenmare', who explained that on account of expenses connected with new convent buildings, she could not afford to buy a copy. Lecky sent her one, which she later quoted in the preface of her book *The Liberator: His Life and Times* (1872), in order to illustrate a typical Englishman's prejudice. When Lecky corrected her about his nationality, she apologised and offered to do so by a letter to the newspapers (Lecky correspondence, TCD, nos 66, 83).

34. *Nation*, 3 February 1872. This review article was unsigned, but it was possibly the work of the editor and proprietor, A. M. Sullivan, who besides being actively engaged in politics, was the author of popular works on Irish history.

35. MacCarthy, a Cork solicitor and MP, belonged to the moderate and federalist wing of the Home Government Association. He was also the author of *Irish Land Questions Plainly Stated and Answered.*

36. J. G. MacCarthy, *A Plea for the Home Government of Ireland* (3rd edn, 1872), pp. 100-1, 94, 93. The quotation from Lecky is from *Leaders* (1871), p. 197. In MacCarthy's book there are slight but insignificant variations of wording – MacCarthy uses 'strong' where the original reads 'are so powerful', and 'adopted' where the original had 'preferred'.

37. *Memoir*, pp. 76, 77, 80, 88.

38. *Ibid.*, p. 41.

39. *Leaders* (1871) was rewritten in the early years of the Carlyle-Lecky friendship.

40. In 1864 Lecky already held with the political economists, especially J. B. Say, that authors were producers, and if therefore he published a book in his own name, he would 'without too much shame and trepidation' be able to encounter his friends who had gone into the professions. See *Memoir*, pp. 35-6.

41. *Essays*, p. 110.

42. *Ibid.*, p. 115.

43. *Ibid.*, pp. 41-2.

44. *Ibid.*, p. 115.

45. The denunciation of the methods by which the Union was carried run throughout all of Lecky's work on the subject.

46. *Democracy and Liberty* (1913), i, 162.

47. *Essays*, p. 115.

48. *Ibid.*, p. 91. Lecky recommended as an antidote to Carlyle, H. Spencer's *The Man and the State* (*Essays*, p. 109).

49. *Essays*, pp. 113-4. See also *Memoir*, p. 74.

50. *Memoir*, p. 8.

51. H. Allingham and D. Radford (eds), *William Allingham: A Diary*, pp. 177, 262, 277, 241.

52. *Memoir*, p. 92.

53. Wilson and MacArthur, *Carlyle*, vi, 322.

54. Duffy to Lecky, 15 March 1873 (Lecky correspondence, TCD, no. 85).

55. *Macmillan's Magazine*, xxx (June 1874), p. 173. The influence of Carlyle on *The English in Ireland* was noted not only by Lecky and Gavan Duffy but also by A. V. Dicey in *Nation* (New York), xvi, no. 412 (22 May 1872); J. E. Cairnes in *Fortnightly Review*, new series, xvi, no. 92 (August 1874; *Edinburgh Review*, cxxxvii, no. 279 (January 1873); *Dublin Review*, new series, xx, no. 39 (January 1873). Various critics including *British Quarterly*, lvii, no. 94 (April 1873) and *Spectator*, xlv, no. 2318 (30 November 1872) also noted what they called the kind of literary brutality affected by Carlyle and his disciples which would excite more moral disgust were it not perceived to be a slightly ridiculous affectation.

56. Lecky to Froude (draft) June 1874 (Lecky correspondence, TCD, no. 97).

57. *Rationalism*, ii, 358.

58. *Ibid.*, ii, 121-5.

59. *Memoir*, p. 95.

60. Lecky to Booth, *ibid.*, p. 95. To another friend he wrote: 'I am at present trying to write a very severe and angry review of Froude's book about Ireland which is a singularly incontinent and abusive performance which has exasperated me more than I can say.' (Lecky to Wilmot Chetwode, 20 November 1872, quoted in Hyde [ed.], *A Victorian Historian*, p. 85).

61. J. A. Froude, *The English in Ireland* (1872), i, 2.

62. *Rationalism*, ii, 214-5.

63. *Ibid.*, ii, x, 227-8.

64. See, for example, *Rationalism*, ii, 225, 227, 226.

65. *Ibid.*, ii, 226. Froude's essays on the colonies were first published in *Fraser's Magazine* for January and September 1870 and republished in J. A. Froude, *Short Studies on Great Subjects*, vol. II.

66. *Macmillan's Magazine*, xxvii (January 1873), p. 247.

67. *Ibid.*, p. 246.

68. *Ibid.*, p. 247.

69. *Ibid.*, p. 253.

70. It is because Froude's most recent biographer, W. H. Dunn, chooses to regard Lecky's criticisms simply as 'sweeping generalizations' (p. 364) that he misses the significance of the intellectual dichotomy illustrated in the Lecky-Froude controversy. Nor is it enough for Dunn to quote Froude's earlier biographer, Herbert Paul, to the effect that Lecky wrote as an Irish patriot and that Froude wrote as an English one (p. 366). Dunn, while supplying much valuable material on Froude, is too much of an apologist. Paul is fairer to Lecky, although perhaps he wrote too close to the period to get it into fuller perspective.

71. *Macmillan's Magazine*, xxx (June 1874), p. 180.

72. Carlyle to Froude, 20 June 1874 (H. Paul, *Life of Froude*, pp. 242-3).

73. For volume and page references and a more detailed discussion, see my paper 'James Anthony Froude and Ireland' in *Historical Studies: Papers read before the Irish Conference of Historians*, viii, edited by T. D. Williams (Dublin, 1971).

74. J. A. Froude, *The English in Ireland* (1872), i, 2.

75. Lecky to Elisabeth van Dedem (*Memoir*, p. 74).

76. J. A. Froude, *Thomas Carlyle*, ii, 422.

77. *Ibid.* Leslie Stephen, too, accepted the Carlyle-Froude explanation. See his 'Carlyle's Ethics' in *Hours in a Library* (1892), iii, 286-94.

78. *Essays*, p. 113.

79. *Fortnightly Review*, new series, xvi, no. 92 (August 1874), p. 172.

80. So, too, did a more recent commentator on Carlyle's doctrine, Pieter Geyl in his *Debates with Historians* (Fontana Library, 1962), pp. 62-3.

81. J. R. Green used to chaff E. A. Freeman, who had once carried on a notorious literary feud with Froude about 'lying down with Froude' in his later years. See J.W. Thompson, *A History of Historical Writing* (New York, 1942), ii, 316.

82. T. N. Burke, Ireland's *Vindication* (Glasgow, n.d.). For a more detailed discussion of the reactions to Froude, see my paper 'James Anthony Froude and Ireland', in *Historical Studies: Papers Read Before the Irish Conference of Historians*, viii, ed., T. D. Williams.

83. J. P. Prendergast's reply was published in a couple of letters and a series of review articles in *Freeman's Journal*, 11, 19 November 1872, and *Nation*, 16, 23, 30 November, 7, 14, 21, 28 December 1872, 11, 18 January 1873. Taken together, these articles add up to a much more impressive display of knowledge of the historical material than Father Burke showed. Yet the impulsive patriotism, interlaced with frantic name-calling, detracted from the effect of genuine scholarship.

84. Lecky to Duffy, 2 June 1873 (NLI, Duffy correspondence, MS 8005).

85. John Mitchel, *1641: Reply to the Falsification of History by James Anthony Froude, entitled 'The English in Ireland': the Crusade of the Period* (Glasgow, n.d.). The Irish-American library edition (New York, 1873) omitted some of the more strongly worded passages. Mitchel's work was largely indebted to Prendergast's *Cromwellian Settlement* and to Prendergast's review articles in *Nation*.

86. *Essays*, p. 2.

87. *Morals*, i, xii-xiii.

88. *Essays*, p. 11.

89. J. A. Froude, *Short Studies on Great Subjects* (Silver Library edn 1915), i, 35-6.

90. For Edmund Burke's interest in a 'philosophical' history of Ireland, see Walter D. Love's 'Charles O'Conor of Belanagare and Thomas Leland's "Philosophical History of Ireland"', *Irish Historical Studies*, xiii, no. 49 (March 1962), pp. 1-25. For the continuation of the 1641 controversy into the early nineteenth century, see my article 'The Writing of History in Ireland, 1800-1830' in *I.H.S.*, x, no. 40 (September 1957), pp. 347-62.

91. Lecky, *Ireland* (cabinet edn), i, 82; *England* (1878), ii, 155. See also *Macmillan's Magazine*, xxx (June 1874), pp. 179-80.

92. *Essays*, p. 6; *Macmillan's Magazine*, xxvii (January 1873), p. 253.

93. *Essays*, pp. 6-7. The Preface to Lecky's *England* showed the persistent influence of Buckle and the sociological school, for *England* was more concerned with the 'permanent forces' of the nation, with the social, intellectual and religious changes, and with the growth or decline of monarchy, aristocracy, democracy, industry and trade.

94. J. A. Froude, *Short Studies on Great Subjects* (Silver Library edn, 1915), ii, 589, 591-2.

95. *Ibid.*, ii, 572.

96. J. A. Froude, *Short Studies on Great Subjects* (Silver Library edn, 1915), i, 1.

97. Quoted by W. S. Lilly in *Nineteenth Century*, xxxviii, no. 224 (October 1895), p. 269.

98. J. A. Froude in Preface to M. Hickson, *Ireland in the Seventeenth Century*, i, ix.

99. J. A. Froude, *English in Ireland* (1872), i, 83, 134.

100. Justin McCarthy relates in *Galaxy*, xiv, no. 3 (September 1873), pp. 298-9, how Froude published a story of a Kerry eviction without waiting for the details to be checked by the peer (Lansdowne) who was involved, and to whom Froude had sent proofs of the page. The peer and others hastened to contradict Froude's published article. The incident nearly involved Froude in a lawsuit and it led to a cooling in his relations with Lansdowne.

101. J. A. Froude, *The Two Chiefs of Dunboy.*

102. Lecky to Standish O'Grady, 25, 30 March (TCD, Lecky correspondence, nos 2541, 2542).

103. *Ireland,* i, 75, 80-81, 73, 100. The fact that protestant writers like Warner, Carte and Henry Brooks and, in Lecky's own time, Prendergast and Gilbert, distrusted the evidence of these depositions carried much weight with him.

104. *Macmillan's Magazine,* xxvii (January 1873), p. 252.

105. *England,* ii, 127, 168; *Ireland,* i, 46, 100.

106. *England,* ii, 169. It may be significant that Lecky in *Macmillan's Magazine,* January 1873, p. 252, used the following words in a sentence: 'What can be thought of an *historian?*' When he came to rewrite the sentence for his *England* (1878), ii, 127, he used the words: 'The reader must form his own judgement of the *writer...*'. *Writer* had been substituted for *historian* (my italics).

107. *Academy,* new series, xxvi, no. 642 (23 August 1884), pp. 121-2.

108. J. A. Froude in Preface to M. Hickson, *Ireland in the Seventeenth Century,* i, x.

109. M. Hickson, *Ireland in the Seventeenth Century,* i, 121, noted this point.

110. Hickson to Lecky, 1 July 1884 (TCD, Lecky correspondence, no. 263).

111. See S. R. Gardiner, *England* (new edn, 1894), x, 68, and his review of her book in *Academy,* new series, xxvi, no. 638 (26 July 1884), p. 53. An exchange of public letters by Hickson, Gardiner and Lecky followed in *Academy,* new series, xxvi, nos 640, 642, 644, 645, 647 (9, 23 August, 6, 13, 27 September 1884), pp. 95, 121-2, 153-4, 169, 203.

112. *Ireland,* i, 80-1; *Academy,* new series, xxvi, no. 642 (23 August 1884), pp. 121-2.

113. T. Fitzpatrick, *The Bloody Bridge,* p. 72.

114. M. Hickson, *Ireland in the Seventeenth Century,* i, 121-2.

115. S. R. Gardiner, *England* (new edn, 1894), x, 64-5. See also Gardiner to Gilbert, 30 March 1880 (R. M. Gilbert, *Life of Sir John T. Gilbert,* p. 271); 'Lecky's account ... seems to me to be singularly fair and painstaking, in so far as I have yet been able to understand the matter.'

116. *Ibid.;* R. Dunlop, *Ireland under the Commonwealth,* i, cxvii. The argument about the depositions has never been resolved. Hickson, Froude and, to a lesser extent, Bagwell tended to accept at least some of the evidence in them. Prendergast, Gilbert, Lecky, Fitzpatrick and Dunlop minimised their historical value. Both Froude and Dunlop (see Preface to Hickson, *op. cit.,* ix, xii; Dunlop, *Ireland under the Commonwealth,* i, cxviii) called for the publication of an authoritative calendar of the depositions in the manner of the State Papers. This has never been done and Gilbert reported adversely on them to the Historical Manuscripts Commission (see the *Eighth Report on the Historical MSS Commission*). One of the reasons why they were not published is undoubtedly because Froude urged these depositions as an 'eternal witness' of Irish barbarity. Since, as Fitzpatrick said (*The Bloody Bridge,* p. xvi), the 'eternal witness' was urged against a nation and a creed, not simply against those who were suspected of a crime, Froude's point about publication was not well received. See also R. Dunlop, 'The Depositions Relating to the Irish Massacres of 1641' in *English Historical Review,* i, no. 4 (October 1886), pp. 740-4, and his subsequent controversy with Hickson in *English Historical Review,* ii, no. 5 (January 1887), pp. 133-7; no. 6 (April 1887), pp. 338-40; no. 7 (July 1887), p. 527. Dunlop took the line that Gilbert, on the one hand, and Hickson and Froude on the other, represented the two extreme views regarding the credibility and historical importance of the depositions. Dunlop argued that the middle view of Lecky and Prendergast was 'as near the truth as we are likely to get'. Hickson claimed that her views were nearer to Lecky's than to any other.

117. *Ireland*, i, vi.

118. John Mitchel, *History of Ireland*.

119. Prendergast to Lecky, 27 January 1878 (TCD, Lecky correspondence, no. 134).

120. 'Historicus' (i.e. R. Barry O'Brien), *The Best Hundred Irish Books*, p. 5.

121. *The Times*, 29 October, 8 November 1872; *Saturday Review*, xxxiv, no. 88 (2 November 1872), pp. 553-4; *Athenaeum*, no. 2352 (23 November 1872), p. 668.

122. See the summaries of Lecky's case in, for example, *Monitor, An Illustrated Dublin Magazine*, new series, i (March 1879), pp. 181-99; *Nation*, 4 January 1873, 20 June 1874, 1, 8 June 1878.

123. *Monitor*, new series, i (March 1879), p. 198.

124. *Dublin Review*, new series, xx, no. 39 (January 1873), p. 259.

125. See above, p. 77.

126. Gavan Duffy to Lecky, 15 March 1873 (TCD, Lecky correspondence, no. 85).

127. De Vere to Lecky, 28 January 1879 (Hague collection, Lecky correspondence).

128. Lecky to O'Neill Daunt, 7 April 1870 (*ibid.*, no. 167); a copy exists in O'Neill Daunt Journal (NLI MS 3042, appendix).

129. O'Neill Daunt Journal (NLI MS 3042), 19 June 1878; 13 January, 15 May 1879, 17 March 1880.

130. O'Neill Daunt to Lecky, 11 April 1879 (Lecky correspondence, TCD no. 168).

131. *Ibid*.

132. *Nation*, 4 January 1873. Lecky had expressed similar views in *Rationalism*, ii, 6, and *Leaders* (1871), pp. 214, 33.

133. *Nation*, 20 June 1874.

134. *Macmillan's Magazine*, xxx (June 1874), pp. 166, 168, 169.

135. *Irishman*, 13, 20 June 1874; *Flag of Ireland*, 13, 20 June 1874.

136. This passage was a continuous sentence as published in *Macmillan's Magazine*; the *Irishman* presented it as a series of propositions with certain phrases in italics. It is given above as it appeared in the *Irishman*, with the correction of certain misprints.

137. *Macmillan's Magazine*, xxvii (January 1873), p. 257. In denying that Ireland wanted separation, Lecky was in agreement with the *Nation* (11 May 1872) which, in a reply to *Fraser's Magazine*, also denied that Ireland desired separation. See also the denial by John Martin in the *Nation* (25 January 1873). Charles Gavan Duffy was in the habit of making similar denials.

138. *The Times*, 4 April 1874.

139. *Edinburgh Review*, January 1873, p. 150.

140. *Saturday Review*, 2 November 1872, pp. 553-4.

141. *Irishman*, 11 April 1874.

142. Charles Gavan Duffy, 'A Fair Constitution for Ireland', in *Contemporary Review*, lii (September 1887), p. 332.

143. J. L. Whittle, 'the hammer of the ultramontanes' and a staunch unionist, was a younger contemporary of Lecky's at TCD. He wrote on educational topics, taking a line that was opposed to that of the catholic bishops. He was once described by the *Irish Ecclesiastical Record* as 'a catholic graduate of Trinity, though he may have forgotten his catechism while passing through the college' – *Irish Ecclesiastical Record*, ii (March 1866), p. 292.

144. *Quarterly Review*, clxv, no. 330 (October 1887), pp. 502-3.

145. Duffy to Lecky, 7 September 1873 (Lecky correspondence, TCD, no. 88). An extract from Duffy's letter is given above, see p. 228, fn.24.

146. *Month*, x (June 1869); *Dublin Review*, xiii, no. 25 (July 1869), pp. 203-7.

147. *Irish Ecclesiastical Record*, ii (November 1865), pp. 97-8; iv (June 1868), p. 440; vi (October 1869).
148. Lecky to Booth, 24 January 1872 (*Memoir*, p. 83).
149. For the attitude of these bishops to home rule, see E. R. Norman, *The Catholic Church and Ireland in the Age of Rebellion 1859-73*; D. Thornley, *Isaac Butt and Home Rule*.
150. D. Thornley, *op. cit.*, pp. 144-5.
151. H. M. Hyde (ed.), *A Victorian Historian*, p. 81.
152. *Memoir*, pp. 100-1.
153. Lecky to Booth, 26 February 1874 (*Memoir*, p. 101).
154. Lecky to Bowen, 6 July 1874 (*Memoir*, p. 102). John Martin also wrote to O'Neill Daunt saying that he felt uncomfortable about the Irish performance.
155. Whittle to Lecky, 7 January 1888 (Lecky correspondence, TCD, no. 497).

Chapter Five

1. J. W. Thompson, *A History of Historical Writing*, ii, 334.
2. *England*, i, 115.
3. *Memoir*, p. 88.
4. *Ibid.*, p. 103.
5. *Ibid.*, p. 104.
6. *Ibid.*, p. 110.
7. *Ibid.*, pp. 108-9.
8. *Ibid.*, p. 121.
9. *Ibid.*
10. *British Quarterly Review*, LXX, no. 139 (July 1879); *Nineteenth Century*, vi, no. 30 (August 1879), pp. 250-92.
11. *Memoir*, p. 135.
12. *Ibid.*, p. 141.
13. *Ibid.*, pp. 137-8.
14. *England*, iii, 14.
15. H. Butterfield, *George III and the Historians*, pp. 159-66.
16. *Memoir*, p. 160.
17. *Ibid.*, p. 161.
18. Harvey Wish, *The American Historian*, pp. 115, 121, 141, 163, 278, 308.
19. *England*, iii, 181.
20. See below, pp. 112-3.
21. Acton to Lecky, 30 April 1882.
22. *Memoir*, p. 169.
23. *Ibid.*, p. 172.
24. Hedva Ben-Israel, *English Historians on the French Revolution*, pp. 240-3.
25. *England*, vii, 384; *Nineteenth Century*, xxi, no. 124 (June 1887), 932-6; xxii, no. 125 (July 1887), 52-4; xxii, no. 126 (August 1887), 279; *Democracy and Liberty* (1896), i, 132-7.
26. *Freeman's Journal*, cited in *Memoir*, p. 199.
27. *Memoir*, p. 209.
28. *Nation* (New York), 18 December 1890, p. 484.
29. *Quarterly Review*, clxxii, no. 343 (January 1891), 1-32.
30. *Irish Times*, 16 October 1890, p. 5.
31. *Memoir*, p. 210.

32. *Ibid.*, p. 218
33. *Ibid.*
34. *Freeman's Journal,* 8 April 1878, p. 2.
35. *Speaker,* 28 February 1891, p. 258.
36. *British Quarterly,* 1891, p. 642; *Pall Mall Gazette,* 15 October 1891, p. 1.
37. H. Butterfield, *George III and the Historians,* p. 159.
38. *Memoir,* p. 88.
39. *The Times Literary Supplement,* 1937, p. 320.
40. H. Butterfield, *op. cit.,* p. v.
41. G. P. Gooch, *History and Historians in the Nineteenth Century,* p. 367.
42. L. P. Curtis (ed.), *Ireland in the Eighteenth Century* (abridged), p. xxiii, n. 2.
43. Registry of deeds (abstract), 14 June 1881, xxv, no. 87; 15 June 1882, xxxvi, no. 285; 15 June 1882, xxxvii, no. 35; 18 January 1882, xxxvii, no. 34; 19 June 1883, xl, no. 75; 24 September 1883, xlvii, no. 73.
44. Lecky to Booth, 9 September 1865 (*Memoir,* p. 43).
45. Lecky to Booth, 12 August 1869 (*Memoir,* pp. 64-5); *Leinster Express,* 17, 24 July 1869.
46. *Leinster Express,* 24 July 1869.
47. Lecky to Booth, 12 August 1869 (*Memoir,* pp. 64-5).
48. William Phillips of St Germaine's, Portarlington, the owner of 739 acres in Queen's County acted as agent for Lecky (*Return of Owners of Land … 1876*).
49. Lecky to Bowen, 14, 30 March 1870 (*Memoir,* pp. 67-9).
50. Lecky to Countess of Carnwath (his stepmother), 15 April 1881 (*Memoir,* p. 155).
51. Lecky to O'Neill Daunt, 15 October 1880 (Lecky correspondence, TCD, no. 206); Lecky to Countess of Carnwath, 15 April 1881 (*Memoir,* p. 155).
52. *Carlow Sentinel,* 30 January 1904.
53. K. Buckley, 'The Fixing of Rents by Agreement in Co. Galway', in *I.H.S.,* vii, no. 27 (March 1951), p. 168, fn. 64.
54. *Daily Express* (Dublin), 11 November 1895.
55. Lecky to O'Neill Daunt, 14 December 1879 (Lecky correspondence, TCD, nos 179, 180). Also O'Neill Daunt Journal, NLI, MS 3042, see appendix; *Memoir,* pp. 138-40.
56. Lecky to O'Neill Daunt, 22 December 1879 (*ibid.,* no. 183); *Memoir,* p. 140; O'Neill Daunt Journal, NLI, MS 3042, see appendix.
57. Lecky to O'Neill Daunt, 8 February 1880 (*ibid.,* no. 187); *Memoir,* pp. 140-1; O'Neill Daunt Journal, NLI MS 3042, see Appendix.
58. On a number of occasions in the earliest editions of *Leaders* (1861 and 1871), Lecky had referred anachronistically to the 'patriots' of eighteenth-century Ireland as the 'liberal party'. He regarded Gladstone as following in this tradition.
59. O'Neill Daunt Journal, NLI, MS 3042, 11 September 1880. Compulsory sale is precisely what Parnell was demanding in 1880 before the United States Congress (see T. Brown, *Irish-American Nationalism,* p. 103).
60. O'Neill Daunt Journal, NLI, MS 3042, 11 September 1880.
61. Lecky to O'Neill Daunt, 15 October 1880 (*ibid.,* no. 206); *Memoir,* p. 146.
62. O'Neill Daunt to Lecky, 21 September 1889 (*ibid.,* no. 203).
64. Lecky to O'Neill Daunt, 1 October 1880 (*ibid.,* no. 204); *Memoir,* p. 144.
64. Lecky to O'Neill Daunt, 15 October 1880 (*ibid.,* no. 206); *Memoir,* p. 146.
65. Lecky to O'Neill Daunt, 11 December 1880 (*ibid.,* no. 214).
66. Lecky to O'Neill Daunt, 5 April 1881 (*ibid.,* no. 224).
67. Lecky to O'Neill Daunt, 1 October 1880 (*ibid.,* no. 204); *Memoir,* pp. 145-6.
68. Lecky to O'Neill Daunt, 29 September 1881 (*ibid.,* no. 238); *Memoir,* p. 158.

69. Lecky to O'Neill Daunt, 11 June 1882 (*ibid.*, no. 258); *Memoir*, pp. 166-7.

70. Lecky to Booth, 5 March 1884; *Memoir*, p. 175.

71. Lecky to O'Neill Daunt, 22 January 1886 (Lecky correspondence, TCD, no. 358).

72. Lecky to O'Neill Daunt, 16 January 1886 (*ibid.*, no. 351); *Memoir*, p. 186. See also Lecky to O'Neill Daunt, 22 December 1879, 29 September 1881 (*ibid.*, nos 183, 238).

73. See, for example, Lecky to Countess of Carnwath, 15 April 1881, and Lecky to Booth, 24 April, 4 August 1881 (*Memoir*, pp. 155-6).

74. Lecky to O'Neill Daunt, 5 April 1881 (Lecky correspondence, TCD, no. 224); Lecky to Countess of Carnwath, 15 April 1881 (*Memoir*, p. 155).

75. Lecky to Booth, November 1881 (*Memoir*, p. 157).

76. *The Times*, 25 January 1882. In *Democracy and Liberty* (i, 187-99) he characterized the 1881 Land Act as one of the most extreme violations of the rights of property in the history of Irish legislation. He also explained the principle of compensation which he advocated in regard to any interference by the state with landed property (*op. cit.*, i, 191-2).

77. *The Times*, 31 January 1882.

78. *Ibid.*, 3 February 1882.

79. Lecky to Booth, 5 March 1884 (*Memoir*, p. 175).

80. The deputation presented a memorial signed by over two thousand people including farmers, peers, MPs, clergymen of all denominations, bankers, solicitors, physicians and merchants, requesting the government to extend the period for repayments which would mean the lowering of instalments and would facilitate purchase. It also requested that corresponding facilities be extended to landowners to borrow money to pay off incumberance (*Irish Times*, 6 March 1884). A statement submitted to her majesty's ministers by the Irish Landowners' Convention in February 1888 also suggested a government loan at low interest to the landlords to pay off the heavy charges on Irish land. This, too, was warmly approved by Lecky (see *Democracy and Liberty*, i, 201-2).

81. J. Frederick Lecky to Lecky, 15 November 1895 (Lecky correspondence, TCD, no. 981).

82. See MacMurrough Kavanagh's references to the evidence of Lansdowne and Dufferin in his separate minority report drawn up by him as a commissioner on the Bessborough Commission. MacMurrough Kavanagh's report is printed as an appendix (E) to Sarah L. Steele, *Arthur MacMurrough Kavanagh*. The reference to Dufferin and Lansdowne is on p. 314. Lord Dufferin argued in *The Times* (December 1880) that the 'three Fs' even in a modified form implied confiscation. His letter was reprinted by the Irish Land Committee as a pamphlet, no. vi (January 1881).

83. *Leaders* (1861), pp. 211-4.

84. *Ibid.*

85. *Leaders* (1871), p. 254.

86. O'Neill Daunt to Lecky, 17 December 1879 (Lecky correspondence, TCD, nos 181-2).

87. *Leaders* (1871), p. 255.

88. *Ibid.*, pp. 309-10. Later he would add the writings of Lalor and Mitchel to these causes. See *England*, viii, 544-5.

89. *Leaders* (1871), p. xix.

90. *Ibid.*, p. 300.

91. *Ibid.*, p. 252.

92. *Ibid.*, pp. 252-3.

93. Jonah Barrington, *Personal Sketches* (3rd edn, 1869), pp. 301-2.

94. The Hartpole papers, once in Lecky's possession, are now in TCD.

95. Lord Aldborough's Memorandum, 27 January 1797 (Hartpole papers, TCD).

96. Young was also the author of the DNB article on Barrington.

97. *England*, iv, 517; *Ireland*, ii, 263.
98. *Ireland*, i, 292; *England*, ii, 297.
99. *Ireland*, i, 284; *England*, ii, 290.
100. *Ireland*, i, 213-4; *England*, ii, 240. See also *Democracy and Liberty*, i, 181.
101. *Ireland*, i, 293; *England*, ii, 297.
102. *Ibid.*
103. *Ibid.*, i, 291; *England*, ii, 296.
104. *Ireland*, iii, 403; *England*, vii, 160. See also *Democracy and Liberty*, i, 210-11.
105. *Ireland*, iii, 406; *England*, vii, 162.
106. *Ireland*, iii, 401; ii, 6; *England*, vii, 158; iv, 315-6. See also *Democracy and Liberty*, i, 178-80, 204.
107. *Ireland*, iii, 407; *England*, vii, 162; *Democracy and Liberty*, i, 179-180.
108. *Ireland*, iii, 397; *England*, vii, 155.
109. *Ireland*, iii, 415-7; *England*, vii, 170; *Leaders* (1903), i, 25-6.
110. *Ireland*, iii, 409-10; *England*, vii, 164-5.
111. *England*, iii, 184.
112. *Ireland*, iii, 408-12; *England*, vii, 163-4.
113. O'Neill Daunt to Lecky, 17 December 1879 (Lecky correspondence, TCD, no. 181).
114. Lecky to O'Neill Daunt, 22 January 1886 (*ibid.*, no. 358).
115. See the previous chapter.
116. In *The Times* (3 February 1882), for example, Lecky had argued that the 1881 Act deprived landlords in Ireland of part of their property without any compensation. In his history of the eighteenth century, he repeated the point: 'In our own day we have seen a number of valuable legal rights, which, a few years ago incontestably belonged to the landlord, transferred without compensation by English legislation to the tenant.' (*Ireland*, iii, 403; *England*, vii, 159.)
117. Lecky to O'Neill Daunt, 1 October 1880 (*ibid.*, no. 204); *Memoir*, pp. 144-6.
118. *Ireland*, i, 212 ff; *England*, ii, 239 ff.
119. Lecky to O'Neill Daunt, 1 October 1880 (*ibid.*, no. 204).
120. The latter two counties were where Lecky's own lands were situated.
121. This was the position in Lecky's own case.
122. An undated, incomplete and unaddressed draft of a letter by Lecky possibly to O'Neill Daunt (Lecky correspondence, TCD).
123. *Democracy and Liberty*, i, 210-1.
124. He referred his readers, for example, to *The Statements of the Irish Landowners' Convention*, to *The Report of the Land Acts Committee*, to *The Working of the Land Law* (*Democracy and Liberty*, i, 190, 196, 202).
125. *Essays*, p. 88.
126. Lecky's references were to recent studies by P. H. Bagenal, William Dillon and Gavan Duffy (*Ireland*, v, 485-6; *England*, vii, 545-6).
127. *Ireland*, i, 150; *England*, iii, 213.
128. *Ireland*, i, chapter II; *England*, ii, chapter VII.
129. *Ireland*, i, 151.
130. *Ibid.*, i, 279.
131. *Ibid.*, i, 151, 279-80.
132. *Ireland*, i, 278; *England*, ii, 286.
133. Lecky to O'Neill Daunt, 4 June 1882 (*ibid.*, no. 255); O'Neill Daunt Journal, NLI, MS 3042, appendix.
134. *England*, viii, 547; *Ireland*, v, 487-8; *Essays*, pp. 25, 87-8; *The Times*, 13 January, 7 June

1886; *Nineteenth Century*, xix (April 1886), pp. 636-44.

135. *England*, iv, 560; *Ireland*, ii, 317; *Essays*, p. 25.

136. See, for example, *England*, vi, 385; *Ireland*, ii, 427: 'No politician had ever less sympathy, than Grattan with disorder and anarchy: and his whole theory of Irish politics was very far from democratic. From first to last it was a foremost article of his policy that it was essential to the safe-working of representative institutions in Ireland that they should be under the full guidance and control of the property of the country and that the greatest of all calamities would be that this guidance should pass into the hands of adventurers and demagogues.'

137. 'It was necessary to withdraw the direction of affairs from a corrupt but intelligent aristocracy without throwing it into the hands of demagogues and rebels, and it was no less necessary to take some serious step to put an end to the vicious system of religious ascendancy without destroying the healthy and indispensable ascendancy of property and intelligence' (*England*, vi, 455; *Ireland*, ii, 517).

138. *England*, vi, 454; *Ireland*, ii, 516. See also *Essays*, pp. 23, 40, 80.

139. *Memoir*, p. 305. See also *Essays*, p. 28, where he refers to Burke as 'the greatest and truest of our political teachers'; and, p. 54, 'There is no figure in English political history for which I at least entertain a greater reverence than Edmund Burke.'

140. *Ibid.*, p. 306.

141. *England*, 181.

142. *Ibid.*, iii, 207.

143. *Ibid.*, 217

144. *Ibid.*, 196-7. Lecky's attachment to the great historical families may have been among the reasons why, as a young man, he was opposed to life peerages.

145. *Ibid.*, 209.

146. *Ibid.*, 217.

147. *Ibid.*, 212.

148. *Ibid.*, 222.

149. Lord Acton once reproached Dollinger for believing with Burke that representation should always depend on property (Himmelfarb, *Lord Acton*, p. 178). Lecky pointed out (*England*, iii, 208) that Burke, on the contrary, took great pains to refute the idea and to show by arguments from history that the commercial interests and the professions had as much right to representation as the landed gentry. Lecky approved of the representation of the various classes (*England*, iii, 214, ff).

150. *England*, iii, 216.

151. *Ibid.*, 213.

152. *Ibid.*, iii, 222; *Essays*, p. 41.

153. *England*, 221.

154. *Ibid.*

155. See above, p. 57.

156. Acton to Lecky, 30 April 1882 (Lecky correspondence, Vienna).

157. Acton to Mary Gladstone, 27 April, 3 May 1882 (*Letters of Lord Acton to Mary ... Gladstone*, 2nd edn, 1913, pp. 151, 152).

158. *England*, iii, 1-9.

159. See above, p. 90.

160. See Acton's reference to Burke in the second last paragraph of Acton's inaugural lecture on the study of history.

161. Prendergast to Lecky, 2 June 1882 (Lecky correspondence, TCD, no. 254).

162. *England*, iii and v especially.

163. *Minute Book*, College Historical Society, TCD, 2 June 1858.
164. *England*, iii, 5.
165. Lecky to O'Neill Daunt, 16 January 1886 (Lecky correspondence, TCD, no. 351); *Memoir*, pp. 185-6.
166. *England*, viii, 551-2; *Ireland*, v, 493-4.

Chapter Six

1. Lecky to his wife?, 2 October 1885 (*Memoir*, p. 180).
2. Reported widely in all the newspapers; see, for example, *Freeman's Journal*, 23 November 1885.
3. For Lecky's views on the results of the election, see Lecky to Blennerhassett, 2 December 1885 (Blennerhassett papers, Cambridge University Library, add. 7486, no. 52 ([1] E).
4. *Ibid.*
5. Sir Rowland Blennerhassett had studied at Oxford, Louvain and at Munich under Dollinger. He entered parliament as a Liberal MP for Galway in 1865; was MP for Kerry 1874-85. In the 1870s he sympathised with home rule during Butt's leadership of the movement. He also sympathised with the liberal catholicism of Acton and Dollinger. His interests were in the Irish land and university questions. He supported Gladstone's 1873 university bill and anticipated peasant proprietorship in a published memo of April 1884. He was President of Queen's College, Cork, 1897-1904. Like Lecky, he strongly disapproved of Parnellism and was widely believed to have subsidised the forger, Richard Pigott, in his search for evidence against Parnell in *The Times* v Parnell investigation (see R. B. O'Brien, *Charles Stewart Parnell*, ii, 207; Sir John Ervine, *Parnell*, p. 253).
6. Lecky to Lady Blennerhassett, 2 December 1885.
7. Lecky to Booth, 3 January 1886 (*Memoir*, pp. 184-5).
8. *The Times*, 13 January 1886.
9. *England*, iii, 212.
10. Lecky had expressed these points already in a private letter to Booth, 3 January 1886 (*Memoir*, pp. 184-5).
11. Cf. Lecky in *The Times*, 3 June 1886: 'The existing grand juries and the synod of the disestablished church are the bodies which now represent most faithfully the independent element in Grattan's parliament.'
12. Lecky repeated this claim in an article for the *North American Review*, clii, no. 410 (January 1891), pp. 11-26 and reprinted in *Essays* as 'Ireland in the Light of History', p. 87.
13. Cf. also Lecky in *The Times*, 3 June 1886.
14. Liberty in preference to democracy – this was an anticipation of the theme of Lecky's book, *Democracy and Liberty*.
15. The concept 'type' played a big role in Lecky's thought, see above pp. 46-7.
16. Lecky thus was advocating land purchase long before it became general policy.
17. E. Pomeroy Colley to Lecky, 17 January 1886 (Lecky correspondence, TCD, no. 2412).
18. Emily Tennyson to Lecky, 14 January 1886 (Lecky correspondence, TCD, no. 348).
19. Goldwin Smith was the author of *Irish History and Irish Character*. He was also the author of the *Irish Question* (1868). Goldwin Smith contributed articles on Ireland to the *Nineteenth Century* (July 1882, June 1883), to the *Fortnightly Review* (January 1884), and a letter to the *Pall Mall Gazette* (23 March 1882). R. Barry O'Brien used Smith's two earlier books on Ireland to refute the later articles. See R. Barry O'Brien 'Mr Goldwin Smith, Past and Present', in *Fortnightly Review* (February 1884) and republished in O'Brien, *Irish*

Wrongs and English Remedies: With other Essays, pp. 187-99.

20. Goldwin Smith to Lecky, 22 March 1886 (Lecky correspondence, TCD, no. 363).

21. *Memoir*, p. 188.

22. Five thousand copies of the reprint were originally ordered by the secretary of the Irish Loyal and Patriotic Union. See MacDonald to Lecky, 3 February 1886 (Lecky correspondence, TCD, no. 360). For the ILPU, see above pp. 120-1.

23. *Memoir*, p. 191.

24. *The Times*, 4 February 1886.

25. See above pp. 128-9.

26. The ILPU did not originally win the confidence of all unionists. Lecky's friend, Colley, wrote: 'I wonder what is thought of the august body which we here have irreverently dubbed "The Loyal and Idiotic". Their speeches the other day did not read impressively and I hear that as oratory they were wretched. But I feel I should not criticise a genuine effort at unionist organisation, and it may bring out men and qualities which are certainly very much needed'. Colley to Lecky, 17 January 1886 (TCD, Lecky correspondence, no. 2412).

27. O'Brien to Lecky, 30 October 1885 (Lecky correspondence, TCD, no. 337).

28. Irish Loyal and Patriotic Union to Lecky, 15 January 1886 (Lecky correspondence, TCD, no. 350).

29. Lecky to Booth, March 1886 (*Memoir*, p. 190).

30. *Ibid.*

31. Lecky, 'A Nationalist Parliament', in *Nineteenth Century*, xix (April 1886), pp. 636-44.

32. See Lecky correspondence, TCD, nos 367-77.

33. Morris to Lecky, n.d. (Lecky correspondence, TCD, no. 2537.) Michael Morris, Lord Morris and Killanin (1826-1901); belonged to an old Roman catholic family of Spiddal, County Galway; educated TCD; MP for Galway 1865; solicitor-general for Ireland 1866, attorney-general, Lord Chief Justice 1887.

34. Blennerhassett to Lecky, 5 April 1886 (Lecky correspondence, TCD, no. 371).

35. Trevelyan to Lecky, 1 April 1886 (Lecky correspondence, TCD, no. 367).

36. Knowles to Lecky, 3 April 1886 (Lecky correspondence, TCD, no. 369). The article was subsequently recast for a unionist textbook, *The Truth about Home Rule*, edited by Sir George Baden-Powell. It was a rejoinder to the *Handbook of Home Rule* edited by James Bryce, which had used a number of quotations from *Leaders*.

37. Grey was also a friend and admirer of Rhodes, and was friendly with Horace Plunkett and George Russell of the Irish Co-operative Movement.

38. Probably W. H. Hurlbert, author of *Ireland under Coercion* (1888). A former editor of the *New York World*, he was facilitated in his researches on Ireland under the 'coercion' of the Land League agitators by the Chief Secretary, A. J. Balfour. What Ireland needed most, he concluded, was 'two, three, four or five years of a steady and cool administration of the laws in Ireland, by an executive officer such as Mr Balfour seems to me to have shown himself to be ...'. See W. H. Hurlbert, *Ireland under Coercion: The Diary of an American* (2nd edn, Edinburgh, 1889), p. 426. Balfour helped Hurlbert in the hope that his ideas would carry weight in America. See L. P. Curtis, *Coercion and Conciliation in Ireland*, p. 263.

39. Grey to Lecky, 21 March 1886 (Lecky correspondence, TCD, no. 362). I have not discovered that Lecky wrote anything for Grey's plan, but he did contribute anti-home rule material to the *North American Review* in January and March 1891.

40. Lecky to —?, 17 April 1886 (Lecky correspondence, TCD, no. 374). This was probably the Loyal and Patriotic Union meeting at Leeds. The Dublin *Daily Express* (5 May 1886) was among the newspapers that reported the meeting. Goschen was the principal speaker.

41.   *The Times*, 1 May 1886.

42.   *Ibid.*, 3 June 1886.

43.   This letter to *The Times* (3 June 1886) was reprinted and circulated by the ILPU as leaflet no. 142 in their anti-home rule campaign.

44.   *The Times*, 4 June 1886.

45.   *Ibid.*, 7 June 1886. The Liberal Unionist Committee reprinted this letter in leaflet form, as leaflet no. 29.

46.   *Ibid.*, 8, 9 June 1886.

47.   *Ibid.*, 21 June 1892.

48.   *Ibid.*

49   *Liberal Unionist*, no. 22 (1 November 1887).

50.   'An Irish Historian on Home Rule for Ireland', Liberal Unionist pamphlet, no. 33.

51.   'Ireland in the Light of History', in *North American Review*, clii, no. 410 (January 1891), pp. 11-26. This is reprinted in Essays, 'Why Home Rule is Undesirable', in *North American Review*, clii, no. 412 (March 1891), pp. 349-70.

52.   *The Times*, 18 June 1892.

53.   See *Unionist Convention for the Provinces of Leinster, Munster and Connaught, June 1892: Report of Proceedings, Lists of Committees, Delegates … .*

54.   Dowden to Lecky, 8 June 1892 (Lecky correspondence, TCD, no. 708).

55.   Lecky's letter is given in *Unionist Convention for the Provinces of Leinster, Munster and Connaught, June 1892 … pp.* 206-7. It was also published in *The Times*, 24 June 1892.

56.   Dowden to Lecky, 26 July 1892 (Lecky correspondence, TCD, no. 714).

57.   Salisbury to Lecky, 23 March 1892 (Lecky correspondence, Hague).

58.   *Scotsman*, 4 July 1892. The fact that Lecky was paid for this letter (£5. 5. 0) may indicate that it was commissioned.

59.   *Annual Register* 1892, part i, 179.

60.   Elliot to Lecky, 4 July 1892 (Lecky correspondence, TCD, no. 716). Arthur Ralph Douglas Elliot (1846-1923). Born in London, second son of the Earl of Minto; educated at Edinburgh and Cambridge; called to the bar; elected MP for Roxburghshire in 1880 as a Liberal; opposed Gladstone on the home rule question in 1886 and was returned to parliament as a liberal-unionist; founded the Liberal Union Club; lost his seat in 1892; defeated for Durham city by one vote 1895, but returned in the by-election 1898; championed free trade in parliament down to his defeat in the 1906 election; editor of *Edinburgh Review* 1895-1912; author of a life of Goshen. Lecky and he 'frequently sat together' in the House of Commons (*Memoir*, p. 275).

61.   A. V. Dicey, *A Leap in the Dark: A Criticism of the Principles of Home Rule as Illustrated by the Bill of 1893* (1893, 1911), p. 150.

62.   For O'Connor Morris, see above fn. 33.

63.   O'Connor Morris to Lecky, 26 February 1893 (Lecky correspondence, TCD, no. 745).

64.   Aubrey Thomas de Vere (1814-1902). Born at Adare, County Limerick, educated at TCD, an admirer of Newman he became a Roman Catholic 1851. Although a unionist and opposed to violent agitation, his work was inspired by a deep sense of patriotism and sympathy with Ireland.

65.   de Vere to Lecky, 5 March 1893 (Lecky correspondence, TCD, no. 746).

66.   'Light on Home Rule', in *National Observer*, new series, ix, no. 224 (4 March 1893).

67.   *Contemporary Review*, lxiii (May 1893), pp. 626-38.

68.   *Ibid.*, p. 626.

69.   The 'Case against Home Rule' from the international point of view was written by Salisbury; from the Australasian point of view by Sir Julius Vogel; from the military

aspect by General Edward Hamley; from the national aspect by A. J. Balfour; from the transatlantic aspect by Goldwin Smith; from the imperial point of view by Sir M.E. Grant Duff; Lord Fingal dealt with the objections from the catholic standpoint; and Lord Ashbourne from the agrarian point of view.

70. *Pall Mall Gazette*, 24 July 1893.

71. See, for example, *The Times*, 13 January 1886; *Contemporary Review*, lxiii (May 1893), p. 630.

72. *Liberal Unionist*, no. 22 (1 November 1887), p. 63.

73. *Contemporary Review*, lxiii (May 1893), p. 629; *Pall Mall Gazette* (24 July 1893).

74. See chapter six above.

75. *Liberal Unionist*, no. 22 (1 November 1887), p. 63.

76. *Ibid.*; see also *Contemporary Review*, lxiii (May 1893), p. 630.

77. *North American Review*, clii, no. 412 (March 1891), pp. 366-7.

78. In the *Pall Mall Gazette*, 24 July 1893, Lecky, describing the land agitation as the mainspring of the home rule movement, said that Lalor was the 'true originator of the Land League policy'. It was in P. H. Bagenal's *American Irish and their Influence on Irish Politics* (1882, pp. 153-97) that 'the connection between Lalor's teaching and the subsequent land agitation' was first clearly shown, according to Lecky (*Ireland*, v, 485).

79. *North American Review*, clii, no. 412 (March 1891), p. 368.

80. *National Observer*, new series, ix, no. 224 (4 May 1891), p. 1.

81. *Contemporary Review*, lxiii (May 1893), p. 628.

82. *Annual Register 1892*, part i, p. 113.

83. *Scotsman*, 4 July 1892. Acton was perhaps more realistic, if not cynical, when he intimated that he was not particularly worried by the extension of political power to the masses, whom he agreed were 'utterly ignorant' and 'easily deceived by appeals to prejudice and passion'. But he felt that in political philosophy there was a case for the extension, and added: 'The danger is not that a particular class is unfit to govern. Every class is unfit to govern.' Acton distrusted the political wisdom of all classes and therefore saw no reason to trust one class more than another. See Acton to Mary Gladstone, 24 April 1881 (*Letters of Lord Acton to Mary Gladstone*, pp. 90-7).

84. *Contemporary Review*, lxiii (May 1893), p. 630.

85. *The Times*, 21 June 1892.

86. *North American Review*, clii, no. 412 (March 1891), p. 359.

87. *The Times*, 21 June 1892.

88. *Ibid.*

89. *Ibid.*

90. *Contemporary Review*, lxiii (May 1893), p. 632.

91. *Ibid.*, p. 633.

92. See above p. 116.

93. *North American Review*, clii, no. 412 (March 1891), p. 350.

94. *The Times*, 4 February 1886.

95. *England*, v, 509-10.

96. *Pall Mall Gazette*, 24 July 1893.

97. J. Matthews to Lecky, 5 July 1887 (TCD, Lecky correspondence, no. 449). In a memorandum drawn up at the end of his career, Gladstone noted that he had been the subject of censure remarkable for its severity, variety and the eminence of the quarters from which it came. Among his eminent literary critics he included Carlyle, Froude and Lecky. See *Gladstone Papers* (1930), pp. 28-9.

98. *The Times*, 7 June 1886. This letter was published for the Liberal Unionist Committee as leaflet no. 29 and it is reproduced fairly substantially in *Memoir*, pp. 192-4.

99. *Scotsman,* 4 July 1892; *Democracy and Liberty,* i, liv.

100. *Contemporary Review,* lxiii (May 1893), pp. 636-7; *Scotsman,* 4 July 1892.

101. *Scotsman,* 4 July 1892.

102. *Democracy and Liberty,* i, xxxviii.

103. *Ibid.,* i, xxii.

104. *Ibid.,* i, xxxvi. Cf. Goldwin Smith to Lecky, 22 March 1886 (TCD, Lecky correspond-ence, no. 363) – 'I suppose the GOM will have his way, and if he has, the result will be about the most tremendous lesson which the world has ever received on the danger of allowing itself to be guided by rhetoric.'

105. *Scotsman,* 4 July 1892.

106. *Liberal Unionist,* no. 22 (1 November 1887), p. 63; *North American Review,* clii, no. 412 (March 1891), pp. 366-7; *Scotsman,* 4 July 1892.

107. *Pall Mall Gazette,* 24 July 1893.

108. See above footnote 97.

109. *Contemporary Review,* lxiii (May 1893), pp. 636-8.

110. *North American Review,* clii, no. 412 (March 1891), p. 370.

111. *Contemporary Review,* lxiii (May 1893), p. 638.

112. *The Times,* 18 January 1886.

113. *North American Review,* cliii, no. 412 (March 1891), pp. 361-5.

114. *The Times,* 5 May 1886.

115. *Ibid.*

116. Lecky to Gavan Duffy, 8 July 1892 (Gavan Duffy papers, NLI, MS 8005). Lecky's draft of this letter is in Lecky correspondence, TCD no. 754a (there is a synopsis in *Memoir,* p. 239). That Lecky had no objection in principle to a moderate home rule is also asserted in his article 'A Nationalist Parliament', in *Nineteenth Century,* xix (April 1886), pp. 636-44. Commenting on this article, R. Barry O'Brien wrote: 'So far as we can gather ... he would not object to the re-establishment of Grattan's parliament now if its essential features could be restored' (R. Barry O'Brien, *Irish Wrongs and English Remedies,* p. 168).

117. *Memorandum on the Proposed Abolition of the Viceroyalty in Ireland,* p. 3. Lecky's friend, J. P. Prendergast, also felt as Lecky did about the viceroyalty and wrote the *Viceroyalty of Ireland ... Historically Vindicated* (1886) which first appeared as a series of articles in the *Irish Times* and was included in chapter xi of the projected autobiography. See Prendergast papers, King's Inns, Dublin.

118. *An Irish Historian of Home Rule,* Liberal unionist pamphlet, no. 33, p. 1.

119. *The Times,* 13 January 1886.

120. 'A Nationalist Parliament', in *Nineteenth Century,* xix (April 1886), pp. 636-44.

121. *An Irish Historian on Home Rule,* Liberal unionist pamphlet no. 33, p. 4; *National Observer,* ix, no. 224 (4 March 1893), special supplement, p. 1.

122. *Scotsman,* 4 July 1892; *Contemporary Review,* lxiii (May 1893), p. 635.

123. *The Times,* 21 November 1893 devoted three columns to a report of Lecky's lecture. The Prince of Wales, introducing Lecky, said that it was 'a matter of sincere congratulation that so eminent a historian should have consented to open the series of lectures and should have given the cachet of his name to these lectures whereby they could not fail to achieve success.

124. See above p. 70.

125. See above p. 68.

126. *Essays,* pp. 61-2.

127. *Ibid.,* p. 48.

128. *Macmillan's Magazine,* xxvii (January 1873), p. 246.

129. *The Times*, 13 January 1886.
130. *Essays*, p. 58. See also the final paragraph of the last volume of *England*.
131. J. A. Froude, *Short Studies*, ii, pp. 546-7. Cf. also Goldwin Smith, 'Why Send More Irish to the Colonies', in *Nineteenth Century* (June 1883) and R. Barry O'Brien's comments in *Irish Wrongs and English Remedies*, p. 191.
132. *Essays*, pp. 51, 53, 54.
133. *Ibid.*, pp. 61, 62.
134. Other critics of Froude had come round to his views of the Celts. For Goldwin Smith, see above, footnote 132. J.P. Prendergast now, also, believed that the Irish were incapable of governing themselves.
135. *Essays*, pp. 48, 49, 67.
136. *Ibid.*, pp. 51, 54, 56.
137. Hyde Clarke to Lecky, 2 December 1893; George William Young to Lecky, 5 December 1893 (TCD, Lecky correspondence, nos 789, 791).
138. *The Times*, 2 December 1893.
139. *Ibid.*, 4 December 1893.
140. *Ibid.*, 8 December 1893.
141. *Essays*, see Preface.
142. *Ibid.*, p. 67.
143. *Ibid.*, p. 62.
144. *Ibid.*, pp. 44, 50, 53, 67.
145. Lecky to —?, 17 April 1886 (TCD, Lecky correspondence, no. 374), the draft of a letter regretting that he would be unable to take part in an anti-home rule meeting.
146. *The Times*, 13 January 1886.
147. *Ibid.*, 3, 7, 9 June 1886.
148. 'A Nationalist Parliament', in *Nineteenth Century*, xix (April 1886), pp. 636-44.
149. *Ibid.*, 7 June 1886.
150. R. Barry O'Brien, *Irish Wrongs and English Remedies*, pp. 168 ff.
151. 'An Irish Historian on Home Rule', Liberal unionist pamphlet, no. 33, p. 7.
152. *Pall Mall Gazette*, 24 July 1893.
153. *Pall Mall Gazette*, 24 July 1893. Goldwin Smith, too, contributed an article to the *Fortnightly Review* (February 1884) in the hope that it might help to remove from 'the national conscience of a fancied burden of historical guilt' regarding Ireland. See R. Barry O'Brien's comments on Smith's article in *Irish Wrongs and English Remedies*, p. 191.
154. *Pall Mall Gazette*, 24 July 1893.
155. K. Young, *Arthur James Balfour* ... (1963), pp. 119-20; N. Mansergh, *Commonwealth Experiment* (1969), pp. 193-4.
156. This was Lecky's own phrase; see *Rationalism*, i, ix.
157. Quoted in J. W. Thompson, *History of Historical Writing*, ii, 67.
158. This was Lecky's own phrase; see *Essays*, p. 99, and above chapter three, footnote 33.
159. A fault Lecky found with Grattan was that his speeches were overcharged with epigram. See *Leaders* (1871), pp. 109-10.
160. *England*, iii, 237.
161. See above p. 117.
162. See above p. 124.
163. His literary income in 1891 was £2556; in 1887 it was £1543. See TCD MS R.7.45.
164. One correspondent who was at first unable to understand how the author of *Leaders* could be a unionist was satisfied by Lecky's explanation given in *The Times*, 5 May 1886, C. Brooke Hunt to Lecky, 5 May 1886 (TCD, Lecky correspondence, no. 381).

165.   See below pp. 144-5.

166.   R. G. Collingwood, *The Idea of History*, p. 68.

167.   *Rationalism*, i, vi.

Chapter Seven

1.   The Duke of Argyll, *Irish Nationalism: An Appeal to History* (1893), pp. 260-1.

2.   J. P. Prendergast to Lecky, 17 January 1886 (TCD, Lecky correspondence, no. 354).

3.   R. Barry O'Brien, *The Life of Charles Stewart Parnell* (London, 1898), ii, 101-3; 'Irish Wrongs and English Remedies', in *Nineteenth Century*, xviii (November 1885), pp. 707-21.

4.   R. Barry O'Brien, 'Three Attempts to Rule Ireland Justly', in *Nineteenth Century*, xix (April 1886), p. 625.

5.   *Freeman's Journal*, 27 April 1886. This and other articles mentioned above were reprinted in book form; see R. B. O'Brien, *Irish Wrongs and English Remedies* (1887).

6.   Longman to Lecky, 30 April 1886 (TCD, Lecky correspondence, no. 380).

7.   Longman to Lecky, 15 July 1886 (TCD, Lecky correspondence, no. 397).

8.   *The Times*, 1 May 1886.

9.   *Ibid.*, 3, 4, 8 June 1886. Lecky's reply to Harcourt is in *The Times*, 3, 7, 9 June 1886.

10.   W. E. Gladstone, 'Further Notes and Queries on the Irish Demand' in *Contemporary Review*, liii, p. 335 (March 1888); 'Ingram's History of the Irish Union', in *Nineteenth Century*, xxii (October 1887), pp. 456, 457; 'Plain Speaking on the Irish Union', in *Nineteenth Century*, xxvi (July 1889), p. 7; 'Lessons of Irish History in the Eighteenth Century', in James Bryce (ed.), *Handbook of Home Rule*, p. 262 (1887). These articles have been collected in W. E. Gladstone, *Special Aspects of the Irish Question* (1892) (see pp. 157, 180, 225, 314 for references to *Leaders*).

11.   See above, pp. 80, 81.

12.   J. Redmond, *The Truth About '98* (1886), p. 6; A. Webb, *The Alleged Massacre of 1641* (1887), pp. 11-12. Both of these pamphlets were published by the Irish Press Agency.

13.   A. Webb, *op. cit.*, pp. 11-12. In this pamphlet Webb made extensive use of Lecky's *England* to refute the charge of a catholic massacre of protestants in 1641.

14.   J. Redmond, *op. cit*, pp. 6, 7, 12, 13; *Irish Protestants and Home Rule* (1887), pp. 7, 10, 11, 16, 17-18.

15.   *Freeman's Journal*, 2 December 1887.

16.   J. P. Prendergast to Lecky, 3 December 1887 (TCD, Lecky correspondence, no. 490).

17.   The leaflets were collected and published under the general title of *Short Lessons on the Irish Question*, edited by J. J. Clancy.

18.   *Essays*, p. 7.

19.   T. W. Russell, *Ireland and the Empire: A Review 1800-1900* (1901), p. 9.

20.   Fox was the author of *Why Ireland Wants Home Rule; Coercion Without Crime*.

21.   J. A. Fox, *A Key to the Irish Question* (1890), p. 369 and *passim*. In a list of twelve books recommended by Fox to Scottish and English leaders for 'some sound readings in Irish history', Lecky's *England* and *Leaders* were placed respectively second and third after Gladstone's *Speeches on the Irish Question*. See J. A. Fox, *op. cit.*, p. ix.

22.   W.E.H. Lecky, *Clerical Influences* (edited by W.E.G. Lloyd and F. Cruise O'Brien), p. 1.

23.   *Facts and Figures on the Irish Question*. Published by the Ulster Liberal Association, pp. 3-4.

24.   M. McDonnell Bodkin, *Grattan's Parliament: Before and After* (1912), pp. 7, 265 and passim.

25. J. G. Swift MacNeill (1849-1926), son of an Irish clergyman; educated TCD and Christ Church, Oxford. Professor of constitutional and criminal law at King's Inns 1882-88 and professor of constitutional law in UCD from 1909. Joined Butt's Home Government Association and became a member of its council. MP for South Donegal 1887-1918. His propagandist historical work included *English Interference with Irish Industries* (2nd edn, London, 1886); *The Irish Parliament: What it was and What it did* (1885, 1912); *How the Union was Carried* (1887); *Titled Corruption: The Sordid Origin of some Irish Peerages* (1894); *The Constitutional and Parliamentary History of Ireland till the Union* (1917).

26. J. G. Swift MacNeill, *The Constitutional and Parliamentary History of Ireland till the Union*, p. viii. He recommended 'the systematic study of Mr Lecky's writings on Irish history which will in itself be an epoch in the reader's intellectual life' (*ibid.*, p. vi).

27. J. G. Swift MacNeill, 'Hibernia Irredenta; I - Mr Lecky and Irish Affairs', in *Fortnightly Review*, new series, lix, no. 349 (January 1896), pp. 18-27.

28. In the debate on 12 April 1886, during Saunderson's speech Gladstone interjected that it was Pitt's policy that had led to the rebellion. Such an admission from such a source was often referred to by home rulers, not only for example by MacNeill in this article (p. 26), but also by J. Redmond, *The Truth about '98* (1886), p. 5. Both MacNeill and Redmond went on to point out that Lecky had already gravely charged Pitt with the same accusation. See above p. 140.

29. In his letter Harcourt said: 'Of all recent writers upon Irish affairs ... there is none who appears to me more full, more trustworthy, or more satisfactory than Mr Lecky.'

30. The meeting was reported in *The Times*, 18 October 1889.

31. On the suggestion of a waggish friend, MacNeill once sent Lecky a copy of his *Titled Corruption*, which carried a quotation from Lecky's *England* as a frontispiece, stating his obligations to Lecky's researches (J. G. Swift MacNeill, *What I Have Seen and Heard*, pp. 309-10). In reply, while Lecky thanked MacNeill he also reminded him, as MacNeill said, 'somewhat sententiously of the duty of judging men according to the average standard of morality of their day, rather than in accordance with the more enlightened standards of our own time.' MacNeill also contravened a second of Lecky's cardinal rules of historical writing: he had been selective and one-sided, and his abuse of history had been associated with an extensive employment of Lecky's own work. In such circumstances, Lecky's stand in parliament a few years later on the question of MacNeill's being allowed to examine the state papers is hardly to be wondered at.

32. Gwynn to Lecky, 23 March 1903 (TCD, Lecky correspondence, no. 2317).

33. Duffy to Lecky, 14 May 1892 (TCD, Lecky correspondence, no. 2423).

34, O'Brien's article in the *Freeman's Journal* was signed 'Historicus' and submitted to various notable men. The article, together with the comments and a concluding essay by O'Brien were collected and published as a pamphlet, see 'Historicus', *The Best Hundred Irish Books*.

35. 'Historicus' (R. Barry O'Brien), *The Best Hundred Irish Books*, p. 11.

36. *Ibid.*, p. 48.

37. W. E. Gladstone, *Special Aspects of the Irish Question*, p. 225. Also W. E. Gladstone, 'Further Notes and Queries on the Irish Demand', in *Contemporary Review*, liii, p. 335.

38. *Freeman's Journal*, 2 December 1887.

39. *Leaders* (1871), p. xix.

40. *The Times*, 8 October 1889.

41. *Leaders* (1871), p. 194.

42. *The Times*, 3 June 1886.

43. *Ibid.*, 9 June 1886.

44. H.A.L. Fisher, *James Bryce*, i, 338. Cf. also M. McDonnell Bodkin, *Grattan's Parliament: Before and After* (1912), pp. 267-8: 'In a conversation in the White House in Washington, Mr Roosevelt, then President of the United States, declared to the writer of this book that he could not understand how any man who read Lecky's history of the union could be a unionist, "Least of all", he added, "can I understand how the man who wrote it is a unionist".'

45. Lowe to Lecky, 16 June 1886 (TCD, Lecky correspondence, no. 392).

46. O'Neill Daunt to Lecky, 16 March 1862 (TCD, Lecky correspondence, no. 22); O'Neill Daunt, *A Life Spent for Ireland*, pp. 189-90.

47. Lecky, *Leaders* (1903), i, xv. Lecky was probably referring to the comments in J.H. McCarthy, *The Case for Home Rule*, pp. 58-61.

48. John Morley, 'Irish Policy in the Eighteenth Century', in *Fortnightly Review*, new series, xi, 196-203 (February 1872).

49. See especially the final paragraphs of the speech delivered in the House of Commons, 8 April 1886.

50. Lecky to Booth, 11 September 1861, *Memoir*, p. 27.

51. Acton, *Essays on Church and State*, ed. Woodruff, p. 35.

52. W. E. Gladstone, *Special Aspects of the Irish Question*, p. 303.

53. *The Times*, 8 October 1889.

54. See *Essays*, pp. 21-42.

55. *Ibid.*, p. 23.

56. *Ibid.*, p. 25. Cf. also *ibid.*, 40, 80.

57. *Ibid.*, pp. 26-9. Cf. M. Oakeshott: '… at the academic level the study of politics should be an historical study' (*Rationalism in Politics and Other Essays*, p. 130).

58. *Ibid.*, p. 30.

59. *Ibid.*, p. 41.

60. Dicey to Lecky, 17 July 1886 (TCD, Lecky correspondence, no. 398).

61. *Ibid.*, 21 July 1886 (*ibid.*, no. 399).

62. *Ibid.*, 10 November 1886 (*ibid.*, no. 405).

63. *Ibid.*, 25 January 1887 (*ibid.*, no. 417). See also A. V. Dicey, *England's Case against Home Rule* (1887), p. 3.

64. A. V. Dicey, *ibid.*, p. 74.

65. *Ibid.*, pp. 76-7.

66. *Ibid.*, pp. 96-9.

67. Stephen de Vere, like his brother Aubrey, was a convert to catholicism. Although opposed to home rule, he strongly supported the efforts of Gladstone and others to reform the Irish land system. Stephen de Vere, *A Letter on Legislation for Restoration of Evicted Tenants in Ireland, with Some Remarks on the Policy of the English Government in Ireland up to the Present Century* (1895).

68. de Vere to Lecky, 1 April 1895 (TCD, Lecky correspondence, no. 855).

69. Argyll to Lecky, March, April 1890 (*ibid.*, nos 582, 588, 589).

70. Duke of Argyll, *Irish Nationalism: An Appeal to History* (1893), pp. 255-6.

71. Argyll to Lecky, 4 June 1890 (TCD, Lecky correspondence, no. 598). Cf. also Duke of Argyll, *Irish Nationalism*, p. 256.

72. Argyll to Lecky, 26 July 1890 (TCD, Lecky correspondence, no. 606).

73. *Ibid.*, 28 November 1892 (*ibid.*, no. 731). Cf. Duke of Argyll, *op. cit.*, p. 3, where he refers to Gladstone's history as 'inflated fable'.

74. Duke of Argyll, *op. cit.*, pp. 190, 197, 243, 213.

75. *Ibid.*, pp. 191, 243.

76. *Ibid.*, p. 213.

77. *Essays*, pp. 38-9.

78. Duke of Argyll, *op. cit.*, p. 259.

79. Thomas Dunbar Ingram, born in County Donegal in 1826; educated Trinity College, Dublin and Queen's College, Belfast; called to the Bar 1856; professor of Hindu law at Calcutta 1866-77; returned to Dublin and devoted himself to historical research and writing; died 1901.

80. See above, p. 10.

81. Henry Grattan, *Memoirs of … Henry Grattan* (5 vols, Dublin 1839-46); Jonah Barrington, *Rise and Fall of the Irish Nation* (Paris, 1833).

82. W. E. Gladstone in *Nineteenth Century* (October 1887) and reprinted in *Gladstone's Special Aspects of the Irish Question.* Extracts from more favourable reviews were appended to Ingram's *Two Chapters of Irish History.* These extracts commented on the political significance of Ingram's book for the home rule controversy, and some, like the *Spectator*, recommended the book to all who had been affected by the argument that Irish independence had been filched away in 1801 'by the influence of English gold poured into the lap of traitors'. Ingram's anti-bribery thesis gets a measure of support in the work of a modern scholar; see G. C. Bolton, *The Passing of the Irish Act of Union* (1966).

83. W. E. Gladstone, *Special Aspects of the Irish Question*, pp. 136-7. It seemed to J. P. Prendergast that both Gladstone and Ingram were 'curiously ignorant of Irish history'. Prendergast also said that Jasper Joly, who possessed a fine collection of pamphlets on the Union period, declined to loan them to Ingram because they differed on the question of the use of corruption in carrying the Union (Prendergast to Lecky, 18 October 1887, TCD, Lecky correspondence, no. 477).

84. W. E. Gladstone, *op. cit.*, p. 157. Lecky in his *Ireland*, v, 354-5, correcting the figures he had used in *Leaders* and which led Gladstone into error, acknowledged that the correction was the result of the researches of Ingram into the matter which he 'kindly sent' to Lecky.

85. Ingram in *Nineteenth Century*, December 1887.

86. Thomas Dunbar Ingram, *A Critical Examination of Irish History* (1904), i, 11, 14.

87. *Ibid.*, ii, 298.

88. *Ibid.*, i, 12-13.

89. *Ibid.*, ii, 298-9, 309.

90 *Ibid.*; 300, 299, 303, 299.

91. *Ibid.*, i, 28, 159, 167, 177; ii, 299, 307, 308-9.

92. *Ibid.*, ii, 310.

93 *Ireland*, v, 348.

94. Argyll to Lecky, 9 February 1893 (TCD, Lecky correspondence, no. 742).

95. C. Litton Falkiner (1863-1908); educated TCD; called to the bar 1887; employed as an assistant land commissioner; contested elections 1892 as a unionist; worked as an organiser of the Irish Unionist Alliance; secretary to the Royal Irish Academy and of the Lecky memorial committee; killed in a mountaineering accident. See Dowden's memoir in Falkiner's *Essays*, published posthumously. Lecky followed his career as a historian 'with much interest and sympathy' (*Memoir*, p. 351).

96. Falkiner to Lecky, 23 February 1899 (TCD, Lecky correspondence, no. 1680).

Chapter Eight

1. *Forum*, June 1890.
2. *Ibid.*, February 1893.
3. 29 May 1868.
4. *North American Review*, January 1891.
5. *Edinburgh Review*, October 1891.
6. See above, pp. 132-4.
7. *Forum*, February 1900.
8. M. Davitt, 'Plea for Old-Age Pensions', in *Forum*, xxviii, p. 67.
9. *Contemporary Review*, October 1891.
10. *Pall Mall Magazine*, April 1901.
11. 'Israel among the Nations', in *Forum*, December 1893.
12. *The Nation*, vol. xlv, no. 1 (151), 21 July 1887, pp. 54-5.
13. N. Pilling, 'The Reception of the Major Works of W.E.H. Lecky 1865-1896', unpublished M.Phil of London, 1978.
14. C. F. Mullet in H. Ausubel and others (eds), *Some Modern Historians of Britain*, p. 143.
15. J. Morley, 'Lecky on Democracy', in *Critical Miscellanies: Fourth Series* (1908), p. 180.
16. *Democracy and Liberty* (1896), i, 21.
17. *Ibid.*, ii, 102.
18. *Ibid.*, ii, 413.
19. J. Morley, *op. cit.*, p. 179.
20. *Democracy and Liberty*, i, 314-25, i, 37; *Ireland*, ii, 57.
21. *Democracy and Liberty*, ii, 1-13.
22. *Ibid.*, i, 264-66.
23. *Ibid.*, i, 191-96.
24. *Ibid.*, i, 64, 184, 218, 220, 312.
25. *Ibid.*, i, 323, 18.
26. *Ibid.*, i, 215, 24.
27. *Ibid.*, i, 248-9, 261-2.
28. *Ibid.*, i, 239.
29. *Ibid.*, i, 216-52.

Chapter Nine

1. Lecky to Alice Stopford Green, n.d. (NLI MS 15085). Lecky gave the same explanation to Henry Charles Lea. See Lecky to Lea, 7 January 1896; Lecky to Lea, 7 March 1901 (Henry Charles Lea Library, Lecky-Lea correspondence).
2. Lecky to Alice Stopford Green, n.d. (NLI MS 15085).
3. J. G. Swift MacNeill, *op. cit.*, p. 18.
4. For the history of the contest, see especially the *Irish Times* and *Daily Express* for the months October-December 1895 and the contemporary college magazine *TCD*.
5. D. P. Moran, 'The Battle of Two Civilizations', in Lady Gregory (ed.), *Ideals in Ireland* (1901), p. 28.
6. F.S.L. Lyons, *The Irish Parliamentary Party*, 1890-1910, pp. 231-2.
7. W.E.H. Lecky, *Democracy and Liberty*, i, 241.
8. *Ibid.*, i, 28.
9. *Memoir*, pp. 279-80.
10. *Hansard*, 4th series, xxxvii, 495. Henry Lucy reported (*A Diary of the Unionist Parliament*

1895-1900), pp. 16-17) that when the new members were advancing to sign the roll of parliament, there was 'the first approach to a cheer of welcome' as Lecky moved forward.

11. *Ibid.*, 4th series, xlviii, 211.

12. *Ibid.*, 4th series, xlix, 275.

13. J. G. Swift MacNeil, *What I Have Seen and Heard*, pp. 307-8.

14. *Ibid.*, p. 309. Cf. also the amusing account of Lecky in the role of teller given by Henry Lucy, *A Diary of the Unionist Parliament 1895–1900*, pp. 87–8.

15. *England*, iii, 109.

16. *Ibid.*, iii, 203-4. In his address in TCD, 7 December 1897, on the centenary of the death of Burke, Lecky also said of him: 'While maintaining that a member of parliament should always consider himself as a trustee, he maintained also that he should never suffer himself to sink into a mere delegate, abdicating his independence of judgment and accepting binding instructions from his constituents' (*Memoir*, p. 308).

17. *Hansard*, 4th series, xcv, 722; xcvi, 338-9.

18. Horace Plunkett, *Ireland in the New Century*, p. vii.

19. *Ibid.*, pp. 2, 6.

20. Gwynn to Lecky, 23 March 1903 (TCD, Lecky correspondence, no. 2317).

21. Horace Plunkett, *Ireland in the New Century*, see 'dedication'.

22. *Hansard*, 4th series, xxxvii, 494-5.

23. *Ibid.*, xlviii, 1666-1670.

24. *Ibid.*, 197-211.

25. *Ibid.*, lv, 1265-7.

26. *Ibid.*, 1267.

27. *Ibid.*, xlviii, 197-211.

28. Lecky to Lea, 7 January 1896 (Henry Charles Lea Library, University of Pennsylvania).

29. *Ibid.*, 19 May 1896.

30. *Ibid.*, 11 May 1903.

31. *Ibid.*, 7 March 1901.

32. During a debate on a Sunday closing bill for Ireland, when Lecky had moved the second reading, nationalist MPs Daly, Harrington and Clancy cited Lecky's own arguments, in *Democracy and Liberty*, against him. See *Hansard*, 4th series, xlix, 275, 283-4, 303.

33. *Hansard*, 4th series, lxx, 431-3; Lecky to Lea, 14 September 1899 (*loc. cit.*); W.E.H. Lecky, 'Old-Age Pensions', in *Essays*, pp. 298-317; *Report of the Chaplain Committee*.

34. *Hansard*, 4th series, lx, 975.

35. *Ibid.*, lv, 455-9.

36. *The Map of Life*, p. 132.

37. *Ibid.*

38. *Ibid.*, p. 85.

39. *Ibid.*, p. 178.

40. *Leaders* (1871), p. 100.

41. *Hansard*, 4th series, xliii, 231-2.

42. See *Democracy and Liberty*, i, 167-212. The main lines of what he here said were re-echoed in *The Map of Life*, pp. 148-53

43. Democracy and Liberty, i, 176-200.

44. *Ibid.*, i, 202-10.

45. *Ibid.*, i, 175.

46. *Ibid.*, i, 166, 197.

47. *Ibid.*, i, 202.

48. *Ibid.*, i, 176, 200, 182, 188, 192, 208, 209, 212.

49. *Ibid.*, i, 213.

50. *Ibid.*, i, 209, 203.

51. He did claim, however, that the Encumbered Estates Act (1849) had created a multitude of landlords whose interest in the land was 'often' only as 'a commercial investment' (*ibid.*, i, 167-8).

52. L. P. Curtis, *Coercion and Conciliation in Ireland 1880-1892*, pp. 349, 239, 217.

53. He was, however, prepared to concede that 'there can be no doubt that most of the English statesmen who carried the Irish agrarian legislation sincerely believed it' (*The Map of Life*, p. 153).

54. *Memoir*, p. 277.

55. *Hansard*, 4th series, xli, 626.

56. *Democracy and Liberty*, i, 206-9.

57. Lansdowne to Lecky, 18 June 1896 (TCD, Lecky correspondence, no. 1342).

58. Ashbourne to Lecky, 23 June 1896 (*ibid.*, no. 1344). A letter from Salisbury to Lecky, 24 June 1896 (Vienna collection), thanked Lecky for 'the leaflet on the land bill'.

59. As Lecky paid tribute to Carson's legal skill, Michael Davitt praised that of Maurice Healy on the nationalist side (*Fall of Feudalism in Ireland*, p. 684), while Sir Henry Lucy had high praise for Tim Healy (*Diary of a Parliament*, pp. 98-9).

60. *Hansard*, 4th series, xliii, 231-2; 899-900. Lecky was an early advocate of peasant proprietorship (see above pp. 95, 98, 102) and he continued to hold with it even after retiring from parliament. In the year of his death and when one of the greatest of the land bills was under discussion (Wyndham bill of 1903), Lecky wrote to the American historian, Lea: 'I am of course keenly interested in our great experiment in Ireland – turning a landlord country into a peasant proprietary one by a large government grant and an enormous government loan. Its consequences must be most complex and far reaching and with our Irish characters and antecedents, I am not too sanguine about it, but recent land legislation has removed all landed contracts so far from a national economical basis and produced such a hopeless confusion that I believe some great transformation of the kind is inevitable. Once one gets away from the old system of free contracts, market value and supply and demand, it is very difficult to stop on the dangerous path of government regulation and interference. How it will be judged fifty years hence I do not venture to predict' (Lecky to Lea, 11 May 1903, Henry Charles Lea Library).

61. *The Times*, 31 July 1896.

62. *Ibid.*, 1 August 1896.

63. *The Times*, 1 August 1896. Lecky reiterated this verdict in *The Map of Life*, p. 125: 'Parliamentary government has many dubious aspects, but it never appears worse than in the cases which may still sometimes be seen when a government thinks fit to force through an important measure by all-night sittings, and when a weary and irritated house which has been sitting since three or four in the afternoon is called upon at a corresponding hour of the early morning to pronounce upon grave and difficult questions of principle, and deal with the serious interests of large classes.'

64. *Ibid.*, 7 August 1896.

65. Balfour to Ridgeway, 20 October 1896 (quoted in L. P. Curtis, *Coercion and Conciliation in Ireland, 1880-1892*, p. 417).

66. *Hansard*, 4th series, lxxxiv, 1415-8.

67. *Democracy and Liberty*, i, 166.

68. *I.E.R.*, ii (November 1865), p. 97. See also *I.E.R.*, iv (June 1868), p. 440; vi (October 1869), p. 5.

69. *Pastoral Letter of His Grace, the Most Rev. Dr Cullen, Archbishop of Dublin … on the Month of May* (1868), pp. 13-14. Even after his death, Lecky continued to be used as an

argument against the attendance of catholics in TCD. See, for example, M. O'Riordan, *Catholicity and Progress in Ireland* (1905), pp. 168, 171, 356-60, and J. F. Hogan, *Irish Catholics and Trinity College* (1906), pp. 55, 94.

70. W. J. Walsh, *The Irish University Question*, p. 36.
71. *The Times*, 6 February 1873.
72. *Ibid.*
73. *Freeman's Journal*, 10 February 1873.
74. Lecky to Bowen, 25 January 1879 (*Memoir*, pp. 131-2).
75. See footnote 91 below. See also Lecky's evidence before the Robertson Commission in *Royal Commission on University Education in Ireland: Appendix to the Second Report: Minutes of Evidence* (1902), pp. 157-162.
76. *The Times*, 13 December 1895.
77. *Ibid.*, 14 December 1895.
78. *Ibid.*, 19 December 1895.
79. *Ibid.*, 25 December 1895. Lecky's second letter was in *The Times*, 20 December 1895.
80. *Hansard*, 4th series, xlv, 313-9.
81. *I.E.R.*, 4th series, ii (July 1897), pp. 84-9.
82. *Freeman's Journal*, 12 January 1898.
83. *Hansard*, 4th series, lxxxi, 230-7.
84. *Ibid.*, xlv, 313-9.
85. *Ibid.*
86. For Lecky's views on the French and German legislation, see *Democracy and Liberty*, ii, chapter VI.
87. *Freeman's Journal*, 10 February 1873.
88. *The Times*, 13 December 1895
89. See also *Democracy and Liberty*, i, 516 where he wrote; 'Dublin University has the honourable distinction of having long preceded the English Universities in the path of true Liberalism, for even before 1793 Catholics and Non-conformists were admitted among its students. ...'
90. P. J. Joyce, *John Healy, Archbishop of Tuam*, p. 174.
91. Lecky to Salmon, 4 April 1899 (*Memoir*, pp. 316-7).
92. Healy to Walsh, 8 June 1908 (P. J. Walsh, *William J. Walsh, Archbishop of Dublin*, p. 562).
93. P. J. Joyce, *John Healy, Archbishop of Tuam*, p. 165.
94. *The Map of Life*, p. 124.
95. *Ibid.*, p. 177.
96. *Ibid.*, p. 169.
97. *Memoir*, p. 358.
98. *Leaders* (1903), i, xv-xvii.
99. TCD, MS R. 8, 1, p. 194.
100. *Ibid.*, p. 97.
101. *Ibid.*, p. 102.
102. *Ibid.*, p. 92.
103. *Ibid.*
104. *Ibid.*, pp. 75, 102.
105. *Ibid.*, p. 70.
106. TCD, MS R. 8. 1, p. 71. Compare also '[Flood] inoculated the people with the spirit of liberty' (*Leaders* [1871], p. 75); '[Flood] inoculated the protestant constituents' (*Leaders* [1903], i, 48-9).

107. *Ibid.*, p. 81.

108. *Leaders* (1861), p. 73; (1871) p. 80 (1903), i, 56. Lecky's source for the figure 80,000 appears to have been Barrington, *Rise and Fall of the Irish Nation* (1843), p. 160. His source for the figure 40,000 may have been Grattan, *Memoirs of the Life and times of Henry Grattan* (1839), i, 399. Lecky used Barrington's figures for the first edition of *Leaders*, and Grattan's figures in the last edition. Meantime, he had written the history of the eighteenth century and had referred to the volunteers as '... an armed body which already counted more than 40,000 men ...' (England [1882], iv, 500, 494; *Ireland* [1892], ii, 242, 234). Further on he wrote: '... and it was alleged, though probably with some exaggeration, that the volunteers throughout Ireland towards the close of 1781 amounted to not less than 80,000 men' (*England* [1882], iv, 521; *Ireland* [1892], ii, 268).

109. *Leaders* (1903), i, 194-5.

110. *Leaders* (1871), pp. 178-81; (1903) i, 224-5;

111. *Ibid.* (1871), p. 182; (1903) p. 243.

112. At least as early as 1882 Lecky no longer regarded Pitt as the villain he had portrayed in 1871: '... you seem to me to exaggerate greatly – not the stupidity, which would be difficult, but the malevolence of the English government in its later stages ...' (Lecky to O'Neill Daunt, 11 June 1882, in Elisabeth Lecky, *A Memoir*, p. 166).

113. *Leaders* (1903), i, 18, 15, 10.

114. Lecky, *Ireland* (1892), i, 116-35.

115. 'Mr Lecky, in the book published to-day, endeavours to reconcile his "boyish rhetoric" with his later convictions. The attempt is not particularly successful; and the "boyish rhetoric" has the truer ring' (*Freeman's Journal,* 17 March 1903).

Chapter Ten

1. *Nineteenth Century,* xxxviii, no. 224 (October 1895), p. 630.

2. J. M. Robertson, *Buckle and his Critics* (1895), p. 458.

3. *Essays,* p. 20.

4. *Ibid.,* p. 68.

5. J. F. Rhodes, *Historical Essays,* pp. 157-8. For Gardiner, see above p. 76.

6. J. Morley, *Gladstone,* ii, 665.

7. See references to Lecky in Harvey Wish, *The American Historian;* also in H. H. Bellot, *American History and American Historians* (London, 1952).

8. *Essays,* pp. 41-2.

9. *Essays,* pp. 13-14.

10. *Leaders* (1871), pp. 183, 203. See also *Democracy and Liberty* (1898), i, xlix.

11. See above p. 25.

12. W. E. Gladstone, 'Lecky's History of England in the Eighteenth Century', in *Nineteenth Century,* xxi, 928 (June 1887).

13. *Nation,* 1 November 1890.

14. *Essays* (1908), p. 26.

15. *Poems* (1891), p. 22.

16. Fox to Lecky, 4 February 1890 (TCD, Lecky correspondence, no. 574). See also Gavan Duffy to Lecky, 14 May (1892) (TCD, Lecky correspondence, no. 2423); and the tributes by Stephen Gwynn and R. Barry O'Brien in *Memoir,* p. 368.

17. Argyll to Lecky, 26 July 1890; 9 February 1893 (TCD, Lecky correspondence, nos 606, 743).

18. *Essays* (1908), p. 5.

19. *Hibernian*, 2 October 1915.

20. TCD, MS R. 7. 33, p. 45.

21. J. J. Horgan, *Parnell to Pearse: Some Recollections and Reflections*, p. 112; P. Colum, *Arthur Griffith*, p. 85.

22. *United Irishman*, 31 October 1903.

23. D. Ryan (ed.), *Collected Works of P. H. Pearse*: 'The Story of a Success', p. 5. Pearse was mistaken in claiming that Lecky was born in this house.

24. *Dail Éireann Proceedings*, 1919-21, p. 74. According to the minutes of the proceedings, Alderman Thomas Kelly was the only other speaker in the First Dail to make a reference to Lecky (*ibid.*, p. 64).

Bibliography

Bibliography of the Writings of W.E.H. Lecky

BOOKS

Hibernicus   *Friendship and Other Poems* (London, 1859).

Anon.   *The Religious Tendencies of the Age* (London, 1860).

Anon.   *The Leaders of the Public Opinion in Ireland* (London, 1861).

W.E.H. Lecky   *History of the Rise and Influence of the Spirit of Rationalism in Europe* (2 vols, London, 1865).

History of European Morals from Augustus to Charlemagne (2 vols, London, 1869).

The Leaders of Public Opinion in Ireland (London, 1871).

History of England in the Eighteenth Century (8 vols, London, 1878–90; cabinet edition, 7 vols, London, 1892).

History of Ireland in the Eighteenth Century (cabinet edition, 5 vols, London, 1892).

The American Revolution, 1763–1783; Being the Chapters and Passages Relating to America from the Author's History of England in the Eighteenth Century ... arranged and edited with historical and bibliographical notes by James Albert Woodburn (New York, c. 1898).

The French Revolution; Chapters from the Author's History of England During the Eighteenth Century ... *with Historical Notes by Henry Eldridge Bourne* ... (New York, Boston, etc., 1904).'

Poems (London, 1891).

Democracy and Liberty (2 vols, London, 1896).

The Map of Life: Conduct and Character (London, 1899).

Leaders of Public Opinion in Ireland (2 vols, London, 1903).

Historical and Political Essays (London, 1908).

Clerical Influences: An Essay on Irish Sectarianism and English Government edited with an introduction by W. E. G. Lloyd and F. Cruise O'Brien (Dublin, 1911).

ARTICLES, PAMPHLETS, PUBLISHED SPEECHES AND ADDRESSES

A Life Spent for Ireland 1870–1894. Being Selections from the Diary of W. J. O'Neill Daunt, edited by his daughter. Prefatory letter by W.E.H. Lecky (London, 1896).

'A Nationalist Parliament', in *Nineteenth Century*, xix (April 1886), pp. 636–44. Revised and republished in G. Baden-Powell (ed.), *The Truth About Home Rule* (London, 1888).

Address in Answer to Her Majesty's Most Gracious Speech. Wednesday 16 February 1898. Speech in the House of Commons on the Roman Catholic University Question. Reprinted from the *Parliamentary Debates.*

An Irish Historian on Home Rule. Liberal unionist pamphlet, no. 33 (London, 1889). First delivered as a speech in Bermingham, 25 April 1889.

'Art of Writing History', in *Forum*, xiv (February 1893), pp. 715–24. Reprinted in *Essays* as 'Thoughts on History', pp. 1–20.

'Canadian Copyright Act', in *Contemporary Review*, lxvii (April 1895), pp. 481–2.

'Carlyle's Message to his age', in *Contemporary Review*, lx (October 1891), pp. 521–8. Same in *Living Age*, cxci (19 December 1891), pp. 758–62. Reprinted in *Essays*, pp. 104–15.

'Conservatism of the British Democracy', in *North American Review*, clxiv (February 1897), pp. 216–32.

'Dean Milman', in *Edinburgh Review*, cxci (April 1900), pp. 510-27. Reprinted in *Essays*, pp. 249–74.

'Formative Influences', in *Forum*, ix (June 1890), pp. 380–90. Reprinted in *Essays*, pp. 90–113.

'Henry Reeve', in *Edinburgh Review*, xlxxxiii (January 1896), pp. 267–71. Reprinted in *Essays*, pp. 242–8.

Introduction to Democracy and Liberty (London, 1899). Reprinted from the cabinet edition.

'Ireland in the Light of History', in *North American Review*, clii, no. 410 (January 1891), pp. 11–26. Discussion in *ibid.*, clii (February 1891), pp. 247–50. Reprinted in *Essays*, pp. 68–89.

'Israel Among the Nations', in *Forum*, xvi (December 1893), pp. 442–51. Reprinted in *Essays*, pp. 116–30.

Letter of apology for non-attendance at the Dublin Unionist Convention, in *Unionist Convention for the Provinces of Leinster, Munster and Connaught (June 1892): Report of Proceedings, List of Committees, Delegates, etc.* (Dublin, n.d.).

Letter on home rule, in *National Observer*, new series, ix, no. 24 (4 March 1893), special supplement, p. 1.

Letter on Irish ideas, in Charles Buxton, *The ideas of the day on policy* (3rd edn, London, 1868).

Letter on the TCD depositions and the 'massacre' of 1641, in *Academy*, no. 642, new series (23 August 1884), pp. 121–2.

Lord Stratford de Redcliffe, a sketch by A. L. Lee; abridged by permission from 'The Life of Stratford Canning' by Stanley Lane-Poole: with an introduction by W.E.H. Lecky (London, 1897).

'Madame de Stael', in *Forum*, xi (April 1891), pp. 168–82. Reprinted in *Essays*, pp. 131–50. *Memorandum … Irish Land Bill, 1896* (London, 1896). *Memorandum on the Proposed Abolition of the Viceroyalty in Ireland* (privately printed, 1887).

Moral Aspects of the South African War (Women's Liberal Unionist Association, Westminster, n.d.) published also in *Daily News* (London), 10 March 1900, also in America and translated into French and German. 'Mr. Froude's *English in Ireland*,' in *Macmillan's Magazine*, xxvii (January 1873), pp. 246–64; xxx (June 1874), pp. 166–84.

'Mr Gladstone and Income Tax in 1874', in *Nineteenth Century*, xxii (July 1887), pp. 52–4.

'Mr Lecky on Mr Gladstone and the Plain Facts of the Irish Question', a letter to the *Scotsman*, 4 July 1892.

On the Influence of the Imagination in History. A lecture to the Royal Institution of Great Britain, 29 May 1868 (London, 1868).

'Political Outlook', in *Fortnightly Review*, lviii, new series, lii (August 1892), pp. 243–6.

'Queen Victoria as a Moral Force', in *Pall Mall Magazine* (April 1901). Reprinted in *Essays*, pp. 275–97.

'Reminiscences of Lord John Russell', published in Stuart J. Reid, *Lord John Russell* (New York, 1895), pp. 335–9. Review in *Literature*, i, no. 1 (23 October 1897). The reviews are unsigned. It is impossible to be certain which was done by Lecky, but a review is listed in his notebook, MSR. 7.45, TCD. Review of *A History of the Warfare of Science with Theology in Christendom*, by A. D. White, in *The Times*, 8 December 1896.

Review of *Life and Correspondence of the Right Hon. Hugh C. E. Childers, 1827–1896. By his son, Lieutenant-Colonel Spencer Childers, C.B.*, in *Spectator*, no. 3798 (13 April 1901), pp. 534–5.

Review of *Memorials of the Earl of Selborne. Part II. Personal and Political*, in *Spectator*, no. 3678 (24 December 1898), pp. 950–1.

Review of *Mr. Gregory's Letter-Box, 1813–1830*, edited by Lady Gregory, in *Spectator*, no. 3638 (19 March 1898), pp. 410–2.

Review of *Napoleon In Time*, by Arthur Levy in *Pall Mall Gazette*, 30 October 1893.

Review of *With Essex in Ireland*, by E. Lawless, *Nineteenth Century*, xxviii, no. 162 (August 1890), pp. 236–8.

Review of R. Barry O'Brien, *The Life of Charles Stewart Parnell*, in *Spectator*, lxxxi, nos. 3673–4 (19, 26 November 1898), pp. 740–2, 776–8.

Roxborough Road school (Limerick diocesan school), in *Daily Express*, 25 March 1897. Unsigned but see Lecky's letter in *Daily Express*, 20 March 1897, where he says he was enclosing a 'short paper giving the later history of the school', and also his notebook, MS R.7.45, TCD.

'Shall we Give Old-Age Pensions?', in *Independent* (New York), li, p. 2662.

'Sir Edgar Boehm', in *Spectator*, no. 3260 (20 December 1890), pp. 900–1. Unsigned, but listed in Lecky's notebook, MS R.7.45, TCD.

'Sir Robert Peel', in *Edinburgh Review*, clxxiv (October 1891), 295–327. Reprinted in *Essays*, pp. 151–99.

'See Aspects of Home Rule', in *Contemporary Review*, lxiii (May 1893), pp. 626–38.

Speech on Financial Relations (England and Ireland) Thurs. 22 March 1900. Reprinted from the *Parliamentary Debates*.

Speech on Financial Relations (Great Britain and Ireland). Wednesday 31 March 1897. Reprinted from the *Parliamentary Debates*.

Speech on home rule delivered at Nottingham, 24 October 1887, published in *Liberal Unionist*, no. 22 (1 November 1887).

Speech on Local Government (Ireland) Bill, Monday 21 March 1898. Reprinted from the *Parliamentary Debates*.

Speech on nomination for the TCD parliamentary seat. Reported in *Daily Express*, 2 December 1895.

Speech on Sale of Intoxicating Liqueurs (Ireland) Bill, Wednesday 12 May 1897. Reprinted from the *Parliamentary Debates*.

Speech on Taxation (Ireland), Monday 4 July 1898. Reprinted from the *Parliamentary Debates*.

Speeches and Addresses of Edward Henry XVth Earl of Derby, K.G. Selected and edited by Sir T. H. Sanderson, K.C.B., and E. S. Roscoe. With a prefatory memoir by W.E.H. Lecky (2 vols, London, 1894). Revised and reprinted in *Essays*, pp. 200–41.

Speeches in parliament. Reported in *Hansard's Parliamentary Debates*, fourth series, for the years 1896–1902.

'Tendencies in Ireland', in *Daily Express* (Dublin), 20 August 1898.

'The Advertisement Nuisance', in *New Review*, ix, no. 54 (November 1893), pp. 466–8.

The Basis of an English-Speaking Alliance (n.d.).

'The Case Against Home Rule. vii – From the Historical Point of View', in *Pall Mall Gazette*, 24 July 1893.

The Empire: Its Value and Its Growth, an inaugural lecture, delivered at the Imperial Institute (London, 1893). Reported in *The Times*, 21 November 1893. Published in *Essays*, pp. 43–67.

The French Revolution by Thomas Carlyle. With a critical and biographical introduction by William Edward Hartpole Lecky ... (New York, 1900).

The History of the Decline and Fall of the Roman Empire, by Edward Gibbon, ed., by J. B. Bury with an introduction by the Rt Hon. W.E.H. Lecky (New York, 1906–7). See the same also in *Historians and Essayists*, iv (New York, 1905), Warner classics.

'The History of the Evangelical Movement', in *Nineteenth Century*, vi, no. 30 (August 1879), pp. 280–92. A reply to W. E. Gladstone's criticism in a review of Lecky's *England*.

'The Irish Local Government Act', in *Irish Ecclesiastical Gazette*, 3 March 1899, pp. 166–7.

The Political Value of History, a presidential address delivered at the Birmingham and Midland Institute, 10 October 1892 (Birmingham, 1892). Reprinted in *Essays*, pp. 21–42.

The Prose Works of Jonathan Swift ... edited by Temple Scott, with biographical introduction by W.E.H. Lecky (London, 1897–08).

'Three Books on Irish History', a review in *Pall Mall Gazette*, 27 October 1893. The books were P. W. Joyce, *A Short History of Ireland*, P. Dwyer (ed.), *The Siege of Derry in 1689*; T. Davis, *The Patriot Parliament of 1689*.

'Why Home Rule is Undesirable', in *North American Review*, clii, no. 412 (March 1891), 349–70.

'Why I Oppose Old-Age Pensions', in *Forum*, xxviii, no. 6 (February 1890), pp. 687–700. Reprinted in *Essays*, pp. 298–317.

LETTERS IN NEWSPAPERS

Letters to *The Times*

6 February 1873	University education.
25 January 1882	The Case of the Irish Landlords.
3 February 1882	The Case of the Irish Landlords.
13 January 1886	Home Rule. Reprinted in pamphlet form for the Irish Loyal and Patriotic Union.
4 February 1886	Home Rule. Signed 'An Old Whig'.
5 May 1886	Reply to John Morley.
3 June 1886	Controversy with Sir Wm. Harcourt. Reprinted as leaflet no. 142 by the ILPU.
7 June 1886	Controversy with Harcourt. Reprinted as leaflet no. 29 by the Liberal Unionist Committee.
9 June 1886	Controversy with Harcourt.
21 June 1892	Reply to Gladstone.
24 June 1892	Letter to the Dublin Unionist Convention.
4 December 1893	Scotland and the Empire.
22 March 1894	Irish Vote on First Reform Bill.
30 October 1895	TCD Parliamentary Seat.
14 December 1895	TCD – Reply to Bishop O'Dwyer.
20 December 1895	TCD – Reply to Bishop O'Dwyer.
13 May 1896	Irish Land Bill. Signed 'Unionist'.
1 August 1896	Irish Land Bill.
11 February 1898	Public Libraries, Authors, Publishers.
9 May 1898	South African Debate – A Correction.
16 July 1900	Contentious and Non-Contentious Legislation.
13 May 1902	Judge O'Connor Morris.

Letters to the *Daily Express*

31 October 1895	TCD Parliamentary Seat.
6 November 1895	Reply to schoolmistress association on the questio of university education for women.

13 November 1895   Two letters from Lecky about his religion.
18 November 1895   Letter to the electors of the University of Dublin.
20 March 1897   Limerick Diocesan School – Reply to Bishop O'Dwyer.
Note: Lecky's poems published originally in various magazines have not been
    included as separate items.

A: MANUSCRIPT SOURCES

I   Lecky Correspondence. Trinity College, Dublin. This collection contains
     between two and three thousand separate items. It consists mainly of letters to
     Lecky from various correspondence, but occasionally there are drafts of
     Lecky's replies. The collection is arranged chronologically and has been cata-
     logued by Mr Wm O'Sullivan.
II   Lecky Papers. Trinity College, Dublin. This collection consists of Lecky's
     manuscript notebooks, commonplace books, diaries, drafts of some of his
     work, marginalia, etc.
III Other Collections Containing Lecky Material

(a) In Ireland

W. J. O'Neill Daunt Journal. National Library, Dublin, MS 3042. In the
     Appendix to this journal are copies of a few letters from Lecky to Daunt. The
     journal itself in a number of entries has references to Lecky and his work.
Gavan Duffy Papers. National Library, Dublin. MS 8005. Letters from Lecky to
     Gavan Duffy, 1873–93.
Alice Stopford Green Papers. National Library, Dublin. MS 15085. Seven letters
     from Lecky, 1877–1895.
Hartpole Papers. Trinity College, Dublin. Contains material relating to the lands
     which Lecky inherited.
J. P. Prendergast Papers. King's Inns Library, Dublin.
National Library, Dublin. Besides the collections listed above the National
     Library also contains the odd letter from Lecky in a few other collections.
Registry of Deeds. King's Inn, Dublin. Contains material relating to Lecky's
     property.
Trinity College, Dublin. Minute books of the College Historical Society.

(b) In Britain

Blennerhassett Papers. Cambridge University Library. Add. 7486 no. 52 (1) E.
     Relevant envelope marked '1 Ch. Lady Blennerhassett. Her letters from Eng-
     lish friends and letters of the King: then Prince of Wales (Edward VII)'.
     Contains eight items from Lecky to Lady Blennerhassett.
Dixon Papers. Cambridge University Library. Three letters from Lecky to James
     Dixon, surgeon, 1878, 1882.
Gladstone Papers. British Museum, Letters to Gladstone 1879–81. Add. MSS
     44460, ff. 206, 226; 44469, f. 57.
Salisbury Papers. Christ Church, Oxford. Nine items from Lecky, 1892–.

Bodleian Library, Oxford. Letters from Lecky to a few correspondents including Sir H. Taylor, H. H. Milman, Mary Seton Watts, Sir Henry Lee.

British Library, London. Besides the letters to

Gladstone a couple of other items from Lecky, including the autographed manuscript of *Morals.*

National Library of Scotland, Edinburgh. Letters to various correspondents.

(c) In Europe

Hague and Vienna Collections. Some forty-four autograph letters from famous contemporaries to Lecky, divided into two lots known as the Vienna and Hague collections, and in possession of Baron Braun of Vienna, a relative of Mrs. Lecky's family, now on microfilm, TCD.

(d) In USA

Lecky-Lea Correspondence. In the Henry Charles Lea Library, University of Pennsylvania, Philadelphia. Contains over thirty letters from Lecky to the American historian, Lea. On microfilm, UCD.

The following institutions contain a small number of letters and other miscellaneous items by Lecky.

Cornell University Library, Ithaca, New York.

Duke University Library, Durham, North Carolina.

Library of Congress, Washington, DC.

Henry E. Huntingdon Library and Art Gallery, San Marino, California.

Houghton Library, Harvard University, Cambridge, Mass.

Massachusetts Historical Society, Boston, Mass.

New York Public Library, New York.

Pierpont Morgan Library, New York.

University of Texas Library, Austin, Texas.

Yale University Library, New Haven, Connecticut.

B: PRINTED MATERIAL

(i) Correspondence of Lecky

H. M. Hyde (ed.). *A Victorian Historian: Private Letters of W.E.H. Lecky, 1859–1878* (London, 1947).

[Elisabeth Lecky] *A Memoir of the Right Hon. William Edward Hartpole Lecky ... By His Wife* (London, 1909).

(ii) Parliamentary Proceedings

Dail Eireann, Miontuairisc an Chéad Dála, 1919–21; Minutes of the Proceedings of the First Parliament of the Republic of Ireland, 1919–21, Official Record (Dublin).

Hansard's Parliamentary Debates, third series, 1830–91, vols i–ccclvi (London, 1831–91).

Hansard's Parliamentary Debates, fourth series, 1892–1908, vols i–cxcix (London, 1892–[1909]).

(iii) Parliamentary papers and royal commissions

Gilbert, J. T., Report on the manuscripts of Trinity College, Dublin in *Eighth report of the royal commission on historical manuscripts: report and appendix – part I* [c 3040], H.C. 1881, pp. 572–624.

Report from the select committee on aged deserving poor; together with the proceedings of the committee, minutes of evidence, and appendix, H.C. 1899 (296), viii. For draft report proposed by Lecky see pp. xxvii–xxxii.

Return of owners of land … in Ireland. [C1492] H.C. 1876.

Royal commission on university education in Ireland: Appendix to the second report: Minutes of evidence [cd. 900], H.C. 1902.

(iv) Select list of diaries, correspondence, memoirs, biographies etc. containing contemporary material relating to Lecky.

Acton, Lord, *Letters of Lord Acton to Mary, daughter of the right hon. W. E. Gladstone,* ed. Herbert Paul (London, 1904).

Acton, Lord, *Selections from the correspondence of the first Lord Acton,* eds J. N. Figgis and R. V. Laurence (London, 1917).

Allingham, W., *William Allingham: a diary,* eds H. Allingham and D. Radford (London, 1907).

Argyll, Duke of, *George Douglas eight Duke of Argyll, K. G., K. T. (1823–1900). Autobiography and memoirs.* Edited by the Dowager Duchess of Argyll (2 vols, London, 1906).

Daunt, W. J. O'Neill, *A life spent for Ireland. Being selections from the journals of the late W. J. O'Neill Daunt.* Edited by his daughter (London, 1896).

de Burgh, U. H. H., *The landowners of Ireland: an alphabetical list of the owners of estates of 500 acres or £500 valuation, with the acreage and valuation in each county* (1878).

Duffy, C. G., *Conversations with Carlyle* (London, 1892).

Dunn, W. H., *James Anthony Froude: a biography, 1818–1856* (Oxford, 1961).

Dunn, W. H., *James Anthony Froude: a biography, 1857–1894* (Oxford, 1963).

Ferguson, Lady M. C., *Sir Samuel Ferguson in the Ireland of his day* (2 vols, London, 1896).

Fitzpatrick, W. J., *The life of Father Thomas N. Burke, O.P.* (2 vols, London, 1885).

Froude, J. A., *Thomas Carlyle: a history of his life in London 1834–1881* (2 vols, London, 1884).

Gardiner, A. G., *Life of Sir William Harcourt* (2 vols, London, 1923).

Gilbert, R. M., *Life of Sir John T. Gilbert* (London, 1905).

Healy, T., *Letters and leaders of my day* (London, 1928).

Hone, J., *W. B. Yeats 1865–1939* (London, 1962).

Hurlbert, W. H., *Ireland under coercion: the diary of an American* (2nd edn, Edinburgh, 1889).

Lucy, H. W., *A diary of the unionist parliament 1895–1900* (London, 1901).

Lucy, H. W., *The Balfourian parliament 1900–1905* (London, 1906).

MacNeill, J. G. Swift, *What I have seen and heard.* (London, 1925).

Morley, J., *Recollections* (2 vols, London, 1917).

Morley, J., *The Life of William Ewart Gladstone* (3 vols, London, 1903).

Morris, W. O'Connor, *Memories and thought of a life* (London, 1895).

Norton, C. E., *Letters of C. E. Norton,* with a biographical comment by his daughter, Sara Norton (London, 1913).

Paul, H., *The life of Froude* (London, 1905)

Skelton, J., *The table-talk of Shirley* (London, 1895).

St Aubyn, G. R., *A Victorian eminence: the life and works of H.T. Buckle* (London, 1958)

Steele, S. L., *The Rt Hon. Arthur Mac Murrough Kavanagh* (London, 1891).

Wilson, D. A. & Mac Arthur, D. W., *Carlyle* (6 vols, London, 1923–34).

Who was who 1897–1916 (London, 1920).

Yeats, W. B., *Autobiographies* (London, 1955).

(v) Select list of contemporary and near contemporary works including commentaries and reviews relating to Lecky.

Anon., 'Mr Gladstone and Mr Lecky', in *Saturday Review* lxiii, no. 1649 (4 June 1887), pp. 786–7.

Anon., 'Mr Lecky and the study of history', in *Spectator,* lxix (15 Oct. 1892), pp. 524–5.

Anon., 'Mr Lecky and Dublin University', in *Spectator,* lxxv (9 Nov. 1895), pp. 632–3; (23 Nov. 1895), p. 724; (30 Nov. 1895), p. 757.

Anon., Review of Lecky's *England* vols v, vi (1887), in *Quarterly Review,* clxv. no. 329 (July 1887), pp. 1–36.

Anon., 'W.E.H. Lecky', in *John Bull,* lxxi, no. 3672 (4 April 1891), p. 216.

Anon., 'W.E.H. Lecky', in *Speaker,* ii, no. 44 (1 Nov. 1890), pp. 486–7.

Argyll, Duke of, *Irish nationalism: an appeal to history* (London, 1893).

Bagenal, P. H., *The American-Irish and their influence on Irish politics* (London, 1882).

Barlow, W., *College Historical Society Address* (1856).

Barrington, J., *Rise and fall of the Irish nation* (Paris, 1833).

Barrington, J., *Personal sketches of his own times* (2 vols, 2nd edn, London, 1830).

Bodkin, M. McDonnell, *Grattan's parliament: before and after* (London, 1912).

[Booth, A.] A College Friend, 'Early recollections of Mr Lecky', in *National Review,* xliii, no. 253 (March 1904), pp. 108–22.

Brabourne, Lord, *Facts and fictions in Irish history: a reply to Mr Gladstone.* Reprinted from *Blackwood's Magazine* (Oct., Nov. 1886).

Bridgett, Rev. T. E., '"Infamous publications": who wrote them' (Dublin, 1872). Reprinted from *Irish Ecclesiastical Record.*

Brownson, O. A., 'Lecky on morals', in *The works of Orestes A. Brownson* (Detroit, 1884). xiv, pp 379–414. Reprinted from *Catholic World.*

Bryce, J. (ed.), *Handbook of home rule* (London, 1887).

Buckle, H. T., *History of civilization in England* (2 vols, London, 1857, 1861).

Burke, T. N., *Ireland's vindication: refutation of Froude and other lectures* (Glasgow, n.d.).

Clancy, J. J. (ed.), *Short lessons on the Irish question; or the leaflets of the Irish Press Agency,* i. nos 1–102 (London, 1890).

Cullen, Archbishop Paul, *Pastoral letter of his Grace, the Most Rev. Dr Cullen, Archbishop of Dublin ... on the month of May* (Dublin, 1868).

Cusack, M. F., *The liberator: his life and times* (Kenmare, 1872).

Daubeny, C. G. B., *Christianity and rationalism ...* (London, 1867).

Daunt, W. J. O'Neill, *Eighty-five years of Irish history, 1800–1885* (2nd edn, 2 vols, London 1886).

Davitt, M., 'A plea for old-age pensions', in *Forum,* xxviii (Feb 1890) pp. 677–86.

Dicey, A. V., *A leap in the dark: a criticism of the principles of home rule as illustrated by the bill of 1893* (London, 1893).

Dicey, A. V., *England's case against home rule* (London, 1887).

Duffy, C. G., 'A fair constituion for Ireland', in *Contemporary Review,* lii (Sept. 1887), pp 301–32.

Dunlop, R., 'The depositions relating to the Irish massacres of 1641', in *English Historical Review,* i, no. 4 (Oct. 1886), pp 740–4; ii, no. 6 (April 1887), pp. 338–40.

Eliot, G., 'The influence of rationalism', in *Fortnightly Review,* i. (1865), pp. 43–55. Reprinted in G. Eliot, *Essays* (London, 1884, pp. 200–28).

Fitzpatrick, T., *The bloody bridge and other papers relating to the insurrection of 1641,* (Dublin, 1903).

Fox, J. A., *A key to the Irish question* (London, 1890).

Froude, J. A., Preface to M. Hickson's, *Ireland in the seventeenth century.*

Froude, J. A., *Short studies on great subjects* (Silver Library edn, London, 1915).

Froude, J. A., *The English in Ireland in the eighteenth century* (3 vols, London, 1872–1874).

Froude, J. A., *The two chiefs of Dunboy, or an Irish romance of the last century* (London, 1889).

[Froude, J. A.,] '*Thumping English lies': Froude's slanders on Ireland and Irishmen.* With preface and notes by Colonel James E. Mc Gee (New York, 1872).

Gardiner, S. R., Letters on the T.C.D. depositions and the 'massacre' of 1641, in *Academy,* no. 642 (23 August. 1884), p. 121; no. 645 (13 Sept. 1884), p. 169.

Gardiner, S. R., Review of Lecky's, *The political value of history,* in *English Historical Review,* viii (April 1893), pp. 394–5.

Gardiner, S. R., Review of M. Hickson's *Ireland in the seventeeth century,* in *Academy,* new series, xxvi, no. 638 (26 July 1884), p. 53.

Gibson, E., *College Historical Society Address* (10 Nov. 1858).

Gladstone, W. E., 'Lecky's history of England in the eighteenth century', a review in *Nineteenth Century,* xxi, no 124 (June 1887), pp. 919–36.

Gladstone, W. E., 'Lessons of Irish history in the eighteenth century', in J. Bryce (ed.), *Handbook of home rule.*

Gladstone, W. E., 'Mr Lecky and political morality', in *Nineteenth Century,* xxii (Aug. 1887), pp. 279–84.

Gladstone, W. E., *Special aspects of the Irish question* (London, 1892).

Gregory, Lady A., (ed.) *Ideals in Ireland* (London, 1901).

Hickson, M., *Ireland in the seventeenth century* (2 vols, London, 1884).

Hickson, M., Letters on the T.C.D. depostiions and the 'massacre' of 1641, in *Academy,* no. 640 (9 August 1884), p. 95; no. 644 (6 Sept. 1884), pp. 153–4; no. 647 (27 Sept. 1884), p. 203.

Hickson, M., 'The depositions relating to the Irish massacres of 1641', in *English Historical Review*, ii, no. 5 (Jan. 1887), pp 133–7; no. 7 (July 1887), p. 527.

Hogan, J. F., *Irish catholics and Trinity College* (Dublin, 1906).

Ingram, J. Kells, *Outlines of the history of religion* (London, 1900).

Ingram, T. Dunbar, *A critical examinaiton of Irish history; being a replacement of the false by the true* (2 vols, London, 1900).

Ingram, T. Dunbar, *A history of the legislative union of Great Britain and Ireland* (London, 1887).

Ingram, T. Dunbar, *Two chapters on Irish history* (London, 1888).

Lawless, E., 'W.E.H. Lecky: a reminiscence', in *Monthly Review*, xiv, no. 41 (Feb. 1904), pp. 112–126.

Lilly, W. S., 'The new spirit in history', in *Nineteenth Century*, xxxviii, no. 224 (Oct. 1895), pp. 619–633.

Lloyd, W. E. G., and O'Brien, F. Cruise (eds), *Clerical influences: an essay on Irish sectarianism and English government. By W.E.H. Lecky.* (Dublin, 1911).

Mc Carthy, J., 'Mr John [sic] Anthony Froude', in *Galaxy*, xiv, no. 3 (Sept. 1872), pp. 293–303.

Mc Carthy, J. H., *The case for home rule* (London, 1887).

McCarthy, J. G., *A plea for home government of Ireland* (3rd edn Dublin, 1872).

Mc Dermott, G., 'A reply to Mr Lecky', in *North American Review*, clii, no. 411 (Feb 1891), pp. 247–250.

Mc Donnell, J., *The Ulster civil war of 1641 and its consequences* (Dublin, 1879).

Mac Neill, J. G. Swift, 'Hibernia irredenta: l – Mr Lecky and Irish affairs', in *Fortnightly Review*, new series, lix, no. 349 (Jan. 1896), pp. 18–27.

Mac Neill, J. G. Swift, *How the union was carried* (London, 1887).

Mac Neill, J. G. Swift, *The Irish parliament what it was and what it did* (2nd edn, London, 1912).

Mac Neill, J. G. Swift, *The constitutional and parliamentary history of Ireland till the union* (Dublin, 1917).

Mac Neill, J. G. Swift, *Titled corruption: the sordid origin of some Irish peerages* (London, 1894).

Mitchel, J., *1641: reply to the falsification of history by James Anthony Froude, entitled 'The English in Ireland': The crusade of the period* (Glasgow, n.d.).

Monteagle, Lord, 'A beginning of conciliation', in *New Ireland Review*, i, no. 3 (May 1894), pp. 133–7.

Morley, J., 'Irish policy in the eighteenth century', in *Fortnightly Review*, new series, xi (Feb. 1872), pp. 196–203.

Morley, J., 'Lecky on democracy', in *Critical Miscellanies,* iv (London, 1908); also in *The works of Lord Morley,* xv (London, 1921), pp. 23–58. Reprinted from *Nineteenth Century.*

Morris, W. O'Connor, *Ireland 1798–1898* (Innes, 1898).

O'Brien, R. Barry, *Irish wrongs and English remedies, with other essays* (London, 1887).

[O'Brien, R. Barry,] 'Historicus', *The best hundred Irish books* (Dublin 1886). Reprinted from *Freeman's Journal*.

O'Riordan, M., *Catholicity and progress in Ireland* (London, 1905).

Parnell, A., 'Mr Lecky on the Earl of Wharton', in *Atheneum*, no. 3, 411 (11 March 1893) pp. 312–3.

Plunket, D. R., *College Historical Society Address* (9 Nov. 1859).

Plunket, H., *Ireland in the new century* (London, 1904).

Prendergast, J. P., *The Cromwellian settlement of Ireland* (London, 1865; Dublin, 1875).

Redmond, J., *Irish protestants and home rule,* Irish Press Agency leaflet no. 19 (London, 1887).

Redmond, J., *The truth about '98,* Irish Press Agency (London, 1886).

Reid, M., 'Our young historians; account of lectures on history by W.E.H. Lecky and J. A. Froude', in *Living Age,* cxcvi (11 March 1893), pp. 694–701. Also printed in *Macmillan's Magazine,* lxvii, no. 398 (Dec 1892), pp. 91–98.

Reports of the Irish landowners convention (Dublin, 1887–1919).

Robertson , J. M., *Buckle and his critics: a study in sociology* (London, 1895).

Rolleston, T. W., 'The Irish parliament and its struggle for reform 1782–1793', in *Westminster Review,* cxxxiv, no. 4 (Oct. 1890), pp. 377–390.

Russell, T. W., *Ireland and the empire: a review 1800–1900* (London, 1901).

Sibley, N. W., 'Mr Lecky on Junius', in *Westminster Review,* cxlvii, no. 1 (Jan. 1897), pp. 57–70.

Smith, Goldwin, 'Mr Lecky on Pitt', in *Macmillan's Magazine,* lxii, no. 376 (Feb. 1891), pp. 241–48.

Stephen, J. F., 'The study of history', in *Cornhill Magazine,* iii (June 1861) pp. 666–80. Republished in *History and Theory,* i, no. 2 (1961), pp. 186–201.

Stephen, L., 'Carlyle's ethics', in *Hours in a library* (3 vols, London, 1892), iii, pp. 286–94.

Unionist convention for provinces of Leinster, Munster & Connaught (June, 1892): Report of proceedings, lists of committees, delegates etc. (Dublin, n.d.).

Walker, H., 'The Rt. Hon. W. E. Hartpole Lecky', in *Good Words,* xl (1899), pp. 114–19.

Walshe, R., *College Historical Society Address* (9 Nov. 1864).

Walsh, Archbishop W. J., *The Irish university question: the catholic case: selections from the speeches and writings of the Archbishop of Dublin: with a historical sketch of the Irish university question.* (Dublin, 1897).

Webb, A., *The alleged massacre of 1641.* Irish Press Agency (London, 1887).

Whittle, J. L., 'The Irish parliament and the union', in *Quarterly Review,* clxv. no. 330 (Oct. 1887), pp 500–34.

Willis, Freeman C., *College Historical Society Address* (1860).

Woodlock, B., *Catholic university education in Ireland, a letter to Mr Cogan, M.P.* (Dublin, 1868).

Note on the above

Most of the reviews of Lecky's books have not been itemized separately. Many of the major reviews are listed in Poole's *Index to periodical literature* and *Nineteenth century reader's guide to periodical literature*. For a detailed list of the reviews of Lecky's major works see Norman Pilling, 'The reception of the major works of W.E.H. Lecky 1865–1896' (M.Phil, 1978, London).

(vi) Obituaries

The Academy and Literature, lxv, no. 1643 (31 Oct. 1903), pp. 471–2. Signed T.W.S. (Sir Thomas Snagg).

American Historical Review, ix, no. 2 (Jan 1904), p. 413.

Atheneum, no. 3966 (31 Oct. 1903), pp. 583–4. Reprinted in *Living Age*, ccxxxix (28 Nov. 1903), pp. 569–71.

Bookman, xviii (Dec. 1903), pp. 338–9.

Dial, xxxv, no. 417 (1 Nov. 1903), pp. 295–7.

Nation, lxxvii, no. 2000 (29 Oct. 1903), p. 337. F. J. Mather Jr.

Spectator, xci, no. 3931 (31 Oct. 1903), pp. 693–4.

The Times 24 Oct. 1903, p. 10 [E.D.J. Wilson]

C: SELECT LIST OF LATER WORKS RELATING TO LECKY

Aspiz, H., 'Lecky's influence on Mark Twain', in *Science and Society*, xxvi, no. 1 (Winter 1962), pp. 15–25.

Auchmuty, J. J., 'The Lecky-Lea correspondence in the Henry Charles Lea Library of the University of Pennsylvania, Philadelphia, U.S.A.', in *Hermathena* xcii (Nov. 1958), pp. 45–61.

Ausubel, H., Brebner, J. B., Hunt, E. (eds), *Some modern historians of Britain: essays in honour of R. L. Schuyler* (New York, 1951).

Baker, N., 'Lecky and the *Annual Register* in Perspective', in *Studies in Burke and His Time*, xiv (Winter 1972–3), pp. 171–7.

Beckett, J. C., 'The Irish parliament in the eighteenth century', in *Proceedings and reports of the Belfast Natural History Society*, second series, v (1950/1–1954/5) pp. 17–37.

Bellot, H. H., *American history and American historians: a review of recent contributions to the interpretation of the United States* (London, 1952).

Ben-Israel, Hevda, *English historians and the French Revolution* (London, 1968).

Bowle, J., *Politics and opinion in the nineteenth century* (London, 1954).

Brinton, C. C., *English political thought in the ninteenth century* (New York, 1962).

Brinton, C. C., *History of western morals* (London, 1959).

Burns, R. E., 'The Irish penal code and some of its historians', in *Review of Politics*, xxi, no. 1 (Jan 1959), pp. 276–99.

Butterfield, H., *George III and the historians* (London, 1957).

Curtis, L. P. Jr., 'Lecky Vindicated', in *Studies in Burke and His Time*, xiv (Spring, 1973), pp. 267–94.

Ensor, R. C. K., 'Some political and economic interactions in later Victorian England', in *Transactions of the Royal Historical Society,* 4th series, xxi (1939), pp. 17–28.

Fraser, P., 'The Liberal-Unionist alliance, 1886–1904', in *English Historical Review,* lxxvii, no. 302 (Jan. 1962), pp. 53–78.

Franqueville, C. F. Comte de, *Notice sur la vie et les travaux du tres-honorable W.E.H. Lecky* (Paris, 1910).

Gooch, G. P., *History and historians in the nineteenth century* (London, 1913).

Gooch, G. P., 'Some great English historians, ii', in *Contemporary Review,* clxxxxi (Jan. 1957), pp. 19–24.

Hirst, W. A., 'The centenary of Lecky the historian', in *Nineteenth Century,* cxxiii, no. 734 (April 1938), pp. 494–8.

Keir, D. L., 'Froude and Lecky on eighteenth century Ireland', a paper read to the Ulster Society for Irish Historical Studies, 18 June 1941, in *Bulletin of the Irish Committee of Historical Sciences,* no. 14, pp. 4–5.

Lippincott, B. E., 'William Lecky', in *Victorian critics of democracy: Carlyle, Ruskin, Arnold, Stephen, Maine, Lecky* (Oxford Univeristy Press; University of Minnesota Press, 1938), pp. 207–43.

Love, W. D., 'Charles O'Connor of Belanagare and Thomas Leland's "philosophical" history of Ireland', in *Irish Historical Studies.* xiii, no. 49 (March 1962), pp. 1–25.

Mc Cartney, D., 'James Anthony Froude and Ireland: a historiographical controversy of the nineteenth century', in *Historical Studies,* vii, ed. T. D. Williams (Dublin, 1971).

Mc Cartney, D., 'Lecky's *Leaders of Public Opinion in Ireland*', in *Irish Historical Studies,* xiv, no. 53 (March 1964), pp. 119–41.

Mc Cartney, D., 'The writing of history in Ireland, 1800–1830', in *Irish Historical Studies,* x. no. 40 (Sept. 1957), pp. 347–62.

Mc Dowell, R. B., Review of J. J. Auchmuty, *Lecky: a biographical and critical essay,* and of H. Montgomery Hyde (ed.), *A Victorian historian: private letters of W.E.H. Lecky, 1859–1878.,* in *Irish Historical Studies,* v, no. 20 (Sept. 1947) pp. 357–60.

Maehl, W. H. 'Gladstone, the liberals and the election of 1874', in *Bulletin of the Institute of Historical Research,* xxxvi, no. 93 (May 1963), pp. 53–69.

Maxwell, C. Review of *Lecky* by J. J. Auchmuty, in *Hermathena,* lxviii (Nov. 1946), pp. 84–6.

Minnick, W. C., 'The Froude-Burke controversy', in *Speech Monographs,* xviii, no. 1 (March 1951), pp. 31–6.

Mullen, J. C., 'Lecky as plagiarist: *The Annual Register* and the American Revolution', in *Studies in Burke and His Time,* xiii (Spring 1972), pp. 193–202.

Mullett, C. F. , 'W.E.H. Lecky', in *Some modern historians of Britain,* eds H. Ausubel & others (New York, 1951).

Mulvey, H., 'The historian Lecky: opponent of Irish home rule', in *Victorian Studies,* i, no. 4 (June 1958), pp. 337–51.

Phillips, W. A., *Lecky: a lecture in celebration of the centenary of Lecky's birth* (Dublin, 1939).

Pilling, N., 'Lecky and Dicey: English and Irish Histories', in *Eire–Ireland,* xvi, no. 3 (Autumn 1981), pp. 43–56.

Prothero, G. W., 'W.E.H. Lecky', in *Dictionary of National Biography, Second Supplement,* (London, 1912), ii, 435–40.

Rhodes, J. F., 'William E. H. Lecky', in *Historical essays* (New York, 1909).

Roach, J., 'Liberalism and the Victorian intelligentsia', in *Cambridge Historical Journal* xiii, no. 1 (1957), pp. 58–81.

Skotheim, R. A., *American intellectual histories and historians* (Princeton University Press, 1966).

Thompson, J. W., *A history of historical writing* (2 vols, New York, 1942).

Wish, H., *The American historian* (New York, 1960).

Wyatt, A., 'Froude, Lecky and "the humblest Irishman"', in *Irish Historical Studies*, xix, no. 75 (March 1975), pp. 261–85.

Wyatt, A., 'Lingard, Lecky, Irish History and 1641', in *Eire–Ireland,* xxiii, no. 1 (Spring 1988), pp. 22–34.

D: THESES

Dineen, Yvonne, 'The problem of political stability in a democratic age: the ideas of W.E.H. Lecky' (Ph.D., 1986, University of Wales, Swansea).

Hill, P. C., 'W.E.H. Lecky: Historian; an historiographical analysis of the works of W.E.H. Lecky'. (Ph.D., 1971, University of Toronto).

Hindman, R. S., 'In search of the young Lecky' (Ph.D., 1975, University of Chicago).

Pilling, N., 'The reception of the major works of W.E.H. Lecky 1865–1896' (M. Phil, 1978, London).

Index